Character Merchandising

Character Merchandising

Second edition

John N Adams
of the Inner Temple Barrister, Professor of Intellectual Property
at the University of Sheffield, Director of the
Intellectual Property Institute

with

an Introduction by
Iain Baillie
of Ladas & Parry, London

a Chapter on Taxation by
Peter Stevens
of Manches, London

Precedents prepared by, and in consultation with,
Bernard Nyman
of Manches, London

a Chapter on France by
Jacques Mazaltov
Avocat au Barreau, Paris

a Chapter on Germany by
Bettina Kormanicki
of Wessing Berenburg-Gossler Zimmerman Lange, Frankfurt

Butterworths
London, Edinburgh, Dublin
1996

United Kingdom	Butterworths a Division of Reed Elsevier (UK) Ltd, Halsbury House, 35 Chancery Lane, London WC2A 1EL and 4 Hill Street, Edinburgh EH2 3JZ
Australia	Butterworths, Sydney, Melbourne, Brisbane, Adelaide, Perth, Canberra and Hobart
Canada	Butterworths Canada Ltd, Toronto and Vancouver
Ireland	Butterworth (Ireland) Ltd, Dublin
Malaysia	Malayan Law Journal Sdn Bhd, Kuala Lumpur
New Zealand	Butterworths of New Zealand Ltd, Wellington and Auckland
Singapore	Reed Elsevier (Singapore) Pte Ltd, Singapore
South Africa	Butterworths Publishers (Pty) Ltd, Durban
USA	Michie, Charlottesville, Virginia

A CIP Catalogue record for this book is available from the British Library.

First edition   1987

ISBN 0 406 07767 3

Printed and bound in Great Britain by Mackays of Chatham PLC, Chatham, Kent

Preface to the second edition

The first edition of this work appeared in 1987 under the title 'Merchandising Intellectual Property'. Although the purist might insist that the former title was more accurate, and that to use the title 'Character Merchandising' for a book which sets out to cover the whole merchandising field is wrong, the fact is that 'Charcter Merchandising' will for most people more readily identify their object of enquiry. Accordingly, I have changed the name to 'Character Merchandising', though the scope of the work remains the same as in the previous edition.

Since the first edition, we have had a new Copyright Act, and a new Trade Marks Act. These have necessitated complete rewrites of the first three Chapters. A brave, possibly foolhardy, attempt has been made in Chapter 1 to spell out in tabular form the effect of the implementation of the Duration of Copyright Directive. The result of the Regulations implementing that Directive is that UK copyright law has attained a level of quite exceptional complexity, and the situation in relation to the connecting factors dealt with in Chapter 2 is scarcely less so. There have been major rewrites in virtually all the remaining Chapters carried over from the previous edition. Chapter 9 by Peter Stephens of Manches, London, dealing with taxation, is entirely new. The Precedents section has been substantially revised and expanded by Bernard Nyman of Manches, London, in consultation with myself. Finally, Part II, dealing with other jurisdictions, is entirely new, the Chapters on France and Germany being contributed by Jacques Mazaltov, and Bettina Kormarnicki of Wessing Berenburg-Gossler Zimmermann Lange, Frankfurt, respectively. I would also like to thank Professor Sam Ricketson of Monash University and Professor Jim Lahore of Queen Mary & Westfield College, for their help with the Chapter on Australia, Sylvana Conte, of Goodman, Phillips & Vineberg, Montréal for her help with the Chapter on Canada, and Professor Oliver Goodenough of the Vermont Law School for his help with the Chapter on the USA.

In addition to the above, I would also like to thank Jack Black of Radcliffes Grossman & Block, Michael Flint of Denton Hall, and Adrian Sterling of Lamb Chambers, Temple, London, for their help on the two copyright Chapters, and Alison Firth of Queen Mary & Westfield College for her help on the two trade mark Chapters. I would also like to thank my colleagues at the Faculty of Law, University of Sheffield: Geraint Howells, and Jeremy Scholes for their help on Chapters 7 and 8 respectively. Last, but by no means least, I would like to thank my colleagues at 1 Raymond Buildings, Gray's Inn: Christopher Morcom, Guy

Preface to the second edition

Tritton and Roger Wyand for their help throughout, but in particular, Michael Edenborough for his help on the section of Chapter 1 which deals with the duration of copyright. Needless to say, responsibility for errors and omissions is mine.

John N Adams
April 1996

Preface to the first edition

Merchandising has grown rapidly in the United Kingdom over the last decade, notwithstanding certain legal difficulties. Some of these difficulties have been of the industry's own making. In particular, American forms and practices have been adopted with little regard to local conditions. The *Holly Hobbie* case is the most notorious example of the problems to which this can lead. The fact is, however, that provided merchandisers are prepared to adapt to local conditions, operations which are perfectly satisfactory from a legal point of view, can be set up in the United Kingdom. There has hitherto been no specialised text dealing with the particular problems which arise in relation to merchandising in the United Kingdom. This book aims to fill this gap, and to offer the information in a concise and readily accessible way by providing checklists, etc. Not only has there been little to refer to for guidance of the relevant legal principles in this field, but there have been few precedents of agreements suitable for local conditions from which to work. Again, it is hoped that the precedents provided in this volume will at least provide some guidance. Finally, because many people who work in the industry (especially overseas traders) do not have ready access to legal sources, very full Appendices are provided containing the statutory and other texts to which they may have occasion to refer – a sort of 'instant library' of source materials, as it were.

Writing the first book in a field is always difficult. As the seventeenth century bibliographer Thomas Bassett wrote 'To do a thing first, and to do it properly, is more than (perhaps) any has as yet to do; and therefore this [work] may well be capable of emendment [sic] or additions at least'.

The law in this book is stated as at 1 February 1987.

John N Adams

March 1987

Contents

Contents

Contents

CHAPTER 17   UNITED STATES   302
Copyright   302
Designs   306
Passing off and unfair competition   307
Trade marks   308
Defamation   309
Invasion of privacy   310
Expropriation of personality and violation of a right to publicity   311
Conclusion   312

SECTION III   PRECEDENTS

Table of statutes

References in this Table to *Statutes* are to Halsbury's Statutes of England (Fourth Edition) showing the volume and page at which the annotated text of the Act may be found.
References in **bold** type indicate where the section of an Act is set out in part or in full.
References are to paragraph numbers. References in *italics* refer to the page numbers of the Precedents.

Table of statutes

Table of statutes

Table of statutes

Table of statutes

Table of Statutory Instruments, International Conventions and European Legislation

Table of Cases

Table of cases

Table of cases

Table of cases

Decisions of the European Court of Justice are listed below numerically. These decisions
are also included in the preceding alphabetical list.

Table of cases

Merchandising: an historical survey

by Iain C Baillie

Early history

The use of 'characters', ie fictional persons or situations, for the marketing of products, probably first originated in the toy industry, which is still one of the major markets. That famous character 'Santa Claus' is recorded in various toys back to the beginning of the nineteenth century and probably also in the eighteenth century. The classic figure 'Punch', apart from his historic significance as a puppet figure, appears in other toys and models at least as far back as the early nineteenth century. If one can regard certain incidents in the Bible as creating 'characters' then toy Noah's Arks can be traced back to Germany in the sixteenth and seventeenth centuries. There is a reference in 1642 to a sign of a Noah's Ark in a toy shop in Germany. In the mid-nineteenth century children's china was made with scenes from Charles Dickens' works. The use of personalities for toys is evidenced by a clockwork figure of General Grant smoking a cigarette made in 1877, and there is a portrait doll from about 1864 representing the famous Swedish singer Jenny Lind. When she visited the United States in 1840 thousands of paper portrait dolls made in Germany were sold during her visit. One of the first characters from comic strips, namely the 'Yellow Kid', was made into a jigsaw puzzle in 1896.

A form of reverse character merchandising was the use in the 'Pets Grocery Stores' and other products made by the firm of Mason and Parker of toy packets bearing the names of real products, such as Fels-Naphtha Soap, Uneeda Biscuits, and Van Camps Pork and Bacon.

That ever popular toy the teddy bear was initially named after President Theodore 'Teddy' Roosevelt as a result of a cartoon in 1903 in the Washington Post by the cartoonist Clifford Berryman showing 'Teddy' Roosevelt refusing to shoot a bear cub. 'Alice In Wonderland' figures for soft toys were produced prior to World War I, and later, in 1923, a 'Peter Pan' model was made by Chad Valley.

One of the first major examples of character merchandising must have been the works of Beatrix Potter. As Margaret Laine in the book *The Magic Years of Beatrix Potter,* records: 'In 1903 after the success of the book *Squirrel Nutkin,* her characters "Peter Rabbit" and "Nutkin" had become nursery heroes. Soft "Peter Rabbits", made of velvet and fur appeared in Harrods and a squirrel named "Nutkin" had been bought by Mr Potter in the Burlington Arcade'. As Miss Laine comments 'A tiresome lady, who seems never to have heard of the tricky question of copyright, was proposing to design a nursery wallpaper with a frieze of Beatrix Potter animals'. Miss Potter was 'astonished and delighted by her success though she was understandably irritated by the wallpaper lady'.

Beatrix Potter is reported to have attempted to produce a 'Peter Rabbit' soft toy. Not only, however, were attempts to manufacture hindered by the monopoly of the European market by German manufacturers, but some of these manufacturers pirated her characters and she found the pirated versions on sale here in London. This led her in 1910 to support tariff reform, but there is no report as to whether she sued the pirates.

Establishment of character merchandising

However, it was probably in 1934, with the first appearance of 'Mickey Mouse' and, later on, of the other Disney characters, that the concept of character merchandising expanded to become a significant part of merchandising. Spreading out from toys to clothing and other articles for children, the industry started to gather momentum.

Thus, the concept of 'characters' started to grow at the end of the last century with the popular magazines and comic strips. Then, with the arrival of films, later radio and finally television and with the growth of marketing and advertising, character merchandising made more and more impact. Stemming both from the sponsorship concept and the toy concept there came the association of more and more goods with characters and manufacture of goods 'embodying' these characters.

Finally, in the mid 1960s there came to be a recognised industry of character merchandising and the growth of character merchandising agents, who have now established themselves as a recognised professional group.

Commercial potential

The commercial potential is obviously immense. In 1974 a Disney Productions' Annual Report indicated royalty revenues of over $15,000,000, while in 1978 the Disney Merchandising Division sold $27,000,000 in merchandise; in 1975, sales of 'Womble' products were quoted at £18,000,000 and in 1978 *Star Wars* was quoted at one point as having made $25,000,000 from box office revenue and $22,000,000 from licensed goods. Cy Schneider in Advertising Age, 30 April 1979, states that Kenner Products sold over $100,000,000 worth of *Star Wars* merchandise (mostly toys and games). He also points out that *Mary Poppins* by Walt Disney was a saleswoman for 46 manufacturers and sold everything from umbrellas to luggage to shoe polish. His estimate, in the USA, for retail value of licensed goods and services from cartoon characters in 1978 was $2.1 billion and for 1979, $3.1 billion. There is no need to go far to see the volume of 'Peanuts' goods, particularly 'Snoopy' goods.

A 1981 US campaign for a US character 'Strawberry Shortcake' (a little girl) projected a life of at least 25 years and a multitude of licensing potentials.

The same success has been evidenced by more recent major film productions such as Jurassic Park and other spectacular films of this nature. The 'Star Trek' series of television programmes and film productions are another example of very successful merchandising.

Therefore, although character merchandising has, perhaps, a long history and has grown substantially from the 1930s (Mickey Mouse is now well over 50), nevertheless it is only since the 1970s that character merchandising has become the major and established field of marketing which it is now. Although perhaps the original rapid growth in this field has somewhat plateaued, nevertheless it is still a major merchandising (promotional) activity which will continue for as long as one can foresee. New exploitable entities will arrive so long as the movie and TV industries release products which have a major impact. Also, as will be indicated, other entertainment media contribute their share to this activity. The publication each year of two or three guides to licensable products is one measure of this continued input.

Sources of characters

The present sources of characters tend to be from television and films. Major examples in the film industry were, of course, *Star Wars*, *Star Trek* and *Jurassic Park*. Examples from television are so numerous as hardly to need mentioning. For instance, there was the very popular *Kojak* which has become enshrined in the law on this field. The series *6 Million Dollar Man* which created the trade mark 'Bionic' as distinct from the original somewhat limited meaning of this word is an obvious example of the effect of this medium. The classic character creations from the comic strips, are also still very popular. 'Superman' and 'Batman' came from the comic strips into radio and television shows and finally to the major films, starting with *Superman — The Movie*, creating character merchandising based both on the original comic strip figure and on the materials from the film. 'Wonderwoman' is another example of movement from the comic strip to television, as is 'The Incredible Hulk'.

Equally, there are characters created in books, such as 'James Bond', ie 'Agent 007', the character created by Ian Fleming, which was enlarged by the series of very successful films. The theatre, though not so significant a source, has resulted in, for example, 'Peter Pan'. Children's books are, of course, still a very fruitful source of such characters and one need only mention Beatrix Potter and 'Peter Rabbit', and also 'Winnie -the-Pooh' and 'Paddington Bear'. In Great Britain, there was the 'Mr Men' series, another typical example of book characters moving into character merchandising.

A classic example of cartoon popularity is, of course, 'Peanuts', with the inimitable 'Snoopy' .

Merchandising does not necessarily always involve a character. Thus, the film *Jaws* appears to have been merchandised by the symbol of the film, ie the rising shark symbol. We shall see later there is a problem when the characteristic that becomes fixed in the public mind is merely a word or title, such as 'Jaws'.

The creation of characters is, of course, not confined to the areas of communication industries, ie books, comic strips or cartoons, films television and radio. Other industries can create characters, and an example would be the greeting card industry, where classic instances are 'Holly Hobbie' and 'Strawberry Shortcake'.

Characters from advertising

A new development also is the creation in advertising of characters which develop a life independent of the original product and move into the area of character merchandising. This, apparently at the present time, appears to be primarily a British phenomenon, although one can think of the Exxon (Esso) tiger and the Kellogg's 'Tony The Tiger'. Examples for instance, in Britain, were 'Buzby' and the Typhoo Tea character 'Gnu'. Indeed, some old characters such as the 'Bisto Kids' were modernised and used for merchandising as well as their original function of selling the goods with which they were first associated.

Traditionally the advertising industry seems to have viewed with some suspicion the use of characters in marketing and there is, perhaps, some vagueness in the boundary between character merchandising and the creation for advertising purposes of a particular character relating to one product. In so far as character merchandising law is concerned, the problem arises when a character, which has gained some public recognition in advertising one specific product of one manufacturer, is then applied by that manufacturer or others for the sale of other products; generally this only happens when the character achieves some form of independent life and public recognition, apart from the product which was originally advertised, though this in itself can, clearly, create problems.

Famous entities

A growing field is the application of the techniques developed in 'character merchandising' to merchandise products based on the reputation of real life entities. A prime example, of course, is the growing use of the Olympic image not only for sponsorship but by direct merchandising. Famous sportspersons are spreading the use of their identity beyond mere sponsorship of goods directly related to their sporting activity. Programmes were based on such famouse race horses as Red Rum, and there have been promotions based on famous buildings either in terms of their real identity or in their fictional identity, for example Castle Howard in Brideshead Revisited.

Market for character merchandising

The market for character merchandising tends to be primarily directed at children and teenagers which is of considerable significance in regard to the areas for which trade mark protection might be sought, as will be seen later in the discussion on trade mark registration. Nevertheless, there are markets directed at adults, for example in the toiletries field, and certainly the character merchandising industry is always pushing more widely the nature of products to which the characters can be applied. Thus the book, Country Diary of an Edwardian Lady, created a major marketing programme specifically directed at a female market over the age of 30.

While the 'blockbuster' feature characters attract attention and create the immense returns, it can be seen that a wide variety of characters can, by careful merchandising directed at the correct market, secure a valuable return in royalties. Even an unsuccessful film can sometimes secure a significant return by merchandising. Thus, *Sergeant Peppers Lonely Hearts Club Band* did not have the success as a film compared to *Grease* or *Saturday Night Fever* but nevertheless had a very successful merchandising return.

The scope of merchandising

The term 'character merchandising' has become somewhat suspect in that it is not adequate to cover all of the entities which are promoted using this selling technique. Some organisations such as opera houses and other prestigious entities are somewhat reluctant to be associated with an activity they associate with cartoon characters. For that reason, it is becoming more customary to refer to the commercial activity as Reputation Licensing or, because it includes use of copyright and other non-reputation rights, Image Licensing. The term character merchandising is, however, still often retained as a useful if somewhat old-fashioned phrase.

This broader concept of commercial promotion can then be broken down into two areas:

(a) Commercial promotion by the owner of the rights itself, namely the owner of a trade mark or other reputation characteristic or copyright, in the promotion of related products by the same entity. Here the main difficulty is usually the extension of reputation and the maintaining of a barrier against attempted encroachment by others. This will be explored in this work under rights which are created by trade mark protection and goodwill protection.

(b) The passing of these rights to others to promote their activities. It is in this field that one has so many different so-called activities ranging from the old-fashioned character merchandising to sponsorship, endorsement, collegiate licensing and brand licensing. All of these names really do not indicate any major difference in activity but rather differences in the nature of the entity being used for promotion. The same rules will generally apply, although some additional requirements will exist when one is using the reputation of a real life person such as a sportsperson or a real life entity such as a horse or famous building or events such as the Olympic Games.

It is the increasing realisation by owners of entities having a major public reputation that there is an exploitable asset in the reputation itself which continues to expand the boundaries of this business activity quite apart from the continuing creation of new exploitable products in those fields such as films and television which have historically been exploited in this way.

Introduction

The terms 'character merchandising (or marketing)', 'personality (or reputation merchandising)', or simply 'merchandising', from a commercial point of view cover closely related fields, which, however, from a legal point of view, are very different. 'Character merchandising' involves the use in the marketing or advertising of goods or services of a fictional personality or situation. 'Personality merchandising' involves the use of the true identity of an individual, or occasionally an animal, in the marketing or advertising of goods or services. Between these two types, lies a rather unclear area where fictional characters played by real actors are used. In these cases it is difficult to separate the actor from his screen personality. To many people the fictional character is real. In addition to these situations, there is another type of merchandising operation which is becoming increasingly prevalent at the present day. That is, the use of famous trade marks to sell products far removed from their original associations. For example, Coca-Cola has been used to sell items of clothing, and similarly Kodak. Some of these uses, as eg Coca-Cola on T shirts, are simply a form of advertising. In other cases, when more obviously trade mark use of the original mark is being made, it is really a case of the trade mark owners seeking to exploit the reputation which attaches to their famous marks. Since, as we shall see, the goodwill attaching to those marks enables the proprietors, rightly, through the action of passing off to enjoin their use by third parties in fields somewhat removed from those covered by the original registrations, there would appear to be no objection, whether legal or otherwise, to the trade mark proprietors being able to extend their registrations to cover such fields. This type of operation presents, in the main, only the problems generally encountered in trade marks law which are adequately covered by existing texts, it is not a primary concern of this book. The focus of this book is character and reputation merchandising, and the particular problems involved in these operations.

Probably the characteristic common to both of these kinds of operation, is the importance of the character, or whatever, *as a commodity in its own right,* independent of the goods, or services, to which it is attached, or with which it is associated. No doubt the goods or services may themselves be desired, *but so also of itself is the character.* In this respect, there is an obvious difference between characters and trade marks. Classically, trade marks were an indication to the public about the origin of goods, a symbol to facilitate consumer choice. A residual element of this classical concept of a trade mark is still alive in the United Kingdom. However, whilst superficially it may seem reasonable to insist upon something like the classical concept of a trade mark, in the real world things are not ordered in quite such a straightforward way, and such insistence is less persuasive. As with characters, some trade marks become valued by consumers as commodities in their own right, as things independent of the product to which they were originally attached — as eg Coca-Cola, and it becomes very difficult realistically to separate this aspect from their true trade mark aspect. Similarly, in the case of some characters, where over the years a reputation for good quality associated with them (as a result of well-run merchandising operations) has grown up, a distinct trade mark aspect has come to attach to the characters.

When we turn to personality merchandising, we find both the commodity aspect and the consumer choice aspect, inextricably intertwined. Products were commended by persons of consequence from the earliest days of advertising (and before advertising in the modern sense came into existence). Today, endorsement of products, especially sports goods by well-known sportsmen, is much the same thing. By contrast, in much of the merchandising involving pop stars, it is the commodity element which is dominant.

Whilst the common basis of all true merchandising is the subject of the operation as a commodity in its own right, the uses to which this form of activity is put differ widely. People such as sportsmen, whose effective working lives in the activity for which they have become known is necessarily rather short, use merchandising as a way of maximising their incomes in the brief periods during which they flourish. Similar uses are made of it in the constantly changing entertainment world. It also provides a valuable spin-off for the motion picture industry, especially in these days of small cinema audiences (not to mention video piracy). It has also proved of value in fund raising for many charities and non-profit making organisations – eg the World Wild Life Fund panda has been extensively merchandised, and the National Trust now have many shops and products bearing their name. The National Football League in America runs a very extensive operation, and no doubt the time may come when some of our professional sports associations may do likewise (some operate in a small way already).

From a legal point of view, it is the subject of a merchandising programme as a commodity in its own right, which presents difficulties. The concept simply does not fit comfortably into the existing intellectual property categories, and the various types of merchandising operation each present their own special difficulties.

Although the phrases 'character merchandising', 'personality promotion or marketing' etc tend to be used both in relation to the licensing *and* the selling of goods to which the reputation is attached, it is obviously necessary from a legal point of view to distinguish the two. For that reason, it would perhaps be better to use the terms 'character' or 'reputation *licensing*' to distinguish that aspect of the arrangement. Certainly in a legal agreement one should never use the word 'merchandising' to define the transfer of rights from the owner of the reputation to the licensee. This matter of terminology can also be a matter of some delicacy when dealing with prestigious cultural organisations, where resistance may be encountered if their licensing activities are described as 'merchandising'. It will be much more acceptable to describe them simply as 'licensing'. This book is concerned with both the licensing and selling operations, and the phrase 'merchandising' provides a convenient umbrella for this combination, however, the distinction mentioned above should be borne in mind, at least when drafting agreements.

Most merchandising operations involve three key persons: the owner of the property to be merchandised; the licensees, who will use and market the goods or services to which the property is attached; and the agents who will negotiate the licences. Obviously, other important people will be involved, such as distributors, but these three lie at the heart of the operation, and it is with their problems, and especially those of the owner and agent, with which this book is concerned.

ENGLAND AND WALES

Part A

Acquisition of merchandising rights

Chapter 1

Copyright, registered designs and patents

COPYRIGHT
Introduction

1.1 As explained in the title on the previous page, the key to a successful merchandising operation is the possession of property rights which will enable the merchandiser to prevent piracy. Of these property rights, in most cases the most important is copyright. Copyright can subsist in literary, dramatic, musical and artistic works. Artistic works are, perhaps, the most important for present purposes. They include drawings, photographs and works of artistic craftsmanship. Thus, copyright can be used to enjoin the production by pirates of such things as heat transfers (for T-shirts, etc), soft toys, dolls, items of clothing[1] etc. In the United Kingdom, copyright in such original works is covered by the Copyright, Designs and Patents Act 1988. That Act also provides for the subsistence of copyright in a miscellany of things, which used under the previous Act, the 1956 Act, to be referred to as 'Part II' works. These works are derivative, and in many countries are protected by neighbouring rights, rather than copyright. Such works include sound recordings, films, TV and radio broadcasts, and the published editions of works.

1 Eg *Radley Gowns Ltd v Costas Spyrou* [1975] FSR 455; *Aljose Fashions Ltd v Alfred Young & Co* [1978] FSR 364, CA.

1.2 The plan of this chapter is first of all to give a general outline of the UK law of copyright under the Copyright, Designs and Patents Act 1988, and then to consider in more detail the subsistence of copyright in the various items which commonly feature in merchandising programmes.

1.3 At the outset, however, it may be worthwhile offering a caution. Although copyright can in principle afford protection to many different items, this protection will be valueless at the end of the day if the merchandiser is unable to prove title to the copyright. It is, unfortunately, only too commonly the case that the question of ownership is only properly broached when it is necessary to stop piracy. The result can be that the merchandiser will discover at this stage that it has no rights upon which to rely. Title to copyright must be established at the outset. We offer suggestions on this point later.[1]

1 See para 1.81 et seq.

UK copyright law in outline

1.4 The basic rule under the transitional provisions of the 1988 Act is that copyright subsists in an existing work after the commencement of the Act only if it subsisted immediately before commencement. The commencement date was 1 August 1989. Accordingly it is necessary to consider some of the provisions of the 1956 Act in order to determine in relation to a work created before that date, whether or not copyright subsisted on that date, and to whom it belongs.[1]

1   See para 1.48 et seq; 1.93 et seq.

1.5 Copyright confers a property right in original literary, dramatic and artistic works.[1] 'Artistic works' include photographs (as noted above) and sculptures, as well as graphic works.[2] Copyright also subsists in sound recordings, films, broadcasts and cable programmes,[3] as well as in the typographical arrangements of published editions.[4]

1   1988 Act, s 1(1)(a).
2   1988 Act, s 4(1)(a).
3   1988 Act, s 1(1)(b).
4   1988 Act, s 1(1)(c).

1.6 Copyright arises automatically: since the UK adheres to the Berne Convention, no registration or other formality is necessary. The basic rule is that the first owner of the copyright in a work is its author,[1] except for works created by employees in the course of their employment.[2] In the nature of things, different rules apply to determine the ownership of derivative works. Some of these will be considered later. The duration of copyright for original works was 50 years from the end of the calendar year in which the author died.[3] The Term Harmonisation Directive,[4] is implemented by the Duration of Copyright and Rights in Performances Regulations (the 'Duration of Copyright Regulations').[5] Under the Directive,with effect from 1 July 1995, the basic copyright term is increased to the life of the author plus 70 years. Unfortunately, the Regulations implementing this change are only effective in the UK from 1 January 1996.[6] Any copyright owner prejudiced by this non-implementation, will have a claim against the UK government under the principle established in *Francovich v Italy*,[7] because the act of publication would have infringed had the Directive been implemented.[8]

1   1988 Act, s 11(1).
2   1988 Act, s 11(2) – there are other exceptions not relevant for present purposes.
3   1988 Act, s 12(1).
4   No 93/98/EEC OJ L 290, 24.11.93, p 9.
5   1995/3297.
6   Ibid, Reg 1(2).
7   Case C-6/90 [1993] 2 CMLR 66. Applied *Brasserie du Pêcheur SA v Federal Republic of Germany*; *R v Secretary of State for Transport, ex p Factortame*: C-48/93, [1996] All ER (EC) 301.
8   Copyright, Designs and Patents Act 1988, s 18.

1.7 When the creator exploits an artistic work industrially, the period of copyright protection is reduced to 25 years from the end of the calendar year in which articles embodying the work are first marketed.[1] This is obviously of considerable importance in relation to long term merchandising properties. The effect of Schedule 1, paragraph 14(1) of the 1988 Act is that for works in which copyright subsisted on 1 August 1989, and which were being exploited industrially on that date (eg toy representations of the work were being manufactured by a licensee), protection will cease after 1 August 2014. Attempting to prolong this period by making minor changes to the work will not succeed in attracting new copyright protection unless a fresh work has been created.[2] When only part of an artistic work is exploited industrially, the above provisions apply only to the part so exploited.

1   1988 Act, s 52(1) and (2) – see para 1.57 below.
2   *Interlego AG v Tyco Industries Inc* [1989] AC 217, [1988] RPC 343.

1.8   Copyright can be infringed in a number of ways. One of the most important of the acts restricted by copyright is copying the work, either directly or indirectly.[1] Literary characters as *such* do not enjoy copyright.[2] The same is true of characters in films. It should be noted, however, that unauthorised use of still frame would infringe the copyright in the film.[3] Therefore, an image of a character in a film cannot be exploited without permission.

1   S 17 – see on indirect copying *King Features* para 1.17 below.
2   See below para 1.40.
3   S 17(4). This was the case under the 1956 Act also *Spelling Goldberg Productions Inc v BPC Publishing Ltd* [1981] RPC 283.

1.9   Copyright is of little assistance to real persons seeking to control the exploitation of their images.[1] A photograph of a person attracts copyright, but, in the absence of contractual provisions to the contrary, where freelance photographers are used, this vests in the creator of the work, the photographer.[2] It is therefore the photographer who has the right to exploit the image.[3] If a photograph or film is commissioned for private and domestic purposes, the commissioner has a right to prevent copies being issued to the public, being exhibited or shown in public, or being broadcast or cablecast,[4] but photographs which do not fall within this limited exception need the consent of the photographer for publication, reproduction, or other exploitation.

1   See para 1.35.
2   1988 Act, s 11(1).
3   Under the Copyright Act 1956 the owner of a photograph commissioned for money or money's worth was the commissioner – s 4(3). This provision was clearly contrary to the Berne Convention. However, it governs works commissioned before 1 August 1989, but which were made after commencement – 1988 Act, Sch 1, para 11(2).
4   1988 Act, s 85.

Types of property subject to copyright

DRAWINGS

1.10   Drawings, such as of cartoon characters, form one of the commonest types of property merchandised. Drawings are protected as 'artistic works' under section 4(1) of the 1988 Act. The term 'artistic work' should not be understood as entailing any requirement that the work in question should qualify as fine art. The subsection makes it clear that protection is afforded 'irrespective of artistic quality'. Protection is even afforded to purely technical drawings.[1]

1   But note the effect of 1988 Act, s 51 discussed below.

1.11 The fact that the original drawing is very simple does not matter. The 'Saint' symbol consisting of a matchstick man with a halo is a perfectly good subject for copyright. As Megarry J said in *British Northrop Ltd v Texteam Blackburn Ltd:*[1]

'It may indeed be that something may be drawn which cannot fairly be called a drawing of any kind: a single straight line drawn with the aid of a ruler would not seem to me a very promising subject for copyright. But apart from cases of such barren and naked simplicity as that, I should be slow to exclude drawings from copyright on the mere score of simplicity.'[2]

1   [1974] RPC 57 at 68. See also *Chas Walker & Co Ltd v British Picker Co Ltd* [1961] RPC 57.
2   This dictum reflects the fact that the originality threshold in UK law is very low – see *Ladbroke (Football Ltd) v William Hill (Football) Ltd* [1964] 1 WLR 273; *Bookmakers' Afternoon Greyhound Services Ltd v Wilf Gilbert (Staffordshire) Ltd* [1994] FSR 723.

1.12 Although in other contexts the effect of European harmonisation may be to raise the originality threshold,[1] for present purposes the above dictum still seems to be correct. It may be, however, that the simpler the drawing, the more difficult it will be as a matter of evidence to prove infringement.[2]

1   See the Software Directive 91/250/EEC; and the draft Database Directive.
2   *Duriron Co Inc v Hugh Jennings & Co Ltd* [1984] FSR 1. See also *Kenrick & Co v Lawrence & Co* (1890) 25 QBD 99.

1.13 If a fictional character in a literary work is represented in the form of a drawing, that drawing will qualify for protection under the rubric of artistic works, irrespective of artistic quality.[1] Thus unauthorised reproduction of a cartoon figure, for instance, can be prevented.[2] Likewise, the use of a drawing on a T-shirt, similar to the drawing used by the copyright owners of the film 'Jaws' for publicity purposes, infringed.[3]

1   1988 Act, s 4(1)(a).
2   See *King Features Syndicate v O and M Kleeman Ltd* [1940] Ch 806 – see below.
3   *Universal City Studios Inc v Mukhtar and Sons Ltd* [1976] 2 All ER 330, [1976] FSR 252.

1.14 A fictional character which does not begin life as a drawing, but is represented only in the form of a three-dimensional object, such as a puppet, will be protected only if it can be classified as a sculpture, or if it has sufficient artistic merit to be called a work of artistic craftsmanship. This is dealt with below.[1]

1   Para 1.23 et seq.

1.15 An important feature of the law is that, subject to a special provision in the Act discussed below, copyright in a two-dimensional artistic work is infringed by reproduction in either two or three-dimensional form. Not only may copyright owners sue if their drawings are copied in two-dimensional form, they also have a remedy if their two-dimensional works are reproduced in three dimensions and *vice versa*.[1] Thus, the copyright in a drawing of a character will be infringed not only when it is copied as a drawing, or reproduced on a T-shirt, but also when it is used as the basis for a three-dimensional object such as a toy or a doll.

1   1988 Act, s 17(3).

1.16 Section 51 of the Copyright, Designs and Patents Act 1988 has the effect that copyright in a design document or model for anything other than an artistic work is not infringed by an article made to the design. Few drawings used in merchandising are *for* things which of themselves would be artistic works (works of artistic craftsmanship or sculptures would almost certainly be the relevant categories), and it has been argued that copying a design document or model which was not *for* an artistic work, would not infringe because of this provision.[1] The potential consequences of this ill-worded provision being interpreted in this way would be catastrophic. Since this would effect a fundamental change in the law, it is unlikely to have been intended. The better view is that cartoon drawings, not being at the outset drawings *for* anything except themselves, do not fall within this provision.[2]

1   Christie [1989] EIPR 253.
2   See Dworkin and Taylor [1990] EIPR 33.

1.17 Two further problems need to be discussed in relation to drawings: protection will be of little value if it is only direct copying of specific drawings which can be enjoined; and it will be of little value if it cannot be used to enjoin the production of such things as soft toys based on the characters, as these are often the most important type of goods dealt in. We will deal with each of these problems in turn.

1.18 Although it is commonly said that there can be no copyright in an idea as such, but only in the expression of an idea, this is a misleading statement[1] and should in any event not be taken as implying that there cannot be infringement where, although no particular drawing is copied exactly, the allegedly infringing copy has a strong family resemblance to the original character. The case of *King Features Syndicate Inc v O and M Kleeman*[2] provides a good illustration of this point. This case was under the Copyright Act 1911, but the essential point of the case is relevant to the interpretation of the present Act. The plaintiffs owned the copyright in a number of drawings of a strip cartoon 'Popeye the Sailor'[3] which appeared in various American and Canadian newspapers. The plaintiffs granted licences to British firms to make and sell dolls, mechanical toys, brooches and other articles featuring the figure of 'Popeye'. The defendants, who had refused to accept the plaintiffs' licensing terms, imported and sold without authorisation, 'Popeye' dolls, toys and brooches. The plaintiffs claimed an injunction for infringement of their copyright. The Court of Appeal held that the defendants' dolls (but not their brooches) were reproductions in a material form of the plaintiffs' original artistic work, even though they were not copied directly from any particular sketch. It was also suggested that the designer of the doll had not in fact copied any sketch at all, but a doll made by one of the plaintiffs' licensees. This argument did not avail the defendants either. As Clauson LJ said:[4]

'There can be no doubt at all that a figure which in fact reproduces an original artistic work consisting, in substance, of a sketch of that figure, is none the less a reproduction of the original artistic work, because the maker of it has copied it not directly from the original but from some representation derived directly or indirectly from the original work.'

So far as the brooches were concerned however, his Lordship was unable on a careful comparison with the various drawings to find sufficient similarity to satisfy him that they were such reproductions as to infringe the plaintiffs' rights in any of the drawings put in evidence. The House of Lords, however, unanimously differed from this view, and held that the brooches also infringed the plaintiffs' copyright.

1   See Laddie, Prescott and Vitoria *Modern Law of Copyright* Butterworths 1995, para 2.73 et seq.
2   [1940] Ch 806. On appeal to House of Lords [1941] AC 417.
3   As to the significance of 'Popeye' in the history of merchandising see Phillips 'Elzie Segar: Intellectual Property Creator Extraordinary' (1986) 12 EIPR 373.
4   *King Features Syndicate Inc v O and M Kleeman Ltd* [1940] Ch 806 at 816.

1.19   It will have been noted that the infringing items in this case were three-dimensional objects, not other drawings, yet this fact did not help the defendants notwithstanding that the Copyright Act 1911 simply enjoined reproduction in 'in any material form'. The wording of the Copyright Act 1988 is absolutely specific, however, as was the 1956 Act.[1] Section 17(3) provides that in relation to an artistic work, copying includes the making of a copy in three dimensions of a two-dimensional work and the making of a copy in two dimensions of a three-dimensional work.[2]

1   1988 Act, s 3(5)(a) and 48(1).
2   1988 Act, s 17(3).

1.20   To summarise therefore:
    (1) if the allegedly infringing work reproduces a substantial part of the original, then it will be held to be an infringement even though it does not exactly reproduce any particular drawing and even though it may have been copied indirectly rather than directly;
    (2) in the same way, three-dimensional reproductions can infringe as well as drawings and other two-dimensional reproductions.
The difference between two and three-dimensional reproductions, as was pointed out in the *Popeye* case,[1] is that in the case of the latter there may be more difficulty in forming a conclusion on the degree of resemblance between the infringing article and the original work. Indeed, section 9(8) of the Copyright Act 1956 provided that:

'The making of an object of any description which is in three-dimensions shall not be taken to infringe the copyright in an artistic work in two-dimensions, if the object would not appear, to persons who are not experts in relation to objects of that description, to be a reproduction of the artistic work.'

1   See above.

1.21 In *Merlet v Mothercare*[1] the Court of Appeal upheld a defence based on this sub-section, on the ground that the product, a baby cape with a hood, would not be recognised as a reproduction of the cutting pattern in which the plaintiff's copyright lay. Although the 1988 Act contains no equivalent of section 9(8), it is believed that on similar evidence the outcome would be the same. Had the plaintiff been able to rely on a proper set of drawings to which a resemblance would have been apparent, the outcome would have been different.[2] Certainly, this defence did not cause difficulty for the plaintiffs in *British Leyland Motor Corpn v Armstrong Patents Co Ltd*[3] (where the objects in question were exhaust pipes for cars).

1   [1986] RPC 115.
2   See also *Johnstone Safety Ltd v Peter Cook (International) plc* [1990] FSR 161.
3   [1986] AC 577, [1986] RPC 279.

1.22 It is instructive in this connection to compare *McCrum v Eisner*[1] in which reproduction model soldiers in a different pose from the plaintiff's were held to be non-infringing, with *Mirage Studios v Counter-Feat Clothing Co Ltd* in which it was held that there was an arguable case that the defendant's figures resembling the plaintiff's 'Ninja Turtle' characters, infringed even though they were not exact reproductions.[2] The difference between the two cases, it may be suggested, lies in the fact that where a figure is standard, as in the case of a soldier, relatively minor changes will suffice to distinguish, whereas if the figure is fanciful, much greater differences will be needed.

1   (1917) 87 LJ Ch 99.
2   [1991] FSR 145.

WORKS OF ARTISTIC CRAFTSMANSHIP

1.23 Again, we must not be misled by the word 'artistic', for whilst the protection afforded to works of artistic craftsmanship by section 4(1)(c) of the 1988 Act does not extend to works 'irrespective of artistic quality',[1] many kinds of object such as models, puppets etc which can form the basis of valuable merchandising operations are protected.

1   See 1988 Act, s 4(1)(a), para 1.10 above.

1.24 The meaning of 'works of artistic craftsmanship' was discussed by the House of Lords in *Hensher Ltd v Restawhile Upholstery (Lancs) Ltd.*[1] The alleged work of artistic craftsmanship in that case was the prototype for a popular suite of furniture. It was held that in determining whether or not a work was a work of artistic craftsmanship, the court should not make an aesthetic judgment, but should view the matter generally in accordance with all the evidence. On the evidence however, the appellants had failed to establish that their suite was regarded as of artistic character. Lord Reid said:[2]

> 'I think one must avoid philosophic or metaphysical argument about the nature of beauty, not only because there does not seem to be any consensus about this but also because those who are ignorant of philosophy are entitled to have opinions about what is artistic. I think that by common usage it is proper for a person to say that in his opinion

a thing has an artistic character if he gets pleasure or satisfaction or it may be uplift from contemplating it. If any substantial section of the public genuinely admires and values a thing for its appearance and gets pleasure or satisfaction, whether emotional or intellectual, from looking at it, I would accept that it is artistic although many others may think it meaningless or common or vulgar.'

He found, however, that in the present case there was no evidence at all that anyone regarded the appellants' furniture as artistic. The appellants' object was to produce something which would sell. He also pointed out that whilst the author's intention might be a pointer, the thing produced must itself be assessed without giving decisive weight to the author's scheme of things. The other members of the House reached the same conclusion that the furniture had not been shown to be artistic, but no clear consensus emerges as to what the proper approach should be. Lord Morris and Lord Dilhorne thought it was a question of fact to be decided on the evidence. Lord Simon, with an eye on the history of the provision, thought that it depended upon whether or not the work was made by an artist craftsman, and Lord Kilbrandon that the true test was whether the author had been consciously concerned to produce a work of art. Whilst these differences of approach raise fascinating questions when applied to the products of whole schools of twentieth century art (eg does Marcel Duchamp's lavatory pan qualify as a work of artistic craftsmanship, or Andy Warhol's Brillo pad boxes?), it seems reasonably clear that most types of work which are likely to be the subject of merchandising such as the props from science fiction movies, are likely to qualify as works of artistic craftsmanship because they are works of imagination and fantasy.[3] There could be uncertainties, however, and the safe advice must be, wherever possible, to rely on copyright in drawings so that it is clear that the question of artistic quality is not in issue.[4]

1   [1976] AC 64.
2   Ibid at p 78.
3   See *Shelley Films* para 1.25 below.
4   See para 1.10 et seq.

1.25 In *Shelley Films Ltd v Rex Features*[1] it was held to be arguable that a film set recreating an historic scene and consisting of numerous components artistically arranged, was a work of artistic craftsmanship. By the same token, it is likely that fanciful props will be held to be works of artistic craftsmanship, but not ordinary costumes,[2] though possibly elaborate suits of armour, and fanciful costumes of the sort used in science fiction films and the like, might be held to be. In the case of plastic objects, the moulds will often be prepared from drawings, in which case protection will be afforded to the products via those drawings, as explained above. It sometimes happens though that the moulds are hand-carved from photographs. In this case, there is no reason why they should not qualify as sculptures and enjoy protection as such.[3]

1   [1994] EMLR 134.
2   *Merlet v Mothercare* [1986] RPC 115.
3   1988 Act, s 4(1)(a) and 4(2). See *Martin v Polyplas Manufacturers Ltd* [1969] NZLR 1046; *Wham-O Manufacturing v Lincoln Industries* [1985] RPC 127 (NZ).

PHOTOGRAPHS AND FILMS

1.26 Photographs are a very common category of merchandised property.[1] They enjoy copyright as artistic works under section 4(1)(a) of the 1988 Act in the same way as drawings. The definition in the 1988 Act includes electronic photographs: it is

> 'a recording of light or other radiation on any medium on which an image is produced or from which an image may by any means be produced, and which is not part of a film.'[2]

1   See eg *Duomo Inc v Giftcraft* (1984) 1 CPR (3d) 165.
2   1988 Act, s 4(2).

1.27 Cinematograph films are separately protected under the 1988 Act.[1] 'Film' is defined to mean

> 'a recording on any medium from which a moving image may by any means be produced.'[2]

The soundtrack of a film is protected as a sound recording.[3]

1   1988 Act, s 1(1)(b).
2   1988 Act, s 5(1).
3   1988 Act, s 5(1).

1.28 Copying in relation to a film includes making a photograph of the whole or any substantial part of any image forming part of a film.[1]

1   1988 Act, s 17(4).

1.29 Films, including their soundtracks, were protected under section 13 of the 1956 Act. It had been doubted whether the definition of 'cinematograph film' in section 13(10) was apt to cover 'stills' from films. The Court of Appeal held however that it did.[1] Films made before the commencement of the Copyright Act 1956 were protected under the Copyright Act 1911 either as dramatic works or as a series of photographs:[2] there was no equivalent of section 13. The sound tracks were protected under the provisions for mechanical instruments.[3]

1   *Spelling Goldberg Productions Inc v BPC Publishing Ltd* [1981] RPC 283 – see para 1.8 above.
2   Copyright Act 1956, Sch 7, para 14. See eg *Pathé Pictures Ltd v Bancroft* (1933) Macg Cop Cas 403; *Nordish Films v Orda* (1922) Macg Cop Cas 337.
3   Copyright Act 1911, s 19.

1.30 The most troublesome questions in relation to photographs are usually about ownership of copyright. In the case of freelance photographers, not working to commission, the position is straightforward: as noted above, they, as authors, are the owners of the copyright.[1]

1   1988 Act, ss 9(1) and 11(1).

1.31 Because the transitional provisions do not affect the ownership of works created before 1 August 1989, it is necessary to be aware of the old provisions governing the ownership of photographs. Under the 1956 Act, 'author' was defined in relation to a photograph, as meaning the person who, at the time when the photograph was taken, was the owner of the material on which it was taken.[1] A 'photograph' meant any product of photography or of any process akin to photography, other than a part of a cinematograph film.[2] Thus, where a negative was used, the photograph was the negative, not the print which was simply a copy. The same thing applied in the case of photography using media other than photographic film or plates to record the image. An exception to this basic rule was that the commissioner of a photograph for money or money's worth was its owner under the 1956 Act.[3] However, in the absence of evidence that this was the case at the time the photograph was taken, the photographer, as the owner of the film on which the photograph was taken, was the owner.[4]

1   Copyright Act 1956, s 48(1).
2   Ibid.
3   S 4(3). The same provision applied to commissioned portraits.
4   *Apple Corps v Cooper* [1993] FSR 286 – the cover photograph for the album 'Sergeant Pepper's Lonely Hearts Club Band' taken by the deceased father of the defendant.

1.32   In the case of photographs taken by employees, again the position is clear. Section 11(2) of the 1988 Act has the effect that where it is made by the author in the course of his employment, his or her employer is the first owner of the copyright subject to any agreement to the contrary. The position was the same under the 1956 Act.[1]

1   S 4(4).

1.33   Under the 1956 Act, where a celebrity was requested by a photographer to give a sitting without any charge being made for the taking of the photographs, copyright would vest in the photographer,[1] notwithstanding that the celebrity might subsequently have purchased copies. Had the subject commissioned the photographs for money or money's worth, however, the subject, as commissioner, would be the copyright owner, as explained above. Other consideration than money might suffice to vest the copyright in someone other than the photographer, as owner of the film, if it was clear that that was the intention of the parties.[2] Thus permitting the photographer to go on to premises for the purposes of taking the photograph could be consideration, although the old case of *Stackemann v Paton*,[3] which was decided under the pre-1911 law, would possibly have been decided differently under the 1956 Act.[4] In that case a photographer was permitted to go on to school premises, for the purposes of taking photographs of the pupils. It was held that copyright vested in the proprietors of the school.

1   *Ellis v Marshall (H) & Son* (1895) 64 LJQB 757; *Melville v Mirror of Life Co* [1895] 2 Ch 531 (decided under old law but still good on this point).
2   The wording of s 4(3) of the 1956 Act required the payment of money *or money's worth*.
3   [1906] 1 Ch 774.
4   Fine Arts Copyright Act 1862, s 1 used the words 'good or valuable consideration', which could be broader than 'money or money's worth', in the present Act. However, as Holmes pointed out, anything can be consideration if it is so intended – *The Common Law* (1881) Little, Brown & Co, p 295. It really is a question of the intention of the parties to be gathered from all the surrounding facts.

1.34   Because of a practice common in the pop world, the abolition of the 'money or moneys' worth' provision will have little effect on the ownership

of that important category of merchandisable property, photographs of pop
stars. In their early days, groups are taken by their managers to freelance
photographers. The understanding is that these photographers will take
the photographs free, using their own film. The photographers then try
to sell the photographs through agencies to periodicals, merchandising
companies (who produce posters and the like), and other media likely to
buy the pictures and give them publicity. It seems clear that under the
general principles of copyright law outlined above, the copyright belongs
to the photographers. Moreover, since the whole object of the exercise is
to generate publicity for the groups, to which end the photographer will
be expending time and money in reliance on his understanding with the
group's manager that he is free to deal in the photographs, it seems also
to be reasonably clear that the managers would in general be *estopped* from
asserting any form of right to prevent the photographers from trying to
sell the photographs.[1] Usually, the point at which groups would want to
assert some sort of right to the photographs is when they have become
successful. Since, however, the photographers have expended their time
and money in promoting the photographs (which may well have
contributed to the group's fame) precisely on the basis that if this happens,
they will have a valuable commodity, it would seem quite inequitable were
the groups to be permitted to do so. In addition to the estoppel argument,
it would be possible for a court to imply a contract from the surrounding
circumstances to give effect to the intention of the parties. The inequitable
features found potentially to exist in a copyright assignment between a
group and its manager in *Clifford Davis Management v WEA Records Ltd*[2]
do not exist, and there is furthermore no inequality of bargaining power
since the groups negotiate with the photographers through their managers
who are experienced men of business, and the purpose of the arrangement
is to promote the groups' trade not to restrain it. The moral is, that if a
group's management wish to impose conditions which will limit in time,
or otherwise restrict the use that may be made of such photographs, they
should do so expressly at the time the photographer is engaged, and should
do so in writing. Such agreements are met with in practice. A typical
restriction would be on the use of the photographs for posters.

1   The principle of proprietory estoppel is applicable to intellectual property rights – see
    eg *Bulmer Ltd and Showerings Ltd v Bollinger SA and Champagne Lanson Père et
    Fils* [1978] RPC 79 at 135-6. On proprietory estoppel see especially *Inwards v Baker*
    [1965] 2 QB 29; *Ives Investments Ltd v High* [1967] 2 QB 379.
2   [1975] 1 All ER 237. See also *Schroeder Music Publishing Co Ltd v Macaulay* [1974]
    3 All ER 616.

1.35 Photographs of a face, even elaborately made up, do not infringe any
copyright,[1] however photographs of copyright items such as clothing[2] taken
otherwise than in a public environment where photography is permitted
could infringe copyright. Photographs of cartoon drawings and the like
would also in similar circumstances infringe copyright. Where copyright
material is exposed in a public place by the owner in circumstances where
photography can reasonably be expected, then a licence to take
photographs will be implied. Whether in such cases the photographer will
always be free to sell his pictures must be doubted. It must depend on the
surrounding facts, eg you would always be free to sell a photograph which
reproduced incidentally an advertising hoarding,[3] you might be free to sell

the photographs taken at a fashion show where photography has been permitted,[4] but circumstances could be envisaged where it is clear that photographs are permitted to be taken for private use only.

1　There is no copyright in a face – *Merchandising Corpn of America Inc v Harpbond Inc* [1983] FSR 32 ('Adam Ant').
2　But see above.
3　See eg *Vincent v Universal Housing* (1928-35) Macg Cop Cas 275 (photograph of garden protected as architectural work).
4　Similarly, in the case of public events such as football matches – *Krouse v Chrysler Canada Ltd* (1973) 40 DLR (3d) 15.

MUSIC AND LYRICS

1.36　Musical scores are protected under sections 1(1) and 3(1) of the 1988 Act. 'Musical work' means a work consisting of music, exclusive of any words or action intended to be sung, spoken or performed with the music. Any lyrics involved enjoy separate protection under sections 1(1) and 3(1) as literary works.

1.37　The music and lyrics involved in merchandising operations are usually those from the soundtracks of films. Under the 1956 Act 'cinematograph film' was defined to include the sounds embodied in any soundtrack associated with the film, thus the acts restricted by section 13(1) in relation to a cinematograph film, were also restricted in relation to its soundtrack.[1] These acts were making a copy of the film; causing it to be seen or heard in public; broadcasting it and causing it to be transmitted to subscribers to a diffusion service. Consequently, in relation to any unauthorised acts of this sort, there would be an infringement of section 13 as well as of section 2 which protected the underlying musical or literary works. Under the 1988 Act, films and sound recordings are separately protected under section 5, so that the copyright in the sound-track is independent of that in the film. The underlying musical or literary works continue to enjoy their own copyright, as explained above.

1　It would appear that the s 2 copyright in the music, and any s 12 copyright in a pre-existing sound recording incorporated on the soundtrack could also have been infringed, and with regard to the sound recording in circumstances where the copyright in the soundtrack itself was not infringed – s 13(9). Where records made from the soundtrack were released the relevant copyrights were s 2 and s 13 (see s 12(9)). If the record and soundtrack were made simultaneously, the relevant provisions were probably ss 2, 12 and 13. The soundtracks of films made before 1 June 1957 were protected under the Copyright Act 1911, s 19.

1.38　Even very short passages consisting of one or two notes can infringe copyright in a musical work,[1] and the work itself can similarly consist of only a note or two.[2]

1　*Lloyd v Lord David Dundas* (1985) Times, 13 June, p 5 (four notes).
2　Even a single note, required to be rendered in a particularly distinctive way, might be a musical work.

1.39　The effect of the Duration of Copyright Regulations[1] and the Copyright Rights in Performances Regulations[2] is that significant changes have been made as to the ownership of the copyright in a film. The basic provision of the 1988 Act was that the person by whom the arrangements necessary for the making of the recording of film were undertaken was the owner – ie the producer.[3] The effect of the Regulations is dealt with at the end of this chapter.[4]

1   1995/3297.
2   Expected to come into force by the end of 1996.
3   1988 Act, s 9(2)(a).
4   Paras 1.48 et seq; 1.93 et seq.

BOOKS, SCRIPTS AND CHARACTERS

1.40 The definition of literary works is very broad and includes works that are expressed in any material form, such as novels, irrespective of their literary merits. Dramatic works also attract copyright irrespective of their quality. An important limitation upon the scope of protection is that there is no copyright in literary or dramatic characters as such, nor in their names.[1] There is no copyright in ideas and it is thought that merely to appropriate a character from eg a literary work, amounts to the copying of an idea rather than the expression of the idea, even where the author has described the character in some detail. Although there is some US case law supporting the proposition that independent copyright protection can subsist in such cases,[2] it is unlikely that an English court would follow it.[3] Copyright subsists only in the book, play or film as a whole and the characters depicted in such works are not protected outside the context of the plot, location, narrative and incidents contained in the work. The reason why names as such are unprotected by copyright is that the only way in which they could qualify would be as literary works and, in order to qualify as a literary work, the work must provide information, instruction or pleasure in the form of literary enjoyment. It is thought that names generally cannot satisfy this requirement.[4] There is a possibility, however, that names or short titles consisting of words which are represented in a visually striking and artistic manner may attract copyright protection as artistic works. This will not prevent others using the name provided they avoid copying the graphic style in which it is written.

1   *Exxon Corpn v Exxon Insurance Consultancy International Ltd* [1982] Ch 119. This is not the case in some other countries eg in France fictional characters enjoy protection as such – see [1986] Revue Internationale du Droit d'Auteur 18. See also Chapter 15 – France.
2   See Chapter 17 – United States.
3   See *Brigid Foley Ltd v Ellott* [1982] RPC 433. However in *Autospin (Oil Seals) v Beehive Spinning* [1995] RPC 683 Laddie J did not rule out the possibility that a three-dimensional work might infringe a literary work, but it would appear that the description would have to be much more exact than is usual in the case of a literary work (the work in question in that case dealt with technical subject matter – which was obviously a material fact).
4   See *Exxon* above.

1.41 It not infrequently happens that a successful book can be converted into a television or film script. The first question which arises, is whether or not this could be done without authorisation without infringing the copyright in the original work. Section 21(1) of the 1988 Act expressly provides that restricted acts include making any adaptation of a work, and section 21(2) has the effect that the same acts are restricted in relation to the adaptation as in relation to the original. 'Adaptation' is defined by section 21(3) as follows:

> 'In this Part "adaptation" –
> (a) in relation to a literary or dramatic work, means –
>   (i) a translation of the work;
>   (ii) a version of a dramatic work in which it is converted into a non-dramatic work or, as the case may be, of a non-dramatic work in which it is converted into a dramatic work;
>   (iii) a version of the work in which the story or action is conveyed wholly or mainly by means of pictures in a form suitable for reproduction in a book, or in a newspaper, magazine or similar periodical;
>   ....'

1.42 Thus, if a novel is converted into a film script without permission, there will be copyright infringement. Similarly, if the work started off as a dramatic work, eg a film script, a non-dramatic work produced from it is an 'adaptation'. The fact that in either case translation may be involved does not matter. Copying of dialogue from the original book is obviously an infringement, but so also will be the borrowing of incidents and situations on a scale sufficient to suggest copying even in the case of works of non-fiction. Thus in *Harman Pictures NV v Osborne*[1] the plaintiffs owned the film rights in Cecil Woodham-Smith's book, *The Reason Why*, which dealt with the events leading up to the charge of the Light Brigade. The defendants produced a screenplay based on this historical incident. There was a marked similarity between the choice of incidents in the book and in the screenplay. The defendant alleged that the screenplay was based on independent research from common sources, but adduced no evidence of these researches. It was held that the similarities between the incidents and situations in the two works afforded prima facie evidence of copying. A purely pictorial adaptation of a literary or dramatic work would amount to infringement under these subsections.

1   [1967] 1 WLR 723. See also *Poznanski v London Film Production Ltd* (1937) MacG Cop Cas [1936-45] 107; *MacGregor v Powell* (1936) MacG Cop Cas [1936-45] 233; *Ravenscroft v Herbert and Anor* [1980] RPC 193.

1.43 Fanciful posters, eg of *Lord of the Rings* characters, using merely their names, do not infringe the copyright in the literary work. There is no copyright in the name of a character as such,[1] though unauthorised use of a character associated with the plaintiff can amount to passing off.[2] Under the principles explained above, however, the use of a character in situations taken from the copyright work, can amount to infringement.

1   *Exxon Corpn v Exxon Insurance Consultants International Ltd* [1981] 1 WLR 624.
2   See Chapter 4.

Games

1.44 Games can be an important part of merchandising programmes, or in rare cases can form the basis of a programme. Some aspects of games, especially board games, may be patentable,[1] but, subject to this, copyright and trade mark law provide the most obvious sources of protection. Copyright cannot protect the idea of a game, but it can protect the expression of the idea in the rules, and the design of boards, counters, and other items used in the game. Thus in *Horn Abbott v W B Coulter Sales*[2] an interlocutory injunction was granted to the proprietors of the copyright in the question cards used in the game of 'Trivial Pursuit', against the manufacturers of two similar games 'Golden Trivia' and 'Junior Trivia'. On the other hand, although 'Trivial Pursuit' was registered as a trade mark, an interlocutory injunction was not granted to restrain the defendant from using its two names on the ground that there was a serious issue as to whether passing off was not the appropriate remedy.[3]

1   See para 1.91.
2   (1984) 77 CPR (2d) 145.
3   Under the Trade Marks Act 1994 there would presumably be infringement of the registered mark in such a case – see Chapter 3.

1.45   The rules of a game are not patentable,[1] but they can attract copyright. Thus in *Caley & Sons Ltd v Garrett & Sons Ltd*[2] although the game was very simple, to the extent that the defendant could argue that anyone describing it would have to use similar words, the defendant was nevertheless held to have infringed the plaintiff's copyright in his instructions for a similar game. The game in that case was used to promote sales of the plaintiff's chocolate. It was very simple, and consisted of a monochrome map of England with circles over the site of various unmarked towns. Each game had printed on it the name of a town and a colour. If a pencil were punched through the correct circle on the monochrome map, this colour would appear and the winner would be entitled to free chocolate on tendering the correctly punched map. The argument that anyone setting out to explain such a simple game, and the manner of playing it, would have to use similar words, failed.

1   See eg *University of London Press Ltd v University Tutorial Press Ltd* [1916] 2 Ch 601; *Antocks Lairn Ltd v Bloohn Ltd* [1972] RPC 219.
2   (1936-45) Macg Cop Cas 99. See also *Elanco v Mandops* [1979] FSR 46.

1.46   The software for computer games is protected under section 3(1)(b) of the 1988 Act as literary works. The problems to which this gives rise in relation to infringement are only just coming before the courts of this country.[1] It must be remembered, however, that in the present context it is likely that the graphics will be of most interest, and these are protected separately under the 1988 Act either as artistic works or films.

1   See *John Richardson Computers Ltd v Flanders* [1992] FSR 391; *IBCOS Computers v Barclays Mercantile Highland Finance* [1994] FSR 275. There is fairly extensive US case law which is discussed in these cases.

TV AND RADIO BROADCASTS

1.47   These are not a very probable basis, *in themselves*, for merchandising programmes, and any aspects of them that are eg art work, films or theme music, are likely to enjoy other copyright protection as explained above. Broadcasts made by the BBC and the ITA after 1 June 1957 enjoyed UK copyright under section 14 of the Copyright Act 1956. The relevant provisions of the 1988 Act replacing them are sections 6 and 7.

Term of copyright

INTRODUCTION

1.48 This is a topic of quite *exceptional* complexity. A tabular representation of what appears to be the present situation appears at the end of this chapter. The text attempts to explain how this representation was arrived at. It should be noted that it deals with works which came into existence after the commencement of the 1911 Act, ie 27 April 1912.

ORIGINAL LITERARY, DRAMATIC, MUSICAL AND ARTISTIC WORKS

Literary, dramatic and musical works (known author)

1.49 The basic term of copyright for published or unpublished literary, dramatic, and musical works created after 1 January 1996[1] is 70 years from end of the calendar year in which the author died.[2] The new provisions also apply to existing copyright works[3] (ie works in which copyright subsisted immediately before 1 January 1996),[4] to existing[5] works which first qualify for copyright protection after 1 January 1996,[6] and to existing works in which UK copyright had expired before 31 December 1995,[7] but which were still protected in another EEA state under legislation relating to copyright or related rights[8] on 1 July 1995 ie copyright in such works is revived.[9] The owner of the revived copyright is the person who was the owner of the copyright immediately before it expired.[10] If the date on which copyright would have expired under the provisions of the 1988 Act is later than the date on which it would expire under the new provisions, copyrights continues to subsist until that later date.[11]

1   The Duration of Copyright and Rights in Performances Regulations 1995, SI 1995/3297 (the 'Duration of Copyright Regulations'), Reg 16(a).
2   1988 Act, s 12(2) as amended by the Duration of Copyright Regulations 1995, SI 1995/3297.
3   Ibid, Reg 16(c), subject to Reg 15(1) which has the effect of preserving any longer term a work would have enjoyed under the 1988 Act. This is dealt with further below.
4   Defined in ibid, Reg 14(1)(b).
5   Defined in ibid, Reg 14(1)(a) to mean, in relation to a work, made before commencement ie 1 January 1996.
6   Reg 16(b).
7   Reg 16(d). This should have read 'on or before', but as presently drafted it excludes everything in relation to which copyright expired *on* 31 December 1995. This means that those works for which copyright would have expired on 31 December 1995, ie the author of which died in 1945, do *not* revive their copyright. Rather, the new extra term applies to works whose author died in 1946 or later (unless protected in another EEA state on 1 January 1995). See RSC Ord 3, r 2(3) and note 3/2/7.
8   Eg not patents, registered designs, confidential information, but quaere unregistered design protection, and moral rights. Quaere also 'publication rights', lending rights, etc.
9   Reg 16(d).
10 Reg 19(1).
11 Reg 15(1).

1.50 This means that a number of works in the public domain in the UK before 1 January 1996 are now back in copyright. The situation where copyright is revived requires special treatment. It is dealt with at paragraph 1.76 below. Where the copyright term is extended, an owner of the copyright for less than the full term provided under the 1988 Act gains nothing: the extended term forms part of the reversion.[1] The copyright owner immediately prior to 1 January 1996 is the owner of any reversion.[2]

1   Reg 18(2).
2   Reg 18(1).

1.51 For works *unpublished* etc at the author's death, *prior* to the commencement of the 1988 Act on 1 August 1989, copyright continued indefinitely. Under the 1956 Act, copyright continued to subsist until the end of 50 years from the end of the calendar year in which the first of the following events occurred:[1]
   (a) publication;
   (b) performance in public;
   (c) records of the work were offered for sale to the public;
   (d) the work was broadcast, or included in a cable programme.[2]

Thus, the copyright in the 'Country Diary of an Edwardian Lady' which formed the subject of some very successful merchandising, bears the copyright date '1977' because although the work was written in the early years of this century, it was not published until 1977, and that is the date from which the 50 year term began to run.

1   Copyright Act 1956, s 2(3).
2   Added by Cable and Broadcasting Act 1984, s 57, Sch 5, para 6 and Sch 6.

1.52 Under the transitional provisions of the 1988 Act, the copyright in works unpublished at the author's death,[1] expired at the end of 50 years from the end of 1989 when the Act came into force.[2] It should be noted, however, that works created after 1 August 1989 and before 1 January 1996 which are unpublished *and* anonymous seem to have an indefinite copyright. Section 12(2) of the 1988 Act specified a term of 50 years from the end of the calendar year in which such a work was first made available to the public, but it did not specify for such works that remained unpublished. Thus under the 1988 Act unpublished, anonymous etc works enjoyed indefinite copyright. Regulation 5 of the 1995 Regulations substitutes a new section 12(3)(a) for section 12(2). This provides a term of 70 years from the end of the year in which such works were *made*. But this provision did not come into effect until 1 January 1996,[3] and presumably the normal presumption against retroactive operation of statutory provisions applies, especially as the Regulations affect property rights.[4]

1   Ie works in relation to which none of the acts listed in s 2(3) of the 1956 Act had been done – these are set out above.
2   Copyright, Designs and Patents Act 1988, Sch 1, para 12(4)(a).
3   Reg 1(2).
4   There is a possible argument that as Reg 15(1) only preserves any longer term if such term was defined under the previous legislation, and as the 1988 Act did not define a term (it was silent), Reg 15(1) does not apply, and so Reg 16(c) applies instead, and the term is 70 years from when made (new s 12(3)(a)), or if made available to the public during that time, 70 years from the end of the calendar year in which it was so made available (new s 12(3)(b)).

1.53 The Duration of Copyright Regulations do not expressly deal with these transitional provisions for works unpublished at the author's death. However, as noted above, they provide that copyright shall continue to subsist until the date on which it would have expired under the 1988 Act if that date is later than the date on which copyright would expire under the new provisions.[1] Thus, Edith Holden, the author of the 'Country Diary' died in 1920 so that the only surviving term is that provided under the provisions of the 1956 Act[2] and the transitional provisions of the 1988 Act so that the term would expire in 2027, ie 50 years from the end of the year of publication.[3] If she had died in 1945, her work would, in principle, get the benefit of the general extension to 70 years pma because it would still be in copyright up to the end of 1995,[4] and thus the copyright would be extended for an extra 20 years, but since that would mean copyright would expire in 2017, whereas under the transitional provisions of the 1988 Act it would expire in 2027, ie 50 years from the end of the year of publication which was 1977, the effect of Regulation 15(1) is that the copyright owners would have got the benefit of the longer term conferred by the 1988 Act.

1   Reg 15(1).
2   Which left the perpetual copyright in unpublished works untouched, but had the effect that once an unpublished work was published the term began to run, and the work enjoyed a term of protection of 50 years from the date of publication ie 1977-1956 Act, s 2(3) (see para 1.51 above).
3   1988 Act, Sch 1, para 12(2)(a).
4   'Existing copyright work' is defined as a work in which copyright subsisted immediately before the commencement of the Regulations on 1 January 1996 – Reg 14(1)(b).

1.54 The case of 'Peter Pan' by Sir J M Barrie is anomalous: although under the 1956 Act copyright expired on 31 December 1987, there is a right to a perpetual royalty on public performances, commercial publications, broadcasts and cable transmissions of the play.[1] Of course, the effect of the Duration of Copyright Regulations is to revive copyright in any event, and since the rights enjoyed under the revived copyright by virtue of section 16 of the 1988 Act are more extensive than those enjoyed under Schedule 6 of the 1988 Act, it may still be relevant to consider the effect of the revival of copyright in this work.[2]

1   Copyright, Designs and Patents Act 1988, s 301 and Sch 6, para 2(1).
2   In this case copyright would revive under Reg 16(d).

Artistic works, known author (excluding photographs and engravings)

1.55 Again, it is necessary to consider whether or not copyright subsisted immediately before 1 January 1996. Under the 1956 Act, whether published or not and whether or not in existence on 1 June 1957, the term was the normal 50 years from the end of the calendar year in which the artist died.[1] As in the case of literary, dramatic and musical works, this is increased to 70 years pma by the 1988 Act as amended by the Duration of Copyright Regulations[2] (the transitional provisions of the Copyright Designs and Patents Act 1988, Sch 1, para 12(2)(a) do not pertain to artistic works). The position in the case of anonymous artistic works is set out below.[3]

1   Copyright Act 1956, s 3(2),(3), (4), and Sch 7, para 2 which excludes photographs that
     were taken before commencement (1 June 1957) from these provisions.
2   1988 Act, s 12(1), and s 12(2) (as amended).
3   Para 1.65 – for photographs see para 1.66.

1.56   Unregistrable designs enjoyed the full copyright term.[1] The effect
of section 51 of the 1988 Act is to withdraw protection from functional
works, which are now protected by design right.[2] Under the transitional
provisions, copyright in such works continues to subsist and to be
enforceable for ten years from 1 August 1989.[3] The Duration of Copyright
Regulations do not affect this. The effect of section 10 of the 1956 Act (as
amended by the Design Copyright Act 1968) was to reduce the period of
protection in respect of artistic works registrable as designs to 15 years.[4]
This 15 year period continues to apply to those articles exploited before 1
August 1989.[5]

1   *Amp Inc v Utilux Pty Ltd* [1970] RPC 397, [1970] FSR 162, CA; affd [1972] RPC 103,
     [1971] FSR 572, HL.
2   See 1988 Act, s 213, and para 1.16.
3   1988 Act, Sch 1, para 19(1) – licences of right have been available since 1 August 1994;
     ibid sub-paras (2) and (3).
4   It did not reduce the term to 15 years, it had the effect that after 15 years it was not
     an infringement to do something which would have been a restricted act.
5   1988 Act, Sch 1, para 20(1). Para 20(a) applies 25 year term to works exploited after
     commencement.

1.57   Of considerable importance for present purposes is that fact that
the term is cut down to 25 years when a work is exploited industrially.
Section 52 provides as follows:

   (1) This section applies where an artistic work has been exploited, by
        or with the licence of the copyright owner, by –
        (a) making by an industrial process articles falling to be treated
             for the purposes of this Part as copies of the work, and
        (b) marketing such articles, in the United Kingdom or elsewhere.
   (2) After the end of the period of 25 years from the end of the calendar
        year in which such articles are first marketed, the work may be
        copied by making articles of any description, or doing anything for
        the purpose of making articles of any description, and anything
        may be done in relation to articles so made, without infringing
        copyright in the work.
   (3) Where only part of an artistic work is exploited as mentioned in
        subsection (1), subsection (2) applies only in relation to that part.

The effect of this provision is that although the artistic copyright in a work
survives for the normal 70 years pma, if that is the relevant term, others
will be free to copy that part which has been exploited industrially. The
result of this is that the effective term for merchandised artistic works is
25 years. The section applies only where articles are marketed as
mentioned in section 52 above after 1 August 1989.[1] Thus the copyright
in a 'Country Diary' is unaffected by them, to the extent that no articles
have been made from particular artistic works contained in it since 1
August 1989.

1   Copyright, Designs and Patents Act 1988, Sch 1, para 20(2).

Photographs with a known author

1.58 In order to determine whether or not copyright subsisted immediately before 1 January 1996, it is necessary to look at the former rules.

1.59 Photographs taken before 1 June 1957 (whether published or not), enjoyed a term of 50 years from the end of the calendar year in which they were taken, and this continued to apply after the coming into force of the 1956 Act.[1] For photographs taken after 31 May 1957, the term was 50 years from the end of the calendar year in which they were first published.[2] *Unpublished* photographs taken after that date potentially enjoyed perpetual copyright, but became subject to the transitional provisions of the 1988 Act, so that copyright will expire 50 years after the end of 1989, the year in which the 1988 Act came into force.[3] Under the transitional provisions of the 1988 Act *published* photographs in which copyright subsisted on 1 August 1989 became subject to the usual 50 year pma term.[4]

1   See Copyright Act 1956, Sch 7, para 2 and s 3(3) and (4) and 1988 Act, Sch 1, para 12(2)(c).
2   Copyright Act 1956, s 3(4)(b).
3   1988 Act, Sch 1, para 12(4)(c).
4   1988 Act, Sch 1, para 12(6).

1.60 Again, if the effect of the transitional provisions of the 1988 Act is to extend the term for unpublished photographs beyond 70 years pma (ie 50 years from 1 August 1989 is the greater term), the copyright owner[1] will retain the benefit of such extension.[2] Otherwise, if 70 years pma would provide a longer term, the owner will get the benefit of the new term provided copyright subsisted immediately before 1 January 1996.

1   See paras 1.30 et seq and 1.98 as to who the owner of the copyright in such photographs is.
2   1988 Act, Reg 15(1).

1.61 The above provisions do not apply to computer generated photographs for which the term remains 50 years from the end of the calendar year in which made.[1]

1   See 1988 Act, s 12(7) as amended by SI 1995/3297, which in essence replaced s 12(3) to the same effect.

Engravings with a known author

1.62 Under the 1911 and 1956 Acts, the term for *published* engravings was 50 years pma,[1] but if the engraving had *not* been published before the death of the author, copyright continued to subsist until 50 years from the end of the calendar year of publication.[2] Otherwise, unpublished engravings enjoyed indefinite copyright. Schedule 1, paragraph 12(2)(b) of the 1988 Act tells us that copyright continues to subsist until it would have expired under the 1956 Act, and that this is the 50 year period mentioned in section 3(4) of the 1956 Act if it has begun to run (because the work has been published after the death of the author). For unpublished works the author of which had died, Schedule 1, paragraph 12(4)(b) of the 1988 Act made this 50 years from the end of 1989. If the effect of the 1995 Regulations is that a life plus 70 years is the longer term, that is the term,[3] but if 50 years from the end of 1989 is greater, the copyright owner gets the benefit of the longer term.[4]

1 1911 Act, s 3; 1956 Act, s 3(4).
2 1911 Act, s 17(1); 1956 Act, s 3(4)(a).
3 1988 Act, s 12(2) as amended.
4 Reg 15(1).

1.63 Engravings to which the 50 year pma term applied get the benefit of the term extension,[1] but where the copyright owner would have enjoyed a greater term under the previous law, the benefit of that greater term is preserved by the Regulations.[2]

1 1988 Act, s 12(1) and (2) as amended by SI 1995/3297.
2 Reg 15(1).

Anonymous or pseudonymous works, literary, dramatic, musical or artistic works (other than photographs but including engravings)

1.64 Anonymous or pseudonymous works are thosewhere there is insufficient evidence available for a reasonable person to identify the author.[1] The rules to determine whether or not copyright subsisted on 1 January 1996 are as follows. Whether the work was published *before* or *after* 1 June 1957: the term was 50 years from the end of the calendar year in which the work was *first published*.[2] Under the 1988 Act (before amendment) it was 50 years from the end of the calendar year in which it was made available to the public.[3] 'Made available to the public' in the case of a literary, dramatic or musical work includes performance in public, being broadcast or included in a cable programme service, and in the case of artistic works being exhibited in public, being included in a film shown to the public, and being included in a broadcast or cable programme service.[4] Under the transitional provisions of the 1988 Act, if the work was published before 1 August 1989, copyright expired when it would have expired under the 1956 Act,[5] but for works unpublished at that date, it was 50 years from the end of 1989, the year in which the 1988 Act came into force,[6] or if made available to the public before that date, 50 years from the end of the year when this occurred.[7] The new term provided under the Regulations is 70 years from the end of the calendar year in which the work was made, or if during that period the work is made available to the public (which still has the same meaning as under the 1988 Act),[8] 70 years from the end of the calendar year in which it was made available to the public.[9]

1 1988 Act, s 9(4) and (5).
2 1956 Act, Sch 2, para 1.
3 1988 Act, s 12(2) (before amendment).
4 1988 Act, s 12(2)(a) and (b) respectively (before amendment).
5 1988 Act, Sch 1, para 12(3)(a).
6 1988 Act, Sch 1, para 12(3)(b).
7 1988 Act, Sch 1, para 12(3)(b) proviso.
8 1988 Act, s 12(5) as amended.
9 1988 Act, s 12(3) as amended.

1.65 *Unpublished* anonymous works made between 1 August 1989 and 1 January 1996 appear to enjoy perpetual copyright. Unpublished anonymous works made after 1 January 1996 are subject to section 12(3) of the 1988 Act (as amended) and the term is 70 years from the end of the calendar year in which the work was made, or if made available to the public, 70 years from the end of the calendar year in which it was made available. The Copyright, Designs and Patents Act 1988, Schedule 1, paragraph 12(3)(b) by its terms only applies to works made *before* 1 August 1989. Again, the 1988 Act in its original form appeared to confer an indefinite term on such unpublished works,[1] and if the argument suggested above is correct,[2] works created between 1 August 1989 and 1 January 1996 enjoy indefinite copyright. Of course, if the author of the work becomes identified before such date, the normal 70 years pma term will apply.[3]

1 Ie by only making the duration referrable to 'making available to the public' and not to the date of creation.
2 Para 1.52
3 Ibid, Reg 5(1) substituting a new s 12(4).

Anonymous or pseudonymous photographs

1.66 As noted above, *published* photographs taken prior to 1 June 1957 enjoyed a term of 50 years from the end of the calendar year in which they were taken, and this applied whether or not the photograph was anonymous.[1] This term is now extended to 70 years by section 12(3) of the 1988 Act (as amended by the Duration of Copyright Regulations) provided the work satisfies the requirements set out in Regulation 16.[2] Unpublished, anonymous photographs made after 1 January 1996 enjoy a term of 70 years.[3] Photographs *published* between 1 June 1957 and 1 August 1989 enjoyed a term of 50 years from the end of the calendar year of publication,[4] and this is now increased to 70 years by section 12(3) of the 1988 Act (as amended). Anonymous *unpublished* photographs *whenever made* where the 1956 Act[5] was the relevant one enjoyed a term of 50 years from the end of 1989, which is increased to 70 years from the end of the calendar year in which they were made by section 12(3)(a) of the 1988 Act, as amended. Anonymous and pseudonymous photographs made between 1 August 1989 and 1 January 1996 appear, for the reason given above, to enjoy indefinite copyright while they remain unpublished.[6]

1 1956 Act, Sch 7, para 2 and s 3(3)(a).
2 See para 1.49.
3 1988 Act, s 12(3)(a) as amended.
4 1956 Act, s 3(4)(b).
5 1956 Act, s 3(4)(b).
6 Para 1.52.

DERIVATIVE WORKS

Sound recordings (other than film sound tracks)

1.67
(a) Made before 1 June 1957, 50 years from the end of the calendar year in which they were made.[1]
(b) Those made on or after 1 June 1957, 50 years from the end of the calendar year in which they were first published.[2]

1 1956 Act, Sch 7, para 11 and 1956 Act, s 12(3).
2 1956 Act, s 12(3).

1.68 *Unpublished* sound recordings made on or after 1 June 1957 (but before 1 August 1989) enjoyed at term of 50 years from the end of 1989.[1] The 1988 Act, as amended by the Duration of Copyright Regulations, makes the term 50 years from the date the sound recording is made, or if released, 50 years from the end of the calendar year of release.[2]

1 1988 Act, Sch 1, para 12(5)(a).
2 1988 Act, s 13A(2)(b) as amended by SI 1995/3297. This could result in a sound recording getting 132 years protection. A sound recording made on 1 June 1957, but remaining unpublished, had copyright until 1 August 1989, which is extended to 2039. If it is published just before that date, the term is extended to 2089.

Cinematograph films

1.69 In order to determine whether or not films enjoyed copyright protection on 1 January 1996 the following rules apply. It must be noted that the rules for films made prior to the commencement of the 1911 Act are different, and are not dealt with here.

1.70 For a film to be protected *as such* under the 1956 Act, ie it was made after 1 June 1957 but before 1 August 1989, copyright continued to subsist: (a) if registrable under Part II of the Films Act 1960 (formerly Part III of the Cinematograph Films Act 1938), until registered; (b) if not registrable, copyright subsisted until publication: thereafter for 50 years from the end of the calendar year of registration or publication respectively.[1] The 1988 Act preserves this position with regard to films whose copyright would expire 50 years from registration or publication.[2] Under the 1956 Act the copyright in unpublished, unregistered, films continued indefinitely,[3] but the effect of the transitional provisions of the 1988 Act is that it will expire 50 years from 1 August 1989, unless the film was published, in which case the term was 50 years from the end of the calendar year in which publication took place.[4]

1 1956 Act, s 13(3)(a) and (b) (as amended). Pre-1 June 1957 films were protected as photographs and dramatic works and there was separate protection for sound tracks which was the same as for sound recordings – as explained in para 1.29 above. It must be remembered that so far as publication is relevant, many films would not have been sold or let on hire to the public. Such films would not have been 'published' within the meaning of the Copyright Act 1956, s 13(10), and they probably would not have been so far as the 1911 Act was concerned.
2 1988 Act, Sch 1, para 12(2)(e).
3 1956 Act, s 13(3)(a) and (b).
4 1988 Act, Sch 1, para 12(5)(b).

1.71 The effect of the Duration of Copyright and Rights in Performances Regulations is that copyright expires at the end of the period of 70 years from the end of the calendar year in which the death occurs of the last to die of the following persons:[1]
- (a) the principal director;
- (b) the author of the screenplay;
- (c) the author of the dialogue;
- (d) the composer of the music specifically created for and used in the film.

1 1988 Act, s 13B(2) as amended by SI 1995/3297, Reg 6.

1.72 If the identity of one or more of the above persons is known and the identity of one or more others is not, the reference in that subsection to the death of the last of them to die is to be construed as a reference to the death of the last whose identity is known.[1] If the identity of none of the above is known, then the term is 70 years from the end of the calendar year in which the film was made, or if during that period the film is made available to the public by being shown in public or broadcast or included in a cable programme or service, the period is 70 years from when such making available to the public occurred.[2]

1   1988 Act, s 13B(3) as amended by SI 1995/3297, Reg 6.
2   1988 Act, s 13B(4) and (6).

1.73 The new provisions are linked to changes in the ownership in the copyright in films. This is dealt with elsewhere.[1]

1   Para 1.93 et seq.

Film sound tracks under the Duration of Copyright Regulations

1.74 The effect of the Duration of Copyright Regulations is to apply the rules for the extension of copyright in films set out in the previous section, to film sound tracks. Section 5B(5) of the 1988 Act as amended by the 1995 Regulations provides that 'Nothing in this section affects any copyright subsisting in a film sound track as a sound recording'.[1] Section 5B(2), however, provides that the sound track accompanying a film shall be treated as part of the film for the purposes of Part I of the Act. Where subsection 5B(2) applies, references to showing a film include playing the sound track to accompany the film, and references to playing a sound recording do not include playing the film sound track to accompany the film.[2] Copyright does not subsist in a sound recording to the extent that it is taken from a previous film.[3] Regulation 26 provides that the new provisions relating to the treatment of film sound tracks apply to existing sound tracks as at 1 January 1996. The owner of the copyright in a film has, as from this date, corresponding rights as copyright owner in any existing sound track, but this is without prejudice to any rights of the owner of the copyright in the sound recording as a sound recording.[4]

1   As to this see paras 1.27 and 1.29 above.
2   1988 Act as amended by SI 1995/3297, s 5B(3).
3   1988 Act as amended by SI 1995/3297, s 5B(4).
4   Reg 26(2).

Broadcasts

1.75 The duration of copyright under the 1956 Act for television and sound broadcasts is 50 years from the end of the calendar year in which the broadcast was first made.[1] The 1988 Act did not alter this, but additionally provided that in the case of a cable transmission, it is 50 years from the end of the calendar year in which the work was first broadcast in a cable transmission.[2] The Copyright Duration Regulations do not affect this, but do provide for term comparison where the author of the broadcast is not a national of an EEA state.[3] The author in this case is entitled to the term of protection conferred by its national law, provided that does not exceed the period of protection which EEA nationals would enjoy.[4]

There is a saving where the application of such term comparison would cause a breach of the UK's international treaty obligations.[5]

1   1956 Act, s 14(2). There was no separate copyright in broadcasts before the 1956 Act.
2   1988 Act as amended s 14(2) (formerly s 14(1)).
3   1988 Act, s 14(3) as amended by SI 1995/3297, Reg 7.
4   Ibid.
5   S 14(4) of the 1988 Act as amended by SI 1995/3297, Reg 7.

REVIVAL OF COPYRIGHT

1.76 The increase of the term of protection to 70 years would obviously cause problems to those who having relied on the expiry of copyright eg to manufacture articles bearing a character drawing, would now find themselves technically infringing. Regulation 24(1) accordingly provides:

> 'In the case of a work in which revived copyright subsists any acts restricted by the copyright shall be treated as licensed by the copyright owner, subject only to the payment of such reasonable royalty or other remuneration as may be agreed or determined in default of agreement by the Copyright Tribunal.'

1.77 This statutory licence also extends to those who, whilst not at 1 January 1996 involved in a restricted act, subsequently wish to commence to do so. In this case in order to avail himself of the statutory licence, notice must be given to the copyright owner of such intention and stating when it is intended to commence such acts.[1] If such notice is not given, the acts in quesion will be treated as unlicensed.[2] Once notice is given, a reasonable royalty must be arrived at as above.

1   Reg 24(2).
2   Reg 24(3).

CONCLUSION

1.78 The above is only a brief summary of a complex topic, but in view of the popularity of 'nostalgia' items from the 1920s, 1930s and 1940s the subsistence of copyright in many pre-1956 items may be important.

1.79 It must be borne in mind that each newly drawn picture of a cartoon character carries its own copyright provided it amounts to a new artistic work.[1] Thus, as styles of art change slightly over the years, the newly drawn cartoons creating new copyright can give new life to old characters, thought subject to the caveat noted above.[2]

1   See para 1.7.
2   See ibid.

1.80 Although all copyrights are of limited duration, as we shall see, trademark protection, and the protection afforded to goodwill through passing off, can be indefinite. Thus, although the copyright in the Beatrix Potter characters had expired under the former provisions, Frederick Warne registered the characters as trade marks. This would only protect against trade mark infringement, of course, but as explained in chapter

4, the provisions of the Trade Marks Act 1994 define infringement more broadly than did the 1938 Act. The Beatrix Potter characters are now back in copyright because of the implementation of the Term Directive.

CREATION OF COPYRIGHT

1.81 No formality is necessary to acquire United Kingdom copyright. It is desirable however to put third parties on notice that a work is subject to copyright, and some formula such as 'Copyright X Co 1985' may be used. Alternatively, the symbol '©', followed by the name of the copyright owner and the date, may be used. For the purposes of international protection, the use of this symbol may be essential.[1] Although there are no formalities required to be observed under United Kingdom law, as a matter of good housekeeping practice, certain procedures should be adopted in order to facilitate the enforcement of rights if action needs to be taken against infringers. First, all copyright material to be merchandised must be carefully identified. The identity of the artist or author should be established and, most importantly, the rights of the owner. If different artists are to be employed, then each individual's work must be separately identified. For set photography, a written exclusive agreement and an agreed set of photographs must be drawn up; all others should be destroyed or retained by the owner of the film or programme. If a property of one type, for example, a stage play, is to be made into a film, then the allocation of rights must be carefully analysed. This may appear elementary, but unfortunately in the frenetic world of entertainment the rules are not always followed. It is particularly important that one be able to demonstrate the chain of title in original copyright from the artist through the various owners to the present owner of the copyright. For some comic strip characters, who like 'Mickey Mouse' are getting on in years, various artists may have been employed over the years and ownership may have passed through various companies. Tracing the artist and his employer at the relevant time will be greatly facilitated if the original artwork contains the name of the artist, the date and a statement ' X Co'. This will also greatly assist in tracing the devolution of the copyright where a number of companies have been involved with the production of the cartoon character over the years. It is useful to have a standard collection of cartoons, ie a number of frames in which the character is shown in standard poses with identification of where these first appeared and other information such as the name of the artist, date etc. This avoids the problem of having to select actual cartoons for the purposes of infringement proceedings (and the selection may have to be done at very short notice). As we have seen, the fact that the infringing work does not exactly copy any particular drawing does not matter. Such a standard set of drawings can obviate the necessity for repetitive analysis of numbers of old cartoons.

1   Though there are few countries which now adhere solely to the Universal Copyright Convention under which the use of this symbol can be required.

1.82 Where artwork is prepared by agencies or other persons not in the employment of the proposed copyright owner, it is important that a clear agreement should be reached at the outset that the copyright will vest in the commissioner of the work. The provisions of section 4(3) of the Copyright Act 1956 vesting the copyright in photographs, or the painting or drawing of a portrait, or the making of an engraving, in the person commissioning the work, did not appear to cover other types of work. Nor did section 4(4) help if the person preparing the artwork was an independent contractor. As we have seen, there is no equivalent to section 4(3) in the 1988 Act. Although the commissioner of a design is the owner of the design right under section 215(2) of the 1988 Act, both the unimportance of design right for present purposes, and uncertainties about its scope particularly because of section 51, make it advisable in *all* cases to have a clear agreement governing the matter. Precedent 3 is an example of such an agreement.

1.83 Publicity materials must be carefully identified and copyright retained. For example, on publicity stills at least a minimum copyright notice as follows is extremely important:

'© [owner – date]. This material is released for publicity purposes only in relation to the film "X" and for use in normal editions of regular magazines, newspapers and periodicals. No licence is given for release to others or for use in any commercial manner or for use in any non-regular publication.'

Materials such as transparencies which are too small to carry the full copyright notice, should be released only in envelopes with the full copyright notice and on the transparencies should be: '[© owner – date]; released for publicity only; not for commercial use'.

1.84 Tracing title to copyright can often be a problem because of the absence of a registration system. It is accordingly advisable to keep on file a record of licences, assignments etc, and, indeed, all correspondence which might have a bearing on the matter. Although, as explained later,[1] registration is no longer a requirement in the United States, it can be useful for the purposes of evidencing title.

1 Chapter 17 – United States.

CROWN COPYRIGHT AND PARLIAMENTARY COPYRIGHT

1.85 Crown copyright applies to a work made by an officer or servant of the Crown in the course of his or her duties.[1] It vests in the Crown and subsists for 125 years from the end of the calendar year in which the work was made, or, if the work was published commercially,[2] before the end of 75 years from the end of that calendar year, 50 years from the end of the calendar year in which it was first so published.[3] This is unaffected by the Term Directive. Crown copyright is subsumed by Parliamentary copyright.[4] Under section 165, works made by or under the direction or control[5] of either House of Parliament enjoy Parliamentary copyright which subsists for 50 years from the end of the year in which the work was made.[6]

1   1988 Act, s 163(1).
2   As to which see s 175(2).
3   1988 Act, s 163(3).
4   1988 Act, s 163(6).
5   See 1988 Act, s 165(4).
6   1988 Act, s 165(3).

REGISTERED DESIGNS

1.86   The law relating to registered designs is regulated by the Registered Designs Act of 1949, as amended by the Copyright, Designs and Patents Act 1988. It confers a monopoly right, lasting up to 25 years, which is enforceable against even those who independently produce the same or a similar design for the goods covered by the registration. 'Design' is defined as features of shape, configuration, pattern or ornament, applied to an article by any industrial process, being features which in the finished article appeal to, and are judged by, the eye.[1] In order for a design to be registered, it must be new:[2] aesthetic considerations must normally be taken into account to a material extent by the customer when choosing an article of the kind in question.[3] Registered designs can be used to protect items such as brooches and toys representing fictional characters.[4] Whether, in any particular situation, the advantages of registration outweigh the disadvantages of the inevitable cost and delay inherent in it,[5] depends to a large extent on the durability and the popularity of the character in question (though the uncertainties created by section 51 of the 1988 Act mentioned above are leading many people to register designs to be on the safe side).

1   Registered Designs Act 1949, s 1(1) as amended by the Copyright, Designs and Patents Act 1988.
2   1949 Act, s 1(2) – as to the meaning of 'new' see the following paragraph.
3   1949 Act, s 1(3).
4   See *Dean's Rag Book Co v Pomerantz & Sons* (1930) 47 RPC 485.
5   Though it should be noted that the UK Registry is both one of the fastest, and cheapest, in the advanced industrial world.

1.87   At first glance, the requirement that the design be new creates an obstacle to the protection of characters. The reason for this is that a design is not new if it has already been registered or published in the UK in respect of the same or any other article. Since, in the case of character merchandising, most designs begin life as a drawing, such as a cartoon, this could pose a problem. However, this is avoided because a design will be treated as new despite earlier publication of a corresponding artistic work, provided there has not been manufacture and sale of articles to which the design or a similar design has been industrially applied. Industrial application has been taken to refer to application to more than 50 articles.

1.88   Changes in the UK law on industrial designs will have to be made when the EC's Designs Directive comes into force. At the moment it looks likely that this will be during 1996. There is also a Regulation providing for EU designs which parallels the Directive. The two measures are, however, going through under different procedures and at the time of writing, there are differences between them. Presumably these will be removed at the end of the day.

1.89 Copyright only protects against copying. A registered design can be infringed, however, by a similar design arrived at independently because the right conferred is equivalent to a patent. Moreover, the defence open to innocent importers, sellers and other dealers under sections 22 and 23 of the 1988 Act, has no equivalent in relation to registered designs. Of more practical importance in the merchandising context, however, is the fact that title to a design is certain: as with trade marks, it is proved by the entry on the register. Given that designs are relatively simple to register, and that it is fairly inexpensive, the certainty of title provided by registration may be worth having. On the other hand, if cumulating exemptions under the Restrictive Trade Practices Act 1976 are likely to cause problems (highly improbable), registration should be avoided.[1]

1   See para 8.12 et seq.

1.90 The Registered Designs Act 1949, as amended by the Copyright Designs and Patents Act 1988, provides for monopoly protection for up to 25 years[1] for a new design. Trade marks may be registered as designs.[2] Purely functional articles cannot be registered as designs, but may benefit under the design right provisions of the 1988 Act.[3]

1   Registered Designs Act 1949, s 8 as amended by s 269 of the Copyright, Designs and Patents Act 1988.
2   *Sobrefina SA's Trade Mark Application* [1974] RPC 672.
3   S 213 et seq.

PATENTS

1.91 These are not very common in merchandising programmes, and are not considered further. They raise no special difficulties, and reference may be made to the standard works where they are involved. The fact that tax needs to be deducted at source from patent royalies needs to be borne in mind.[1] Competition law (especially EEC) is also an important consideration.[2]

1   See Income and Corporation Tax Act 1988, ss 348, 349 and 350.
2   The terms of any licence should comply with Commission Regulation No 240/96.

MORAL RIGHTS

1.92 An innovation made by the 1988 Act was the introduction of moral rights. This was required in order to comply with Article 6bis of the Berne Convention.[1] The rights are:
  (1) to be identified as author[2] – this rights needs to be asserted;[3]
  (2) to object to derogatory treatment;[4]
  (3) not to have a work falsely attributed to you;[5]
  (4) privacy of certain photographs and films commissioned for private and domestic purposes.[6]

The right to object to false attribution lasts for 20 years pma, but the other rights subsist for the full copyright term of 70 years pma. These rights can be waived, or acts which would otherwise infringe, licensed.[7]

1 Paris Act 1971.
2 1971 Act, s 77.
3 1971 Act, s 78. Certain categories of work are also excepted from the right, including works created in the course of the author or director's employment where copyright vested in the employer – s 79.
4 1971 Act, s 80 – there are exceptions to the right, and where the copyright vested in the author or director's employer, it does not apply unless they are identified (s 82).
5 1971 Act, s 84.
6 1971 Act, s 85.
7 See Precedent 3, clause 8.

OWNERSHIP OF COPYRIGHT
Under the 1988 Act

1.93 The 'author' of a work is the first owner of any copyright in it.[1] 'Author' in elation to a work means the person who creates it. Before amendment by the Duration of Copyright and Rights in Performances Regulations 1996[2] this was:

    (a) in the case of a sound recording or film, the person by whom the arrangements necessary for the making of the recording of film are undertaken;

    (b) in the case of a broadcast, the person making the broadcast *[ie the person transmitting the programme, if he has responsibility to any extent for its contents, and any person providing the programme who makes with such a person the arrangements necessary for its transmission]*[3] or, in the case of a broadcast which relays another broadcast by reception and immediate re-transmission, the person making that other broadcast;

    (c) in the case of a cable programme, the person providing the cable programme service in which the programme is included;

    (d) in the case of a typographical arrangement of a published edition, the publisher.[4]

In the case of a literary, dramatic, musical or artistic work which is computer-generated,[5] the author is the person by whom the arrangements necessary for the creation of the work were undertaken.[6]

1 1988 Act, s 11(1).
2 SI 1995/3297.
3 1988 Act, s 6(3).
4 1988 Act, s 9(2).
5 As to the meaning of this term, see 1988 Act, s 178.
6 1988 Act, s 9(3).

The Effect of the Copyright and Related Rights Regulations

1.94 Copyright and related rights regulations modify the scheme set out above as follows. The 'author' of a sound recording is still the producer, but in the case of a film it is the producer and the principal director.[1] A film is to be treated as a work of joint authorship within the meaning of section 10 of the 1988 Act, unless the producer and principal director are the same person.[2] Where a film is made by an employee in the course of employment, the first owner of the copyright in it is his employer.[3]

1   Reg 18(1) substituting s 9(2)(aa) and (ab) for s 9(2)(a).
2   Reg 18(2).
3   1988 Act, s 11(2) as amended by Reg 18(3).

1.95   In infringement proceedings brought with respect to a film, where copies issued to the public bear a statement that a named person was the producer or director[1] of a film, that statement is admissible as evidence of the facts stated and is presumed to be correct until the contrary is proved.[2] Section 105 which contains a similar presumption with regard to films shown in public, broadcast or included in a cable programme, is amended in the same way, and it is further provided that the presumption applies where a named person was the principal director of the film, the author of the screenplay, the author of the dialogue or the composer of the music specifically created for and used in the film.[3]

1   Ie the principal director – s 105(6) added by Reg 19(4)(c).
2   1988 Act, s 105(2)(a) as amended by Reg 18(4)(a).
3   1988 Act, s 105(5)(a) as amended by Reg 18(4)(b), adding also s 105(5)(a)(aa).

1.96   A definition of 'producer' is added to section 178. 'Producer' in relation to a sound recording or a film means the person by whom the arrangements necessary for the making of the sound recording or film are undertaken.[1]

1   Reg 18(5).

1.97   These provisions concerning the authorship of films come into effect in relation to films made on or after 1 July 1994, but it is not infringement of any right which the principal director has by virtue of the Regulations to do anything after their commencement in pursuance of arrangement for the exploitation of the film made before 19 November 1992, though this does not affect the principal director's right to equitable remuneration under section 93B.[1]

1   Reg 14(1) inserts the new s 93B into the 1988 Act.

1.98   Regulation 19 clears up some of the uncertainties in relation to the ownership of the copyright in photographs following the Duration of Copyright and Rights in Performances Regulations. Regulation 15 of those regulations provided that any longer term of copyright enjoyed under the 1988 Act, continued to be enjoyed.[1] Regulation 16 extended the term of a life plus 70 years pma to works made after commencement, existing works qualifying for protection after commencement and works in which copyright expired before 31 December 1995 but still protected in another EEA state on 1 July 1995.[2] Regulation 19 provides that the ownership of copyright for the purposes of Regulations 15 and 16, or 19(2)(b), of the Duration of Copyright Regulations,[3] is to be determined in accordance with the rules of section 9 of the 1988 Act set out above, and not the rule set out in Schedule 1, paragraph 10 of the 1988 Act, which provides that ownership is to be determined in accordance with the law in force at the time the work was made.

1 See para 1.60.
2 It also applied the new provisions to works subject to Regulation 15.
3 Ie the extended term.

TABULAR REPRESENTATION OF THE EFFECT OF DURATION OF COPYRIGHT REGULATIONS

Original works

LITERARY, DRAMATIC AND MUSICAL WORKS (KNOWN AUTHOR)

1) Works *published* **during the author's lifetime**

Provided in copyright in another EEA state on 1 July 1995, date of publication immaterial	70 years pma

2) Works *unpublished* **at the author's death**

Published between 1 June 1957 and August 1989	50 years from publication etc *if* longer than 70 years pma
Unpublished at 1 August 1989	50 years from end of 1989 *if* longer than 70 years pma
Other *unpublished* works	70 years pma

ARTISTIC WORKS, KNOWN AUTHOR (EXCLUDING PHOTOGRAPHS AND ENGRAVINGS)

Whenever created, published or unpublished	70 years pma

PHOTOGRAPHS (EXCLUDING COMPUTER GENERATED), AND ENGRAVINGS WITH A KNOWN AUTHOR

1) Photographs with a known author

Taken before 1 June 1957	50 years from end of calendar year taken
do. *published* 1 June 1957 – 1 August 1989	50 years from end of calendar year of publication
Taken after 1 June 1957 *unpublished* at 1 August 1989	50 years from end of 1989
Whenever taken *published* prior to 1 August 1989	70 years pma *if* longer than above terms
All other photographs	70 years pma

2) Engravings with a known author

Published after death of author but before 1 August 1989	50 years from end of calendar year of publication
Published before death of author	70 years pma *if* longer than above
Unpublished	70 years pma *if* longer than 50 years from the end of 1989

ANONYMOUS OR PSEUDONYMOUS WORKS, LITERARY, DRAMATIC, MUSICAL OR ARTISTIC WORKS (OTHER THAN PHOTOGRAPHS BUT INCLUDING ENGRAVINGS)

Published before 1 August 1989	50 years from end of calendar year in which published
Existing but unpublished at 1 August 1989	50 years from end of calendar year in which made available to public
Unpublished other than made between August 1989 and 1 January 1996	70 years from end of calendar year in which made *if* greater than above
Unpublished made between 1 August 1989 and 1 January 1996	Possibly indefinite copyright
Unpublished made after 1 January 1996	70 years from end of year in which made
Made available to public after 1 August 1989	70 years from end of calendar year when made available to public

ANONYMOUS OR PSEUDONYMOUS PHOTOGRAPHS

Taken prior to 1 June 1957	70 years from end of calendar year when taken
Made available to public between June 1957 and 1 August 1989	70 years from publication
Unpublished taken before 1 June 1957	70 years from end of 1989
Taken between 1 August 1989 and January 1996 but not made available to the public	Possibly indefinite copyright
Made after 1 January 1996	70 years from end of year of making

Derivative works

Sound recordings (other than film sound tracks)

Made before 1 June 1957	50 years from the end of the calendar year in which they were made
Made between 1 June 1957 and August 1989 and *published*	50 years from the end of the calendar year in which they were first published
Made after 1 June 1957 and *un-published* at 1 August 1989	50 years from end of 1989
Unpublished made after 1 August 1989	50 years from the end of the calendar year in which the recording was made, or if released before the end of that period, 50 years from the end of the calendar year in which the recording was released

Cinematograph films

[It must be noted that the rules for films made prior to the commencement of the 1911 Act are different, and are not dealt with here.]

Rules for films prior to 1 January 1996

Made before 1 June 1957	[see photographs and sound recordings]
Made after 1 June 1957: if registrable under (Part III of the Cinematograph Films Act 1938) Part II of the Films Act 1960	until registered
if not registrable	until publication thereafter for 50 years from the end of the calendar year of registration or publication respectively
Films *unpublished* at 1 August 1989	50 years from the end of 1989 or, if published, 50 years from end of calendar year in which publication took place

Rules for films under the Duration of Copyright Regulations

Films made after 1 January 1996, first qualifying for copyright protection after that date, existing copyright works, and films in which copyright had expired before that date but which were still in copyright in another EEA country

70 years from the end of the calendar year in which the death occurs of the last to die of the following persons:
(a) the principal director;
(b) the author of the screenplay;
(c) the author of the dialogue;
(d) the composer of the music specifically created for and used in the film.[1]

If the identity of one or more of the above persons is known and the identity of one or more of the others is not the reference in that subsection to the death of the last of them to die is to be construed as a reference to the death of the last whose identity is known. If the identity of none of the above is known, then the term is 70 years from the end of the calendar year in which the film was made, or if during that period the film is made available to the public by being shown in public or broadcast or included in a cable programme or service, the period is 70 years from when such making available to the public occurred.[2]

1   1988 Act, s 13B(2) as amended.
2   1988 Act, s 13B(3) as amended.

FILM SOUNDTRACKS UNDER THE DURATION OF COPYRIGHT REGULATIONS

[The effect of the Duration of Copyright Regulations is to apply the rules for the extension of copyright in films set out in the previous section, to film sound tracks, both existing at 1 January 1996 and created thereafter.]

Broadcasts

Television or sound and cable transmission after 1 June 1957

50 years from the end of the calendar year in which the broadcast was first made[1]

1   1988 Act, s 14(3) as amended.

Chapter 2

Subsistence of copyright (connecting factors), and international aspects of copyright, trade marks, patents and designs

COPYRIGHT

Introduction

2.1 This chapter is not concerned with the subsistence of the copyright *term*: the term of UK copyright enjoyed by various categories of works was dealt with in the previous chapter.[1] In this chapter we are concerned with the question as to what connecting factors must exist for a work to enjoy UK copyright at all. This is an area which can raise complexities which are no less difficult to resolve than some of the problems that can be encountered in relation to the duration of copyright.

1   Para 1.48 et seq.

2.2 The basic rule is set out in Schedule 1, paragraph 5(1) of the 1988 Act, which provides that copyright subsists in an existing work after the commencement of the Act (1 August 1989) only if it subsisted immediately before commencement. In consequence, it is still necessary sometimes to grapple with the old rules to determine whether or not copyright subsisted at 1 August 1989. For obvious reasons, those contained in the 1956 Act are the most important now, and it is proposed to focus on these. The provisions of the 1911 Act are dealt with in the standard texts.[1] A checklist is provided at paragraph 2.35 et seq. The situation with regard to the United States is considered separately – paragraph 2.52 et seq.

1   See *Copinger on Copyright* 13th edn 1992, eg para 4.102 et seq (literary, dramatic, musical and artistic works – in the latest edition the relevant transitional provisions are to be found in the individual chapters dealing with categories of works – there is useful overview in the previous edition at para 1084 et seq); Laddie, Prescott & Vitoria *Modern Law of Copyright* 2nd edn, 1995 para 4.105 et seq; Sterling & Carpenter *Copyright Law in the United Kingdom* 1986 para 2A01 et seq.

The Copyright Conventions

2.3 The United Kingdom is a member both of the Berne Union[1] and the Universal Copyright Convention. Most countries of the world are members of either or both Conventions.[2] Since the accession of the United States to the Berne Convention, that has been much the more important of the two Conventions.

1   Works of foreign authors made before 1 July 1912 depended upon the provisions of
     the International Copyright Act 1886 which implemented the Berne Convention, and
     the Copyright Act 1911, s 24. The position is complex – see *Laddie, Prescott and Vitoria*
     op cit, para 4-108 et seq. The present Berne text to which the United Kingdom adheres
     is the 1971 Paris one. The UCC text is the 1971 Paris one.
2   There is a problem that some countries still adhere only to earlier versions of the
     Conventions, and accordingly, because of the principle of national treatment, the rights
     conferred may be less than under the present versions.

2.4 Under Article 4 of the Berne Convention (1971 Paris text), authors
who are nationals of any of the countries of the Union enjoy in countries
other than the country or origin of the work, for their works whether
unpublished or first published in a country of the Union, the rights which
their respective laws grant to their nationals, as well as the rights
specially granted by the Convention: the famous principle of 'national
treatment'.

2.5 The country of origin in the case of unpublished works is the country
to which the author belongs. In the case of published works, the country
of origin is generally the country of first publication, though there are
special provisions to cover the problem of simultaneous publication in
several countries. The literary and artistic works covered by the
Convention are listed (non-exhaustively) in Article 2. The minimum term
of protection under Article 7(2) is the life of the author plus 50 years, but
may be longer if the country in which protection is claimed grants a longer
period. In the case of films, members of the Union may provide that the
term shall expire 50 years after the work has been made available to the
public with the consent of the author, or 50 years after the making if not
so made available.[1] For photographs and works of applied art the minimum
term is 25 years from their making.[2] It should be noted that Article 7(8)
provides that the term of protection in the country where copyright is
claimed does not exceed that fixed in the country of origin unless the
legislation of the former country provides otherwise – the principle of 'term
comparison'. The Universal Copyright Convention (UCC) is broadly
similar, but the minimum period of protection is only the life of the author
plus 25 years.[3] Furthermore, under the UCC, the use of the symbol © on
all published copies of the work accompanied by the name of the copyright
proprietor and the year of first publication will satisfy the formality
requirements of any member state.[4]

1   Art 7(2).
2   Art 7(4).
3   Art IV.
4   Art III.

2.6 When a country accedes to the Berne Convention, its operation is
retrospective so far as works not in the public domain through expiry of
the term in the country of origin are concerned.[1] If, however, a work has
fallen into the public domain through the expiry of the term, in the country
where protection is claimed, it is not protected anew.[2] But the conditions
of application of this principle are for determination in the countries
concerned.[3] The UCC is not retrospective, and accordingly it is important
to know the date on which the Convention came into force in the acceding
country. This is the relevance of the date stated against the name of certain

countries in the statutory instruments dealing with the application of the Copyright Acts to other countries.

1   Art 18(1).
2   Art 18(2).
3   Art 18(4).

Subsistence of copyright under the 1956 Act

2.7   How to approach the subject:
   (1) As noted at the beginning of this Chapter, works must qualify for United Kingdom copyright by virtue of a 'connecting factor' which may be satisfied either by the *author* satisfying certain criteria to connect him or her to a country qualifying under (2) below, *or* by virtue of the work being *published* in such a country. Obviously, in the case of unpublished works, the connecting factor must be associated with the author, but in the case of published works, the connecting factor for works first published after 1 June 1957, can be associated with *either* the author, *or* the place of publication. For works first published before that date, it is publication alone in a country qualifying under (2) below which matters.
   (2) The countries (other than the United Kingdom) with which it is necessary to establish a connecting factor are those countries to which the Copyright Act 1956 extended or applied, or was deemed to extend. This is dealt with in paragraph 2.23 below.

SUBSISTENCE OF UNITED KINGDOM COPYRIGHT ON 1 AUGUST 1989 (ASSUMING TERM HAS NOT EXPIRED)[1]

Unpublished works

2.8   The 1956 Act was retrospective as to works enjoying copyright at the date of its commencement,[2] and the effect of extending it to countries which were not covered by the Copyright Act 1911 (only Sabah and Zanzibar) would appear to have been to bring into copyright works in the public domain in the United Kingdom (though presumably not so as to make acts done whilst works were in the public domain infringements). The author must have been a 'qualified person' at the time the work was made.[3] So far as individuals, as opposed to corporations,[4] were concerned, 'qualified person' was defined by section 1(5) as follows:
   (1) a British subject
   (2) a British protected person
   (3) a citizen of the Republic of Ireland
   (4) a person domiciled in the United Kingdom
   (5) a person resident in the United Kingdom
   (6) a person domiciled or resident in another country to which United Kingdom copyright extended or was deemed to extend.

1   As to expiry of term see para 1.48 et seq.
2   Sch 7, para 45(1).
3   Copyright Act 1956, ss 2(1), 3(2), 12(1) and 13(1).
4   The position regarding corporations is explained below – para 2.15

2.9   The term 'British subject' included every person who was a citizen of the United Kingdom and Colonies, or who under any enactment for the

42

time being in force in specified countries was a citizen of one of those countries.[1] There was also a class of British subjects without citizenship.[2]

1   British Nationality Act 1948, s 1(1) as amended. The specified countries are Canada, Australia, New Zealand, India, Ceylon, Cyprus, Nigeria, Sierra Leone, Ghana, Malaysia, Tanzania, Jamaica, Trinidad & Tobago, Uganda, Kenya, Malawi, Zambia, Malta, Gambia, Guyana, Singapore, Botswana, Lesotho, Barbados, Swaziland, Mauritius, Tonga, Fiji, Bahamas, Bangladesh, Seychelles, Solomon Islands, Tuvalu & Kiribati.
2   Ibid, ss 13 and 16.

2.10   A 'British protected person' was a person who was a member of a class of persons declared by Order in Council made in relation to any protectorate, protected state, mandated territory or trust territory, to be, for the purposes of that Act, British protected persons by virtue of their connection with that protectorate, state or territory, or was a British protected person by virtue of the Solomon Islands Act 1978.

2.11   'Domicile' was, and is, a common law concept. A domicile of origin in the United Kingdom (or other relevant country) was, and is, acquired by virtue of the fact of having been born in the United Kingdom. A domicile of choice in the United Kingdom (or other relevant country) was, and is, acquired by a settled intention to make the United Kingdom a person's sole or principal residence.[1]

1   *Re Fuld's (No 3) Estate, Hartley v Fuld* [1968] P 675.

2.12   'Residence' denoted the place where an individual ate, drank and slept, or where his family or his servants ate, drank or slept:[1] in effect the author's home at the relevant time.

1   *R v Overseers of Norwood* (1866) LR 2 QB 457; *Sinclair v Sinclair* [1968] P 189.

2.13   The relevant time for fulfilling the above conditions as to domicile, residence etc was the time when the work was 'made'. When was a work deemed to have been made? In the case of literary, dramatic, musical or artistic works, whose making extended over a period of time, the requirement was that the author was a qualified person for a substantial part of the period of making.[1] 'Making' in relation to literary, dramatic or musical works meant the reduction to writing or some other material form.[2] In the case of sound recordings, 'making' meant the production of the first record embodying the recording.[3] There was no definition of 'making' in relation to an artistic work or a cinematograph film in the 1956 Act, but the maker of a cinematograph film was the person by whom the arrangements necessary for the making of the film were undertaken.[4]

1   Copyright Act 1956, ss 2(1) and 3(2).
2   Ibid, s 49(4).
3   Ibid, s 12(8).
4   Ibid, s 13(10).

2.14   As to the devolution of copyright on the death of the author, reference should be made to the standard works.[1]

1   See *Copinger* para 5-2 and 5-4; *Laddie, Prescott and Vitoria* para 12-1 et seq.

Corporations

2.15 In the case of corporations, the test of qualification under the 1956 Act was place of incorporation: was the corporation incorporated in the United Kingdom at the time the work was made, or in a country to which the Act has been extended or is deemed to extend?[1]

1   See para 2.23.

2.16 A corporation could not be a 'qualified person' in respect of every type of work. Here is a checklist of works of which it could, or could not, be an author:[1]
   (1) Literary, dramatic and musical works – no
   (2) Artistic works – no, except photographs (which include films made before commencement of 1956 Act)[2]
   (3) Sound recordings and films made after 1 June 1957 – yes
   (4) Broadcasts and cable transmissions - yes
   (5) Published editions – yes

1   Note: test of qualification prior to commencement of the Copyright Act 1956 was different in relation to photographs from that under the 1956 Act – see below.
2   1 June 1957 – see also para 1.29.

2.17 Corporate bodies then, could not be authors of artistic works.[1] In the case of photographs, however, (which, as noted above, include the photography involved in films made prior to the commencement of the 1956 Act) the 'author' was the *'person'* who at the time when the photograph was taken, was the owner of the material on which it was taken,[2] and this *could* include corporations. It is to be noted that in relation to photographs taken before 1 June 1957 the requirement was that the corporation should have had an established place of business in, rather than be incorporated in, a country to which the 1956 Act extended, or was deemed to extend.[3]

1   The term is not defined in the Copyright Act 1956 but both normal usage and the fact that s 3(3)(c) refers to the 'death' of the author, it would appear that only individuals are contemplated. Similarly, s 4(4) refers to works made 'in the course of the author's employment'.
2   Copyright Act 1956, s 48(1); Copyright Act 1911, s 21.
3   Copyright Act 1956, Sch 7, para 39(4) applied the definition 'qualified person' contained in s 1(5) to photographs taken, and sound recordings made before 1 June 1957, but substituting the requirement of an established place of business for the requirement of incorporation in the relevant country.

2.18 A corporation could be a 'qualified person' with regard to sound recordings, and post-May 1957, cinematograph films, in relation to which the relevant term was 'maker' not 'author'[1] as well as to published editions in relation to which the qualified person is the publisher).[2] In the case of post-May 1957 cinematograph films, 'maker' meant person by whom the arrangements necessary for the making of the film were undertaken.[3]

1   Copyright Act 1956, ss 12(1) and 13(1).
2   Ibid, s 15(1).
3   Ibid, s 12(10).

Published works

2.19 In the case of literary, dramatic and musical works first published before 1 June 1957, and artistic works first published before that date, the position was the same as in the case of post-1957 works where the author was not a qualified person, ie place of publication is what mattered (see below).[1] In the case of works published on or after 1 June 1957 if the author of a work was a qualified person when it was made, the work would enjoy United Kingdom copyright under the 1956 Act, *wherever it was published*. This is also the case, where the author died before publication, and he was a qualified person immediately before his death.[2] Where, however, the author was not a qualified person, copyright would nevertheless subsist if the work was first published in the United Kingdom or the other countries to which the relevant provisions of the 1956 Act had been extended or applied, or was deemed to extend or apply.[3]

1   Sch 7, para 1; Copyright Act 1911, s 1.
2   Copyright Act 1956, ss 2(2)(c) and 3(3)(c).
3   Ibid, ss 2(2)(a), 3(3)(a) – for extension countries see para 2.23.

2.20   The above applied to photographs,[1] even if taken before 1 June 1957. Films made after May 1957[2] and sound recordings,[3] even if made before 1 June 1957,[4] were treated in a similar manner so far as connection by place of publication was concerned. Otherwise the requirement was that the maker should have been a qualified person at the time of making.[5] Broadcasts were not protected at all prior to the commencement of the 1956 Act, or the date of its extension or application to the relevant country.

1   Copyright Act 1956, Sch 7, paras 39(4) and 45. Including films made before 1 June 1957: ibid, Sch 7, paras 14 and 16.
2   Ibid, s 13(1) and (2). Most films were unpublished – see para 2.21 below.
3   Ibid, s 12(1) and (2).
4   Sch 7, para 39(4) had the effect that in relation to unpublished photographs taken, and sound recordings made (whether published or not) before 1 June 1957 corporations qualified by established place of business rather than place of incorporation.
5   In relation to sound recordings, see Sch 7, paras 11, 12, 13 and 45.

Publication

2.21   'Publication' involved in the case of literary, dramatic or musical works, or an edition of such a work, or an artistic work, issue of reproductions of the work to the public.[1] A sound recording was published if records embodying the recording, or any part of it, were issued to the public.[2] A cinematograph film was published if copies of the film were sold, let on hire, or offered for sale or hire to the public,[3] thus many films would not have been published. The performance of literary, dramatic or musical works or the issue of records of them, the exhibition of artistic works, or the issue of photographs of works of art such as sculptures, was not publication.[4] The requirement in section 49(2)(c) of the 1956 Act that publication should involve the issue of 'reproductions' to the public, probably excluded single reproductions, and certainly excluded oral reproductions. The private circulation of manuscripts etc was not issue to the public. In *Merchant Adventurers Ltd v M Grew & Co Ltd*[5] it was held that drawings for electric light fittings for public lighting were published by the sale to the public of the fittings made from the drawings, since section 48(1) of the Copyright Act 1956 defined 'reproduction' to include three-dimensional reproduction of two-dimensional artistic works.

1   Copyright Act 1956, s 49(2)(c).
2   Ibid, s 12(9).

3 Ibid, s 13(10).
4 Ibid, s 49(2)(a).
5 [1972] Ch 242.

2.22 The reproduction of a work had to be issued to the public to constitute publication. Probably, an offer or exposure for sale was not publication of itself, though any consequent sale which resulted in the issue of reproduction of the work, would be.[1] In *British Northrop Ltd v Texteam Blackburn Ltd* Megarry J had held that offering the work to the public did amount to publication, however, and that the place of first publication was the place where copies were first put on offer to the public.[2]

1 *Infabrics Ltd v Jaytex Ltd* [1980] 2 All ER 669 at 676.
2 [1974] RPC 57.

2.23 Where works were published simultaneously ie within 30 days of each other in more than one country, the earlier publication did not prevent the later one, eg in the United Kingdom, from being treated as the first publication.[1] Under the 1911 Act, the same applied, but the relevant period was 14 days.[2]

LIST OF COUNTRIES TO WHICH THE 1956 ACT EXTENDED, OR WAS DEEMED TO EXTEND:[3]

Antigua
Barbados
Bermuda (*6 August 1962*)[4]
Botswana (Bechuanaland) (*4 December 1965*)[3]
British Antarctic Territory
British Indian Ocean Territory (*14 May 1984*)[3]
British Virgin Islands (*11 October 1962*)[3]
Cayman Islands (*4 December 1965*)[3]
Channel Islands
Falkland Islands (*10 June 1963*)[3]
Gambia
Gibraltar (*1 June 1960*)[3]
Grenada (*1 January 1966*)[3]
Guyana (British Guiana) (*5 February 1966*)[3]
Hong Kong (12 December 1972)[3]
Isle of Man (31 May 1959)[3]
Jamaica
Kiribati
Lesotho
Montserrat (*5 November 1965*)[3]
Pitcairn Islands
St Helena (*10 June 1963*)[3]
St Kitts-Nevis-Anguilla
St Lucia (*5 November 1965*)[3]
St Vincent (*5 July 1967*)[3]
Sabah (North Borneo) (6 August 1962)[5]
Sarawak (*1 January 1960*)[6]
Seychelles (*10 June 1963*)[3]

Sierra Leone[7]
Singapore
Solomon Islands
Somalia[8]
Swaziland
Tanzania[9]
Trinidad and Tobago
Turks and Caicos Islands
Tuvala
Uganda (*1 January 1962*)[10]
Zanzibar (*1 January 1962*)[11]

1   Copyright Act 1956, s 49(2)(d).
2   Copyright Act 1911, s 35(3).
3   See 1956 Act, Sch 7, para 39.
4   This date is relevant for broadcasts – see para 2.40.
5   No United Kingdom copyright existed in this territory prior to this date.
6   See n 4 above.
7   Prior to commencement of Sierra Leone Copyright Act 1965.
8   Probably prior to 10 December 1963 only in relation to that part of Somalia which was the Somaliland Protectorate.
9   Prior to coming into operation of the Tanzanian Copyright Act 1966 – as to Zanzibar, see below.
10 See n 4 above.
11 See n 4 above.

2.24   Where the 1911 or 1956 Acts were extended by Order in Council to countries which were formerly British dependent territories, the 1988 Act preserves such extension.[1] The 1988 Act itself may be extended to any of the Channel Islands, the Isle of Man and any colony, in which case it takes effect as part of the law of that country to the extent that it is not modified by any relevant sovereign legislation.[2] If a country to which the Act has been extended ceases to be a colony, the Act continues to apply until revoked.[3]

1   Sch 1, para 36.
2   S 17(4)8.
3   1988 Act, s 158.

APPLICATION COUNTRIES

2.25.   Both Copyright Conventions were implemented by section 32 of the Copyright Act 1956, and the Orders made thereunder, adding countries subsequently adhering to these Conventions. Further Orders have been made under the 1988 Act. The 1993 Order is the most recent.[1]

1   Copyright (Application to Other Countries) Order 1993, SI 1993/942, as amended.

Problems with corporations as makers of unpublished pre-1957 photographs, films and sound recordings

2.26   There was an unfortunate lacuna in the transitional provisions of the 1956 Act as regards corporations which were not deemed to be resident in a country to which the Copyright Act 1911 extended because they had no established place of business within them prior to the commencement

47

2.26 *Subsistence of copyright*

of the 1956 Act (27 September 1957 or such later date specified in Schedule 2 of the Copyright (International Conventions) Order 1979). If a company was incorporated in a country which adhered to either copyright convention, the Copyright Act 1956 applied to it,[1] because the Act is applied as if the company were incorporated in the United Kingdom. There was no equivalent provision deeming corporations resident where the established place of business criterion was material as it was in the case of unpublished photographs taken or sound recordings made (published or unpublished) before the commencement of the 1956 Act. However, our obligations under both Conventions would seem to be to accord protection to such photographs or sound recordings of corporations with established places of business in member states of the respective Conventions, and it is submitted that they ought to have enjoyed United Kingdom copyright.[2]

1   See below.
2   S 32(1)(d).

2.27   This same problem exists in relation to films, which as we have seen were treated either as a sequence of photographs, or as dramatic works under the 1911 Act[1] (a corporation could not of course be the 'author' of a dramatic work so that the problem does not arise in that regard). The problem also arises in relation to the soundtracks of such films.

1   See para 1.29 above.

The 1988 Act

CONNECTING FACTOR

2.28   As under the 1956 Act works must qualify for United Kingdom copyright by virtue of a 'connecting factor' which may be satisfied either by the *author* satisfying certain criteria to connect him or her to a country qualifying under paragraph 2.31 below, *or* by virtue of the work being *published* in such a country.

Qualifying country and qualifying individual

2.29   Section 206 of the Act provides:

'(1)   In this Part –
"qualifying country" means –
(a) the United Kingdom,
(b) another member State of the European Economic Community [EU], or
(c) to the extent that an Order under section 208 so provides, a country designated under that section as enjoying reciprocal protection;
"qualifying individual" means a citizen or subject of, or an individual resident in, a qualifying country; and
"qualifying person" means a qualifying individual or a body corporate or other body having legal personality which –
(a) is formed under the law of a part of the United Kingdom or another qualifying country, and
(b) has in any qualifying country a place of business at which substantial business activity is carried on.

48

(2)   The reference in the definition of "qualifying individual" to a person's being a citizen or subject of a qualifying country shall be construed –
(a) in relation to the United Kingdom, as a reference to his being a British citizen, and
(b) in relation to a colony of the United Kingdom, as a reference to his being a British Dependent Territories' citizen by connection with that colony.'

2.30   The 1988 Act applies to literary, dramatic, musical or artistic works, sound recordings, films or editions first published in the relevant country (in the case of UCC countries not adhering to Berne only if published after the date specified in brackets in Schedule 1 of the 1993 Order).[1] The Act also applies to works of citizens of, subjects of, persons domiciled or resident in, the relevant country, but in the case of countries which adhered only to the UCC only if the work remained unpublished at the date specified in brackets. In the case of corporations, the connection with the relevant country was probably (see below) principal place of business in respect of photographs and sound recordings (published or unpublished) made prior to the commencement of the 1956 Act and place of incorporation thereafter.[2]

1   See para 2.25 above.
2   See para 2.26 above.

2.31   The following is a list of application countries enjoying protection. Where a date in Roman type appears against a country's name, that is the relevant date at which the work must have remained unpublished for the purposes of the UCC. Protection for sound recordings, broadcasts and cable programmes is dealt with in the following way. Those countries enjoying full protection for sound recordings are marked '*', and those enjoying full protection in respect of broadcasts are marked '†', and the relevant date shown in *italics* in the brackets following the symbol.[1] Some countries which appeared on the list of extension countries, also appear on this list. Presumably the rights conferred under these provisions are cumulative in such cases, though this no longer appears to have much practical importance.

Albania
Algeria (28 August 1973)
Andorra (27 September 1957)
Antigua and Barbuda† *(1 January 1996)*
Argentina*† *(2 March 1992)*
Australia (including Norfolk Island)*† *(30 September 1992)*
Austria*† *(9 June 1973)*
Bahamas
Bahrain† *(1 January 1996)*
Bangladesh*† *(1 January 1996)*
Barbados*† *(18 September 1983)*
Belarus *(25 December 1991)*
Belgium† *(8 March 1968 – television; 1 January 1996 – non-television)*
Belize† *(1 January 1996)*
Benin

Bolivia*† *(1 January 1996)*
Bosnia-Herzegovina
Botswana† *(1 January 1996)*
Brazil*† *(29 September 1965)*
Brunei Darussalam† *(1 January 1996)*
Bulgaria*† *(31 August 1995)*
Burkina Faso*† *(14 January 1988)*
Burundi† *(1 January 1996)*
Cameroon
Canada† *(1 January 1996)*
Central African Republic† *(1 January 1996)*
Chad
Chile*† *(5 September 1974)*
China
Colombia*† *(17 September 1976)*
Congo*† *(18 May 1964)*
Costa Rica*† *(9 September 1971)*
Côte d'Ivoire† *(1 January 1996)*
Croatia
Cuba† *(1 January 1996)*
Cyprus, Republic of† *(5 May 1970 – television; 1 January 1996 – non-television)*
Czech Republic*† *(1 January 1993)*
Denmark (including Greenland and Faeroe Islands)*† *(1 February 1962 - television, 1 July 1965 - non-television)*
Djibouti† *(1 January 1996)*
Dominica† *(1 January 1996)*
Dominican Republic (8 May 1983)*† *(27 January 1987)*
Ecuador*† *(18 May 1964)*
Egypt† *(1 January 1996)*
El Salvador*† *(29 June 1979)*
Estonia
Fiji*† *(11 April 1972)*
Finland*† *(21 October 1983)*
France (including all Overseas Departments and Territories)*† *(1 July 1961 – television; 3 July 1987 – non-television)*
Gabon† *(1 January 1996)*
Gambia
Georgia
Germany*† *(21 October 1966)*
Ghana*† *(1 January 1996)*
Greece*† *(6 January 1993)*
Guatemala (28 October 1964)*† *(14 January 1977)*
Guinea† *(1 January 1996)*
Guinea-Bissau† *(1 January 1996)*
Guyana† *(1 January 1996)*
Haiti (27 September 1957)
Holy See
Honduras*† *(16 February 1990)*
Hungary*† *(10 February 1995)*
Iceland*† *(15 June 1994)*
India*† *(1 January 1996)*

Indonesia*† *(1 June 1957)*
Ireland, Republic of*† *(19 September 1979)*
Israel† *(1 January 1996)*
Italy*† *(8 April 1975)*
Jamaica*† *(27 January 1994)*
Japan*† *(26 October 1989)*
Kampuchia (27 September 1957)
Kazakhstan (25 December 1991)
Kenya† *(1 January 1996)*
Korea, Republic of† *(1 January 1996)*
Kuwait† *(1 January 1996)*
Laos (27 September 1957)
Latvia
Lebanon
Lesotho*† *(26 January 1990)*
Liberia
Libya
Liechtenstein† *(1 January 1996)*
Lithuania
Luxembourg*† *(25 February 1976)*
Macau† *(1 January 1996)*
Macedonia
Madagascar
Malawi*† *(22 June 1989)*
Malaysia*† *(1 June 1957)*
Maldives† *(1 January 1996)*
Mali† *(1 January 1996)*
Malta† *(1 January 1996)*
Mauritania† *(1 January 1996)*
Mauritius† *(1 January 1996)*
Mexico*† *(18 May 1964)*
Moldova*† *(5 December 1995)*
Monaco*† *(6 December 1985)*
Morocco† *(1 January 1996)*
Mozambique *(1 January 1996)*
Myanmar† *(1 January 1996)*
Namibia† *(1 January 1996)*
Netherlands (including Aruba and Dutch Antilles)*† *(7 October 1993)*
New Zealand*† *(1 January 1996)*
Nicaragua† *(1 January 1996)*
Niger*† *(18 May 1964)*
Nigeria*† *(29 October 1993)*
Norway*† *(10 August 1968 - television, 10 July 1978 - non-television)*
Pakistan*† *(1 January 1996)*
Panama (17 October 1962)*† *(2 September 1983)*
Paraguay*† *(26 February 1970)*
Peru*† *(7 August 1985)*
Phillipines*† *(25 September 1984)*
Poland† *(1 January 1996)*
Portugual† *(1 January 1996)*
Romania† *(1 January 1996)*
Russian Federation

51

Rwanda
St Kitts & Nevis
St Lucia† *(1 January 1996)*
St Vincent and Grenadines† *(1 January 1996)*
Saudi Arabia (13 July 1994)
Senegal† *(1 January 1996)*
Sierre Leone† *(1 January 1996)*
Singapore† *(1 June 1957)*
Slovak Republic*† *(1 January 1993)*
Slovenia† *(1 January 1996)*
South Africa† *(1 January 1996)*
Soviet Union (27 May 1973)
Spain*† *(19 November 1971 - television, 14 November 1991 - non-television)*
Sri Lanka† *(1 January 1996)*
Surinam† *(1 January 1996)*
Swaziland† *(1 January 1996)*
Sweden*† *(1 July 1961 - television; 18 May 1964 - non-television)*
Switzerland*† *(24 September 1993)*
Taiwan, territory of (10 July 1985)*
Tajikistan (25 December 1991)
Tanzania† *(1 January 1996)*
Thailand*† *(1 January 1996)*
Togo† *(1 January 1996)*
Trinidad and Tobago† *(1 January 1996)*
Tunisia† *(1 January 1996)*
Turkey† *(1 January 1996)*
Uganda† *(1 January 1996)*
Ukraine
United States of America (including Puerto Rico and all territories and possessions† *(1 January 1996)*
Uruguay*† *(4 July 1977)*
Venezuela† *(1 January 1996)*
Yugoslavia
Zaire
Zambia† *(1 January 1996)*
Zimbabwe† *(1 January 1996)*

1   See Copyright (Application to Other Countries) Order 1993, SI 1993/942 as amended.

The problem of countries which change borders/ governments

2.32 'Country' was defined in section 48(1) of the 1956 Act to include 'any territory'. It would appear, therefore, that if the work originated in a territory to which the Berne Convention applied, it would be subject to copyright, no matter that when it was first published the territory formed part of a country which was not a member of the Union. For example, a work first published in either the Federal Republic or the GDR would be subject to copyright, because both states were adherents to the Berne Union as is their successor (the fact that the former German state, the

Third Reich, was also an adherent does not matter). By contrast, a work first published in a part of Poland which after the Second World War became part of the USSR would not be subject to copyright, because the USSR was a member only of the UCC to which it adhered in 1973, and the UCC is not retrospective. On the other hand, Poland before the war was a member of the Berne Union, and it seems unfair that an author once protected by virtue of the former Polish state's adherence to the Convention, should lose copyright by virtue of the annexation of a part of his country. It could be argued that a work once subject to copyright by virtue of being published in Poland as a country (no matter where in Poland) would still enjoy copyright. This interpretation was borne out by the First Schedule of the Copyright (International Conventions) Order 1957[1] which listed the Federal Republic and the state of Berlin and Pakistan as having ratified the 1928 version of Berne. Neither of these states existed in 1928. It must therefore be that these states were *deemed* adherents. If this is correct, it could be that the view of the UK draftsmen at the relevant time was that under the international law doctrine of state succession,[2] once UK copyright subsisted, we were bound to go on recognising an author's rights even though the state in which he was now domiciled had not adhered to either of the copyright conventions. This is now a matter of some importance having regard to the changes which have taken place in eastern Europe in recent years. It would follow from this argument that *even in the absence of a statutory instrument covering the situation* UK courts *should* continue to recognise copyright once it has subsisted in the UK. Works created *after* the change of sovereignty would, of course, be subject to the ordinary rules.

1   SI 1957/1523.
2   As to which see the leading case of *US v Perchman* 7 Pet 31 (1830); and Restatement 3d at para 208 et seq.

2.33   Fortunately, many of the above complexities have disappeared because most of the states occupying the territory of the former Soviet Union have now adhered to the Berne Convention, and the Berne Convention is retrospective. This is a complex topic, and for further discussion reference should be made to the standard works.[1]

1   See para 2.32, n 2 above.

EXAMPLE

2.34   It may help to explain the working of these very complex provisions and doctrines to give an example.

Igor is a best selling Russian author who has lived in Belarus throughout his life, and whose surrealist novels have been translated into many languages, including English. His first book, 'The Filing Cabinet Drawer' was published in Moscow in 1960. His second book, 'Secrets of a Card Index' was published in Moscow in 1970 and translated into English by Pat, an Australian living in Melbourne, and published in London in 1975. His latest work, 'The Private Life of a Database', was published in Belarus in 1990. If a UK film company wanted to make a film based on these works, would they require a copyright licence from Igor or Pat?

It is necessary to consider each of these three works separately.

   (1) The USSR did not adhere to the Universal Copyright Convention until 27 May 1973, and *that* is the relevant date specified in the Copyright (Application to Other Countries) Order 1993.[1] The UCC is not retropective, consequently the first work is not protected in the UK.

   (2) The same applies to the underlying copyright in the second book as the USSR, of which Belarus formed part, did not adhere to the UCC until 27 May 1973. The only argument arises from the question as to whether or not publication of the translation in London in 1975 (by which date the USSR had adhered to the UCC) could have conferred rights on Igor – after all, the selection and arrangement is his. Under the 1988 Act, section 3(2) and (3), the recordal of an unprotected work in writing creates a copyright which belongs to the author, and a long shot argument that the translation created a new copyright might have been based on these provisions had they been in force in 1975, which, of course, they were not. There was no equivalent provision in the 1956 Act, however. Would the common law have reached a similar conclusion? There seems to be no authority.

   (3) Igor at the relevant time was domiciled in Belarus, and the place of first publication was Belarus. Although the Russian Federation had adhered to the UCC and has now adhered to Berne, Belarus as a separate entity has only adhered to UCC from 25 December 1991, and Igor's third book was written before that date. If Belarus adheres to Berne, and this is recognised in a UK statutory instrument, Igor will enjoy UK copyright, but at the time of writing this has not happened. Had he enjoyed UK copyright in either of the two earlier works at the time Belarus became independent, it is arguable that under the international law doctrine of state succession, he should continue to enjoy it.[2] Such enjoyment would be independent of any statutory instrument recognising the fact, being based on international law doctrine.

If he enjoyed UK copyright in any of his novels, he would, in principle enjoy the moral right to object to derogatory treatment conferred by section 80 of the 1988 Act. He would also enjoy this moral right in any work in which UK copyright subsisted on 1 August 1989, which could mean that he had this moral right in the second novel. This moral right is, of course, waivable. The relevant UK copyrights will require licences from Pat and, if they subsist, Igor, because the making of a film is a reproduction of the underlying works.[3] The publisher's copyright in the typographical arrangements is *not* relevant, because that will not be infringed by the making of the film.

1   SI 1993/942.
2   See 2.32.
3   See eg *Harman Pictures NV v Osborne* [1967] 2 All ER 324.

Subsistence of United Kingdom copyright: Checklist[1]

NOTE

2.35 This Checklist answers the question as to whether or not copyright subsisted on 1 August 1989 (a matter which was regulated by the prior law) because of the basic rule set out in the transitional provisions of the 1988 Act that if copyright subsisted on that date, it continued to subsist under the 1988 Act.[2] Separately, however, a work may enjoy copyright under the 1988 Act, by virtue of its extension to a particular country by the Copyright (Application to Other Countries) Order 1993 (as amended). [Taiwan needs special consideration because it was brought into the UK copyright scheme though not a member of either convention – see para 2.48 below.]

1   This Checklist is valid after 24 January 1980. See Copyright (International Conventions) Order 1979.
2   As suggested above (para 2.32) if a work ever enjoyed copyright under the former law, it should continue to enjoy it.

Unpublished works created before 1 August 1989 (not being special category works, broadcasts or sound recordings)

2.36   Was the author, maker etc a qualified person at the time the work was made? – see paragraph 2.8 et seq. If so, the work enjoys United Kingdom copyright, subject to the copyright term still subsisting.[2]

1   See Copyright Act 1956, ss 33 and 39(1)(a).
2   See para 1.48 et seq above.

Unpublished works created after 1 August 1989

2.37   Was the author a qualifying person? – see para 2.29.

Published works created before 1 August 1989 (not being special category works[1] broadcasts[2] or sound recordings[3])

Post 1956 published works (ie post May 1957)
2.38
    (1) All works and published editions of works first published on or after 1 June 1957 if the author, maker etc was a 'qualified person' or a 'specified person'[4] enjoy UK copyright wherever published subject to the copyright term still subsisting – see paragraph 2.8 et seq
    (2) All works and published editions of works first published in countries to which the 1956 Act extended or applied enjoy United Kingdom copyright subject to the copyright term still subsisting – see paragraph 2.23

1   See para 2.45 below.
2   As to which see para 2.40 below.
3   See para 2.43 below.
4   See para 2.8 above.

Pre-1957 published works (ie pre-1 June 1957)
2.39   All other works (not broadcasts)[1] if the work was first published in a country to which the 1956 Act extended or applied, or was deemed to extend enjoy United Kingdom copyright subject to the copyright term still subsisting – see paragraph 2.19.

1   See para 2.40 below.

Broadcasts

2.40   Enjoyed United Kingdom copyright as from the commencement of the 1956 Act ie 1 June 1957, or the date of its extension or application to the relevant country – see paragraphs 2.23 and 2.31.

Works not benefiting from protection under any of the above categories (not being sound recordings)

2.41 Such works are in the public domain in the United Kingdom, unless the relevant country, or its successor, is listed in the 1993 Order without a date in roman characters because it has since adhered to the Berne Convention. If a date appears in roman characters, the work must have been created after that date because the UCC is not retrospective.

Sound recordings made before 1 August 1989

2.43 Copyright subsisted in a sound recording if it fulfilled *either* of two criteria:
- (1) the maker was a qualified person or a specified person at the time it was made (see para 2.36 above), or
- (2) if the recording was published in a country specified in paragraphs 2.23 or 2.31 above (but only in the case of countries listed in paragraph 2.31 after the date shown in brackets).

2.44 Corporations qualified by place of incorporation after the relevant commencement date, principal place of business before that date.[1]

1   But see para 2.26 above.

Exceptions to above (other than Singapore, Taiwan and the United States)

2.45 If the work was first published in Syria, Ruanda-Burundi, Papua New Guinea or Western Samoa, it enjoyed United Kingdom copyright only if publication took place during the period when the country was included in the relevant Order.[1]

1   Indonesia was also in this category – included Part I SI 1957/1523, deleted SI 1960/200 as from 19 February 1960; Syria – included Part I SI 1957/1523, deleted SI 1962/397 with effect from 11 March 1962; Indonesia – West Irian included with New Guinea in SI 1957/1523 not included in SI 1964/690 (with effect from 21 May 1964) or subsequent Orders; Papua New Guinea – Naura and Papua New Guinea included in SI 1957/1523, SI 1964/690 and 1972/673 but not included in SI 1979/1715 (with effect from 24 January 1980); Samoa – included in SI 1957/1523 and SI 1964/690, deleted SI 1972/673 with effect from 31 May 1972; Ruanda-Burundi – included in SI 1957/1523, but not in SI 1964/690 (with effect from 21 May 1964). Rwanda is included in the 1993 Order – see para 2.31 above.

2.46 Works protected under the Copyright Act 1911 by virtue of the author's citizenship of, residence or domicile in or first publication in Korea, Japanese Saghalien, Kwangtung, Leased Territory of Formosa, were not mentioned in the Orders made under section 32 of the Copyright Act 1956.[1] Some of these countries, eg Taiwan (formerly Formosa) are now included in the 1993 Order under new names,[2] but otherwise works in this category would not be protected.

1   The same would appear to apply to Estonian and Latvian works.
2   See para 2.31

Published works created after 1 August 1989

2.47 Was the work first published in the UK or a country to which the 1988 Act extends? – see paragraph 2.31. If qualification is by place of publication alone, and a date appears in brackets after the name of the country in the table in paragraph 2.31, publication must have taken place on or after that date if qualification is by place of publication alone.[1]

1   Unless publication took place within 30 days in another country for which no date is specified – 1988 Act, s 155(3).

SINGAPORE AND TAIWAN[1]

2.48. Taiwan is now included in the 1993 Order, but the position with regard to Taiwan was and is anomalous because it was not a signatory to either Copyright Convention, but it was treated as an application country for the purposes of the former United Kingdom copyright law.

1   See Copyright (Taiwan) Order 1985, SI 1985/2722.

2.49 Literary, dramatic, musical or artistic works, sound recordings, cinematograph films or published editions first published in Taiwan, enjoyed copyright as though they had first been published in the United Kingdom. However, the relevant date for the purposes of the transitional provisions in Schedule 7 of the 1956 Act was 10 July 1985.

2.50 The 1956 Act also applied in relation to persons who were citizens or subjects of China, being citizens or subjects also at the same material time or resident or domiciled in Taiwan, as it applied to British subjects. Singapore is also a special case, being party to neither Convention but being treated as though it were a member of Berne for the purposes of UK law.

2.51 For corporations the relevant consideration was clearly incorporation in Taiwan after 10 July 1985.

UNITED STATES

2.52 Because of its importance in merchandising, a summary of the position in regard to United States as well as United Kingdom copyright is included here. The complexity of the American position will also serve to illustrate the care which needs to be observed in attending to the international aspects of the protection of any given property.

United Kingdom protection for unpublished American works and for works first published in the United States

2.53 The United States ratified the Universal Copyright Convention in 1955. It became a party to the Berne Convention from 1 March 1989 so that US works are now subject to UK copyright whenever made. Prior to that, the situation was exceptionally complex. Unpublished American literary, dramatic, musical and artistic works were given the protection of the 1911 Act, by an Order in Council dated 3 February 1915 made under section 29 of the Act.[1] Provided the author was a subject of or resident in the United States, and provided the American copyright had not expired by 27 September 1957, the work was protected by the 1956 Act.[2] Otherwise, subject to the exceptions outlined below, works first published in the United States before 27 September 1957 were not protected in the United Kingdom, as the Universal Copyright Convention was not retrospective.

1   SR & O 1915/130.
2   SI 1979/1715. Works published in the specified area within 14 days of US publication were deemed first published here and benefited from the Copyright Act 1911, s 35(3).

2.54 By an Order in Council of 9 February 1920,[1] the 1911 Act was applied to works first published in the United States between 1 August 1914 and the termination of the war on 10 January 1920 (which had not been republished in the British Empire other than in the self-governing dominions, prior to 2 February 1920), provided the work was published in the United States not later than six months after the termination of the war, ie 10 July 1920.[2] Similar provisions were made for works first published in the United States between 3 September 1939 and 29 December 1950. To benefit from this Order, the work had to be published not later than 28 December 1950.[3]

1   SR & O 1920/257.
2   There is a defect in the drafting of the Order which seems to suggest that British publication should have occurred between 2 February and 10 July 1920. This literal reading cannot be right and would probably not be followed.
3   SR & O 1942/1579, SI 1950/1641, repealed by SI 1957/1523.

Pre-1957 sound recordings, photographs and films

2.55 An unpublished literary, dramatic, musical or artistic work made by a United States citizen or person resident in the United States before 27 September 1957 enjoyed copyright by virtue of the 1915 Order,[1] but lost it (subject to benefiting from the special wartime arrangement) on first publication prior to that date. The same applied in the case of unpublished photographs (and therefore films). However, in the case of sound recordings first published in the United States before 27 September 1957 copyright would not have been lost because a relevant consideration was whether the maker was a citizen of or resident in the United States at the time, and not merely whether the work was published in a country to which the 1956 Act applied.[2] If a film maker were a corporation the relevant consideration was established place of business in the United States at the time of making prior to 27 September 1957.[3] After that date, the relevant consideration was that the maker was incorporated in the United States. However, in all cases the question needed to be asked whether or not the corporation was the person entitled to copyright. Thus for pre-1957 films, the relevant consideration was ownership of the film stock,[4] or commissioner of the film (in relation to which the position was the same as in relation to photographs under the 1956 Act).[5]

1   SI 1915/130.
2   See SI 1979/1715, art 4(1)(b) which says 'copyright shall not subsist by virtue of this Part of this Order in any such work or other subject-matter *by reason only* of its publication [in the United States], and Copyright Act 1956, Sch 7, para 39(4).

3 This is probably the test – see para 2.26. Under the Copyright Act 1911 the letting of films for hire was not thought to amount to publication.
4 Copyright Act 1911, s 21.
5 See para 1.26 et seq.

Protection of works of United Kingdom nationals under United States law

2.56 The protection of British works in the United States depends, of course, upon American law. After the Chace Act 1891, foreign nationals could obtain protection for their works in the United States. This was replaced by the Copyright Act 1909 and by a Presidential proclamation under which the citizens of certain foreign countries, including Britain, might acquire statutory protection for their works in the same way as American citizens.

2.57 Works subject to copyright were: literary works; musical works and any accompanying words; dramatic works and any accompanying music; pantomimes and choreographic works; motion pictures and other audio-visual works; and sound recordings.[1]

1 United States Code, s 102.

Unpublished works
2.58 Unpublished works created on or after 1 January 1978 were subject to statutory copyright protection 'without regard to the nationality or domicile of the author'.[1] Works created before 1 January 1978 (the date the current statute came into effect) were protected by common law rather than statutory copyright, but thereafter became subject to statutory copyright.[2] Once a work was published however, anywhere in the world, it became subject to the national origin requirements.

1 1976 Act, ss 104 and 302(a).
2 Ibid, s 303.

Published works
2.59 A work published in the United States by a US national, did not acquire copyright protection unless the registration requirements of US copyright law had been complied with. However, works published by nationals of Convention countries, enjoyed protection subject to compliance with the formalities under the Convention.

2.60 Foreign authors who were domiciled in the United States at the time of first publication anywhere in the world, were entitled to claim statutory copyright in the same way as United States citizens.[1] Works first published in the United States were also entitled to statutory protection irrespective of the author's nationality or domicile.[2] This applied to works published after 1 January 1978. For works subject to the Copyright Act 1909, there was no statutory copyright if the author was neither domiciled in the United States at the time of publication, a national of a Universal Convention country, or a national of a proclamation country and if the work was not first published in a UCC country *other* than the United States. Section 9(b) of the Copyright Act 1909 permitted the President to issue a proclamation under which the nationals of certain foreign countries, might acquire statutory protection for their works in the same way as works of nationals of the United States. A proclamation was issued covering Great Britain and her possessions and colonies. The effect of this was to confer upon British citizens the right to acquire statutory copyright in the United States.[3]

1   Ibid, s 104(b)(1).
2   Ibid, s 104(b)(2).
3   With effect from 1 July 1909.

2.61   By an amending Act of 1919, authors who, owing to war conditions had been unable to register their copyright in the United States before first publication abroad might obtain copyright by taking steps to acquire United States protection within 15 months of the declaration of peace. A similar provision was enacted by an Act of 1941 and the benefit of this provision was extended to United Kingdom citizens by a proclamation of 1944. The benefit of this proclamation extended to works published outside the United States on or after 3 September 1939. The benefit of this proclamation expired on 29 December 1950.

2.62   Under all of the above provisions the formalities of United States law had to be observed. The United States adhered to the Universal Copyright Convention on 16 September 1955. Works then enjoying protection in another Convention country were to enjoy 28 years' protection from the date of their first publication abroad, without further formality. The Convention came into force between the United Kingdom and the United States on 27 September 1957.

2.63   For British works published after accession, it was not necessary to register at the Copyright Office at Washington. In order to be eligible for exemption from the registration requirements, all copies of post-accession works had to bear from the time of first publication the symbol '©' accompanied by the name of the copyright proprietor and the year of first publication, placed in such manner and location as to give reasonable notice of the claim of copyright.

2.64   For works requiring protection by registration, the term of copyright in the United States was 28 years from the date of first publication with the right of renewal for a second period of 28 years. All renewal copyrights which would have expired between 19 September 1962 and 31 December 1976 were extended.

2.65   Section 104A of the Copyright Act 1976 now restores copyright to foreign works still protected in the source country, but in the public domain in the United States. There are three requirements for the resurrection of copyright:
   (1)   The work must have at least one author or right holder,[1] who must take steps to get on the 'Lazarus list' as explained below. Such author or right holder must at the time the work was created have been a national or domiciliary of an eligible country ie essentially a member of the Berne Union, the World Trade Organisation or the beneficiary of a special presidential proclamation.
   (2)   The work must be an original work which has not fallen into the public domain in the source country.

(3) If the work was published, it must have been published in an eligible country, and not in the United States until more than 30 days later. In practice, this will often be virtually impossible to ascertain. Presumably, where there is no clear evidence on this question, the claimant must be given the benefit of the doubt.

1   Ie a person who owns the rights in a sound recording. The position of parties who have acted in reliance on a work being in the public domain is dealt with below.

2.66 These provisions are effective from 1 January 1996.[1] The above provisions do not resurrect the copyright in works of US authors which have fallen into the public domain. The benefit is limited to the works of the categories of foreign authors specified. Such works coming back into copyright enjoy the remainder of the term they would have enjoyed if they had not gone into the public domain. Those published after 1 January 1978 will enjoy the remainder of the full copyright term of a life plus 50 years. For those published before that date the period was a 28 year term followed by a 47 year term, ie 75 years. Thus the legislative commentary gives the example of a French short story published in 1935 without the required copyright notice. It will be treated as if it had both been published with the proper copyright notice, and properly renewed, so that the copyright will expire in 2010, 75 years from when US copyright protection would have come into existence. Title to the copyright vests in the original author or rights holder, and devolves according to the law of the source country. Contractual dealings will be given effect to according to their terms.

1   This is controversial. It is arguable that they should have come into force on 1 January 1995, the date the GATT/TRIPs Agreement came into force.

2.67 Parties who have relied on a work being in the public domain in the US have one year's immunity from infringement claims, which runs from the date the reliance party receives notice of the intention to enforce copyright, or it receives constructive notice through publication in the Federal Register of notices of intent to enforce copyright (the 'Lazarus list'). The first of these lists was published in May 1996, and it is therefore important that copyright owners get on to this list. The procedure for doing so was effective from 1 October 1995.

2.68 Derivative works, such as films, created before the coming into force of the Uruguay Round Agreements Act on 8 December 1994 are treated somewhat differently. If, for example, a European film in the public domain had been remade in the US, the reliance party which remade the film can continue to market it in the US, but it must pay the copyright owner a reasonable remuneration for use. This would apply also to musical works incorporated into the film, which had been in the public domain in the US: the copyright owner is entitled to reasonable remuneration. If a reasonable remuneration cannot be fixed, compensation is to be set by the Federal Court. Some Constitutional difficulties have been raised concerning the above legislation. Only time will tell whether or not these are real.

The 'manufacturing' requirement
2.69 Until the 1891 Act, copyright protection extended only to citizens or residents of the United States. When this was changed in 1891, the requirement exacted by the printing industry was that books, photographs,

chromolithographs, and lithographs were required to be 'printed from type set within the United States, or plates made therefrom, or from negatives, or drawings on stone made within the limits of the United States', otherwise these works did not qualify for copyright protection. The notice of intent must identify the title of the restored work, including an English translation of the title and any alternative by which the work is known[1] and be signed by the owner of the restored copyright or of the exclusive right therein or by the owner's agent.[2]

1   Copyright Act 1976, s 104A(e)(1)A.
2   Ibid, s 104A(e)(1)B.

INTERNATIONAL PROTECTION OF TRADE MARKS, DESIGNS AND PATENTS

2.70   The United Kingdom is a party to the International Convention for the Protection of Industrial Property, the Paris Convention, of 1883. This has been revised on several occasions, the last revision being at Stockholm in 1967. The United Kingdom ratified the revised Convention in 1969. Under Article 4 of the Convention, any person who has duly filed an application for a trade mark (or a design) in one of the countries of the Union, or his successor in title, enjoys, for the purpose of filing in the other countries, a right of priority during the period fixed by the Convention. By Article 4C, the period of priority for trade marks is six months.[1] The period for designs is the same. The period for patents is twelve months. The period runs from the day after the date of filing, unless this day was an official holiday, or a day when the Office was not open for the filing of applications, in which case it runs from the first following working day.

1   It is debatable whether the Convention priority period extends to service marks. This ultimately depends on municipal law eg in Germany it does not, see Heil Strohele 'Protection of Service Marks in Germany' (1979) IIC 689, 694. As to the United Kingdom and countries to which priority is being accorded see Trade Marks Act 1994, s 55 and SI 1986/1303.

2.71   Registration of trade marks through the Community Trade Marks Office at Alicante, and the International Bureau, at Geneva, is dealt with at paragraph 3.69.

Chapter 3

Trade marks and service marks

INTRODUCTION

3.1 As already pointed out, some merchandising is primarily concerned with the extension of registrations for well-known marks. For this type of operation, the immediate cost effectiveness of obtaining the additional registrations may not be of primary importance. For ordinary merchandisers, however, where at the outset the potential of a property is somewhat problematic, the expense of a programme of trade mark registration may not be felt to be justified. We believe, however, in view of the fact that it is not always possible to predict which properties will be short-lived and which long-lived, and the greater ease and cheapness of the system of registration introduced by the Trade Marks Act 1994, it will often be prudent at the outset to apply at least for some registrations.

3.2 There were two principal problems with UK trade marks law in this field. The first was the limited types of mark which were registrable, shapes, for example, could not be registered as such.[1] The second was the restrictions placed on licensing under s 28 of the Trade Marks Act 1938, in particular as interpreted in the *Hollie Hobby* case.[2] The Trade Marks Act 1994 has effectively eliminated these problems.

1   *Coca-Cola Co's Application, Re* [1986] 2 All ER 274, [1986] FSR 472.
2   *Re American Greetings Corpn's Application* [1984] RPC 329.

3.3 The purpose of this chapter is not to give a detailed exposition of the law relating to trade and service mark registration in the United Kingdom, since this is dealt with in the standard texts.[1] It is simply to attempt to sketch the salient features of the new law, with overseas readers especially in mind, and to draw attention to those aspects which are particularly problematic in relation to merchandising.

1   See Firth, 'Trade Marks: The New Law', Jordans, Bristol, 1995; Morcom, 'The Trade Marks Act 1994', Butterworths, London, 1994.

FRAMEWORK OF THE TRADE MARKS ACT 1994 AND ITS LEGISLATIVE CONTEXT

Introduction

3.4 The new trade marks law not only implements the Trade Marks Directive of 21 December 1988,[1] it goes much further and effects the first major overhaul of the UK law on registered trade marks for nearly 90 years. The 1938 Act was a very conservative measure. It was also in places obscurely drafted and difficult to understand. The practice on registrability evolved by the Registry was set out in a bumper fun book called the 'Work Manual' (which incidentally got no mention at all in the standard practitioner work on the 1938 Act, *Kerly on Trade Marks*, even though it was essential reading for practitioners). It was in the Manual that one discovered such gems as that in determining whether a name was in its ordinary signification a surname,[2] the Registrar would, *inter alia*, look in the London telephone directory, and if it was a word having no other meaning, such as 'Schlitz', consider it prima facie registrable in Part A if it appeared five times or less, and in Part B if it appeared 15 times or less. For names with another meaning, such as 'Bush' the figures were 50 and 100 times respectively. This somewhat curious result was a way of implementing the requirements of the 1938 Act, but it must be admitted that the result was bizarre.

1   89/104.
2   See 1938 Act, s 9(1)(d).

3.5   In 1974 the Mathys Committee recommended very few changes in the law, apart from the introduction of registration for service marks,[1] which was eventually implemented in 1984 by the cumbersome mechanism of having a second Act for service marks paralleling the 1938 Act for goods. It is symptomatic of the change which has overcome our conservative organs of government in the last decade or so, that not only are the minimal changes required to implement the mandatory provisions of the Directive being made, but a major modernisation is being undertaken which adopts the optional provisions of the Directive[2] and goes much further. Thus the very restrictive licensing provisions contained in section 28 of the 1938 Act, which presented especial problems in the merchandising context, have gone. In place of nanny Registrar, proprietors will have to look after their marks themselves, and ensure that their licensees do not endanger their registrations. The UK also at last unequivocally complies with the requirements of Article 6bis of the Paris Convention in protecting well-known foreign trade marks.

1   They also recommended the abolition of the division of the register into Parts A and
     B, which is implemented by the 1994 Act – see below.
2   As recommended by the White Paper of September 1990.

3.6   A welcome, and long overdue, reform effected by the new law is the abolition of the distinction between Part A marks and Part B marks. Apart from the fact that the Registry applied different criteria for the admission of marks to one part or the other, no one was ever been able to establish how *in practice* you were worse off with a Part B registration, since section 5(1) of the Act told us that registration in Part B conferred a 'like right' to registration in Part A.[1]

1   There were some differences. For example, Part A marks became invulnerable after
     seven years, and some argued that Part B marks could not be infringed by importing
     a reference. The former was of little practical importance, and the latter view was
     almost certainly wrong.

3.7 Perhaps the greatest change is that instead of a mark having to *qualify* for registration as under the old Act,[1] marks are registrable unless *excluded* from registration on the absolute or relative grounds set out in sections 3 and 5. The situation under the old law was that many marks which secured registration in other countries, were excluded from registration here. Accordingly, the common law of passing off played a relatively large role in protecting trade marks. Registration, moreover, only gave the right to sue for infringement in respect of the goods or services specified, and the Registrar often imposed further limitations (for example the well-known 'Penguin' mark for books had a limitation excluding its use on books about birds!). Accordingly, proprietors who had registrations nevertheless often needed to resort to passing off. Under the new law, infringement rights extend to the use of the mark on similar goods and services, and in certain cases, dissimilar goods and services.[2] Furthermore, given that under the new law registration is much easier to secure, the need to rely on passing off will diminish. Indeed it may be that the requirements of the tort of passing off will eventually come to be most frequently referred to in relation to opposition proceedings under clause 5(4)(a) (opposition on the basis of unregistered marks) which requires an opponent to registration to show that the use of the mark in the UK is liable to be prevented, inter alia, by passing off – which is narrower than the old grounds of opposition under section 11 under which it was not necessary to show that the opponent would succeed in a passing off action.[3]

1   Under ss 9 and 10.
2   S 10(3)(b) – this is an attempt to deal with an aspect of the 'dilution' problem mentioned below.
3   See the test laid down in *Re Smith Hayden & Co's Application* (1946) 63 RPC 97; modified in *Berlei (UK) Ltd v Bali Brassiere Co Inc* [1969] 2 All ER 812, [1969] RPC 472.

3.8   To summarise the principal changes which the 1994 Act effects:
   (a) registration is easier to obtain, and without unnecessary limitations;[1]
   (b) the rights conferred by registration are not restricted to the specifications of the goods or services in respect of which the mark is registered, but extend to similar, and in some cases dissimilar goods and services;
   (c) an effect of the above is that the right to oppose on the basis of a prior registered mark is rather broader than under the old section 12, which required that the earlier proprietor's registration be for the same goods or descriptions of goods;[2]
   (d) on the other hand the right to oppose on the basis of an unregistered mark is narrower than under the old section 11;
   (e) the former restrictive provisions on licensing have gone;
   (f) there is only one undivided register of marks.
Given the extent of the changes outlined above, established operations with a range of marks registered under the 1938 Act, should review their portfolios of registrations in the light of the new provisions.

1   See para 3.12 et seq.
2   Though it should be noted that in *British Sugar plc v James Robertson & Sons* [1996] RPC 281, Jacob J suggested that the considerations a court should have in mind in judging whether goods are 'similar' are similar to those which the court had in mind in judging whether goods were 'of the same description'.

Outline of the United Kingdom registration system

3.9 Registrations are secured by application to the Trade Mark Registry. The United Kingdom Registry is a division of the Patent Office. The procedural aspects of registration are governed by the Trade Marks Rules 1994. Additionally, the new law makes provision for two alternative routes to registration through the Community Trade Marks Office and the Madrid Protocol, mentioned later.

3.10 A foreign applicant for registration must be represented in the United Kingdom. There is no limitation on the persons who can represent applicants before the Trade Mark Registry. Usually, however, the applicant will employ a specialist to conduct the application. Firms of patent attorneys, as well as firms of trade mark attorneys, specialise in this sort of work, and there are also some firms of solicitors. Some firms of American lawyers with offices in London also undertake this work, principally, but not exclusively, on the behalf of American clients. Because of the peculiar problems involved in merchandising, it is desirable to find a firm which has some specialised knowledge of the field, and in particular, knowledge of the law of copyright.

3.11 An application for a mark is filed for goods or services in one or more relevant classes of the International Classification. There are 34 classes for goods, and 8 for services. Usually it will be desirable to file in a number of different classes in order to cover the variety of goods or services in which the business proposes to deal. The classes tend to be rather broad, and generally it will be necessary to limit the application to specified goods within that class. A major procedural improvement effected by the new law is that it is no longer necessary to file separate applications for each class. Because of the arbitrary nature of some of the classifications, it can sometimes occur that goods or services of a similar description in trade and on which the mark is likely to be used, may nevertheless fall into different classes for the purposes of classification. A guide is published by the Registry listing goods and services in alphabetical order with their classifications. An application should be filed by the party who has used or intends to use the mark.

DEFINITION OF 'TRADE MARK'

3.12 A trade mark consists of:

'... any sign capable of being represented graphically which is capable of distinguishing goods or services of one undertaking from those of other undertakings.

A trade mark may, in particular, consist of words (including personal names), designs, letters, numerals or the shape of goods or their packaging.'[1]

The above definition covers marks used in relation to both goods and services. The cumbersome arrangement of having separate definitions in separate Acts for trade marks and service marks has gone. Although at first sight it might appear that the definition excludes the possibility of audio and olfactory marks, it seems clear from the White Paper that this was not the intention of the draftsman.[2] Provided such marks can be represented graphically for registration purposes, it would appear that they might be registrable, and could be infringed by audio or olfactory reproduction. Thus a bar of music might be registrable, and be infringed eg by unauthorised use in a radio commercial. Such marks have been recognised in some countries, and it appears that the government wants to leave open the possibility of their being registrable here. There is some doubt whether slogans are registrable. However, given that these do not appear to be ruled out by the absolute or relative grounds of refusal set out below, and that they may function in the market as trade marks, there seems to be no good reason for supposing they are excluded.[3]

1   Trade Marks Act 1938, s 1(1).
2   See White Paper, para 2.06.
3   See paras 3.13 and 3.32.

ABSOLUTE GROUNDS FOR REFUSAL OF REGISTRATION

3.13   A mark which falls within the Act's definition of 'trade mark' is registrable, unless excluded from registration on either the absolute or relative grounds set out in sections 3 and 5. These are set out in section 3(1) which provides:

'The following shall not be registered –
(a)   signs which do not satisfy the requirements of section 1(1),[1]
(b)   trade marks which are devoid of any distinctive character,
(c)   trade marks which consist exclusively of signs or indications which may serve, in trade, to designate the kind, quality, quantity, intended purpose, value, geographical origin, the time of production of goods or of rendering of services, or other characteristics of goods or services,
(d)   trade marks which consist exclusively of signs or indications which have become customary in the current language or in the *bona fide* and established practices of the trade:
Provided that, a trade mark shall not be refused registration by virtue of paragraph (b), (c) or (d) above if, before the date of application for registration, it has in fact acquired a distinctive character as a result of the use made of it.
(2)   A sign shall not be registered as a trade mark if it consists exclusively of –
(a)   the shape which results from the nature of the goods themselves,
(b)   the shape of goods which is necessary to obtain a technical result, or
(c)   the shape which gives substantial value to the goods.
(3)   A trade mark shall not be registered if it is –
(a)   contrary to public policy or to accepted principles of morality, or
(b)   of such a nature as to deceive the public (for instance as to the nature, quality or geographical origin of the goods or service).
(4)   A trade mark shall not be registered if or to the extent that its use is prohibited in the United Kingdom by any enactment or rule of law or by any provision of Community law.'

1   Set out in para 3.12 above.

3.14   As under the previous law, and as required by the Paris Convention, specially protected emblems such as national symbols continue to be unregistrable.[1] Applications for registration must be made in good faith. *John Batt* type activities, ie stockpiling trade mark registrations with the intention of dealing in them rather than using them in relation to goods or services, would presumably fall foul of the requirement contained in section 3(6) that an application for registration must be made in good faith.[2]

1   S 3(5).
2   See *John Batt & Co v Dunnett*1899] AC 428.

Signs which do not satisfy the requirements of section 1(1)

3.15   This provision needs little comment. The overriding requirement that the sign can be represented graphically is discussed above.

Marks devoid of distinctive character

3.16   Paragraph 3 of the Statements on Article 3(1)(b) of the Directive from which this provision derives states that 'a trade mark is devoid of distinctive character if it is not capable of distinguishing the goods or services of one undertaking from those of other undertakings'. This simply repeats Article 2 of the Directive on which section 1(1) is based, and so adds little to section 3(1)(a). Presumably this provision is meant to make it clear that generic names for goods or services, purely laudatory names such as 'perfection',[1] or descriptive names such as 'king size' for cigarettes are unregistrable. In *British Sugar plc v James Robertson & Sons*[2] Jacob J held that the word 'Treat' for dessert sauces was improperly registered. However, words refused under the old law, as being merely phonetic equivalents of descriptive terms such as 'Orlwoola', may be registrable provided evidence that they have acquired a distinctive character is filed,[3] but because of section 3(3)(b) mentioned below, it may be necessary to volunteer a limitation of its use to woollen goods.[4]

1   See *Perfection Trade Mark* (1909) 26 RPC 837.
2   [1996] RPC 281
3   *Orlwoola Trade Mark* (1909) 26 RPC 683.
4   Under s 13. It is believed, however, that the Registry will not require disclaimers on *ex parte* applications, but they may be necessary in oppositions. Even with a disclaimer, however, there will be a problem in relation to infringement with such marks, because, 'Orlwoola' could clearly be infringed by use on polyester articles of clothing – see s 10(3). There is also the problem of the Trade Descriptions Act 1968 under s 3(4) mentioned below.

Signs designating characteristics of the goods

3.17   Signs excluded under section 9(1)(d) of the old Act as having a 'direct reference to the character or quality of the goods' (or services) or being in their ordinary signification geographical names, could be excluded from registration under section 3(1)(c).[1] Although it was hoped that the Registry would cease to apply its somewhat mechanical guidelines on what was in its 'ordinary signification' of geographical name or surname, since the words 'ordinary signification' do not appear in the new section, it would appear that they are continuing to apply fairly mechanical *de minimis* criteria for both types of marks, even though surnames are not mentioned in section 3.[2] In both cases it is, of course, possible to file evidence of distinctiveness. Thus 'York' for trailers would now be registrable.[3]

1   They may also, in certain cases, be excluded under s 3(4) discussed below.
2   And note s 11(2).
3   *York Trailer Holdings Ltd v Registrar of Trade Marks* [1982] 1 All ER 257, [1984] RPC 231.

Signs customary in the trade

3.18   Signs which have become generic, or which have come into general use in the trade can be refused under section 3(1)(d). It is not clear whether it is signs customary in the current language or in the *bona fide* and established practices *of the trade* only, which are excluded under this provision, or signs customary in the current language (of the public in general), *or* in the *bona fide* and established practices of the trade. Revocation because a mark has become generic is limited to marks which have become common names *in the trade* for a product or service for which it is registered.[1] For this reason, it may be that the former reading is the correct one. Thus, goods which the public habitually refer to generically, but which the trade would always refer to by their correct trade name, would not be barred from registration. It is difficult to see how such signs which have become generic could qualify as distinctive under the proviso, and evidence filed to counter objection under this head will presumably be directed at showing the objection was unfounded.

1   S 46(1)(c).

The proviso

3.19   At present, the only guidance as to the evidence of use necessary to acquire the distinctiveness necessary for a mark to qualify for registration under the proviso, is contained in the Draft Trade Marks Registry Work Manual of June 1995. Chapter 6, paragraph 4.2.2 and Chapter 7 are of some help, but it is likely to be some time before a body of decisions has built up which will be of real help in particular cases.

Marks contrary to public policy or morality, or deceptive

3.20   Under section 11 of the old Act, marks could be refused registration if their use would be contrary to law or morality. The word 'Hallelujah' was refused on this ground.[1] Presumably such a word would be unregistrable under section 3(3)(a). It is unlikely that in practice this ground of refusal will be of very much significance. Section 3(3)(b) which prevents registration of marks of such a nature as to deceive the public (for instance as to the nature, quality or geographical origin of the goods or services), requires no further comment.

1   *Hallelujah Trade Mark* [1976] RPC 605.

Marks whose use would be contrary to law

3.21   The United Kingdom enactments which would be relevant for the purposes of section 3(4) include the Trade Descriptions Act 1968,[1] the Anglo-Portuguese Commercial Treaty Acts 1914 and 1916 (meaning of 'port' and 'madeira' as applied to wine), the 'Anzac' (Restriction on Trade

Use of Word) Act 1916, and the Geneva Conventions Act 1957. So far as
EC law is concerned, the wine regulations are an obvious example,[2] and
the Regulation on the protection of geographical indications and
designations of origin for agricultural products and foodstuffs.[3]

1   The registration of '*Orlwoola*' mentioned above, without a limitation to woollen goods,
    would possibly be contrary to this section.
2   Eg Reg 823/87 applied in *Taittinger SA v Allbev Ltd* [1993] FSR 641.
3   Reg 2081/92.

Types of registrable mark

3.22   The Addendum to the Draft Work Manual referred to in paragraph
3.19 is a useful guide as to which marks are acceptable, and which are
not, and should be consulted on all borderline cases. The following is simply
a non-exhaustive list of some of the types of marks used in merchandising
operations.

Names

3.23   Name marks, whether real or fictitious, are very important in all
kinds of merchandising. So far as the Trade Marks Registry is concerned,
it does not matter whether a name is fictitious in the context of the film
or TV series (or whatever) from which it is taken, the question is whether
its registration would cause prejudice to third parties bearing the same
name. In *Games Workshop Limited and anor v Transworld Publishers Ltd*[1]
the first plaintiffs were involved in publishing books and in making and
selling games bearing the words 'DARK FUTURE' for which they had a
registration in relation to publications, magazines, books, manuals, rule
books for playing games and other things, including games etc. The second
plaintiff was the first plaintiff's agent and licensee. The defendant
published novels entitled 'Dark Future 1: The Revengers', 'Dark Future
2: Beyond the Grave', 'Dark Future 3: The Horned God', and 'Dark Future
4: The Plague'. It was held by the Court of Appeal that there was a seriously
triable issue that the defendant's use was use as a trade mark within the
meaning of the 1938 Act. In deciding not to abrogate the interlocutory
injunction granted at first instance, the Court took into account, inter alia,
damage to the first plaintiff's licensing prospects. Trade mark use is not,
it would appear, required under the new Act.[2]

1   [1993] FSR 705.
2   See now *British Sugar plc v James Robertson & Sons Ltd* [1996] RPC 281, criticising
    this aspect of *Bravado Merchandising Services v Mainstream Publishing* ('Wet Wet
    Wet') [1996] FSR 205.

Signatures

3.24   Signatures are quite frequently met with in personality
merchandising, especially in the field of sport. In the ordinary world of
commerce, signature marks are not usually very valuable because the
protection they afford is so narrow. Such a mark cannot be used to stop a
person using the same name with a sufficiently different signature.
However, in the context of personality merchandising, they can be quite
valuable as the public will tend to identify the signature as well as the
name.

3.25 The fact that the person whose signature the mark is has ceased to be proprietor, does not invalidate the mark. Whilst the mark obviously cannot be used to stop him from using his own signature bona fide, it is difficult to envisage circumstances in which it could be used as a mark bona fide on goods within the registrations. In the case of unregistered marks, where the person whose signature the mark is has ceased to be connected with the business using it, the fact that the signature has become associated with particular goods, and has acquired goodwill, may be a ground for refusing registration to the person whose signature it is. The *Re Barry Artist Trade Mark* case[1] provides a good illustration of this.

1   [1978] RPC 703.

Words not being names
3.26 Words which have a common English meaning can, under certain circumstances, be registrable as trade marks. Thus, under the former Act, the word 'Bionic' was accepted for a variety of merchandise for the purposes of a merchandising operation based on the TV series 'Six Million Dollar Man'. Under the new Act such words will qualify for registration, unless falling into one of the excluded categories set out above. It may also be recalled, that it is possible in the case of marks excluded under section 3(1)(b), (c) or (d) to adduce evidence that the mark has in fact acquired a distinctive character.

Symbols and device marks
3.27 Symbols and device marks are an important element in many examples of successful merchandising operations. Examples include the World Wild Life Fund panda, and the National Football League shield. They may enjoy copyright protection additionally, of course, but as explained at paragraph 1.57 the effect of section 52 of the Copyright, Designs and Patents Act 1988 will usually be to cut down the period of protection to 25 years from the end of the calendar year in which the work was first marketed. Trade marks, by contrast, in principle (ie as long as they are used etc), stay on the register for as long as renewal fees are paid. Initials such as 'NFL', may themselves be separately registrable as a mark (see below).

Portraits
3.28 Similarly, portraits too enjoy copyright protection, subject to the limitation noted in the previous paragraph. Portraits being distinctive graphic signs[1] are, in principle, registrable. The protection afforded by such a registration is quite narrow: any infringement would have to bear a substantial similarity to the registered portrait. However, in the merchandising context, this may be of less importance than in an ordinary commercial context.

1   See 1994 Act, s 1(1).

Initials
3.29 Subject to section 3(1)(c), combinations of letters are registrable. If there is a problem with section 3(1)(c), it is possible to file evidence of acquired distinctiveness in order for the mark to qualify for registration under the proviso.

Numerals
3.30 Again, subject to section 3(1)(c), numerals may also be registered as marks. In relation to section 3(1)(c), the point made in the previous paragraph concerning acquired distinctiveness also applies.

Shapes
3.31 There is quite a lot of useful guidance about marks consisting of three-dimensional shape marks in the Addendum to Chapter 6 of the Trade Marks Registry's Draft Work Manual, and for borderline cases that should be consulted, in particular at page 129. The use in section 3(2) of the word 'exclusively' should be emphasised.[1] Combinations are not excluded under this provision. Paragraph 4 of the Statements state that where goods are packaged, the 'shape of goods' includes their packaging. This must be the case for such things as liquids which cannot be marketed without a container of some sort. Goods and containers of distinctive appearance, not dictated entirely by function, are not excluded under this provision. Where a shape is functional, but one of a limited number of possible technical solutions, so that there can be said to be some arbitrary element present, registration ought surely to be refused on this ground, otherwise a limited number of manufacturers could monopolise a design field?[2] The words 'gives substantial value to the goods' are presumably meant to indicate that distinctive features which make the product a better product in the functional or aesthetic sense, are excluded under this provision – they may after all be protectable as designs, or even patentable. On the other hand, if Reckitt & Coleman had before marketing applied to register a plastic lemon under a provision equivalent to this one, it could be argued that it should be excluded under this provision, otherwise they would acquire the exclusive right to use lemon shaped objects in relation to lemon juice.[3] But if this reading is right, they could not even get registration on evidence of distinctiveness under the proviso to section 3(1). It should be noted that signs excluded under this sub-section (as under the following one) cannot be made registrable by filing evidence of distinctiveness. So far as containers are concerned, and indeed certain other shapes which may give rise to problems at the borderline, reference should be made to the Addendum to the Draft Work Manual, notably, so far as containers are concerned, at page 23. The registration of the *Coca-Cola* bottle, foreshadowed on page 18, has now occurred.

1   In a case involving 'twirled snacks' the Dutch Supreme Court held that the value of the crisp lay in its eating qualities rather than shape – Hoge Raad, 11 November 1983, NJ (1984) 203, BIE (1985) 23; Kamperman Sanders *Some Frequently Asked Questions about the Trade Marks Act 1994* (1995) 2 EIPR 67.
2   See eg the passing-off case of *Hodgkinson & Corby Ltd and Roho Inc v Wards Mobility Services Ltd* [1995] FSR 169. In this case, however, it should be noted that Jacob J rejected the distinction between capricious additions and integral features, because both can function as trade marks. This is surely correct, and the doctrine of aesthetic functionality adopted by some US courts it is submitted is wrong – see eg *Pagliero v Wallace China* 198 F 2d 339 (1952) where a floral pattern on china was denied protection.
3   Under s 9(1).

RELATIVE GROUNDS FOR REFUSAL

3.32 Section 5 sets out what are called "relative grounds for refusal of registration". It provides:

'(1)   A trade mark shall not be registered if it is identical with an earlier trade mark and the goods or services for which the trade mark is applied for are identical with the goods or services for which the earlier trade mark is protected.

(2)   A trade mark shall not be registered if, because

(a)   it is identical with an earlier trade mark and is to be registered for goods or services similar to those for which the earlier mark is protected, or

(b)   it is similar to an earlier trade mark and is to be registered for goods or services identical with or similar to those for which the earlier trade mark is protected,

there exists a likelihood of confusion on the part of the public, which includes the likelihood of association with the earlier trade mark.

(3)   A trade mark which

(a)   is identical with or similar to an earlier trade mark, and

(b)   is to be registered for goods or services which are not similar to those for which the earlier trade mark is registered,

shall not be registered if, or to the extent that, the earlier trade mark has a reputation in the United Kingdom .... and the use of the later mark without due cause would take unfair advantage of, or be detrimental to, the distinctive character or the repute of the earlier trade mark.

(4)   A trade mark shall not be registered if, or to the extent that, its use in the United Kingdom is liable to be prevented

(a)   by virtue of any rule of law (in particular, the law of passing off) protecting an unregistered mark or other sign used in the course of trade, or

(b)   by virtue of an earlier right other than those referred to in subsections (1) to (3) or paragraph (a) above, in particular by virtue of the law of copyright, design right or registered designs.'

3.33   Earlier trade marks, for the purpose of these provisions, include well-known trade marks entitled to protection under the Paris Convention,[1] but also, it would seem, marks which are less than well-known marks since the word used is 'reputation'. There are no clear criteria as to what amounts to a well-known mark, nor when, in relation to dissimilar goods, the use of the later mark would take unfair advantage of, or be detrimental to, the distinctive character of the earlier mark. There is clearly a continuum between well-known marks, and those simply enjoying a reputation.[2]

1   Under s 56 proprietors of such marks are accorded special protection.
2   It is hoped that mechanical rules of the sort operated in Germany, where a distinction is drawn between well-known marks and famous marks, will not be developed. 40% recognition is required for a mark to qualify as the former, and 80% as the latter.

3.34   Section 6 provides that 'earlier trade mark' means a registered trade mark, an international trade mark (UK),[1] and a Community trade mark,[2] all having application dates prior to that of the mark applied for. The grounds for refusal set out in sub-sections 5(1) to (3) are reflected in the definition of 'infringement' contained in sub-sections 10(1) to (3). Under the previous law, it was not necessary for there to be potential infringement for registration to be refused.[3]

1   Ie marks which will be protected under the Madrid Protocol – s 53.
2   S 51.
3   Under s 12.

Judging similarity

3.35   Again, there is some useful guidance to be obtained from the Trade
Mark Registry's Draft Work Manual, section 4.4. So far as sub-sections
5(2) and (3) are concerned, there is no guidance in the Act as to when marks
are similar. Nor is there guidance in the Act as to when goods or services
are to be regarded as 'similar' for the purposes of section 5(2). The new
provisions appear to require appraisal of the likelihood of confusion in all
the circumstances of the case. According to the Statements, paragraph 5(a),
goods may be considered as similar to services in appropriate
circumstances. The concept of 'likelihood of association' has been developed
by Benelux case law, to which the Directive is heavily indebted. Thus 'Anti-
Monopoly' for a game was held to infringe the registration 'Monopoly'
because anyone seeing the mark applied to a game would think of
Monopoly.[1] In *Wagamama Ltd v City Centre Restaurants*[2] Laddie J held,
obiter, that the words 'likelihood of association' added nothing to the words
'likelihood of confusion'[3] and declined to follow the 'statements'annexed to the
minutes of the Council Meeting at which the Directive was adopted as a guide
to interpretation. These make it clear that the words 'likelihood of association'
were derived from Benelux law.Under the old Act there were cases deciding
whether goods were of 'the same description'.[4] In *British Sugar plc v James
Robertson & Sons Ltd*[5] Jacob J suggested the considerations the court had to
bear in mind in these cases are similar to the considerations it must bear in
mind in deciding whether goods are 'similar'.

1   *Edor Handelsonderneming BV v General Mills Fun Group* (1978) Nederlandse
    Jurisprudentie 83.
2   [1995] FSR 713.
3   See para 3.52.
4   Eg *Jellinek's Application* (1946) 63 RPC 59.
5   [1996] RPC 281.

3.36   In judging similarity with an earlier mark, the case law under the
previous Act will presumably continue to have relevance. Thus if goods
are expensive, and of a sort usually selected after deliberation, a greater
degree of similarity may be permissible, than in the case of goods bought
with little thought or close examination such as those displayed in a super-
market.[1] In relation to word marks, Parker J observed:

> You must take the two words. You must judge them, both by their look
> and by their sound. You must consider the nature and kind of customer
> who would be likely to buy those goods. In fact you must consider all
> the surrounding circumstances; and you must further consider what
> is likely to happen if each of those trade marks is used in a normal
> way as a trade mark for the goods of the respective owners of the
> marks.[2]

1   See *Pianotist Co's Application* (1906) 23 RPC 774; *Lancer Trade Mark* [1987] RPC 303.
2   *Pianotist* (above) at p 777.

3.37   Regard is to be had to the idea of the mark: the two marks placed
side by side may exhibit significant differences, and yet the main idea left

in the mind may be the same, so that a person buying the goods without having the two side by side to make a comparison, might be deceived into buying the wrong goods.[1] Marks tend to be remembered imperfectly by general recollection rather than by photographic recall.[2] Resemblance with reference to the ear, as well as the eye, must be considered, because goods are ordered, for example, by telephone.[3] Importance may be attached to the resemblance between first syllables, because of the tendency in English to slur terminations.[4] Regard must be had to the appearance the marks will have in actual use, when fairly and honestly used.[5] The respective colours of the two marks can be an important consideration.[6]

1 See eg *Barker's Trade Mark* (1885) 53 LT 23 'Hunstman' and 'Sportsman' for cherry brandy.
2 *Aristoc v Rysta* (1945) 62 RPC 65, 73 per Luxmore LJ.
3 See eg *Phillips Trade Mark* [1969] RPC 78.
4 See eg *Capsuloid Co Ltd's Application* (1906) 23 RPC 782 – 'Tablones' too near 'Tabloids'.
5 *Re Smith Hayden & Coy Ltd's Application (Ovax)* (1945) 63 RPC 97.
6 *Worthington & Co's Trade Mark* (1880) 14 Ch D 8 – too close resemblance to the Bass red triangle.

3.38 The existence of a number of marks, of a somewhat similar nature, may have the effect that the public will appreciate finer distinctions between them,[1] but the fundamental question is still whether the mark applied for will lead to deception.[2] Under the new law *the onus will be on the opponent to show that it will do so.*

1 *In the Matter of Helena Rubinstein Ltd's Application for a Registered Trade Mark 'Skin Dew'* [1960] RPC 229.
2 *Taylor's Drug Co's Application* (1923) 40 RPC 193 – 'Germocea' refused because of existing registrations for 'Germolene' and 'Homocea'.

3.39 The question as to whether resemblance to an earlier mark is likely to lead to deception or confusion, is one for the tribunal adjudicating the case to decide, not witnesses.[1] On the other hand, the tribunal must take account of evidence showing that there has been no confusion.[2]

1 See eg *Berlei (UK) Ltd v Bali Brassiere Co Inc* [969] 2 All ER 812, [1969] RPC 472.
2 See eg *Kidax Ltd's Application* [1960] RPC 117, 122 – 'Kidax'/'Kiddies Daks'.

3.40 Under section 8 the Secretary of State may by order provide that a trade mark shall not be refused registration on any of the 'relative' grounds mentioned in section 5 unless objection on that ground is raised in opposition proceedings by the proprietor of the earlier right. The idea is to permit abolition of the power of the Registrar to refuse to register marks on relative grounds. However, this will not be possible until ten years after the coming into force of the Community Trade Mark system.

EXTENT OF PROTECTION REQUIRED

3.41 It is important to decide at the outset how much protection is necessary, because, although a single application under the new law can cover a number of different classes, nevertheless, the fees payable depend upon the number of classes applied for. The fact that part of the property forming the basis of the licensing programme is subject to copyright protection, can be a reason for cutting down the number of registrations. In the case of cartoon characters, for example, it is probably only going to be worthwhile to register the *name* of the leading character or characters. In the case of films and television series, it is usually worthwhile registering the title of the film (if possible), given the general absence of protection for it otherwise. Similarly, in the case of human characters in such films and series, trade mark registration will be virtually the only protection.

3.42 Licensing programmes are very varied, and it is impossible to give advice which will cover all cases. However, as a general rule the most important classes for initial consideration are:

Class 6	metal badges
Class 9	films, records etc
Class 14	watches, clocks and jewellery
Class 16	posters, books, magazines, publications, comics, stationery, printed materials, paper badges, stickers and transfers
Class 20	mirrors, furniture etc
Class 24	bed linen
Class 25	clothing
Class 26	cloth badges, buckles, belts etc
Class 28	toys and games
Class 30	food products and confectionery.

3.43 Service mark registrations are likely to be much less important than trade mark registrations. Sometimes the names of personalities and fictional characters are used as the names of restaurants etc, and in such cases a registration in Class 42 could obviously be of value, but it must be remembered that there must still be bona fide intention to use a mark, merely the hope that it might be licensed, it will be refused registration; and if registered, it may be liable to removal for the same reason by virtue of section 2. Probably the type of merchandising where service mark registrations are likely to play the most important role are in merchandising sporting personalities, in which such things as franchised coaching centres could be important. If such things are envisaged, a Class 41 registration should be sought. Curiously enough, the classification makes no provision for retail services per se and at present the Registry is not intending to follow the practice of some countries in permitting registration in Class 42 (Miscellaneous). Accordingly, the only registrations available are in respect of the goods in which a shop trades and to which it applies its own marks ie own brands. Again, the possibility of licensing sports shops could be important to the merchandising of sports personalities, and the present prohibition on the registration of retail services is a nuisance. The DTI has said that it will look again at this exclusion, but no change is as yet forthcoming.

PRACTICE ON APPLICATIONS

3.44 Detailed consideration of the practice on applications to register marks is beyond the scope of this work. The fact that a mark may have been registered in other countries is no guide as to its registrability in the United Kingdom, indeed evidence of such registrations will be dismissed as irrelevant in the absence of detailed information as to the law and facts pertaining to the registrations in those foreign territories. Presumably, however, the practice in other EU states may have some relevance, since the object ofthe Directive is harmonisation. The practice of the Community Trade Mark Office could also, for the same reason, be relevant.

PROTECTION OF MARKS

3.45 One of the most important matters in relation to marks used in merchandising, is still to ensure that they are properly used. Thus, there may be a question as to whether a mark in Class 25, registered for items including T-shirts, is actually being used as a trade mark when it appears as the design on the front or back of the shirt.[1] The best plan is to use the device on the label of the shirt as well. This advice will apply to many situations in the merchandising context, where there may be an argument as to whether the mark is being used as a decoration rather than as a mark.

1   See para 3.52 below.

3.46 It is important to ensure that the relevant marks are used in such a way that distinctiveness is not weakened by their use alongside other matter which detracts from that distinctiveness. Thus, to return to our T-shirts example, any label sewn in bearing the mark should be in substitution for any mark of the original manufacturer. It is also good practice to indicate the fact that the device or whatever, is a mark by '™' or '®', although under United Kingdom law neither is required. It may be argued that strictly speaking neither form should be used in respect of unregistered marks, to the extent that the use of either might suggest to the public at large that the mark was registered. The convention amongst trade mark practitioners is, however, that '™' can be used for unregistered or registered marks, and '®' for registered marks.

3.47 Where a manufacturer wants to be identified on the product, some formula such as 'X ™' manufactured by A & Co under licence from the B Co' should be used. Cross-reference should be made to paragraph 7.16 et seq for a discussion of the liability of the trade marker of goods under the Consumer Protection Act 1987.

NON-USE

3.48 Failure to use a mark for five years up to one month before the date of application for removal, renders it liable to be removed from the Register for non-use.[1] It will commonly be the case in merchandising that a number of identical or very similar marks will have been registered in respect of various goods (and services). Some of these may not have been used during the relevant period, but some of them may have been on goods of the same description. In such circumstances, the tribunal can refuse to remove the unused marks. It would appear from the *Kodak / Kodiak* case,[2] that an applicant who seeks to remove a mark which is registered for a range of goods, on the ground of non-use, must specify the goods in respect of which he alleges non-use. In that case incidentally, the question was raised, but not decided by Whitford J, as to whether or not use on T-shirts was trade mark use.

1 S 46.
2 *Greb Industries' Application* (8 February 1985, unreported). See, however, para 3.52 below.

THE PROBLEM OF PRE-EMPTION BY THIRD PARTIES

3.49 Many merchandised properties first become successful overseas, especially in the United States. It can happen, that by the time it is decided to secure trade mark registrations in this country, some third party has registered the relevant marks. If in such a case, the marks infringe no copyright, or other property right in the United Kingdom of the party seeking rectification, rectification may be refused. The famous *Rawhide* case[1] illustrates the problem. In this case, the applicant made a practice of registering in advance, the titles of American television series, not yet known in this country. Cross J held that since the proprietors of the relevant series could not claim to own the mark in this country, it was open to the applicants to choose it. If it could be shown that the work was registered without a bona fide intention to use, the situation will be different.[2]

1 [1962] RPC 133.
2 In *Rawhide*, the applicant's contingent intention to use depending on the film being shown in England was insufficient to give them standing as proprietors of a mark proposed to be used by then within s 17 of the 1938 Act.

3.50 If the foreign proprietor actually has a reputation in this country, this may be a ground for refusing registration, or for expunging a mark. The 1994 Act expressly protects well known trade marks,[1] and furthermore, reputation in the UK is a ground for opposition based on section 5(3).

1 S 56.

POLICING MARKS WORLDWIDE

3.51 The *Rawhide* type of activity is potentially very damaging for merchandisers, particularly when it is borne in mind that many jurisdictions favour the first party to register, even as against parties already trading in the jurisdiction under the relevant mark. In such jurisdictions, the six month Convention priority period could be important if sufficiently early notice of the application is obtained, and rapid action is taken. One way of obtaining such early warning is to place the mark with one of the worldwide trade mark watch services. For a relatively small sum, a watch can be maintained on the mark in all classes of the classification system in over 140 jurisdictions throughout the world. It may also be advisable to maintain a watch on attempts to register marks as company names.

THE EFFECT OF REGISTRATION

Rights conferred by a registered trade mark

3.52 The proprietor of a registered trade mark has 'exclusive rights' in the mark, which are infringed by use of the mark in the United Kingdom without his consent.[1] The use does not appear to have to be trade mark use, as it did under the old Act. Any use suffices, provided it is an act amounting to infringement within section 10. Section 10(4) gives examples of infringing uses.[2] These include affixing the mark to goods or their packaging; offering or exposing the goods for sale, putting them on the market or stocking them for those purposes under the sign; importing or exporting goods under the sign; and, using the sign on business papers or in advertising. The infringing use does not have to be visual or graphic, an oral use, eg describing unmarked goods as being goods of a particular registered proprietor, would appear to infringe,[3] or storing the sign in a computer.[4] This raises the interesting question as to whether use of a registered trade mark as a design on a T-shirt would now infringe. In *British Sugar plc v James Robertson & Sons Ltd*[5] Jacob J held that when considering infringement under section 10(2) three questions need to be asked, namely (1) was the sign used in the course of trade? (2) are the goods for which the sign was used, similar to those covered by the registration? and, (3) was there a likelihood of confusion because of that similarity? Putting this together with the views expressed by Laddie J in *Wagamama Ltd v City Centre Restaurants*[6] that to interpret section 10(2) in the way in which it has in some Benelux cases[7] would create a new type of monopoly not related to the proprietor's trade, but in the mark itself. This monopoly could be likened to a quasi-copyright in the mark, but which, unlike copyright, would be of no fixed duration. In conclusion, it would appear that use of a mark in an ordinary 'T-shirt' manner, would not infringe.

1   S 9(1).
2   It should be noted that the words in this subsection 'in particular' seem to mean 'inter alia'.
3   See ss 10(4)(b) and 103(2).
4   S 103(2).
5   [1996] RPC 281.
6   [1995] FSR 713.
7   As to interpretation, see para 3.67.

3.53 Such rights of the proprietor have effect from the date of registration, and this is the date of filing the application for registration as under the old law.[1] The absence of the word 'registered' to qualify the word 'proprietor' may indicate, that unlike the old law,[2] it is open to such persons as assignees whose title has not yet been registered under section 25, to sue for infringement.[3] A person infringes a registered trade mark if he uses in the course of trade a sign which is identical with the trade mark in relation to goods or services which are identical with those for which it is registered.[4] He also infringes if he uses an identical mark in relation to goods or services which are similar to those for which the mark is registered, or a similar mark for identical or similar goods or services to those for which the mark is registered, so that there exists a likelihood of confusion on the part of the public, which includes a likelihood of association with the mark.[5] A person also infringes a registered mark if he uses in the course of trade a sign which is identical with or similar to the trade mark, and is used in relation to goods and services which are *not* similar to those for which the trade mark is registered, where the trade mark has a reputation in the United Kingdom and the use of the sign, being *without due cause*, [emphasis supplied] takes unfair advantage of, or[6] is detrimental to, the distinctive character or the repute of the trade mark.

The emphasised words suggest that where, as in '*Lego*',[7] the defendant has in good faith used his own name on a range of goods, there might be a defence under this sub-section.

1   Ss 9(3) and 40(3).
2   There were, however, some decisions even under the old law that 'proprietor' was not limited to 'registered proprietor'.
3   But note s 25(4).
4   S 10(1).
5   S 10(2).
6   S 10(3) – it is not clear whether or not the 'or' is disjunctive, so that either unfair advantage *or* detriment suffice. These words also appear in the proviso to s 10(6). If 'detrimental' is to be read disjunctively, that might enable action to be taken against 'dictionary' uses under this provision (as well, possibly, under s 10(2)). Art 10 of the Community Trade Mark Regulation (EC 40/94) deals with dictionary uses specifically.
7   [1983] FSR 155.

3.54   A person who applies a registered trade mark to material intended to be used for labelling or packaging goods, as business paper, or for advertising goods or services, is to be treated as a party to any use of the material which infringes the registered mark in certain circumstances.[1] These are that when he applied the mark he knew or had reason to believe that the application of the mark was unauthorised by the proprietor or licensee.[2] This latter provision is limited to the application of the *registered* mark, and does not cover use of a similar mark, unless the differences are sufficiently slight not to be noticeable by the consuming public, presumably. This has the curious result that this type of infringement is more narrowly defined than the criminal offence provided for in section 92, where it is sufficient that the mark applied is 'likely to be mistaken for' a registered mark.

1   S 10(5). It is to be noted that under this provision, it appears to be the registered trade mark, not a similar mark, which has to be applied.
2   Ibid.

3.55   Section 10(6) provides that the use of the registered mark by any person for the purpose of identifying goods or services as those of the proprietor or licensee[1] is not prevented by the previous provisions, but such use other than in accordance with honest practices in industrial or commercial matters shall be treated as infringing the registered trade mark, if the use without due cause takes unfair advantage of, or is detrimental to, the distinctive character or repute of the trade mark.[2] The reference to 'honest practices' is to be found in the Directive, and ultimately derives from Article 10bis(2) of the Paris Convention. The application of these words will depend on the facts of each case, but may well be affected by any code of practice adopted for the relevant trade. In *Chanel Ltd v Triton Packaging Ltd*[3] the defendants operated a multi-level marketing scheme selling imitations of leading brands of perfume, including the plaintiffs'. Each distributor received a confidential manual which contained a comparison chart showing the defendants' perfumes, identified by code numbers, with the corresponding well-known brand names, including the plaintiffs'. Millett J held that the comparison chart was 'freighted with the goodwill attached to the [plaintiffs'] brand names', and held there to be infringement by importing a reference.[4] Such conduct would seem, probably, to fall within section 10(6), but was its use 'otherwise than in accordance with honest practices'? No one, after all, was deceived by the use, although, clearly the use was detrimental to the distinctive character or repute of the mark.

1   Does this exclude the goods of other companies *associated with* the proprietor? If it does, it may be that the use of the trade mark in relation to goods first marketed by a foreign associated company can be prevented. In *Revlon Inc v Cripps & Lee Ltd* [1980] FSR 85 it was held that the UK proprietors of the mark 'Flex' for shampoo could not use the mark to prevent the importation of Flex shampoo manufactured by a member of the same group of companies in the USA. If the wording of s 10(6) excludes the goods of associated companies, in a *Revlon* type situation there would be no defence under s 10(6), and given that the exhaustion defence contained in s 12(1) is supposed now in any case limited to goods first marketed in the EC, the result would now be different. It may be noted, however, that it is arguable that the Directive does not preclude national laws retaining a doctrine of international exhaustion – see Shea (1995) 10 EIPR 463. If this argument is correct, s 12(1) might be read as not being intended to abolish international exhaustion. As to the exhaustion defence, see para 3.61 below.
2   This provision is inconsistent with the draft Directive on comparative advertising, and may have to be revised in due course.
3   [1993] RPC 32.
4   Under s 4(1)(b) of the 1938 Act.

Use of own registered trade mark

3.56   Section 11(1) provides that a registered trade mark is not infringed by the use of another registered trade mark in relation to goods or services for which the latter is registered. The sub-section cross-refers expressly to section 47(6) which concerns declarations of invalidity, the effect of which is that the registration is deemed never to have been made, so that a mark, the registration of which was declared invalid, would not benefit from this section. There is no cross-reference to section 46 concerning revocation. These take effect only from the date of the application for revocation, or at an earlier date if the registrar is satisfied that grounds for revocation existed at an earlier date.[1] Presumably, in either case, the defendant is not protected if a previously registered trade mark is used after registration ceased to have effect.

1   S 46(6). The effect of this would appear to be that an unused trade mark could be infringed, if the infringement takes place before an application for revocation has been made, unless the Registrar is prepared to order that revocation is effective from a date prior to the act of infringement.

Use of own name etc and descriptive and other indications

3.57   Section 11(2) contains further restrictions on the rights of the proprietor.[1] It provides that a registered mark is not infringed by:

'(a)   the use of a person of his own name or address,
(b)   the use of indications concerning the kind, quality, quantity, intended purpose, value, geographical origin, the time of production of goods or of rendering of services, or other characteristics of goods or services, or
(c)   the use of the trade mark where it is necessary to indicate the intended purpose of a product or service (in particular accessories or spare parts),
provided the use is in accordance with honest practices in industrial or commercial matters.'

The words in the final qualification appear also in section 10(6), and what was said above about them is relevant here too. These provisions are similar to the *bona fide* use provisions contained in section 8 of the 1938 Act, and it is likely that they will be applied in much the same way. Paragraph 7 of the Statements to the Trade Marks Directive 1989 (EC 89/104) say that the words 'his own name' apply only in respect of natural persons (so that the defence is not open to legal persons). English law does not, however, generally distinguish between natural and legal persons.[2] It may be therefore that the courts will hold that the defence is open to corporations provided that their use is *bona fide*. There seems to be no very good reason for it not being.

1   It is derived wholly from the Directive, Art 6.1.
2   Interpretation Act 1978, s 5 and Sch 1.

3.58   The wording of sub-section 11 (2)(b) is similar to the absolute ground for refusal to register descriptive matter set out in section 3(1)(c). The effect of the proviso in sub-section 11(2)(c) requiring the use to be 'necessary' is similar to the requirement under the 1938 Act that the use be 'reasonably necessary'.[1]

1   S 4(3)(b).

Use of an earlier right applying in a particular locality

3.59   Section 11(3) provides that a registered trade mark is not infringed by the use in the course of trade in a particular locality of an earlier right which applies only in that locality. 'Earlier right' means an unregistered trade mark or other sign continuously used by a person (or a predecessor in title of his) from a date which is prior to the earlier of the use of the registered trade mark by the proprietor (or a predecessor in title of his) from a date which is prior to the earlier of the use of the registered trade mark by the proprietor (or a predecessor in title) or the registration of the trade mark. The earlier right is regarded as applying in a locality if, or to the extent that, its use in that locality is protected by virtue of any rule of law, in particular the law of passing off.

3.60   This provision is derived from Article 6.2 of the Directive which is believed to have been intended to address a particular situation which arises under German law. It is not clear how it may apply in the United Kingdom. Presumably, it will only be relevant to service marks since use in relation to goods is not usually confined to a particular locality.[1] As we have seen, unregistered rights can form the basis of opposition proceedings under section 5.

1   See *Chelsea Man Trade Mark* [1989] RPC 111.

Exhaustion of rights

3.61   Section 12 has generally been thought to effect a significant change from previous United Kingdom law. It provides that a registered trade mark is not infringed by the use of the trade mark in relation to goods which have been put on the market in the European Economic Area under that trade mark by the proprietor or with his consent, and this has generally been taken to modify the former doctrine of 'international exhaustion'. The problem is whether or not this is intended to preclude the possibility of international exhaustion by first marketing outside the EU. It has been argued that the Directive does not intend so to limit exhaustion.[1] It was also noted above that the defence contained in section 10(6) of using a sign to identify goods as those of the proprietor or licensee, does not appear to extend to another company in the same group. Thus to market Brazilian 'Colgate' toothpaste made by a sister company as 'Colgate' toothpaste in the UK, would not benefit from s 10(6) and would, in principle, infringe.[2] On the other hand, the words 'with his consent' in section 12(1) clearly cover goods marketed within the EU by a licensee, and also, presumably extend to goods marketed by other companies in the same group.

1 See Shea (1995) 10 EIPR 463.
2 See the passing off case of *Colgate-Palmolive Ltd v Markwell Finance Ltd* [1989] RPC 497 – it should be noted that the goods imported by the defendant in that case, although manufactured by a sister company of the plaintiff in Brazil, and lawfully bearing the 'Colgate' trade mark, were of an inferior quality to the goods marketed by the plaintiff in the UK (in *Spalding (AG) v A W Gamage* (1915) 32 RPC 273 the plaintiffs were able to enjoin the sale of an inferior discontinued line of goods which had been sold as scrap).

3.62 Sub-section (2) provides that exhaustion does not apply where there exist legitimate reasons for the proprietor to oppose further dealings in the goods, in particular where the condition of the goods has been changed or impaired after they have been put on the market. The jurisprudence the European Court of Justice has developed in relation of parallel import cases under Article 36 will no doubt provide guidance as to how this provision is to be interpreted.[1] The common law doctrine of international exhaustion will remain relevant in passing-off cases.[2]

1 See eg *Hoffmann-La Roche v Centrafarm*:102/77 [1978] 3 CMLR 217; *Centrafarm v American Home Products*:3/78 [1979] 1 CMLR 326. There are also rulings due from the Court in *Bristol-Myers v Paranova*: C-427/93, C-429/93 and C-436/93; and *Eurim-Pharm Arzneimittel GmbH v Beiersdorf AG*: C-71/94, C-72/94 and C-73/94. In *IHT International Heiztechnik GmbH v Ideal Standard GmbH*: C-9/93 [1994] 3 CMLR 857 the ECJ held that national rules allowing a ban on imported goods which might be confused with domestic goods were compatible with the Treaty of Rome. This was so even where the mark in the exporting country had been freely assigned by a sister company of the registered proprietor in the country of import – a further indication of the retreat from the doctrine of 'common origin' laid down in *Café Hag*:192/73 [1974] 2 CMLR 127, and overruled in *CNL-Sucal v HAG*: C-10/89[1990] ECR I-3711.
2 See *Champagne Heidsieck v Buxton* (1930) 47 RPC 28; *Revlon v Cripps & Lee* [1980] FSR 85; *Colgate-Palmolive Ltd v Markwell Finance Ltd* [1989] RPC 497.

Transitional provisions

3.63 Schedule 3, paragraph 4(1) provides that sections 9 to 12 discussed above apply in relation to existing registered marks. Section 14 which provides that infringement of a registered trade mark is actionable by the proprietor applies in relation to infringements after the commencement of the 1994 Act. The old law applies otherwise.[1] These transitional provisions give rise to an obvious question as to what happens when the infringement started under the old provisions, and continued under the new. Presumably, the acts have to be considered separately under the old law, and under the new.

1   It is not an altogether happy way of implementing the obvious intention of this provision to provide that the 1938 Act is repealed (Sch 5) but to provide that the old law 'continues to apply'.

3.64   It is not infringement to continue after commencement any use which did not amount to infringement of an *existing* registered trade mark under the old law.[1] This protection is limited to infringement of existing registered marks, and there is some doubt whether it correctly implements Article 5.4 of the Directive, which seems to be intended to protect existing users against any infringement actions in respect of *any* trade marks, whether registered before or after the commencement of the new law.[2] This provision also gives rise to a problem in relation to section 5(2) of the 1938 Act. That provided that no injunction or other relief could be granted in relation to infringement of a Part B mark, if the defendant established certain facts. It did not, however, provide that there was no infringement. Perhaps the problem is academic, because there was no case in this country where this 'defence' succeeded in relation to a Part B mark where it would not have succeeded in relation to a Part A mark,[3] but there does appear to be a lacuna in the transitional provisions.

1   Ie, a mark registered at the commencement of the 1994 Act – Sch 3, para 4(2).
2   Existing users can, of course, oppose applications for registration under s 5.
3   There was an Australian case *Hammond v Papa Carmine Pty* [1978] RPC 697.

Disclaimers

3.65   Section 13 provides for an applicant to accept voluntarily a disclaimer, or a territorial or other limitation. The registrar's power to insist on these has gone, and as noted above, they will not be required in *ex parte* applications. Presumably, in practice, therefore, such voluntary acceptance of a disclaimer is most likely to occur when opposition proceedings are settled by the parties. Disclaimers under the old law continue to apply.[1]

1   Sch 3, para 3(2).

SOME PROBLEMS UNDER THE NEW LAW
Searching

3.66   The result of the new law is that registrations are much easier to obtain, and confer a wider protection.[1] Infringement is extended to 'similar goods', and in the case of marks having a reputation in the UK (whatever that means)[2] to dissimilar goods and services. It may extend beyond identical or similar signs where there is a likelihood of confusion, to those where there is a likelihood of association.[3] Moreover, such things as shapes are registrable. Searching the register under the old system was relatively straightforward, both because the specifications of goods strictly defined

3.66 *Trade marks and service marks*

proprietors' rights, and because the range of marks was more limited - shapes of containers, for example, could not be registered.[4] Under the new law it is, however, necessary for a person selecting a new mark to be concerned not only with the specifications of goods for which marks are registered, but marks for similar and in certain cases, dissimilar goods. Of course, under the old regime, a proprietor unable to sue for infringement because the defendant was using a similar mark on goods outside the registration might nevertheless sue in passing off, but at least *searching the Register* was fairly straightforward. On the other hand, many more marks will now be registered, and it was always inherently difficult to be certain that there were no unregistered marks which could cause problems. It may be therefore that the additional search costs for registered marks will be justified by the reduction in the possibility of having a passing off action brought by a proprietor of an unregistered mark. A further problem in searching is caused by the fact that shapes are registrable. For example, it should be possible to register the distictive shapes of certain breakfast cereals and biscuits. But searching shapes is technically more difficult than searching two-dimensional devices.

1   S 10.
2   See para 3.53 above.
3   The views expressed by Laddie J in *Wagamama Ltd v City Centre Restaurants* [1995] FSR 713 that confusion and association are as to source or origin, were *obiter* given the finding of likelihood of confusion.
4   *Coca-Cola Trade Marks* [1985] FSR 315.

Interpretation

3.67   The Act follows the wording of the Directive quite closely. However, the Directive is not altogether clear on a number of points. As an aid to its interpretation, the Council Meeting at which the Directive was adopted produced an Annex containing 'Statements' explaining what the Council and the Commission intend certain of the provisions to mean. The question was, would the English courts have regard to these where the wording of the Act follows the Directive in the loosening up of the traditional aversion to external aids to interpretation following *Pepper v Hart*?[1] In *Wagamama Ltd v City Centre Restaurants plc* Laddie J observed that in view of the confidentiality of the minutes themselves, and lack of evidence that the statement that '"likelihood of association" is a concept which in particular had been developed by Benelux law' had been entered into them, it would be wrong and dangerous to rely on Chinese whispers as to the origin and meaning of the legislation, no matter how commonly believed. These remarks were *obiter* and other views have been expressed as to the confidentiality of the minutes.[1] No doubt it will ultimately be for the ECJ to rule upon this question, but it must be observed that the Benelux courts themselves seem to be having second thoughts about some of their decisions. English courts, on the other hand, certainly should refer to the Preamble to the Directive, which is helpful on a number of points of interpretation.

1   [1991] 2 All ER 824.
2   See Gielen [1996] 2 EIPR 83.

The international framework of the new law

3.68 The Act made provision both for the UK to adhere to the Protocol to the Madrid Agreement (which came into effect on 1 April 1996), and for the Community Trade Mark. Thus, from 1996 application via the International Bureau in Geneva is an option. The application will designate members states of the Madrid Union, and states adhering to the Protocol, in which registration is being sought. It is interesting to speculate whether the Madrid route will prove as successful as the Patent Co-operation Treaty has been in relation to patent applications. Unfortunately, for the present, the United States seems to have lost interest in it. We must also bear in mind that the initiative for future developments in this field will probably lie with TRIPS. We were in the past able to ignore provisions of the Paris Convention, such as Article 6bis, because there really are no sanctions. TRIPS have teeth, however, and new requirements will have to be complied with, and may effect a significant improvement in this field where uncontrolled piracy is endemic in certain countries.

3.69 The Community Trade Marks Office in Alicante has been accepting applications for registration from 1 January 1996. The advantage offered by registrations through that Office is a European Union wide protection. The terms of the Regulation under which it operates are similar to those of the Directive, and it will be interesting to see the extent to which it develops different practices on certain categories of mark which the UK Registry still finds problematic.

The Olympic Symbols Act 1995

3.70 This Act confers a trade mark-like right on the Olympic symbol, and various words associated with the Olympic Games. The object is to prevent unauthorised commercial exploitation. The rights are vested in the British Olympic Association, and are stronger in some respects than ordinary trade mark rights.

ASSIGNMENTS OF TRADE MARKS

3.71 Section 22 of the 1994 Act states unequivocally that trade marks are personal property. Accordingly, section 24(1) provides that registered trade marks are transmissible by assignment, testamentary disposition or operation of law, in the same way as other personal (or moveable) property. Section 24(2) allows partial assignment or transmission limited to only some of the goods or services covered by the registration, and in relation to the use of the mark in a particular locality or in a particular manner. Sub-section (3) provides that the assignment (or assent) must be in writing, signed by or on behalf of the assignor (or personal representative). It does not need to be signed by the assignee. In England and Wales, the requirement can be satisfied by affixing the seal of a body corporate. An assignment which did not comply with the Act's formalities might be effective in equity, in the same way as an assignment of copyright which does not comply with the 1988 Act's requirements.[1]

1 See *Roban Jig and Tool Co Ltd and Elkadart Ltd v Taylor* [1979] FSR 130; *Richardson (John) Computers Ltd v Flanders* [1993] FSR 497.

Chapter 4

Passing off and unfair competition

INTRODUCTION

4.1 We have already examined the possibilities for protecting merchandising operations through the law relating to registered marks and copyright. Because of the coming into force of the Trade Marks Act 1994, many more kinds of marks are registrable.[1] Accordingly, the need for merchandisers to rely on the law of passing off should in future be considerably diminished. Nevertheless, passing off can be a useful supplement to these rights, notwithstanding the expense which frequently is involved in this kind of action because of the need to assemble evidence of goodwill and confusion if the case goes beyond the interlocutory stage, which fortunately is not often in the present context. The tort could be helpful in the following situations:

(1) there are no relevant registered trade marks,[2] and there is no copyright;

(2) registered trade marks do exist, but the defendant's activities do not infringe them, a situation much less likely to occur, however, under the Trade Marks Act 1994.[3]

1 See para 3.12 et seq.
2 It is to be remembered that although a proprietor's rights have effect from the date of application for registration, no infringement proceedings can be begun until the mark is in fact registered – s 9(3).
3 See Chapter 3.

4.2 The law of passing off provides a limited form of protection for both fictional characters and natural persons. The main function of the law of passing off is to protect the goodwill and reputation that arises in the course of business or trade. While other jurisdictions recognising a tort based upon the English notion of passing off have broadened the law to provide more extensive protection, the courts in the UK have until very recently refused to do so. Although at one time it was thought that developments in the law of passing off presaged the emergence of a general action for unfair competition, this has not materialised. However, the most recent indications are that the courts are willing to develop passing off to take greater account of merchandising.

4.3 In this chapter we will first of all examine the elements of the tort of passing off and its application to merchandising. We will then consider in more detail some aspects of it which give rise to particular problems in the present context. Finally, we will examine the question as to whether or not passing off is likely to develop into a tort of unfair competition.

ELEMENTS OF THE TORT

4.4 To support an action in passing off, the following elements must be established:
  (1) a misrepresentation
  (2) made by a trader in the course of trade
  (3) to prospective customers of his or ultimate consumers of goods or services supplied by him
  (4) which is calculated to injure the business or goodwill of another trader (in the sense that this is a reasonably foreseeable consequence) and
  (5) which causes actual damage to the business or goodwill of the trader by whom the action is brought or (in a *quia timet* action) will probably do so.[1]

Thus first, it must be shown that the plaintiff has built up a reputation and goodwill around a character. Second, it must be shown that there has been a misrepresentation on the part of the defendant which leads the public to assume that there is some connection or association between the two parties. Finally, there must be evidence that the plaintiff's goodwill is likely to be damaged as a result of the defendant's misrepresentation.

1 *Warnink v Townend* [1980] RPC 31 at 99 per Lord Diplock. Lord Fraser's different, and narrower, formulation in the same case has not subsequently been favoured – see *Reckitt & Colman Products Ltd v Borden Inc* [1990] RPC 341.

4.5 In order to show that the plaintiff has the goodwill necessary to sustain a passing off action, there must be evidence that the plaintiff is engaged in a business. Business is understood to include the work done by professionals, sportsmen, artists, cartoonists, writers and performers. The reputation of a trader is normally limited to a name or mark designating his or her goods or services. In the case of performances, films, literary, dramatic or artistic works, the reputation may reside in a character portrayed in the performance or work. If the character attracts the reader, listener or viewer, there is goodwill attaching to that character or to the character's name.

4.6 The need to prove a misrepresentation giving rise to confusion is likely to present plaintiffs in character or personality merchandising cases with difficulty. A misrepresentation is easiest to prove where the defendant exploits a fictional character in a medium similar to that in which it was originally portrayed. Thus an action would probably succeed where the defendant makes a film featuring the popular protagonist of the plaintiff's films.[1] There would be a misrepresentation calculated to cause damage to goodwill; the public would assume there is a connection between the plaintiff's and the defendant's works or business. Members of the public may go to see the defendant's film thinking it to be one of the plaintiff's. The plaintiff's goodwill may be damaged if cinema-goers attend the defendant's film instead of the plaintiff's or, if they are put off, seeing later films made by the plaintiff because of the inferior quality of the defendant's.

1   *Shaw Bros (Hong Kong) Ltd v Golden Harvest HK Ltd* [1972] RPC 559 – the 'One Armed Swordsman' case.

4.7   Apart from the situation described above, it is difficult to prove a misrepresentation that will sustain a passing off suit. The courts have tended to take the view that unless the parties are actually or ostensibly engaged in a 'common field of activity', there is unlikely to be a misrepresentation giving rise to confusion. Although a common field of activity is not a legal element of the tort, its absence may cause an action to fail on the facts. In character and personality merchandising situations, the plaintiff and defendant usually operate in very different fields and this often acts as a major stumbling block to proving that there is any representation that the defendant's acts were either authorised by, or associated with, the plaintiff. Thus the producers of the TV series 'Neighbours' failed to obtain an interim injunction against a magazine calling itself 'Neighbours Who's Who' dealing with characters in the series.[1] If the creator of a fictional character has never traded and built up goodwill in goods other than in relation to the original work, such as the book from which the character derives, the likelihood of confusion will probably not be proved.[2] It has generally been assumed that consumers would not be misled into believing that the use of the character outside the context of the novel in which it features would denote a relationship between its creator and a trade in say, clothing. For example, where the distinguishing feature of a fictional detective appearing in a television series was his fondness for lollipops, it was nevertheless not passing off for traders to use the character's name for their lollipops.[3] The fields of activity of a television studio and a manufacturer of confectionery were too remote from each other to lead to confusion; the evidence did not establish that the public would associate the defendant's goods with the plaintiff's business.

1   *Grundy Television v Startrain* [1988] FSR 581; compare, *BBC v Celebrity Centre* (1988) IPR 133 – injunction against 'A-Z of Eastenders'.
2   *McCulloch v Lew A May (Product Distributors) Ltd* [1947] 2 All ER 845 – 'Uncle Mac'.
3   *Tavener Rutledge v Trexapalm* [1977] RPC 275 – 'Kojak'.

4.8   Where real personalities are concerned, the courts have on occasion said that they would be less reluctant to find confusion; it is thought that the public may well believe that the celebrity in question has endorsed the product or approved the use of his or her name in relation to it. This would be particularly likely if the person is qualified to recommend the goods or business as where, for example, a sportsman's name is used on sporting goods. However, even where the name of a real person is used in merchandising, the difference between the respective fields of activity of the parties can prove decisive. So, for example, it was held that the use of the name of some cartoon characters, the 'Wombles' (which were said to clear up litter and put it to good use) on rubbish skips which the defendants leased was *prima facie* not passing off.[1] This was an interlocutory decision, however.

1   *Wombles v Wombles Skips* [1975] FSR 488.

4.9 Thus it is apparent that the notion of a common field of activity can present problems in merchandising cases. There are a number of circumstances, however, in which the absence of related fields of activity might not prove fatal. Where a mark or name has a very strong reputation, it is easier to show that its exploitation in a different field by someone other than its owner constitutes a misrepresentation calculated to damage goodwill.[1] It is conceivable that this could be of assistance to very well-known personalities or the owners of rights in very well-known fictional figures. In addition, if a mark has been used by the owner or his licensees on diverse goods, the courts are more likely to accept that use in yet another unrelated field will cause confusion. Thus extensive merchandising by the owner of the rights in a character or personality will make it easier to stop unauthorised merchandising.[2]

1 *Lego Systems A/S v Lego M Lemelstrich* [1983] FSR 155.
2 *News Group Newspapers v Rocket Record Co* [1981] FSR 89.

4.10 It has sometimes been argued that the disparity in the parties' fields of activity should not present problems in relation to character or personality merchandising because the public would infer the existence of a link between the parties through some type of licensing arrangement. In the past, since the courts have insisted that the public do not recognise or understand these forms of merchandising, these arguments have seldom been accepted. However, there now appears to be greater readiness on the part of the courts to follow this line of reasoning.[1] In a recent decision, the court suggested that the level of public awareness of merchandising practice is now greater and it found that the practice of licensing the use of characters is known to a substantial number of customers. A plaintiff who had copyright in the drawings of the 'Ninja Turtle' cartoon characters and who had set up an extensive business licensing those characters had an arguable case in passing off, as well as copyright infringement.[2]

1 *IPC Magazines Ltd v Black & White Music Corp* [1983] FSR 348 – 'Judge Dredd'.
2 *Mirage Studios v Counter-Feat Clothing Co Ltd* [1991] FSR 145 – an interlocutory decision, however.

4.11 Another factor which limits the use of passing off actions in relation to character and personality merchandising is that even if a misrepresentation leading to confusion is established, an action for passing off may nevertheless fail because of an inability to prove the likelihood of damage to goodwill. The reason for this is that the range of types of damage recognised in the UK is limited. Damage in the form of diversion of custom from the plaintiff is unlikely to be proved because the plaintiff is generally not in direct competition with the unauthorised merchandiser. On the other hand, the fact that the defendant's goods might be of poor quality may be sufficient to ground an action. Loss of opportunity to expand into the field now occupied by the defendant has been treated as damage to goodwill in some passing off cases ('Judge Dredd' above), but has not yet been fruitfully relied on in the context of character, personality or image merchandising. Loss of royalties or licensing opportunities has been found to support an action in passing off where the merchandising potential of a cartoon character was evident and where the plaintiff was already engaged in extensive licensing.

The licensor's goodwill

4.12 As noted above, passing off may lie where the activity complained of is calculated to damage the plaintiff's goodwill, but where the defendant's activities do not amount to an infringement of the plaintiff's intellectual property.[1] For example, in *Samuelson v Producers Distributing Co Ltd*,[2] the plaintiff owned the copyright in a stage sketch 'The New Car'. The defendants made a film entitled 'His First Car' which differed so substantially from the sketch that it was impossible to maintain that there was infringement of copyright. However, the defendants advertised it in a way which implied clearly that 'His First Car' was a film version of 'The New Car'. The plaintiff succeeded in a passing off action. The damage to the plaintiff's property right was spelled out clearly by Lawrence LJ: 'If the plaintiff had stood by, his exclusive right to make a film version of his sketch would have been rendered valueless'.[3] In another case in the same year, however, *Ormond Engineering Co Ltd v Knopf*,[4] the plaintiffs failed because they failed to show actual or potential damage to their property right. Goods were marketed bearing the legend 'Manufactured under Ormond Patent'. The goods did not infringe the patent, and it was held that even if the words implied that the goods were made under licence from the plaintiffs, no action would lie in the absence of proof of damage. No evidence was given that anyone was misled into buying the articles thinking they were the plaintiff's. We will consider later the evidence which needs to be adduced to support a passing off action. First of all, however, we will consider the circumstances in which a licensor builds up goodwill.

1   See eg *Chappell v Davidson* (1855) 2 K & J 123; *Lawrie v Baker* (1885) 2 RPC 213.
2   [1932] 1 Ch 201.
3   Ibid at 209.
4   (1932) 49 RPC 634.

4.13 There has been considerable debate about the goodwill element in the licensing of unregistered trade marks. Indeed, one extreme view was that the licensing of unregistered trade marks was not possible.[1] However, in *Mirage Studios v Counter-Feat Clothing Co Limited*[2] the Vice-Chancellor held that the plaintiffs, who were merchandising the 'Turtle' characters, were in the business of turning the characters to profit by licensing their reproduction on goods made and sold by third parties. A major part of the plaintiffs' income arose from such licensing, and as a result it was highly foreseeable that the defendants'activities in selling counterfeit 'Turtle' characters would cause loss to the plaintiffs. Whilst being an interlocutory decision this must be treated with some caution, nevertheless, it does suggest when taken along with other cases[3] that English judges are coming to terms with the phenomenon of merchandising, and that we have moved quite a long way from the views expressed by Walton J in '*Kojak*'[4] – these views are quoted below.[5]

1   *Star Industrial v Yap Kwee Kor* [1976] FSR 256. But see the scholarly examination of
     this problem by Shelley Lane 'The Status of Licensing Common Law Marks' 1991.
2   [1991] FSR 145.
3   Notably 'Judge Dredd', *IPC Magazines v Black and White Music* [1983] FSR 348.
4   *Tavener Rutledge v Trexapalm* [1975] FSR 479.
5   Para 4.17.

4.14 *Passing off and unfair competition*

4.14 Another important decision on this issue is the Australian *Muppets* case.[1] In that case, the first plaintiffs, producers of a television show involving animated puppets called 'Muppets', granted licences to manufacturers to make numerous 'Muppet' products. The defendants sold plush toys with physical characteristics similar to those of certain 'Muppet' characters. The Supreme Court of New South Wales found that there was sufficient evidence to enable it to reach the conclusion that the public believed that the plush toys were being sold under licence from the first plaintiffs. The first plaintiffs themselves licensed the manufacture of plush toys under strict quality controls, and this fact, together with the evidence given that the first plaintiff's name was associated with the Muppets and that the public was aware of the practice of licensing in such cases (albeit in a rather general undefined way) enabled the court to conclude that the plaintiffs had a reputation in the merchandise in question. The defendants toys were inferior in quality to those licensed by the plaintiffs, and clearly therefore could have damaged the plaintiffs' reputation. On this ground alone therefore, the court could probably have granted the first plaintiffs an injunction. However, Helsham CJ went on to hold that the first plaintiff and the defendant were operating in a common field of activity. On the facts of the case, for the reasons explained below, this view was almost certainly correct. However, it is to be noted that the New South Wales Court has for some time had a more liberal view of the 'common field of activity' problem than tended to be the case in England until recently. We will now consider this.

1   *Children's Television Workshop Inc v Woolworths (NSW) Ltd* [1981] RPC 187.

The common field of activity problem

4.15 In both of the situations considered, in the previous two sections, there was direct injury to the plaintiff's property, resulting, or likely to result from the defendant's activities. Many activities do not cause such injury, and the real substance of the plaintiff's complaint is that the defendant's activities have the potential to foreclose the plaintiff's possibilities of licensing in fields in which he is not already active. As we will see, if the plaintiff can in fact substantiate his allegation that this will in fact be the result of the defendant's activities, then he should succeed in a passing off action. It is clear that there is no rule of law which requires the parties to be in similar fields. It is probably the case moreover, that now that the activity of merchandising is relatively well known to the public (in a general sort of way), it is easier to prove that the effect of the defendant's activities is to foreclose the plaintiff's licensing programme.[1] An examination of the cases will be helpful in elucidating the nature of this problem.

1   See para 4.11 above.

4.16 In the well-known *Uncle Mac* case,[1] the plaintiff was well known as a children's broadcaster under the name 'Uncle Mac'. The defendants distributed a breakfast cereal under the name 'Uncle Mac's Puffed Wheat'. The cartons bore the statement:

'Uncle Mac loves children – and children love Uncle Mac: Uncle Mac has a wonderful way of brightening any table to which he has been invited.... So introduce Uncle Mac to your family, and when you see how popular he is, be neighbourly and recommend him to your friends.'

Wynn-Parry J based his refusal of an injunction on the fact that the parties had no common field of activity:

'On the postulate that the plaintiff is not engaged in any degree in producing or marketing puffed wheat, how can the defendant, in using the fancy name used by the plaintiff be said to be passing off the goods or the business of the plaintiff?'

1   *McCulloch v Lewis A May (Produce Distributors) Ltd* (1947) 65 RPC 58.

4.17   Similarly, in *Conan Doyle v London Mystery Magazine Ltd*,[1] the plaintiff, the executor of Sir Arthur Conan Doyle, failed to enjoin the defendants from publishing a magazine, the *London Mystery Magazine* from 221B Baker Street, the fictitious address of Conan Doyle's character Sherlock Holmes. It was made clear that the stories themselves contained in the magazine were by a number of authors. There was nothing to lead members of the public to associate them with the works of the late Sir Arthur Conan Doyle. More recently, in the *Kojak* case,[2] the licensed manufacturers of 'Kojak' lollipops, not only failed to get an injunction, but were themselves restrained in favour of unlicensed manufacturers, on proof by the latter that they had built up a reputation in the goods. Walton J held that there was no relevant field of activity either actual or existing in the mind of the public which was common to both the licensors Universal Studios, and to the unlicensed manufacturers. He suggested that:

'there may come a time when the system of character merchandising will have become so well known to the man in the street that immediately he sees "Kojakpops" he will say to himself "they must have a licence from the person who owns the rights in the television series"; but that, by itself, [is not enough, what the person who owns the rights] would have to go on to show is that it had also become so well known that people in the situation of licensors of these names exercised quality control over any product bearing their name, so that as soon as anybody in the street came to the conclusion that a product was licensed by the owners of some series, such as the "Kojak" series, he would say to himself not only, "This must have been licensed by them", but also: "and that is a guarantee of its quality". That point we are miles away from reaching and there is not really a shred of evidence in front of me to that effect.'

These remarks of Walton J must be understood as putting forward as an example, evidence which would have enabled the plaintiffs to succeed in passing off, rather than as laying down a legal principle. It is clear that since the *Advocaat* case[3] at any rate, it cannot be argued that as a matter of law passing off can never be established where the fields of activity are completely different. The question is, whether or not there is likely to be confusion. As Russell LJ observed in *Annabel's (Berkeley Square) v Schock*:[4]

'Is there an overlap in the fields of activity? But, of course, when one gets down to brass tacks this is simply a question which is involved in the ultimate decision whether there is likely to be confusion.'

4.17 *Passing off and unfair competition*

Similarly, in the *Lego* case,[5] Falconer J observed:

'What has to be established by the plaintiff is that there is a real risk that a substantial number of persons among the relevant section of the public will in fact believe that there is a business connection between the plaintiff and the defendant'.

1   (1949) 66 RPC 312.
2   *Tavener Rutledge v Trexapalm Ltd* [1977] RPC 275.
3   *Erven Warnink BV v Townend & Sons (Hull) Ltd* [1979] AC 731.
4   [1972] FSR 261.
5   *Lego Systems A/S v Lego M Lemelstrich Ltd* [1983] FSR 155.

4.18 The plaintiffs in *Lego* were the manufacturers of the well-known children's plastic play bricks. The defendants marketed plastic garden sprays and sprinklers under the same name (under which they were well established in Israel though not in this country). It was held that the plaintiff's reputation was wide enough to extend to goods of the sort made by the defendant. The plaintiff had adduced evidence of confusion amongst a significant number of people. As Whitford J observed in *Stringfellows*:[1]

'We are a long way from the situation which prevailed when Walton J gave judgment in 1975 in the *Kojakpops* case.... That these names thus licensed have in use been taken, rightly or wrongly, by members of the public as some guarantee of quality is undoubted.'

The Court of Appeal reversed Whitford J's decision at first instance granting an injunction to Stringfellows night club restraining the defendants from marketing oven chips under the name 'Stringfellows', inter alia, because the Court did not believe that the evidence showed that the plaintiffs would have been able to exploit merchandising rights in the name 'Stringfellows' but for the defendants' activities.

1   *Stringfellow v McCain Foods (GB) Ltd* [1984] RPC 501.

4.19 It can be said that at the present time it is probably easier to establish the fact that the defendant's activities are likely to foreclose the plaintiff's exploitation of his merchandising rights. Thus in the *Judge Dredd* case,[1] which involved the unauthorised use of a cartoon character's name on a record, Goulding J said:

'at the present time the public know something about the prevalent practice of character merchandising, though most of them probably do not know that term, and I think therefore that both among people of my own age and among young adults such as my own grandchildren and their friends who buy records and read such magazines as these, a substantial number of people will infer that the record has been authorised and approved by the plaintiff'.

1   *IPC Magazines Ltd v Black and White Music Corpn* [1983] FSR 348.

4.20 Where a wide variety of goods are already being marketed under a name, it may be relatively easier to demonstrate that the public are likely to connect the new species with the plaintiff's business. Thus in the *Page*

Three[1] case, the plaintiffs had marketed and sold a wide range of goods under the words 'Page Three', but not as yet records. It was held, inter alia, that the very diversity of goods marketed might make it likely that some members of the public would think that the single record marketed by the defendant bearing the title 'Page Three' was connected with the plaintiffs.

1   *News Group Newspapers v Rocket Record Co* [1981] FSR 89. But the facts must establish deception – compare *Harrods v Harrodian School* (2 April 1996, unreported).

4.21   One objection to the availability of passing off in the above circumstances was raised on behalf of the defendants in *Stringfellow*, but was not dealt with by the Court of Appeal. It was argued that, in the absence of a registered mark, 'Stringfellows', the plaintiff could not grant a licence for the use of his name which would have any legal validity. *Star Industrial Co Ltd v Yap Kwee Kor*[1] was cited in support of this proposition. That case supports the proposition that goodwill can only exist in connection with a business. As a consequence, the position in the case of unregistered marks remains the same as it was in the case of registered marks before the Trade Marks Act 1938,[2] consequently neither assignment in gross nor licensing is possible. It is submitted that whilst assignment in gross is undoubtedly not effective in the case of unregistered marks to confer on the assignee the right to sue in passing off, such an assignment is effective as a licence to protect the assignee from a passing off action by the assignor. In the same way a licence granted as such is effective to protect a licensee from action by his licensor. A more interesting and difficult question is whether or not the goodwill built up by a licensing programme attaches to the licensor's business, or the licensee's. Where the licensor is exercising proper quality control it seems clear that the goodwill attaches to the licensor's business. Thus in the *Muppets* case,[3] evidence was adduced that the plaintiffs did exercise strict quality control, and that they had built up the goodwill necessary to support a passing off action through their licensing programme. Similarly, in another Australian case, *J H Coles Pty Ltd v Need*,[4] the appellant carried on a business under the trade name of 'J H Cole 3d 6d and 1s Stores', and entered into a franchise agreement with the respondent which was later terminated, the appellants were able to restrain the respondent from continuing the business under their name. The Privy Council held that the name was still distinctive of the licensor. A reasonable explanation of this is that because the licensee was required to purchase his stock from the licensor, the licensor controlled quality. Had evidence along the lines of that adduced in *Muppets* been forthcoming in *Kojak*,[5] or in *Wombles*[6] and *Abba*[7] where injunctions were refused, it is submitted that the outcome would probably have been different.

1   [1976] FSR 256, PC.
2   See eg *Re John Sinclair Ltd's Trade Mark* [1932] 1 Ch 598.
3   *Children's Television Workshop Inc v Woolworth's (NSW) Ltd* [1981] RPC 187 – see para 4.14 above.
4   [1934] AC 82, PC.
5   *Tavener Rutledge Ltd v Trexapalm Ltd* [1977] RPC 275.
6   *Wombles Ltd v Wombles Skips Ltd* [1975] FSR 488.
7   *Lyngstad v Anabas Products Ltd* [1977] FSR 62.

SUMMARY

4.22 As explained above, the crucial thing in a passing off action is to adduce the right evidence. It may be helpful at this point to summarise some of the guidance on this question to be drawn from the modern cases.

(1) We have moved to a position where an allegation that the defendant's activities have damaged the plaintiff's goodwill by foreclosing his opportunities for merchandising, sponsorship or indorsement has some prospects of success if supported by adequate evidence that that is in fact the probable effect of the defendant's activities.

(2) If a name is not a household word such as 'Lego', fairly clear evidence that the public do associate the defendant's business with that of the plaintiff is required. If the evidence shows that the defendant could expect to derive some real benefit from the plaintiff's reputation, as a result of their choice of name, as in the *Kodak*[1] or *Harrods*[2] cases (and probably the *Exxon*[3] case) the plaintiff's prospects of success are much improved.

(3) If the licensor has a reputation independently of his licensing activities, and the nature of the defendant's activities is such that although in a different field, the public would be likely to associate the two to the damage of the plaintiff's goodwill or other property right, then the plaintiff's prospects of success are again improved. Thus in *Annabel's*,[4] the association of the defendant's escort agency with the plaintiff's nightclub was fairly natural in a way that the association of oven chips with a night club was not.

1 *Eastman Photographic Materials Co Ltd v John Griffiths Cycle Corpn Ltd* (1898) 15 RPC 105.
2 *Harrods Ltd v R Harrod Ltd* (1923) 41 RPC 74.
3 *Exxon Corpn v Exxon Insurance Consultants International Ltd* [1981] 1 WLR 624.
4 *Annabel's (Berkeley Square) v Schock* [1972] FSR 261.

4.23 Survey evidence can be helpful in supporting the plaintiff's case, as it was in *Lego*.[1] Nevertheless, it is treated with scepticism by some judges.[2] In *Stringfellow*[3] Whitford J declined to rely on the survey evidence on the ground, inter alia, that the mere forms of question in some instances and their particular sequence might influence the answers that were going to be given, leaving aside any question as to intonation or method by which the question is put, and he did not know how careful or otherwise the interviewers might have been in performing their duties. One question however the judge did consider reasonably reliable. At the outset the public were shown a card carrying the word 'Stringfellows', and they were asked what, if anything, this word meant to them. Slade LJ in the Court of Appeal said that in general he had some sympathy with the judge's scepticism as to the evidentiary value of market survey reports in passing off cases for much the same reasons. Nevertheless, in view of the specific agreement of the parties relating to this evidence, he was entitled and bound to treat each of the questionnaire forms as containing true and accurate particulars of the questions asked in the course of each interview and of the answers obtained in response to those questions.

1 *Lego Systems A/S v Lego M Lemelstrich* [1983] FSR 155.

2   It must be remembered that the fashion for this type of evidence spread here from the United States, where juries are used to determine issues of fact. English judges are likely to question the value of such evidence fairly rigorously – for a recent example see *Neutrogena v Golden Ltd (trading as Garnier)* [1995] IPD 18083; IPD 19028, CA.

3   *Stringfellow v McCain Foods (GB) Ltd* [1984] RPC 501.

Reputations built up abroad

4.24   Many properties which it is sought to merchandise in the United Kingdom, have first been merchandised abroad. If these have acquired the status of well known marks within Article 6bis of the Paris Convention, action can be taken under section 56 of the Trade Marks Act 1994. It is not clear what will be considered as being 'well known' for these purposes, but it seems that a mark must be significantly better known than a mark having a reputation for the purposes of sections 5(3) or 10(3).[1] The problem with many kinds of merchandisable properties is that they will not qualify as well known *trade marks*, though they may well have a reputation in this country. The question then arises: will a reputation built up abroad suffice for the purposes of passing off? The question is of some importance as pirates frequently precede the merchandiser into the UK, having identified potentially valuable properties in their home market. In some cases, a trade mark may even have been registered by a third party without authority.[2] It is clear that even if registration is successfully obtained, it will provide no defence to a passing off action.[3] At all events, since the *Budweiser* case[4] it would appear that a reputation in this country, of itself, is not enough. The plaintiff must have goodwill here. That case has resolved the uncertainty arising out of a number of somewhat contradictory interlocutory decisions.[5]

1   Morcom 'A Guide to the Trade Marks Act 1994' para 13.10; Firth 'Trade Marks: The New Law', 1995, para 12.25 et seq. As to ss 5(3) and 10(3) see para 3.32 et seq. WIPO will shortly be producing a study on this question.

2   See eg *Rawhide Trade Mark* [1962] RPC 133 at p 28.

3   Trade Marks Act 1938, s 2.

4   *Anheuser-Busch Inc v Budejovicky Budvar Narodni Podnik (Budweiser)* [1984] FSR 413.

5   *Sheraton Corpn of America v Sheraton Motels Ltd* [1964] RPC 202; *A Bernardin et Cie v Pavilion Properties Ltd* [1967] RPC 581; *Baskins-Robbins Ice Cream Co v Gutman* [1976] FSR 545; *Maxim's Ltd v Dye* [1978] 2 All ER 55; *Metric Resources Corpn v Leasemetrix Ltd* [1979] FSR 571; *Athlete's Foot Marketing Associates Inc v Cobra Sports Ltd* [1980] RPC 343.

4.25   The defendants in *Budweiser* had marketed their beer in the United Kingdom since 1973, but their product was certainly less well known than that of the plaintiffs. At the time of the action, 1979, the plaintiffs' sales in this country had been sporadic and limited, although there had been large sales to American service personnel on American bases in this country. For practical purposes no one could buy the plaintiffs' beer in this country, and it was held that the reputation which their beer had in this country did not constitute goodwill in any relevant sense. The sales on American bases were sales in a separate, artificial and special market, and could not be the foundation for goodwill in a market into which the plaintiffs had never really ventured. Oliver LJ having returned to Lord Macnaughten's definition of goodwill as 'the attractive force which brings in custom',[1] asked the following question:

'what custom in this country in 1973 was brought in by the knowledge of members of the indigenous British public of the plaintiffs' Budweiser beer?'[2]

He continued:

'the answer must be that there was none, because however attractive they may have found the idea of drinking the plaintiffs' beer, they could not get it. In so far, therefore, as anyone was misled by the defendant's use of the name 'Budweiser', the plaintiffs could suffer no damage either by loss of sales, for there were none at that time and none were contemplated, not by loss of reputation, because if there was any such loss (which seems highly improbable) the reputation was quite unconnected with either an ability or a willingness to supply.'

Both O'Connor and Dillon LJJ expressed similar views.

1   *Reuter Co Ltd v Mulhens* [1954] Ch 50; *IRC v Muller & Co's Margarine Ltd* [1901] AC 217 at 223.
2   *Anheuser-Busch v Budejovicky Budvar* [1984] FSR 413 at 469.

4.26   It is to be noted that the Court of Appeal did not hold that in order to succeed in passing off it is necessary actually to have a place of business in this country. Both O'Connor and Dillon LJJ expressed the view that the *Panhard* case[1] was rightly decided. In that case, the plaintiffs, motor car manufacturers, had no business in England nor any agency. Their cars could not be imported into England without a licence from English patentees. There was however an English importer, and individuals bought cars in Paris for import into England. It could be said therefore, that England was one of their markets. O'Connor LJ also expressed the view that the *Poiret* case[2] was rightly decided. In that case similarly, the plaintiff had no place of business here, but he exhibited his goods and sold to customers here either directly or through an agent. Consequently, it could again be said that England was one of the plaintiff's markets. In *Budweiser*, by contrast, the plaintiffs had no market, but only a reputation.

1   *Anciens Etablissements Panhard et Levassor SA v Panhard Levassor Motor Co Ltd* (1901) 18 RPC 405.
2   *Poiret v Jules Poiret Ltd and Nash* (1920) 37 RPC 177.

4.27   The situation which commonly arises in merchandising is that whilst an overseas merchandiser may not at the relevant time have a place of business here, there have been mail order sales. It seems clear that such sales could go towards establishing the goodwill necessary to support a passing off action.[1] In *Sheraton Corpn of America v Sheraton Motels Ltd*,[2] which also lends some support to this view, the plaintiffs secured an interlocutory injunction against the defendants who called themselves 'Sheraton Motels', on evidence of advertising the plaintiff's US hotel chain in this country and the taking of bookings at an office kept by the plaintiffs here. The decision must, however, be regarded as borderline. Another common situation is that the merchandiser, again without a place of business in this country, has begun advertising and other promotional activity, but has not yet begun selling. It would appear that provided the relevant promotional campaign is in preparation for marketing, here, then the fact that marketing has not commenced does not matter. Thus in *Elida Gibbs v Colgate-Palmolive*[3] the plaintiffs had decided to market a new toothpaste called 'Mentadent'. A pre-launch marketing campaign was started in August 1982, and launched to the press in September 1982. The plaintiffs spent a considerable amount of money on the campaign, the public marketing campaign was due to begin on 18 October, but the defendants, in order to pre-empt it, deliberately placed advertisements in newspapers. The plaintiffs were granted an injunction to restrain them. In *My Kinda Bones Ltd v Dr Pepper's Stove Co Ltd*,[4] where the defendants were about to open outlets in this country, but had at the relevant time only advertised, they were able to obtain an injunction. Although both of these cases involved interlocutory applications where special considerations apply, both are consistent with the proposition that goodwill is something attaching to a business. A proposed business, however, suffices. By contrast, in *Budweiser*, the plaintiffs had neither an existing nor a proposed business at the relevant time, merely a reputation.

1   See cases cited at para 4.26, nn 1 and 2, above.
2   [1964] RPC 202.
3   [1983] FSR 95.
4   [1984] FSR 289. See also *W H Allen & Co v Brown Watson* [1965] RPC 191; *BBC v Talbot Motor Co* [1981] FSR 228.

Unfair competition

4.28   Since the *Pub Squash*[1] case there seems to be no possibility in the foreseeable future of a tort of unfair competition based upon the proposition that it is 'unfair to reap what another has sown',[2] developing in the United Kingdom.[3] Under Article 10bis of the Paris Convention, the UK is bound to afford adequate protection against unfair competition, but the present view appears to be that the combination of passing off, trade descriptions law, the Code of Advertising Practice and other measures, the UK does comply with this article.[4] WIPO is currently examining compliance with this article in Convention countries.[5]

1   *Cadbury Schweppes Pty Ltd v Pub Squash Pty Ltd* [1981] RPC 429.
2   See *International News Service v Associated Press* 245 US 215 (1918). An interesting question is whether or not the law of restitution might not be able to fill some of the gaps left by the absence of a tort of unfair competition.
3   See Adams (1985) JBL 26; (1992) 8 EIPR 259.
4   See Protection Against Unfair Competition, WIPO 1994.
5   Ibid.

Malicious falsehood

4.29   The ordinary tort of passing off consists of a representation made by the defendant for trading purposes that his goods are those, or his business is that, of the plaintiff. This rule may be only a special instance of a more general rule that any misrepresentation calculated to give one trader the benefit of another's goodwill is actionable, or even that any misrepresentation calculated to injure another in his trade or business is to be regarded as passing off, at which point passing off shades imperceptibly into the tort of injurious or malicious falsehood.[1] Injurious or malicious falsehood, also known as 'trade libel', is an action which lies for written or oral falsehoods not actionable *per se* nor even defamatory, where they are maliciously published, and where they are calculated in the ordinary course of things to produce, and where they do produce, actual damage.[2] To support the action it was necessary for the plaintiff to prove:

    (1) that the statements complained of were untrue;

    (2) that they were made maliciously, that is to say, without just cause or excuse; and,

    (3) that the plaintiff has suffered special damage thereby.[3]

This third requirement was, however, relaxed by the Defamation Act 1952. As a separate cause of action, this tort is not likely to crop up very frequently in the context of merchandising, but it is necessary to give a short account of it for completeness.

1   *Kerly on Trade Marks* (12th edn 1986), Sweet & Maxwell, para 16.03 citing Parker J in *Burberry's v Cording & Co Ltd* (1909) 26 RPC 693.
2   *Kerly*, op cit, para 18.02.
3   *Royal Baking Powder v White & Crossley* (1900) 18 RPC 95, 99 per Lord Davey; adopted *Reuter v Mulhens* ('*4711*') (1953) 70 RPC 102.

Chapter 5

Other possible sources of protection

5.1 The discussion in this chapter is principally relevant to personality merchandising.

INVASION OF PRIVACY

5.2 In some jurisdictions in the United States the tort of invasion of privacy serves to prevent the appropriation of the plaintiff's name or likeness for the defendant's benefit.[1] Indeed, such appropriation was the first form of invasion of privacy.[2] The tort was introduced by statute in New York,[3] and other jurisdictions followed either through case law or statutes. A celebrated article by Warren and Brandeis[4] was influential in this development.

1 For English literature on the subject see P Russell (1979) 129 NLJ 791; *Privacy* ed J B Young (1979) Wiley & Sons Essay 5 by G Dworkin; Wacks *The Protection of Privacy* (1980) Sweet & Maxwell; J Thomas McCarthy 'Protection of Names and Likenesses' (1986) Trade Mark World (Dec) p 14; O Goodenough *Privacy and Publicity* Intellectual Property Institute 1996 (which covers both the situation in this country and in the USA).
2 See *Prosser on Torts* (5th edn, 1984) West Publishing Co p 849.
3 NY Sess Laws 1903 Ch 132 ss 1–2.
4 'The Right to Privacy' (1890) 4 HLR 193.

5.3 After examining a number of cases on defamation, invasion of a property[1] right and breach of confidence or an implied contract,[2] Warren and Brandeis concluded that in reality these cases were based on a broader principle of 'a right to privacy'. This argument does have some superficial attractions on the basis of the English case law examined by the authors. Thus, leaving aside section 85 of the Copyright, Designs and Patents Act 1988, if you employ a photograher to take your photograph, the use of the negative by him to make further unauthorised prints can, on this basis, be restrained. In *Pollard v Photographic Co*[3] North J expressly based his decision in part on breach of faith. In *Wyatt v Wilson*,[4] Lord Eldon is supposed to have said:

> 'If one of the late King's physicians had kept a diary of what he heard and saw, this Court would not, in the King's lifetime, have permitted him to print and publish it.'

Brandeis and Warren concluded from these cases and other authorities that:

5.3 *Other possible sources of protection*

'the protection afforded to thoughts, sentiments, emotions, expressed through the medium of writing or of the arts, so far as it consists in preventing publication, is merely the instance of the enforcement of the more general right of the individual to be left alone'.[5]

1   Including *Prince Albert v Strange* (1849) 1 Mac & G 25; *Abernethy v Hutchinson* (1825) 3 LJOS Ch 209.
2   *Pollard v Photographic Co* (1888) 40 Ch D 345.
3   (1888) 40 Ch D 345. See also *Argyll v Argyll* [1965] 1 All ER 611. See Copyright Act 1956, s 4(3).
4   Unreported, cited by Cottenham LC in *Prince Albert v Strange*, n 1 above.
5   (1890) 4 HLR 193 at 205.

5.4   The problem is that even if there were 'a right to be left alone', or 'a right to privacy', it is difficult to see how publishing a name invades it. The unauthorised use of a celebrity's name would not appear to involve an invasion of privacy, in that it involves neither intrusion, public disclosure nor the misuse of confidential information.[1] It is unlikely for this reason that the courts in this country would recognise this application, even if such a tort were to develop. In any case, the Calcutt Committee, like the earlier Younger Committee on privacy, did not recommend the introduction of a tort of invasion of privacy.[2]

1   See *Wacks*, op cit, p 18.
2   Report of the Younger Committee Cmnd 5012, 1972; Report of the Calcutt Committee Cm 1102 1990.

5.5   It would appear to be more appropriate to speak of the violation of a celebrity's right to publicity.[1] In other words, the marketing value of a celebrity's name is recognised as a property right.[2] Alternatively, the action can be based on an appropriation of the plaintiff's personality.[3] The basis of such a tort, whatever it is called, is the use of the plaintiff's identity for the defendant's advantage.[4] It must be borne in mind, however, that newspapers and other periodicals repeatedly use the names of famous people in items of news. This helps to sell the newspaper and in turn keeps celebrities in the public view. Clearly, celebrities cannot be allowed to charge for the very publicity which helps to make them celebrities in the first place. The argument that they could charge for such publicity, was met early in the history of invasion of privacy in the United States and it was held that they could not.[5]

1   *Uhlaender v Henricksen* 316 F Supp 1277 (1970); *Cary Grant v Esquire Ltd* 367 F Supp 876 (1973).
2   See *Bela Lugosi v Universal Pictures* 603 P 2d 425 (Cal) (1979) 172 USPQ 541. *Price v Hal Roach Studios* 400 F Supp 836 (1975).
3   *Athans v Canadian Adventure Camps Ltd* (1977) 80 DLR (3d) 583.
4   *Prosser*, op cit, p 851 et seq.
5   *Colyer v Richard F Fox Publishing Co* 146 NYS 999 (1914). The Report by Prof Goodenough cited in para 5.2, n 1 above offers a valuable insight into how the line might be drawn beteen legitimate and illegitimate uses.

5.6   In English law, there is no property in a name as such. Although there is a dictum of Cairns LJ in the old case of *Maxwell v Hogg*[1] to the effect that *Clark v Freeman*[2] might have been decided on the ground that the plaintiff had a property in his name, the position today would seem to be well settled.

1   (1867) 2 Ch App 307 at 310.
2   (1848) 11 Beav 112. In this case a quack medicine was marketed under the name of an eminent physician. An injunction to stop this was refused, Lord Langdale MP considered that the injury to the plaintiff's property or livelihood had to be established at law first.

5.7   Even if a tort of expropriation were to develop in this country, it would have to be subject to some limitations.[1] It is unlikely, however, that any specific tort will develop in the foreseeable future. Protection for the names of personalities must be sought elsewhere therefore.

1   See McCarthy, loc cit, para 5.2, n 1 above.

DEFAMATION

5.8   It can be defamatory to assert that a person has endorsed a product or a service when he has not. In *Tolley v Fry & Sons Ltd*,[1] the plaintiff was a well-known amateur golfer. The appearance of his caricature on a chocolate advertisement carried the innuendo that the plaintiff had allowed his name to be used in return for gain, and prostituted his reputation as an amateur golfer for advertising purposes. In the absence, however, of facts such as those present in this case which make the words defamatory,[2] the mere use of a person's name or portrait for promotional purposes would not of itself be defamatory.

1   [1931] AC 333. See *Dunlop Rubber Co Ltd v Dunlop* [1921] 1 AC 367.
2   See *Gatley on Libel and Slander* (8th edn, 1981) ss 40n, 46 for examples.

5.9   Thus, the marketing of a product bearing the name of a well-known personality without his authority, is not defamatory unless he can show that his professional reputation is damaged.[1] On the other hand, as we have seen, it may amount to passing off.[2]

1   *Clark v Freeman* (1848) 11 Beav 112 at 117; *Dockrell v Dougall* (1899) 80 LT 556; *Corelli v Wall* (1906) 22 TLR 532.
2   See pp 44–45. See also *British Medical Association v Marsh* (1931) 48 RPC 565.

INTERFERENCE WITH A SUBSISTING CONTRACT AND WITH BUSINESS RELATIONS

5.10   If a personality already under contract to sponsor one product is persuaded to break his contract, and sponsor a rival product, this could amount to the tort of interference with a subsisting contract. There may additionally, of course, be a remedy for breach of contract against the personality himself.

5.11   The question is whether, when a merchandiser has become entitled to intellectual property rights under a contract, the marketing of 'bootleg' products infringing those rights could amount to interference with a subsisting contract. This in turn involves the question of whether the tort may be developing into a generalised tort of interfering with business

5.11 *Other possible sources of protection*

relations. In *Keeble v Hickeringill*[1] Holt CJ enunciated a wide principle of liability for intentional harm to economic and trading interests. He held that he who hinders another in his trade or livelihood is liable to an action for so hindering him. However, the growth of a general principle of tortious liability for intentional and malicious interference with economic and business interests was effectively stifled by the House of Lords in the well known case of *Allen v Flood*.[2] More recently, however, the *Island Records* case[3] gave rise to hopes in some quarters that something like Holt CJ's tort might flicker into life again.

1   (1706) 11 East 574n.
2   [1898] AC 1.
3   [1978] Ch 122.

THE *ISLAND RECORDS* CASE

5.12   The *Island Records* case was concerned with the Performers' Protection Acts 1958–1972. These Acts were aimed at stopping pirated recordings by making such pirating activities a criminal offence. Whilst these Acts are peripheral to our present concern, the case is interesting in the context of the development of an 'interference' tort. The defendant had made records of performances in which the plaintiff claimed no copyright at all. It was held that section 1 of the 1958 Act provided only for criminal penalties, but that where a person could show a private right (loss of sales and royalties) was being interfered with by a criminal act, relief would be given to restrain such interference.

5.13   In *RCA Corpn v Pollard*,[1] the Court of Appeal held that it was bound by its own previous decision in the *Island Records* case that the Performers' Protection Acts did not confer a civil right of action for breach of a statutory duty on performers or on record companies, and that the *Lonrho* case[2] had impliedly overruled *Island Records* as regards the wide formulation of the tort of interference with business relations. Slade LJ suggested that in all cases where the tort of interference with contractual relations had been established, there has been interference with the *performance* by a third party of his contractual obligations. There was nothing in the cases to suggest that a defendant is liable merely because he does an act which he knows is likely to render less valuable the plaintiff's contractual rights with a third party, without interfering with that third party's performance.

1   [1983] Ch 135, [1983] FSR 9.
2   *Lonrho Ltd v Shell Petroleum Co Ltd (No 2)* [1982] AC 173.

5.14   The implication of this case is[1] that it is improbable that a generalised tort of interference with business relations is developing. Such a tort could have been useful to a merchandiser who had established licensing arrangements which would be damaged by piratical activities. The tort would have supplemented the tort of passing off.[2]

1   In *Warner Bros Records Inc v Parr* [1982] 2 All ER 455, the defendant had a 'bootlegged' recording made by persons with whom the plaintiffs had recording contracts. The plaintiffs argued that although the Dramatic and Musical Performers' Protection Act 1958, s 1 made such activities a criminal offence only, they were nevertheless entitled

to bring a civil action for damages. It was held, by Julian Jeffs QC, applying dicta in the *Lonrho* case, that the plaintiffs were within the established exceptions to the rule that a statutory obligation could only be enforced in the manner provided by the statute, and the plaintiffs were entitled to damages and an injunction. This decision was not discussed by the Court of Appeal in *RCA v Pollard*, but must be considered doubtful.

2   See para 4.1 et seq.

CRIMINAL AND OTHER REGULATORY PROTECTION

5.15   Criminal and other regulatory protection is dealt with in Chapter 10, and reference should be made to the discussion there.

THE COURT OF CHIVALRY

5.16   Merchandising has become a useful source of additional revenue for such institutions as universities. They affix their coat of arms to a variety of goods, for example glasses, mugs, pens and pencils. The copyright in the coat of arms has frequently expired, or is untraceable (if it ever existed). Usually, no mark will have been registered, and even if it has, there is the problem of whether such uses actually infringe.[1] In any event, the most likely registration will be in Class 41, for the provision of courses of instruction; arranging and giving of lectures; library services and consultancy services; and the provision of sporting activities. However, provided such coats of arms are properly granted by the College of Arms (in Scotland the Court of the Lord Lyon), it is possible to take action through the Court of Chivalry (in Scotland the Court of the Lord Lyon), to restrain the unauthorised use. Thus, Manchester Corporation was able to restrain the use of its arms by the Manchester Palace of Varieties.[2] The Court has the power to grant injunctions.[3]

1   See para 3.52.
2   *Manchester Corpn v Manchester Palace of Varieties* [1955] P 133. this was the first time the Court had been convened since 1737.
3   See Kinsey [1992] Trade Mark World 25. How it would enforce disobedience to its orders is problematic, though as a Royal Court disobedience to its orders ought, in principle, to be punishable as contempt.

SETTING UP THE LICENSING PROGRAMME

Chapter 6

Licensing

INTRODUCTION

6.1 As we have seen, the basic protection for merchandising programmes is under copyright and trade marks law. Copyright licensing presents few problems. The right to grant licences is recognised by section 90(4) of the Copyright, Designs and Patents Act 1988. A licence does not confer any proprietary right on a licensee. The licensor must be joined in any action for infringement,[1] unless the licence is exclusive.[2] It occasionally happens that an exclusive licensee in turn grants an exclusive sub-licence. The question then arises, who is the exclusive licensee for the purpose of taking action. This difficult question is dealt with later.[3]

1   *CBS United Kingdom Ltd v Charmdale Record Distributors Ltd* [1980] 2 All ER 807.
2   Copyright, Designs and Patents Act 1988, s 101(1). The rights of an exclusive licensee are concurrent with those of the proprietor – s 101(2).
3   Para 10.11.

6.2 No particular form is laid down for copyright licences. So long as the agreement has the effect of a licence, ie it operates as an authority to do something which would otherwise be wrongful or illegal,[1] then it will have the desired effect.

1   *Federal Comr of Taxation v United Aircraft Corpn* (1943) 68 CLR 525.

6.3 Subject to questions of title having been properly addressed, copyright licensing is straightforward. More care needs to be taken with the licensing of trade marks, however, because even under the relaxed regime introduced by the Trade Marks Act 1994 it is essential not to endanger the mark, or to cause other problems for the proprietor. The provisions which should be inserted in the licence agreement are discussed below. Section 28(1) of the Act provides that a licence to use a registered trade mark may be general or limited. A limited licence may, in particular,[1] apply in relation to some but not all of the goods or services covered by the registration, or in relation to use of the mark in a particular manner or in a particular locality. The only formal requirement is that in order to be effective, the licence must be in writing and signed, or in the case of a company, sealed,[2] by the licensor.[3] Sub-licensing of trade marks is now permissible,[4] but because of the doctrine of privity of contract the terms of the head licence will not be directly enforceable by the proprietor against the sub-licensee. Accordingly, it is suggested that sub-licensing is best avoided, and should be prohibited by the terms of the licence agreement.

111

If it is envisaged that the licensee will seek other licences, the pitfall of sub-licensing can easily be avoided if the proprietor appoints the licensee an agent for the purpose of granting licences.[5] Licences do not have to be registered, but may be.[6] Although section 28(3) provides that unless the licence otherwise provides, it is binding on the successor in title to the grantor's interest, section 25(3) provides that until application has been made to register the prescribed particulars of a registrable transaction, it is ineffective against a person acquiring a conflicting interest in or under the registered mark in ignorance of it, and a person claiming to be a licensee by virtue of the transaction does not have the protection of sections 30 and 31 (rights and remedies of a licensee). Accordingly, it is in the interest of the licensee that his interest should be registered, and accordingly, it should be the licensee who bears the costs of registration. The procedure for registration is set out in Rules 34 and 35 of the Trade Marks Rules 1994 and the practice is set out at p 19 of Chapter 17 of the Work Manual. The application is made on Form TM50, and can be made even though the application for the registration of the mark is pending. An assignment of intellectual property rights should be made by the assignor with 'full title guarantee' or with 'limited title guarantee',[7] as appropriate.

1   This is the Parliamentary draftsman's translation of *'inter alia'*.
2   This provision does not apply in Scotland.
3   S 28(2).
4   S 28(4).
5   See para 6.8.
6   S 25(1) and (2).
7   See Law of Property (Miscellaneous Provisions) Act 1994.

THE LICENCE AGREEMENT

Preliminary matters

SHOULD THE TRADE MARK LICENCE AND COPYRIGHT LICENCE BE COMBINED?

6.4   The principal reason why some merchandisers used to separate copyright and trade marks licences, appears to have been to keep royalties secret. Royalties were therefore paid on the copyright licence, which was not subject to registration. However, even under the Trade Marks Act 1938, registration of licensees was not mandatory.[1] It was certainly advisable, however, to register some of the licensees as users, in order to benefit from section 28(2), but in those cases the object of keeping royalties secret could be secured, because the Registrar could be required under section 28(7) not to disclose the royalties. Under the 1994 Act there is no problem in this respect. Royalties are not one of the prescribed particulars which need to be furnished to the Registrar when registration of a licence is applied for.[2] Moreover, there are good reasons for combining them. It is desirable to have a single set of quality control provisions in respect of the products, laid down in a single document. There are certainly no tax advantages in separating the licences, since, as explained in Chapter 9, neither trade mark nor copyright royalties are necessarily subject to deduction at source (unlike patent licences). Liability to deduction can arise in relation to copyright and trade mark licences, but ought not to do so.[3] Whilst a combined licence would not qualify for exemption under Schedule 3 of the Restrictive Trade Practices Act 1976, it is highly improbable that this would be of any consequence.[4] In general, therefore, the licences are better combined. Precedent 1 is equally suited to a combined or a separate licence.

1   *Bostitch Trade Mark* [1963] RPC 183.
2   Ibid, s 25 and Trade Marks Rules 1994, r 34.
3   See para 9.108 et seq.
4   See para 8.12.

Who owns the intellectual property?

6.5 It may seem self-evident, but it is something which is not always sufficiently attended to in practice: the licensor must actually have something to licence. Registered trade marks are straightforward, the register provides the evidence of title. Problems can occur in relation to unregistered marks, for it is to be remembered that the prohibition against assignment in gross was only lifted in respect of registered marks by the Trade Marks Act 1938.[1] It is a consequence, however, of the fact that in the absence of goodwill, no passing off action can be brought in respect of such marks. Unless therefore they are subject to copyright protection, they are worthless. It should be noted that dealings between parent and wholly owned subsidiaries are not subject to these restrictions. This prohibition on the assignment of unregistered marks in gross can be a trap in the merchandising context, though there should be less need to rely on unregistered marks since the coming into force of the 1994 Act.

1   S 22(1).

6.6 Not only can problems arise as to the title to unregistered trade marks, but, notoriously, title to copyright can involve difficulties. It is essential therefore that attention be paid to the matters discussed in Chapter 1, to ensure that copyright is actually vested in the intended licensor, and to satisfy potential licensees of this fact.

6.7 As suggested above, it may be advisable to set up a company for the purpose of owning the intellectual property which is separate from the proprietor's trading company (which should be formally licensed to use the intellectual property).

Merchandiser will appoint agent to appoint licensees

6.8 The actual grant of licences in many cases will be negotiated by merchandising agents who specialise in this. The agent should be appointed agent of the owner of the intellectual property for the purpose of negotiating licences of the intellectual property with third parties[1] – never sub-licences, because of the doctrine of privity of contract (as noted above). Such agents do not negotiate the sale and purchase of goods, and consequently the arrangement is outwith the Commercial Agents (Council Directive) Regulations 1993.[2]

1   See Precedent 2.
2   SI 1993/3053, Reg 2(1).

6.9 This really depends upon the length of the proposed licence. Many merchandising licences are for very short terms, and for these purposes an informal licence suffices. This should take the form of an agreement to grant a licence on the licensor's standard form, and an acceptance of these terms by the proposed licensee. In this way, should the property prove unexpectedly long-lived, relations can be formalised. Alternatively, the licence can be formally entered into at the outset. This does have the advantage of obviating a possible argument by the licensee at a later stage that he had not assented to particular terms.

Contents of the agreement

REQUIREMENTS CONTRACT

6.10 Many merchandisers will want to sell their merchandise themselves through a catalogue or shop. For this purpose, the licence should contain a clause requiring the licensee to supply such of the relevant goods to the licensor, or to any person nominated by him, as the licensor should require.[1] The costs of post or transport in the United Kingdom will normally be borne by the customer, and this should be stipulated in the catalogue sent to customers. The licensor company will be liable to the licensee for the price of the goods, plus any costs, in respect of all goods ordered and supplied. Payment of the price of small items is probably most conveniently dealt with by making monthly billings, which again should be stipulated for. It should be noted that the merchandiser, as seller, will incur the usual liabilities of a seller under the Sale of Goods Act 1979 (as amended by the Sale and Supply of Goods Act 1994)[2] and appropriate product liability insurance cover should be taken out.[3]

1   See Precedent 1, clause 8. Although such agreements are very common, it has occasionally been questioned whether such one sided agreements conform to the requirement that each party provide consideration for the other's promise. There is however no reported case in which this argument has succeeded, and in fact these agreements have always been upheld – see Adams (1978) 94 LQR 73. In the present context, the grant of the licence should be sufficient consideration for the keeping open of the continuing offer to supply.
2   And see Chapter 7 below.
3   This is advisable in any event, even if the merchandiser is not selling goods - see Chapter 7 below.

QUALITY CONTROL

6.11 It is absolutely essential both for trade mark and other purposes that the licence contains adequate quality control provisions.[1] There was nothing in the case law even under the 1938 Act to suggest that control should actually be carried out in all respects by the licensor company. In the case of some classes of trade marked goods, this would not be practical. To give an example from outside merchandising, there is only one laboratory in the whole of the United Kingdom capable of giving comprehensive analyses of all kinds of alcoholic beverages, and the fact that many different trade mark owners rely on it in respect of wines, beers etc, clearly does not endanger their marks, as they use it as the only satisfactory method of exercising quality control. What merchandisers must be able to demonstrate, if necessary, is that the arrangements set up by them are such as, in the particular circumstances, *in fact* to secure adequate quality control.[2]

1   See Precedent 1, clause 7.
2   *Re Molyslip Trade Mark* [1978] RPC 211.

6.12   The licensee should be required to supply samples to the licensor, or the monitoring third party, and to make at least a quarterly return of any complaints received in respect of the goods.[1]

1   See Precedent 1, clause 7.2.

THE GOODS

6.13   In the case of registered trade marks, the licensee should be concerned to ensure that the goods to which the licence relates fall within the specification of the goods for which the mark or marks are registered. Where the mark is a character, the licensee should require that the licensor warrants that it has been used as a trade mark in relation to the relevant goods. It has been suggested, for example, that an alternative line of objection open to the Registrar in the *Holly Hobbie* case,[1] might have been that the character was not used as a mark on the relevant goods. Whether or not on the actual facts of that case this was true, because American Greetings did print a trade mark using the character on the back of their greeting cards, for example, the point is worth remembering. Merely representing figures such as Holly Hobbie would not generally be taken to be trade mark use. Registered marks which are not being used as trade marks are vulnerable.[2]

1   *Re American Greetings Corpn* [1984] RPC 329.
2   Registration may be revoked for non-use during the five year period following completion of registration – s 46(1)(a), or it may be cancelled on the ground that the application was made in bad faith – s 47(1).

FAILURE TO SECURE REGISTRATION

6.14   Where new marks are being licensed, for which applications are merely pending, the position in the event that the application to register the marks should fail needs to be considered, and whether or not a term needs to be included to deal with it. If the agreement remains operative in respect of copyright, normally there would be no need to vary the royalties or other provisions, but this should be spelled out.

ADDITIONAL TRADE MARKS

6.15   The licensee should be restrained from itself registering the mark in respect of any goods, in order to guard against his securing registration in respect of goods other than those within the licensor's registrations, though, of course, because of the wider scope of registrations[1] it is now easier for a proprietor to take steps to stop this than it was under the old Act. The question of whether or not the licensee should be given an option in respect of additional marks which the licensor may obtain should also be considered (this of course will only be relevant in respect of fairly long-term licences).

1   See Precedent 1, clause 9.4, and para 3.52 et seq.

NOT TO ENDANGER THE INTELLECTUAL PROPERTY

6.16   The licence should contain standard clauses for the protection of the licensor's intellectual property.[1]

1   See Precedent 1, clause 9.

NOT TO REGISTER ANY NAMES INVOLVED IN THE LICENSING PROGRAMME AS A COMPANY NAME[1]

6.17   The owner of a registered trade mark cannot prevent a company's bona fide use of its own name. Notwithstanding the qualification 'bona fide', it is advisable that licensees be restrained from registering any names used as their company names.

1   See Precedent 1, clause 11.

THE GRANTS

6.18   These can be:
   (a) sole;
   (b) exclusive;
   (c) non-exclusive; or
   (d) a combination of these in respect of different territories.[1]

Care should be taken with all territorial grants to avoid infringement of any relevant competition laws,[2] and in the case of exclusive licences, arguments that there is a transfer which is subject to CTT.[3]

1   See Precedent 1, clauses 2 and 3.
2   See Chapter 8.
3   See Chapter 11.

PRICES

6.19   The prices to be charged by the licensee may be specified, but the provisions of any relevant competition laws again need to be borne in mind.[1] The normal non-exclusive licence does not fall within section 6 of the Restrictive Trade Practices Act 1976, as relevant restrictions as to the goods are accepted only by the licensee, and in the case of exclusive licences a provision under which the licensor binds itself not to license the marks to others in the territory is probably not a restriction as to goods. The Treaty of Rome needs to be borne in mind, on the whole, only in the case of large-scale licensing programmes. Most programmes at the outset will fall within the guidelines provided by the Notice on Minor Agreements. For these purposes the turnover of the parties must exceed ECU300 million or 5% of market share.

1   See Chapter 8.

PAYMENTS AND ROYALTIES[1]

Checklist

6.20
(1) Is an 'up-front' payment to be required on entry into the agreement by the licensee? If so, is it to be set against royalties or other payments made by the licensee?
(2) On what basis is the royalty to be calculated? It should be remembered that the licensee will normally have to pay VAT on the royalties charged to him (input tax) as well as VAT on his sales (output tax).
(3) Are separate royalties payable on the different elements comprised in the intellectual property package? As explained above, unless patents or designs are included (which would be unusual), there would not seem to be any good reason for requiring this.
(4) Is there to be a minimum royalty payment? – and the right of termination by the licensor if the target royalty is not reached? Alternatively, the licensee may wish to be given the right of early termination in cases where a target turnover is not reached.
(5) What records of sales and other dealings are to be kept by the licensees? – the licensor should have the power to inspect these records, and in particular VAT receipts.
(6) Is the licensee going to deal with its subsidiaries? If so, dealings by the licensee with its subsidiaries should be required to be made at arm's length, and the dealings to be treated as ordinary sales for royalty purposes.

1   See Precedent 1, clause 5.

MARKING OF ARTICLES

6.21   The way in which the mark is to be applied to the specified goods, packaging or samples should be stipulated, as well as the mode of use in advertising materials, and the licensee should be enjoined from using any other marks alongside it, unless this has been specifically negotiated by the parties.[1]

1   See Precedent 1, clause 9.2.

INDEMNITY

6.22   The agreement should require indemnity from the licensee in respect of any loss arising from failure by the licensee to comply with the provisions of the licence.[1]

1   See Precedent 1, clause 18.

DURATION

6.23 Term of the licence should always be set out, and any one[1] option for renewal.

1 See Precedent 1, clause 4.2 for example.

TERMINATION

6.24 The agreement should separate breaches which are fundamental and terminate the agreement automatically, from those requiring notice. Failure to comply with the former should lead to automatic termination. Failure to comply with the terms of a notice will be deemed a fundamental breach.[1]

1 See Precedent 1, clause 15.

POST-TERMINATION

6.25 The licensee should be required to cease to apply the mark, and either surrender existing stock or dispose of it within a specified period, eg six months, after termination of the agreement.[1]

1 See Precedent 1, clause 17.

NO SUB-LICENCES

6.26 As explained above,[1] these are inadvisable and the licensee should be enjoined from granting them.[2]

1 Para 6.3.
2 See Precedent 1, clause 9.7.

INSOLVENCY, CHANGE OF MANAGEMENT

6.27 Insolvency, change of management etc – any of these events in the licensee company should terminate the agreement automatically, since in most cases merchandisers will want to have some sort of control over the choice of persons with whom they do business.[1]

1 See Precedent 1, clause 15.3.

INFRINGEMENT

6.28 Subject to the provisions mentioned above concerning exclusive licensees, usually it will be for the licensor and the licensor alone to take action against pirates.[1] As explained above, when he is himself trading in the goods, the licensor should be able to sue in passing off, as well as infringement.[2] As the *Muppets* case[3] shows, it may also be possible for a merchandiser who is purely licensing unregistered marks, to succeed in passing off. This could be important where registrations are pending, because although rights when granted date back to the date of registration,[4] pending registration an unregistered proprietor cannot sue for infringement.[5]

1   See Precedent 1, clause 14.
2   See Chapter 4.
3   *Children's Television Workshop Inc v Woolworths (NSW) Ltd* [1981] RPC 187 discussed at para 4.14.
4   S 9(3).
5   Ibid, the position was the same under the old Act – see *Denny & Sons v United Biscuits (UK)* [1981] FSR 114; *McGregor-Doniger Inc v Sterling McGregor* [1981] FSR 299.

GOODWILL

6.29   The goodwill generated by the licensee's operation should be held by the licensee as a trustee for the licensor.[1]

1   See Precedent 1, clause 9.8.

NOTICES

6.30   The method of serving notices should be specified.[1]

1   See Precedent 1, clause 21.8.

Chapter 7

Liability for defective products

INTRODUCTION

7.1 This Chapter deals with possible ways in which a character merchandiser, or a personality, could become liable in respect of product defects. The important point to realise is that there is this possibility, and proper insurance cover against potential product liability should be considered. The grounds on which such liability could be founded is the subject of this chapter.

7.2 As mentioned in Chapter 6, a merchandiser who is dealing in the products, either in his own right as seller or as agent for his licensees as undisclosed principals, can be liable to customers for defects in the goods supplied. Liability in such cases is under the quality warranties of the Sale of Goods Act 1979, as amended by the Sale and Supply of Goods Act 1994. The merchandiser should have ensured that he has a right of indemnity from the licensee who manufactured the goods, under the express terms of the licence agreement. In the absence of such terms, a merchandiser dealing as agent to sell the goods on behalf of the licensee would have an implied right of indemnity against the licensee.[1] Where the merchandiser sells on its own account as an ordinary retailer, he will similarly be liable under the Sale of Goods Act 1979 but, having acquired the goods under a contract of sale from its supplier, will in turn be able to sue that supplier under the Sale of Goods Act quality warranties.

1 *Bowstead on Agency* (15th edn, 1985) Article 67; Fridman *Law of Agency* (6th edn, 1990) p 180 et seq.

7.3 Liability under the Sale of Goods Act quality warranties does not depend on fault. A retailer can be liable even in respect of latent defects which it had no possibility of discovering. Liability under the Sale of Goods Act quality warranties raises no special problems in relation to merchandising, and it is not proposed to deal further with it at this point. The more problematic areas are those where there is no contractual nexus between the injured party and the merchandiser. What is the position for example where the licensed manufacturer acting on his own account has dealt with the customer? For example, let us suppose a piece of sports equipment bears the name of a well-known sportsman. A defect in a piece of such equipment causes injury to a customer who dealt directly with the manufacturer or his dealers. Since there is no contractual relationship between the sportsman and the customer in such a case, liability would have to depend on negligence on the part of the sportsman eg where the goods have been made to a faulty specification he or she had provided, or upon the existence of one or more of the factors which traditionally have justified liability to third parties for the acts or defaults of another, in particular, control and holding out, and express or implied endorsement of the product.[1] Although this liability is most likely to arise in practice in relation to defective goods, it could in the same way arise in relation to defective services. A licensor can also incur liability under the Consumer Protection Act 1987. We will consider these matters in turn.

1   See Atiyah *Vicarious Liability* (1967) Butterworths, p 15 et seq.

NEGLIGENCE

7.4   In the case of *Junior Books Ltd v Veitchi Co Ltd*,[1] the House of Lords held that a flooring sub-contractor was liable to the owner of the factory in which the floor was laid. The duty of care owed by the contractor as producer, to the owner extended beyond the duty merely to prevent harm being done by faulty work, and included a duty to avoid faults being present in the work or article itself. The liability extended to economic loss to the factory owner caused through the defect. In this case, as in a number of other cases,[2] Lord Atkin's famous formulation of the tort of negligence in *Donoghue v Stevenson*,[3] seemed to have been taken to its logical conclusion. As the law stood therefore, there would, for example, have been the possibility of a merchandiser becoming liable to third parties in respect of economic loss caused through negligence. This could have had far reaching consequences. However, this line of development of the tort of negligence was effectively ended by the House of Lords in *Murphy v Brentwood District Council*[4] and it is now clear that liability will only exist in respect of damage to persons or property (including economic loss resulting from damage to property[5]).

1   [1982] 3 All ER 201.
2   See specially *Dutton v Bognor Regis UDC* [1972] 1 All ER 462; *Anns v Merton London Borough Council* [1977] 2 All ER 492.
3   [1932] AC 562.
4   [1991] 1 AC 398.
5   *Spartan Steel & Alloys Ltd v Martin & Co (Contractors) Ltd* [1977] 3 QB 27; *Muirhead v Industrial Tank Specialities Ltd* [1986] QB 507.

7.5   An exception to the above principle seems to be the result of *Henderson v Merrett Syndicates*.[1] In this case it was held that where a person had held himself out as having certain professional skills, and the plaintiff had relied on this, the defendant was liable for consequential financial loss under the principle of *Hedley Byrne & Co Ltd v Heller & Partners Ltd*.[2] *Hedley Byrne* was a case concerning a negligent misrepresentation, and it must be admitted that the border between *Murphy* and *Henderson* is by no means clearly defined. It is possible, however, that a personality failing to exercise a proper level of professional care in endorsing a product which the public is likely to purchase in reliance on the fact that proper professional care has been taken, could incur liability on the *Henderson* principle, and that this would extend to liability for consequential economic loss. Endorsement of a financial product by a financial journalist might, for example, result in such liability if the product proved defective.

1   [1994] 3 All ER 506.
2   [1964] AC 465.

7.6   What about non-experts? In *Esso Petroleum Co Ltd v Mardon*,[1] Esso were held liable in respect of a forecast of the throughput of a filling station, which proved hopelessly over-optimistic. Although that case might be thought to be distinguishable on the basis that Esso were making a statement about something which the plaintiff could reasonably suppose to be within their field of expertise, the question is really whether or not a reasonable representee would have *relied on* the representation in purchasing the product (or service). Where representations are sufficiently specific about product performance, ie more than mere puffs, it is quite possible that a plaintiff could successfully argue reliance on them. It is not unreasonable in such a case for a member of the public to suppose that the personality making the statement has investigated the product before making it.

1   [1976] QB 801, [1976] 2 All ER 5.

7.7   Liability based on a negligent failure to carry out a right to control quality under the licence agreement, would probably not be sufficient to impose liability in negligence on the merchandiser. A right exercisable vis-à-vis the licensee by virtue of the licence agreement, would seem to be unpromising material on which to found a duty vis-à-vis the public. However, the possibility of liability based on negligence should be distinguished from vicarious liability incurred by virtue of the existence of *rights of control* over the manufacturer *per se*. This is a separate ground of liability, which we must now consider.

VICARIOUS LIABILITY THROUGH CONTROL

7.8   Control over the way in which a person performs his duties has been one of the traditional bases of the doctrine of vicarious liability in tort.[1] A degree of control will usually be exercised by a merchandiser over his licensed manufacturers. Where this is merely by specification, even detailed specification of the goods (or services) to which the name is attached, there is probably no danger of the licensor being held vicariously liable.[2] Traditionally, the independent contractor, for whose defaults the employer is not liable, has been distinguished from the employee for whose defaults the employer is liable, on the basis of the distinction between control by specification and control which goes further.[3]

1   See Atiyah *Vicarious Liability* (1967) Butterworths, p 15 et seq.
2   Unless of course the harm is caused by a defect in the specification itself.
3   *Atiyah*, op cit, p 42.

7.9   As we have seen, where marks are licensed, quality control over the goods (or services) to which the mark is applied must be exercised by the proprietor.[1] Were such control to be held, of itself, to be sufficient for licensors to be held liable in respect of defects in the products to which the mark were applied, the implications would be quite far reaching. It is improbable that a court would want to move in such a direction in the absence of legislation. It might possibly distinguish between such controls as are always necessary to preserve marks, and those which go further. This approach has been adopted by some American jurisdictions. *Nicholls v Arthur Murray*[2] is a well-known example, but the problem with this case is that the judge did not in fact specify which controls he thought went beyond an ordinary trade mark licence. Making such a distinction is always going to create considerable difficulties.

1   Para 6.3.
2   56 Cal Rep 728 (1967).

7.10   In fact it will usually be difficult to distinguish between necessary and unnecessary controls in this respect. One justification for the existence of vicarious liability in tort is that the master, by virtue of his control over his servants, has the opportunity to prevent loss.[1] A possible basis of distinction would be to ask whether the control exercised gave the opportunity to prevent the defect in question arising. Thus controls designed to ensure merely that products conform to a specification would not be sufficient, on this argument, to justify holding a licensor liable for latent defects in goods which had no connection with the way in which their manufacture had been specified.

1   *Atiyah*, op cit, p 15 et seq.

LIABILITY THROUGH HOLDING OUT

7.11   Control *per se* has never been sufficient ground for making a person vicariously liable in tort.[1] Other factors have needed to be present. On the other hand, there is some authority for the proposition that merely allowing a licensee to carry on a business under a name or mark associated with another can be sufficient ground for imposing liability on a licensor.[2]

1   *Atiyah*, op cit, p 15 et seq.
2   See Adams (1981) 3 EIPR 314.

7.12   Some American courts have gone along a similar route in the absence of legislation. Some have held that merely allowing another to use a name or trade mark on a product may be a ground for liability in respect of latent defects.[1] A similar principle has also been applied outside the field of product liability, where a name or mark has been displayed on vehicles involved in an accident or on premises where an accident has occurred. In the case of *Buchanan v Canada Dry*,[2] the defendant moved for summary judgment. Presiding Judge Deen observed that on the evidence adduced by the plaintiff on the issue of control, the court would have been bound to grant the motion. He went on to observe, however, that the record revealed the following:

> The [truck involved in the accident] carried numerous Canada Dry insignias and no [other] markings; the driver's uniform displayed only

Canada Dry insignia; there is no listing in the Atlanta telephone directory [of the truck owner] but there is for 'Canada Dry'; two prominent signs on [the truck owner's building] read 'Canada Dry' and a small sign on the door indicates [the truck owner].

The motion for summary judgment was accordingly dismissed. Whilst none of the above factors alone might demonstrate that the truck owner was Canada Dry's *alter ego*, collectively they were sufficient to defeat the defendant's motion. It did not appear from the record whether or not the presence of these factors were the result of Canada Dry's control, or the truck owner's excessive zeal. Other courts have taken the view that something more than mere permission to use is required.[3] In jurisdictions taking the view that a person who puts out as his own product a chattel manufactured by another is subject to the same liability as though he were manufacturer,[4] even the incorporation of words such as 'made for' has not been necessarily sufficient to avoid liability.[5] Again, however, since the implications of holding an ordinary mark or name licensor so liable would be quite far reaching, it is improbable that English courts would adopt such an approach prior to implementation of legislation.

1   *Slavin v Francis H Leggett & Co* 177 A 120 (1935); *Swift v Blackwell* 84 F 2d 130 (1936). See Miller and Lowell *Product Liability* (1977) Butterworths, pp 182–183.
2   226 SE 2d 613 (1976). For other illustrations of this approach see *Fidelman-Dansiger v Statler Management* 136 A 2d 119 (1957); *Bech v Arthur Murray* 54 Cal Rep 328 (1966); *Gizzi v Texaco* 437 F 2d 303 (1971); *Singleton v International Dairy Queen* 332 A 2d 160 (1975); *Billops v Magness Construction* 321 A 2d 196 (1978).
3   See for example *Sherman v Texas Oil Co* 165 NE 2d 916 (1960); *Coe v Esau* 377 P 2d 815 (1963); *Crittendon v State Oil* 222 NE 2d 561 (1966); *Apple v Standard Oil* 307 F Supp 107 (1969); *Mabe v BP Oil* 356 A 2d 304 (1976).
4   And see Restatement of Torts (2nd edn) para 400.
5   See Miller and Lowell, n 1, above.

7.13   One of the few English cases having a bearing on the subject is *Ready Mixed Concrete (South East) Ltd v Minister of Pensions and National Insurance*.[1] In this case, as in *Canada Dry*, the vehicle was owned by the licensee, but bore the licensor's insignia (and the driver wore a special uniform). The issue was not however vicarious liability, but whether or not the licensee was an 'employed person' for the purposes of the National Insurance Act 1965. It was held that he was not. It is certainly arguable that on the question of national insurance contributions a court might be justified in holding that the parties were independent *inter se*, whilst on the same evidence in the event of the licensor being sued by a third party, holding the licensor liable. Almost certainly, however, as we observed above, at present something more than merely the use of a name or mark associated with another will be required before an English court will be prepared to impose liability on a licensor. What, however, is that something more? None of the factors mentioned by Mackenna J in the *Ready Mixed Concrete* case (agreement to work for a wage etc)[2] will exist in a merchandising licence.

1   [1968] 2 QB 497. See also eg *BSM (1257) Ltd v Secretary of State for Social Services* [1978] ICR 894; *Thames Television Ltd v Wallis* [1979] IRLR 136; *Addison v London Philharmonic Orchestra Ltd* [1981] ICR 261.
2   In fact, more recent cases have moved to a more impressionistic approach in any event – see eg *Market Investigations Ltd v Minister of Social Security* [1969] 2 QB 173 at 184-5; *Lee Ting Sang v Chung Chi-Keung* [1990] 2 AC 374, PC.

LIABILITY THROUGH ENDORSEMENT IN THE ABSENCE OF NEGLIGENCE

7.14   In the absence of negligence, which was dealt with above, the main danger of liability arising in merchandising is probably through the general or specific endorsement of a product. This element is clearly of more significance in the case of personality merchandising, than character merchandising. A general endorsement sufficed to render the defendants liable where the plaintiff had slipped whilst wearing shoes on which the defendants had allowed to appear their 'Good Housekeeping Consumers' Guaranty Seal'.[1] The mere use of a personality's name might similarly be held to amount to a general endorsement, though it is unlikely to be so held in this country at present. In this respect Walton J's remarks in the *Kojak* case, quoted above in a different context,[2] which suggest that the public do not look upon such endorsement as a guarantee of quality, still have some validity. By contrast, in the case of products specifically endorsed by a personality, there might be liability in respect of their failing to live up to the expectations consumers might reasonably have of them as a result of such endorsement. Such liability could be based on finding a collateral contract between the endorser and the public purchasing the products in reliance on the endorser's promise.[3] Clearly, a specific endorsement of the characteristics of a product by a personality, could result in liability if the product is deficient in those characteristics. Thus, a statement by a personality that a paint product is 'guaranteed to give five years of weatherproofing', could give rise to liability under a collateral contract.[4]

1   *Hanbury v Hearst Corpn* 81 Cal Rep 519 (1969).
2   See para 4.17. See, however, remarks of Whitford J and Goulding J quoted at paras 4.18 and 4.19.
3   See eg *Shanklin Pier v Detel Products Ltd* [1951] 2 KB 854; *Andrews v Hopkinson* [1957] 1 QB 229; *Wells (Merstham) Ltd v Buckland Sand & Silica Co Ltd* [1965] 2 QB 170.
4   *Shanklin Pier Ltd v Detel Products Ltd* [1951] 2 KB 854.

7.15   Statements about product performance made by a personality without any basis could after all result in criminal liability under the Trade Descriptions Act 1968 (which applies to false and misleading statements about goods and services).[1]

1   See para 7.5.

LIABILITY UNDER THE CONSUMER PROTECTION ACT 1987

7.16   The most likely way in which a licensor could become liable to consumers in respect of defective products is under the Consumer Protection Act 1987. Part I of the Consumer Protection Act implements EEC Council Directive 85/374. Section 2 of the Act imposes civil liability for damage wholly or partly caused by a defective product. This liability can extend to the producer, *anyone who holds himself out as such by putting his name on a product or by using a trade mark or other distinguishing*

7.16 *Liability for defective products*

mark in relation to the product, or anybody who has imported the product into the EEC in order to supply it to another. Obviously, the way in which merchandisers are most likely to become liable is by using their trade mark in relation to a product. This raises the question of whether liability can be avoided if there is wording on the product which makes it clear that the trade mark proprietor is not the producer. It would seem possible that they can, and certainly, little is to be lost by printing on the product some formula such as 'Produced under licence from XYZ Plc the proprietor of the trade mark 'Golden Widget' by ABC Plc'.[1] Suppliers may become liable if they fail to identify the producer, importer, or their own supplier.

1   See Precedent 1, clause 9.10.

7.17 'Defect' is defined by reference to a standard of safety which persons generally are entitled to expect.[1] Warnings given with the product are taken into account. 'Damage' is limited to death or personal injury, or loss or damage to property ordinarily intended for private use, provided the damages awarded would not exceed £275.[2]

1   S 3.
2   S 5.

7.18 Part II of the 1987 Act implemented the general product safety requirements proposed in the White Paper on the Safety of Goods[1] and incorporates earlier legislation on consumer safety. Section 10 makes it an offence to supply goods which do not comply with the new standard. Goods will not comply if they are not reasonably safe having regard to all the circumstances and this would include, for example, where they do not conform to published standards, or are 'defective'. Section 11 confers, inter alia, powers for establishing standards, giving approvals, requiring product information to be provided etc. These provisions must now, however, be read in the light of the General Product Safety Regulations 1994[2] implementing the EC's Product Safety Directive.[3] These do not repeal the 1987 provisions, but disapply them in certain circumstances. Regulation 5 disapplies section 10 to the extent that it imposed general safety requirements where products were:
  (a) to be placed on the market, offered or agreed to be placed on the market or exposed or possessed to be placed on the market by *producers*; or
  (b) supplied, offered or agreed to be supplied or exposed or possessed to by supplied by *distributors*.

A merchandiser selling merchandise manufactured by a licensee on its own account would be a distributor for these purposes. Regulations 12 and 13 create new offences for producers who place unsafe products on the market, and distributors who supply products which they know, or should have known on the basis of information in their possession, are dangerous.[4] Regulation 13 makes it an offence for any producer or distributor inter alia to offer or agree to place on the market any dangerous product. The penalties for breach of these provisions can include imprisonment as well as, or instead of, a fine. As well as producers and distributors, Regulation 15(1) provides that where the commission of an offence was due to the act or default of some other person in the course of a commercial activity of

126

his, that other person shall be guilty of an offence. Merchandisers might become liable under these provisions eg where the specification laid down in the licence agreement results in an unsafe product.

1   1984 Cmnd 9302.
2   SI 1994/2328.
3   92/59/EEC.
4   Regs 12 and 9(a).

Chapter 8

Competition law

Introduction

8.1 The competition law in operation in the United Kingdom is exceptionally complex. Fortunately, for the most part, it should have little bearing on the usual run of merchandising operations. However, there are pitfalls for the unwary draftsman, and some operations are on a sufficiently large scale to be objects of concern to the enforcement agencies. It is necessary therefore to give a brief account of the laws in order to draw attention to possible dangers especially as this is an area of law which is often forgotten about in practice. The consequences of running foul of competition laws can be serious.

8.2 The laws in operation theoretically are of two kinds: those which designate as problematic certain business practices according to their forms, and those which focus not on the form of the business practice but on its effects. The effects approach is adopted by Article 85 of the Treaty of Rome and the United Kingdom Competition Act 1980. It is also adopted in Article 86 and the United Kingdom Fair Trading Act 1973, though neither of these latter provisions is likely to be of much importance in relation to merchandising except in rare cases. The 'forms' approach is adopted by the United Kingdom Restrictive Trade Practices Act 1976 and the Resale Prices Act 1976. The common law doctrine of restraint of trade also needs to be mentioned. Whether or not, in practice, the distinction between forms and effects is quite so clear cut is another matter. Certainly formalism has on occasion crept into EEC decisions, and could do so in the application of the Competition Act 1980, although there is no evidence of this as yet.

8.3 In this section we focus principally upon the licensing programme which is where problems are most likely to arise. The agreements appointing merchandising agents could theoretically give rise to problems, but in practice are much less likely to do so. Changes to UK law look likely in the forseeable future.

RESTRICTIVE TRADE PRACTICES ACT 1976
Introduction

8.4 For the reasons explained in the following paragraphs, this complex legislation ought not to catch the usual sort of merchandising licence.

Unfortunately, the effect of failing to furnish particulars of a registrable agreement to the Office of Fair Trading is that all relevant restrictions[1] become void. The Act therefore cannot be ignored altogether.

1 See para 8.16.

8.5 The Act, which consolidates earlier legislation,[1] applies to agreements containing specified kinds of restriction as to either goods or services.[2] In the first place, however, to be caught, the agreement must be between two or more parties carrying on business in the United Kingdom either in the production or supply of goods or in the provision of services. Thus, if two parties to an agreement are a party with a goods business in the UK, and another with a services business in the UK, the Act does not apply, no matter what the agreement. Whilst licensing intellectual property rights in this country can amount to carrying on a business in the United Kingdom,[3] it would not appear *of itself* to be a business in either goods or services.[4] Consequently, the Act would not apply. Even if it were held to amount to carrying on a business, in goods or services, so that there would then be two parties carrying on business in goods, or in services, the agreement would probably still not be registrable: two or more parties must accept restrictions, and on the *Ravenseft* principle discussed at paragraph 8.9 below, it can be argued that the licensee of intellectual property is not restricted by the agreement for the purposes of the Act. In the case of trade mark, patent, know-how, and copyright licences, there may in any event be exemption under Schedule 3.[5] Subject to this, it is clear that it does not matter for the purposes of the Act that the parties are carrying on different classes of business, eg that the licensee is a manufacturing company while the licensor is not (though nevertheless dealing in goods).[6] On the other hand, two or more parties must accept relevant restrictions as to the goods, or two or more parties relevant restrictions as to the services.[7]

1 In particular the Restrictive Trade Practices Acts 1956 and 1968.
2 As to the relevant restrictions see para 8.8 below.
3 *Noddy Subsidiary Rights Co Ltd v IRC* [1966] 3 All ER 459 – and see para 9.11.
4 See Annual Report of Director General of Fair Trading 1979, p 36. This Report of course provides guidance only, it is not binding, and, if in doubt, agreements should be notified for safety's sake.
5 See para 8.12 et seq.
6 Restrictive Trade Practices Act 1976, ss 6(2)(b) and 14(4). As explained above, if one of the parties is dealing in goods, and the other services, the Act does not apply.
7 Leisner *Review of Restrictive Trade Practices Policy* (Cmnd 7512) 5–20.

8.6 The Act also applies to information agreements: sections 7 and 12[1] contain a similar set of provisions to sections 6 and 11.[2] The point is that, for example, a non-competitive pricing policy can be achieved by firms by notifying each other's prices, as well as by actually agreeing to follow a common pricing policy. The requirement that a licensee provide an account to the licensor of sales to third parties for the purposes of royalty payments could be an information agreement for this purpose, and if the licensor accepted a relevant information obligation as to goods, the agreement would be registrable. However, there are two possible ways out:
(1) section 9(3) says that where the agreement in question is an agreement for the supply of goods or for the application of any process of manufacture to goods, no account shall be taken of any

term which relates exclusively to the goods supplied, or to which
the process of manufacture is to be applied, in pursuance of the
agreement (section 18(2) contains the equivalent provision in
respect of services);[3]

(2) on the *Ravenseft* principle, the licensee is not restricted anyway.[4]

1 See para 8.8, n 3 below for extent to which these provisions are in operation.
2 Again, there is no aggregation of ss 6 and 7, or ss 11 and 12, respectively, so that only
  if both the licensor and licensee were subject to eg an information obligation, would it
  be necessary to furnish particulars.
3 Though this type of provision could be found in patent pool licensing which can be a
  way of operating a cartel, and the effect of giving this somewhat unclear provision the
  interpretation suggested in the text would be to prevent the Act being effective in such
  a situation.
4 See para 8.9.

8.7 A relevant restriction can still be a restriction even though it is less
than total. In ordinary licensing, it is exclusive territory clauses which are
most likely to render an agreement registrable. These restrict the licensor's
right to carry on business in the licensee's territory. Because, in practice,
there are likely to be restrictions upon the licensee, not to poach outside
his territory, there are restrictions accepted by both parties within the
meaning of the Act.[1] However, in most merchandising licences, the
exclusive territory clause simply amounts to an agreement by the licensor
not to license other users of the intellectual property within the territory,
and there would therefore seem not to be any restrictions as to goods or
services accepted by the licensor for the purposes of the Act. A problem would
arise only if the licensee requires stronger protection, eg because the licensor
is already engaged in the production of the goods elsewhere, and the licensee
does not want them imported into his territory. If the licensor who is also
carrying on business in the United Kingdom accepts such a restriction, the
agreement will be registrable. If such a restriction affects imports from other
EU countries, the agreement will infringe Article 85(1) of the Treaty of
Rome, considered at paragraph 8.22 et seq below.

1 Ie restrictions on 'the areas or places in ... which ... goods are to be supplied or acquired'
  – s 6(1)(f). S 11(2)(e) contains parallel provisions for services.

Relevant 'Restrictions' for the purposes of the Restrictive Trade Practices Act 1976

8.8 The relevant restrictions for the purposes of the Act in relation to
goods, are as follows:

'Section 6(1):
This Act applies to agreements (whenever made) between two or more
persons carrying on business in the United Kingdom in the production
or supply of goods, or in the application to goods of any process of
manufacture, whether with or without other parties, being agreements
under which restrictions are accepted by two or more parties in respect
of any of the following matters –
(a) the prices to be charged, quoted or paid for goods supplied, offered
    or acquired, or for the applications of any process of manufacture
    of goods;

(b) the prices to be recommended or suggested as the prices to be charged or quoted in respect of the resale of goods supplied;

(c) the terms or conditions on or subject to which goods are to be supplied or acquired or any such process is to be applied for goods;

(d) the quantities or descriptions of goods to be produced, supplied or acquired;

(e) the process of manufacture to be applied to any goods, or the quantities or descriptions of goods to which any such process is to be applied; or

(f) the persons or classes of persons to, for or from whom, or the areas or places in, or from which, goods are to be supplied or acquired, or any such process applied.'[1]

There is an equivalent provision for services,[2] and there are equivalent provisions governing information agreements as to goods and services.[3]

1   Restrictive Trade Practices Act 1976, s 6(1).
2   Ibid, s 11(2).
3   Ibid, ss 7(1) and 12(2). The powers under s 12(2) have not yet been exercised, and under s 7(1) they have been exercised in respect of prices charged (not prices paid), and terms and conditions of supply (not purchase).

The *Ravenseft* principle: 'opening the door'

8.9   The licensor owns intellectual property rights, and, until permitted to do so, no one else can lawfully exploit those rights. Once permission is given, a licensee can operate, but only under the terms of the agreement. If he steps outside of the agreement he becomes liable to an action for infringement or passing off. This liability arises under the general law, not under the terms of the agreement: it is simply that the licensee has lost the defence provided by the agreement. Thus if the licensee is licensed to produce and sell 300 'Derby Duck' cuddly toys, and produces and sells 350, he is liable in respect of those unlicensed extra 50.[1] The *Ravenseft* case itself[2] involved restrictive covenants in leases, however the Office of Fair Trading take the view that it is of general application to intellectual property licensing.[3] The principle can also be derived from the earlier *Waste Paper* case.[4] In truth, however, that case seems to embody a slightly different proposition, namely that agreements which merely reproduce duties already imposed by law, eg as to the quality of goods sold, are not restrictive. Whilst the *Ravenseft* principle is logical it may be dangerous to rely on it too much. It is after all inconsistent with the structure of the Restrictive Trade Practices Act 1976: why, for example, if the principle is applicable to intellectual property, do you need the exemptions in Schedule 3? A court could find grounds for distinguishing leasehold covenants from the intellectual property licences.

1   Such a restriction is a relevant restriction within s 6(1)(d) above. But it should be noted that whatever the merits of the 'opening the door' argument under UK law, problems could arise under EU competition law with this kind of restriction.
2   *Ravenseft Properties Ltd v Director General of Fair Trading* [1978] QB 52.
3   Annual Report of the Director General of Fair Trading 1979, p 36.
4   *Re British Waste Paper Association's Agreement* [1963] 2 All ER 424 – see Cunningham *Fair Trading Act 1973* (1974) Sweet & Maxwell, pp 14–16.

Provisions to be disregarded

8.10 Before considering whether or not an agreement needs to qualify for exemption, it is necessary to consider whether or not the relevant restriction can be disregarded under section 9(3) of the 1976 Act. As noted above, this provides that in an agreement for the supply of goods, or for the application to goods of any process of manufacture, no account shall be taken of any term which relates exclusively to the goods supplied, or to which a process of manufacture is to be applied, in pursuance of the agreement (the equivalent provision for services is section 18). The meaning of this arcane provision used to be the subject of some debate. However, in *Re Diazo Copying Materials*,[1] Warner J held that a restriction on a party re-selling goods supplied under the agreement, outside the United Kingdom, was a restriction relating exclusively to the goods supplied thereunder. He declined to deal with an argument based on the *Ravenseft* principle, though he saw difficulties with it. He also declined to deal with an argument based on the second limb of section 9(3). In most merchandising situations, the relevant restrictions will be on the licensee manufacturer. Consequently, it is the second limb of section 9(3) which is most likely to be relevant. Warner J did not explain what difficulties he saw in the application of this provision to the facts in *Re Diazo*, but they may have been connected with the fact that the goods came back to the manufacturer under a buy-back provision. At all events, it can certainly be argued that Warner J's literal reading of the subsection is equally appropriate for the second limb. In consequence, a restriction on a licensee selling the products he manufactures under licence, eg to the United States, can be said to relate exclusively to the goods to which a process of manufacture is to be applied. Similarly, a maximum price term could be imposed, and possibly a minimum price term, but here regard would have to be had to other competition legislation.

1 [1984] ICR 429.

8.11 Section 18 is the equivalent provision relating to services in Part II (but it works somewhat differently).[1]

1 See Korah *Competition Laws of Great Britain and the Common Market* (1982) Martinus Nijhof para 5.6.4.

Exempt agreements

8.12 Schedule 3 of the 1976 Act contains a list of exempt agreements. It is important to note that these exemptions *cannot* be cumulated: it is only possible to benefit from one in relation to any given agreement. Exempted agreements relating to goods include:
  (1) Exclusive dealing[1]
  (2) Know-how agreement[2]
  (3) Trade mark registered user agreements[3] – not, note, unregistered licence agreements, and not registered user agreements in respect of service marks.
  (4) Patent and Registered design licences and assignments[4]
  (5) Licences and assignments of unregistered design right[5]
  (6) Agreements with overseas operations[6]
  (7) Copyright licences and assignments[7]

1   Restrictive Trade Practices Act 1976, Sch 3, para 2.
2   Ibid, para 3.
3   Ibid, para 4.
4   Ibid, para 5.
5   Ibid, para 5B.
6   Ibid, para 6.
7   Ibid, para 5A.

8.13   Exempted agreements as to services include:
    (1) Exclusive supply of services agreements[1]
    (2) Know-how about services agreements[2]
    (3) Agreements with overseas operations[3]

1   Restrictive Trade Practices Act 1976, Sch 3, para 7.
2   Ibid, para 8.
3   Ibid, para 9.

8.14   If an agreement falls within the terms of one of these heads, it may contain the restrictions specified in the relevant paragraph of Schedule 3, and provided it contains no other relevant restrictions (after the application of section 9(3)) the agreement will not be registrable.

8.15   Copyright licences were not originally included, presumably because when the Act was first drafted it was not considered that it would apply to copyright licences anyway. At all events, a new paragraph added by the Competition Act 1980 now exempts copyright licence assignments, and agreements for licences and assignments, provided no relevant restrictions are accepted except in respect of the work or other subject matter in which copyright subsists. In *Academy Sound and Vision Ltd v WEA Records Ltd*[1] the defendants assigned their copyrights and other interests in certain recordings to the plaintiffs. There was a restriction as to the period for which the defendant could sell existing stocks in the United Kingdom and Eire, and a corresponding restriction on the plaintiffs selling into those markets during the same period. It was held that this provision was 'in respect of' the assignment of the copyright, and accordingly was exempted by this provision. The Restrictive Trade Practices Act 1976, accordingly, did not apply to the agreement.

1   [1983] ICR 586.

Time for furnishing particulars

8.16   If an agreement is caught by the Restrictive Trade Practices Act's provisions, particulars of it had to be furnished before the date on which any restriction accepted or any information provision made under the agreement takes effect, and in any case within three months of the day on which the agreement is made. Under the Deregulation (Restrictive Trade Practices Act 1976)(Amendment)(Time Limits) Order 1996[1] the time limit is now three months from the date of the agreement, but during such period it is unlawful to operate the relevant restricition.[2] The furnishing of particulars should generally be done by the licensor (it could be done by the licensee) and accompanied by a certificate in the form prescribed by Form RTP(C), signed by or on behalf of the person furnishing particulars.[3] There is no fee payable. Two copies of the agreement must be furnished. Where the documents do not disclose the name and address of any party to the agreement, two copies of a document indicating that person's name and address must be furnished, but if they exceed 100, individual names and addresses need not be furnished provided two copies of a document indicating their number (or approximate number) is supplied. For standard form agreements such as merchandising licences, once particulars have been furnished as above, all that needs subsequently to be furnished is a memorandum giving the dates of other agreements and the parties to them. This should refer to the agreement particulars of which have been furnished, and state that the new agreement(s) is (are) identical to it.[4] Failure to register renders void all restrictions accepted under the agreement,[5] ie presumably all relevant restrictions.[6]

1   1996/347.
2   Restrictive Trade Practices Act 1976 (as amended), s 27ZA inserted by SI 1996/347.
3   Restrictive Trading Agreements Regulations 1992. This form now asks questions about the economic effect of the agreement.
4   Ibid, Reg 4.
5   Restrictive Trade Practices Act 1976, s 35.
6   Ibid, s 35(1). The new sub-section (1) substitutes 'all' for 'relevant' in the Restrictive Trade Practices Act 1956. Since the 1976 Act is meant to be a consolidation however, presumably no intention existed to change the effect of the section, and there is a possible drafting reason for the change – see Adams and Prichard Jones *Franchising* (3rd edn, 1990) Butterworths, para 2.147.

8.17   Under the Deregulation and Contracting Out Act 1994[1] certain classes of agreement can be exempted by statutory instrument from the need to lodge for registration. The DTI's Consultation Paper of December 1994 proposed to designate the following categories of agreement as non-notifiable:

(1) Agreements where the total UK turnover of the parties is below £20 million.[2]

(2) Agreements where the combined market share of the parties for the products in question is below a threshold likely to be between 5% and 10%.[3]

(3) Agreements corresponding to the categories of agreement benefiting from the EC's block exemptions.[4]

The effect of the partial implementation of these proposals is to exempt a large number of the relatively small percentage of merchandising agreements, particulars of which at present need to be furnished, from the need to notify.

1   S 27A.
2   Restrictive Trade Practices (Non-notifiable Agreements)(Turnover Threshold) Order 1996, SI 1996/348.
3   Not yet implemented.
4   Restrictive Trade Practices (Non-notifiable Agreements)(EC Block Exemptions) Order 1996, SI 1996/349, and Restrictive Trade Practices Act 1976, s 27A inserted by s 10 of the Deregulation and Contracting Out Act 1994.

Registrable agreements and the EU provisions

8.18   The UK Regulations[1] which previously obliged parties to an agreement registrable under the Restrictive Trade Practices Act, which also fell within Article 85 of the Treaty of Rome, to inform the Office of

Fair Trading of any notification of that agreement or other communication with the EC concerning it, have been revoked.[2] Agreements which benefit from the application of a block exemption are also exempt from notification.[3]

1   Registration of Restrictive Trading Agreements (EEC Documents) Regulations 1973, SI 1973/950.
2   SI 1994/1095.
3   SI 1996/349 above. Only Reg 83/83 is likely to be relevant – see para 8.35.

How to approach the Restrictive Trade Practices Act 1976

8.19   If the agreement is not of a class exempted under the Deregulation and Contracting Out Act,[1] ask yourself the following questions:

(1) Is it in an agreement relating to goods? – Part II of the Act applies to agreements relating to goods.
(2) Is it in an agreement relating to services? – Part III of the Act applies to agreements relating to services. An agreement may relate both to goods and to services and therefore come under both Part II and Part III. In this case the application of Part II must be considered separately from the application of Part III.
(3) Are there two or more parties to the agreement carrying on business in the UK *either* in the manufacture or supply of goods *or* in the provision of services? If not, there is no need to worry further about the application of the Act.
(4) Does the agreement contain relevant restrictions accepted by two parties within the meaning of section 6 (or section 11), or does it contain information provisions which may be covered by the Act?
(5) Does the agreement contain restrictions which may be disregarded under section 9?
(6) If there are still restrictions accepted by two or more parties, go to Schedule 3[2] and consider whether or not the agreement qualifies for exemption under any *one* of its heads (you cannot cumulate exemptions).
(7) If the agreement does not qualify for exemption it is probable that particulars must be furnished.

Note: where the licensee is a company, it may be thought desirable to obtain restrictive agreements from individual directors. Such agreements can however result in relevant restrictions being accepted by two or more parties, and thus requires particulars to be furnished.

1   See para 8.17.
2   There are other exemptions contained in the Restrictive Trade Practices Act 1976, s 29 et seq, but they are unlikely to apply in our context.

'EFFECTS' LEGISLATION
Introduction

8.20   Both the Treaty of Rome and the Competition Act 1980 focus on the anti-competitive effects of agreements, rather than on the form of agreements. In either case, the concern is with agreements which have appreciable anti-competitive effects. Few individual merchandising licences are likely to have this, but it is to be noted that it is the cumulative effect of a network of agreements which will be considered, not each agreement in isolation.

8.21 Most lawyers in this country, used to the forms approach, find this type of competition law difficult to come to terms with. It requires consideration of the economic effects of agreements. For the purpose of licensing generally, it is possible to distinguish four types of agreement each with a significantly different economic consequence. However, in the case of merchandising licences, which are usually manufacturing licences, the thing which needs to be watched most closely is the artificial division of markets through the existence of national intellectual property rights and the problems this could cause in relation to EC competition law.

Common Market competition law

INTRODUCTION

8.22 Agency agreements can form an important element in a merchandising programme, and there is at present considerable uncertainty as to the status of agency agreements in EC competition law. In principle, an agent does not have a commercial existence separate from that of his principal and should therefore arguably be seen as part of the principal's business. On this view, the agreement between agent and principal, and any restrictions therein, would not fall within Article 85 at all. Since 1962, however,[1] the EC has held the view that there are circumstances where the agent should be regarded as an undertaking in its own right separate from the principal, with the effect that the laws are in principle applicable both to agency agreements with merchandising agents as well as to the licensing programme set up through these agents. The difficulty lies in telling when an agent will be independent: the test in the 1962 Notice[2] was that the agent accepted a financial risk. This is by no means the whole story now.[3] What follows is a very brief outline of a very complex area of law. For further reading, reference should be made to the standard works.[4]

1   See Notice on Exclusive Agency Contracts 1962 JO [1962] 139/291.
2   Above.
3   See Scholes and Blane 'Practical Law for Companies' IV/II Dec 1993, pp 39-48.
4   Butterworths Competition Law (looseleaf); Bellamy and Child *Common Market Law of Competition* (4th edn, 1993) Sweet & Maxwell, London; Whish *Competition Law* (3rd edn, 1993) Butterworths, London.

8.23 Article 85(1) of the Treaty of Rome prohibits all agreements between undertakings which may affect trade between Member States and which have as their object the prevention, restriction or distortion of competition within the common market. The article lists five groups of agreement which in particular are prohibited. These include agreements fixing selling prices and sharing of markets. Free movement of goods between Member States is an overriding concern of the market, and Articles 30 – 36 of the Treaty of Rome are also important whenever intellectual property is involved. All forms of intellectual property confer national rights, and the existence of such national rights has an inherent tendency to insulate markets. Whilst such property rights must be recognised by virtue of Article 222, it is well established that the protection of this article will be lost if the rights have been *exercised* in such a way as artificially to insulate markets. An important limitation on intellectual property rights is the doctrine of 'exhaustion of rights' under which if goods protected by an intellectual property right have been put into the market in one EU country by the owner of the right or with his consent (eg by a licensee), the rights owner cannot assert his property rights to prevent importation into another.[1]

1   See Adams & Prichard Jones, 'Franchising' (3rd edn, 1990), para 2.79 et seq.

8.24 The principal danger, in our context, is that the existence of separate intellectual property rights in each Member State will inhibit the free movement of goods between those states. As noted above, the existence of those rights is recognised by Article 222 of the Treaty, but Article 36 provides that such rights must not be used as a disguised restriction on trade: markets must not be divided artificially. Most merchandising licences are manufacturing licences, and in addition to the division of markets by virtue of the existence of intellectual property rights, there exists the possibility of markets becoming *de facto* divided by the fact that none of the licensees in the different countries has sufficient capacity to export. Whether or not this is a problem, will of course depend upon the size of the operation, but large operations involving well-known trade marks could run into difficulties if such a set-up is the result of their licensing programme. Because national intellectual property rights tend to insulate markets, attempts to prolong them through devices such as 'no challenge' clauses, in principle, are contrary to Article 85. However, it is permissible to make an agreement terminate on challenge.[1]

1   See Regulation 4087/88, Art 5(f); Precedent 1, clause 15.2.4.

8.25 Most merchandising contracts will not in any event significantly affect trade between Member States. The Notice on Agreements of Minor Importance,[1] which in its current form applies to agreements relating to services as well as goods, provides guidance on this. The Commission takes the view that agreements between undertakings engaged in the production or distribution of goods do not fall under the prohibition of Article 85 *if* the parties involved do not have more than 5% of the total market for the products in question and similar products taking the area of the EC affected by the agreement, *and* the aggregate turnover of the participants does not exceed ECU300 million.

1   OJ 1986 C231/2 updated OJ 1994 C 368/20.

8.26 An agreement which infringes Article 85 is automatically void.[1] Moreover, if not notified, a substantial fine may be imposed,[2] though for a vertical agreement such as a licence, which is not blatantly market insulating, this would, of course, be most unusual.

1   Art 85(2).
2   Reg 17, Art 15(2). Fines do not run for the period during which the agreement is notified – Reg 17(5) – unless the Commission has indicated after preliminary examination that it considers the agreement to infringe Art 85.

8.27 Notification must be made on form A/B.[1] Unless notified, an agreement cannot be granted negative clearance on the ground that the Commission consider that there are no grounds for action,[2] nor exemption under Article 85(3) on the ground, inter alia, that it improves the production or distribution of goods. Block exemption has been given for exclusive distribution and purchasing agreements which satisfy the criteria laid down in Regulations 1983/83 and 1984/83 respectively, but these are unlikely often to be of relevance in the context of merchandising. Certain agreements are excused notification, however.[3] These are agreements where:

(1) the only parties thereto are undertakings[4] from one Member State and do not relate to exports or imports;

(2) not more than two undertakings are parties thereto and the agreements only restrict the freedom of one party as to prices or conditions of business, or impose restrictions on the assignor or user of industrial property rights etc;

(3) they have as their sole object the development of uniform standards, or joint research and development, or specialisation in manufacture (subject to certain limits as to market share etc).

A rather curious distinction has been drawn between agreements which do not affect trade between Member States (not within the prohibition of Article 85 at all) and those which, though they must by definition be capable of affecting trade between EU countries, do not relate to imports and exports (excused from notification under Regulation 17/62 Article 4(2)(1)).[5] In practice, circumstances where it is clearly safe to rely on this exemption do not arise frequently, and it is not much relied on.[6] Agreements excused notification under Regulation 17 are not excused from the Article 85 prohibition and may nevertheless need to be notified for individual exemption under Article 85(3) if a block exemption is not available, where appropriate.[7] Agreements qualifying for block exemption are by definition also excused notification.

1   For procedure see Butterworths Competition Law X [261] et seq.
2   Reg 17, Art 2.
3   Reg 17, Art 4.
4   As to 'undertakings' see *UNITEL*, below. A network of agreements with different parties qualifies – Case 1/70: *Parfums Marcel Rochas Vertriebs-GmbH v Bitsch* [1970] ECR 515.
5   Case 43/69: *Brauerei Bilger Sohne GmbH v Jehle* [1970] ECR 127.
6   See Kerse *EC Anti-Trust Procedure* (3rd edn, 1994) pp 53-55.
7   Case 47/76: *De Norre v NV Brouwerij Concordia* [1977] ECR 65.

The UNITEL case

8.28 The one EEC case having direct bearing on the interpretation of some of these provisions in relation to merchandising is the *UNITEL* case.[1] It must therefore be discussed, although it must be borne in mind that it is only a Commission decision.

1   *Re UNITEL Film-Und Fernse-Produktionsgesellschaft mbH & Co*, Case 78/516 [1978] 3 CMLR 306.

8.29 Radio Televisione Italiana was planning to broadcast a gala performance of Verdi's 'Don Carlos'. Four of the singers had contracts with UNITEL under which they had agreed not to take part in any film or television production of this opera without the consent of UNITEL. Radio Televisione Italiana reported the matter to the Commission, who in turn asked UNITEL for information on various matters. UNITEL objected to this request on five grounds, of which three are material for our purposes:

(1) that artistes were not undertakings for the purposes of Article 85(1);

(2) that the exclusive commitments between UNITEL and its singers qualified for exemption under Regulation 67/67 (the predecessor of 1983/83);

(3) that the exclusive commitments did not affect trade between Member States.

8.30 The Commission reached the following decisions:

(1) that artistes exploiting their talents commercially are undertakings for the purposes of Article 85(1);

(2) that Regulation 1967/67[1] did not apply to the provision of services, so that no exemption could be claimed for the commercial exploitation of artistic performances;

(3) that the contracts might affect trade between Member States for the purposes of Article 85.

This decision has obvious application to some aspects of personality merchandising. Personalities exploiting their talents commercially are 'undertakings' for the purposes of Article 85(1). In consequence, licence agreements etc, entered into by them are subject to the provisions of the Treaty.

1   Now replaced by 83/83.

The Application of Article 85 to manufacturing licences

8.31 Most merchandising licences are manufacturing licences. The intellectual property rights licensed are generally trade marks and copyright. Both of these rights depend upon the national laws of the Member States. Under the international conventions, states are only obliged to accord to nationals of other convention states the same protection that they afford to their own nationals. Of the EC states, only the United Kingdom affords protection of a copyright nature to ordinary industrial designs.[1] Consequently, the fact that a product enjoyed copyright protection in the United Kingdom could not be used to prevent its importation into Germany, where the same protection might only be obtainable through a petty patent. Subject to this, all national intellectual property rights have the inherent tendency to insulate markets. The first limitation to such insulation of markets, at least in relation to copyright, is the doctrine of exhaustion of rights. If goods are put into the market by a person, or by his consent, he cannot assert property rights so as to prevent their importation into another Member State.[2] The situation in relation to trade marks is a little different, because obviously products bearing the same mark may differ. In some early cases, the court came close to propounding a *per se* rule that if trade marks had a common origin, then markets were artificially divided.[3] In the *Terrapin* case,[4] however, the court recognised the importance of the question of the similarity of the products. It also clarified the respective roles of the national courts and the Court of Justice in considering this question:

'It is for the court at first instance, after considering the similarity of the products, and the risk of confusion, to enquire further in the context of this last provision into whether the exercise in a particular case of industrial and commercial property rights may or may not constitute a means of arbitrary discrimination or a disguise restriction on trade between Member States.'

1   See Copyright, Designs and Patents Act 1988, s 213 et seq.
2   Case 78/70: *Deutsche Grammophon GmbH v Metro-SB-Grossmarkte GmbH & Co KG* [1971] ECR 487. *Keurkoop BV v Nancy Kean Gifts BV*: 144/81 [1982] ECR 2853, [1983] 2 CMLR 47.
3   Especially in Case 192/73: *Van Zuylen Freres v Hag AG* [1974] ECR 731.
4   Case 119/75: *Terrapin (Overseas) Ltd v Terranova Industrie CA Kapferer & Co* [1976] ECR 1039. See also Case 24/67: *Parke Davis & Co v Probel* [1968] ECR 55.

8.32 Leaving aside the insulation of markets through the existence of intellectual property rights, it is to be remembered that *de facto* insulation can be the result of setting up a chain of producers, none of whom individually have the capacity to indulge in exports and who have no incentive to do so anyway if local demand is good. If the various licences are exclusive, so that the licensor cannot license further producers, the markets will remain insulated. In such a case the exclusive licence provisions would certainly be contrary to Article 85(1).[1] Non-competition and 'no challenge' clauses,[2] can also contribute to market insulation in such cases. Even in the absence of any restrictive clauses, a course of conduct pursued by a licensor and his licensees to preserve the separation of their markets within the EC would be contrary to Article 85(1).

1   *Re Agreements of Davidson Rubber Co* [1972] CMLR D52.
2   See eg *Vaessen (H) BV v Alex Moris and Moris PVBA*: 79/86 [1979] 1 CMLR 511.

8.33 Restrictive agreements between traders within the EC and traders outside which would bring about an isolation of the EC as a whole, and which would reduce the supply of products originating in the country outside the EC, similar to those protected by a mark within the EC, might affect the conditions of competition within the EC.[1] However, a restriction on exporting from the EC, to such non-Member States, would not have anti-competitive implications, unless its effect was likely to be significantly to prevent parallel imports.[2]

1   *EMI Records Ltd v CBS Grammofon A/S*: 86/75 [1976] ECR 871.
2   See eg *Re Goodyear Italiana SpA Application*: 75/94 (1975) OJ L38/10, [1975] 1 CMLR D31.

8.34 The above is only a sketch of a very complex area. We have endeavoured only to alert the reader to the dangers. For a full exposition, reference should be made to the standard works.[1]

1   See works listed in para 8.22, n 4 above.

Exclusive distribution agreements

8.35 Exclusive distribution agreements may incidentally be entered into in the course of a licensing programme. If so, care should be taken to bring them within the terms of the block exemption Regulation 1983/83.[1] They raise no special problems in this context, and the standard works may be referred to for precedents.[2]

1   See Korah *Exclusive Dealing Agreements in the EEC* (1984) European Law Centre.
2   See Encyclopaedia of Forms and Precedents, vol 1, title 'Agency'.

How to approach Article 85(1)

8.36   Although they may not be directly relevant, the existing block exemptions' lists of 'black clauses' and 'white clauses' can be helpful in providing guidance as to what is likely to be acceptable. Subject to this, the following should be borne in mind:

(1) If the agreement takes the usual form of a licence of intellectual property rights to a manufacturer, it is necessary to consider not only the effect of the agreement itself, but the possible effect of the agreement in the context of a network of other such agreements, on trade between Member States, bearing in mind the guidance provided by the Notice on Minor Agreements.

(2) If Article 85(1) may be infringed, consider whether or not the agreement is likely to qualify for individual exemption under Article 85(3) or under any relevant block exemption. In order to gain individual exemption it must be notified, even if otherwise exempt from the need to notify under Regulation 17, Article 4. Agreements qualifying for block exemption are also excused from the requirement of notification of course.[1]

(3) If it is concluded that the agreement is notifiable this is to be done on form A/B and negative clearance and exemption applied for at the same time.[2]

1   As well as those relating to exclusive distribution on purchasing agreements (Regs 83/83 and 84/83) the only other one likely to be relevant in the present context is that relating to technology transfer agreements – Regulation 240/96.
2   For procedure see Butterworths Competition Law, loc cit, para 8.27, n 1 above.

8.37   The decision whether or not to notify is a strategic one to be taken in the light of the following factors:

(1) In favour of notification –
   (a) you are safe from fines (which can be considerable);
   (b) the agreement can be granted individual exemption, though a 'comfort letter' is the more likely outcome. These simply state that the Commission has closed its file, they do not give conclusive validity to an otherwise void agreement.

(2) Against notification –
   (a) You may be required to modify terms and therefore to have to renegotiate your agreements. Given that some time may have elapsed by the time this occurs, it might have to be done when your relative bargaining strength has weakened. However, it is to be borne in mind, if you do not notify, that 'Euro-issues' could be raised in any litigation with your licensees, and you might then find yourself in a difficult position.

Competition Act 1980

8.38   This Act seeks to control practices which are anti-competitive, ie a course of conduct pursued by a person which of itself, or when taken together with a course pursued by other persons associated with him, may have the effect of restricting, distorting or preventing competition. The Act specifies no particular types of anti-competitive practice (unlike Article 85(1)), but the Office of Fair Trading's Guide to the Act mentions various anti-competitive practices in relation to pricing policy and distribution policy.

8.39 The Competition Act 1980 is unlikely to affect many merchandising arrangements, simply because practices carried on by a person *either* with an annual turnover of less than £10 million *or* less than 25% of market share, are excluded.[1] Even though a group of inter-connected bodies corporate are aggregated for this purpose, it is improbable that their turnover or market share will exceed the limit. Arrangements registrable under the Restrictive Trade Practices Act 1976 are excluded from the purview of the Competition Act 1980. If a practice does fall within the Competition Act 1980, and the Director General in any investigation finds a practice which is anti-competitive and is not satisfied by undertakings, the matter can be referred to the Monopolies and Mergers Commission.

1   Competition Act 1980, s 2(2). Anti-Competitive Practices (Exclusions) Order 1980, SI 1980/979, as amended by SI 1994/1557.

8.40 How to approach the Competition Act 1980:
  (1) Does the agreement require registration under the Restrictive Trade Practices Act 1976? If it does, there is no need to consider the application of this Act (though other provisions including Article 85(1) need to be considered).
  (2) Does the business exceed the thresholds *either* of market share *or* turnover? If not, there is no need to consider this Act further (and it is likely that the agreement will come within the Notice on Minor Agreements for the purposes of Article 85(1), ie there should be no need to notify for negative clearance or exemption, but the application of EC law should nevertheless be separately considered).

8.41 If the agreement could come within the scope of the Act, it is possible meanwhile to carry on safely (though possibly not in relation to the EC provisions), but it may be advisable to think up some arguments that the effects of the agreements are pro-competitive, against the off-chance of intervention by the Director General of Fair Trading.

RESTRAINT OF TRADE AT COMMON LAW

8.42 At common law, all restraints of trade are void in the absence of justifying circumstances,[1] but are not illegal. Typical restraints caught by the doctrine are covenants not to carry on a similar trade within a certain distance of business premises etc, or not to carry on a similar trade for a certain time after the expiry of an agreement. 'Solus' ties are another example. These were the subject of much litigation in the 1960s and provide the principal modern guidance as to the application of the doctrine. It is difficult to pin down its basis. Is it designed to preserve free competition, or to protect the weak from the strong?[2]

1   *Nordenfelt v Maxim Nordenfelt Guns and Ammunition Co* [1894] AC 535.
2   See *Anson on Contract* (ed Guest) (26th edn, 1984) OUP, p 319.

8.43   It is possible to derive some useful guidance as to its application from *Esso Petroleum Co Ltd v Harper's Garage (Stourport) Ltd.*[1] In this case the 'opening the door' principle, previously discussed, was proposed as a limitation to the doctrine, and some guidelines were proposed, the most relevant to our subject being:
   (1)   The court will look not at each agreement separately, but the trading pattern which emerges from a group of similar agreements.
   (2)   The court will consider the benefits received in return for the restraints.
   (3)   Terms requiring approval by the licensor of prospective assignees of the licence, must be reasonable.
   (4)   The court will consider the relative bargaining strength of the parties.

1   [1968] AC 269.

8.44   By far the most likely terms in licences likely to come into conflict with the doctrine are restraints on sales outside a licensee's territory. Given the fact that without the intellectual property licence the manufacturer could not make the goods at all, and the fact that the 'opening the door' principle is recognised in relation to the doctrine of restraint of trade, it should not be arguable that the manufacturer is unreasonably restrained, even without reference to the guidelines set out above. The doctrine is also important in relation to the restraint of trade clauses often imposed on former agents, and this, of course, includes merchandising agents. It is important, therefore, to keep such covenants in restraint of trade to the minimum necessary to protect the merchandiser's legitimate interests presumably in geographical extent, subject-matter and time.[2]

2   See Precedent 2, clause 6.5. It is possible to build in a fall back position into this clause, and in certain cases, this may be desirable. If a number of separate agreements are to be negotiated for the UK, it is advisable to leave the time and extent of the clause blank, and to fill these in in ink as each separate agreement requires. It is unlikely that a standard form clause would otherwise meet every individual circumstance.

Chapter 9

Tax aspects

INTRODUCTION

9.1 It is the object of this chapter to highlight the main areas where United Kingdom taxation impacts on the exploitation of merchandising rights, rather than to provide a comprehensive review of the taxes concerned, and readers requiring a more detailed explanation of the general application of those taxes should refer to one of the many specialist works on the subject.

9.2 As has been seen in the earlier chapters of this work, 'merchandising rights' do not exist as a *sui generis* form of legal protection. A person seeking to control the use of a name or likeness of a real or imaginary character on merchandise produced by others will be relying primarily on the protection afforded to copyright material, trademarks and designs.[1] Goodwill and know-how may also be important.

1 Registered designs are governed by the Registered Designs Act 1949, as amended by the Copyright, Designs and Patents Act 1988. Unregistered design right is protected by Part III of the Copyright, Designs and Patents Act 1988.

9.3 Patent rights are unlikely to be relevant in the context of this work and, although their tax treatment differs in a number of respects from that described in this chapter for other forms of intellectual property, they are ignored for the purposes of this chapter.

9.4 Since character merchandising is a relatively new industry, there have been few tax cases specifically involving it. Tax cases concerning copyright will, of course, be as relevant to forms of merchandising which rely on copyright protection as they are to other forms of copyright material. There is hardly any tax law exclusively relating to trademarks and designs. In practice, care should be taken to distinguish the form or forms of legal protection embodied within a merchandising agreement, as the tax treatment of each may differ but for convenience, the expression 'merchandising rights' is used in this chapter as a generic term covering each such form or forms of legal protection where the tax treatment does not differ.

9.5 The UK taxes which are relevant for present purposes are: income and corporation tax (in relation to which we consider separately the position of the UK resident rights owner whether a creator or otherwise, the overseas rights owner and the licensee of merchandising rights, and then explain the special rules affecting personal appearances in the UK by non-resident entertainers and sports personalities); capital gains tax; value added tax; inheritance tax and, stamp duty.

INCOME AND CORPORATION TAX

9.6 A person exploiting merchandising rights may be doing so in the course of carrying out a trade, profession or vocation[1] or may be exploiting property which he holds as an investment.[2] There may be intermediate Cases to which Schedule D, Case VI[3] applies. This distinction is crucial, as each Case has its own rules for determining how the taxable profits are computed, what expenditure may be deducted from gross income for this purpose, and when the tax due becomes payable. The distinction is also important for withholding tax purposes.[4]

1 The profits of a trade are taxed under Schedule D, Case I, while the profits of a profession or vocation are taxed under Schedule D, Case II. To all intents and purposes, the liability to tax under these Cases is the same. A company can trade, but it does not have the personal qualities to carry on a profession or vocation (*IRC v Peter McIntyre Ltd* (1926) 12 TC 1006). Rights in material produced in the course of a profession or vocation are not 'stock-in-trade', so the rule in *Sharkey v Wernher* [1956] AC 58, 36 TC 275 (which establishes the principle that where a trader takes stock from his business for private use or enjoyment or disposes of stock otherwise than by sale in the normal course of trade, the transfer should be dealt with for tax purposes as if it were a sale at market value) does not apply: *Mason v Innes* [1967] Ch 1079, [1967] 2 All ER 926, 44 TC 326. ICTA 1988, s 775 (see paras 9.32–9.35 post) applies to individuals carrying on activities of any of the kinds pursued in any profession or vocation, but not trade.
2 The income from which may be taxable under Schedule D, Case III as an 'other annual payment': ICTA 1988, s 18(3). See para 9.48 et seq post.
3 See para 9.37 post.
4 See para 9.108 et seq post.

Trade

9.7 'Trade' is defined, rather unhelpfully, by section 832(1) of the Income and Corporation Taxes Act 1988 as including 'every trade, manufacture, adventure or concern in the nature of trade'. There have been numerous cases on the subject, and each case will depend on its own particular facts.

9.8 The question of whether a particular activity constitutes a trade will be decided by the General or Special Commissioners. The primary facts found by the Commissioners, and the inferences to be drawn from those facts, are treated as questions of fact, although the statutory construction of 'trade' is a question of law. This means that, under the principles in *Edwards v Bairstow and Harrison*,[1] the court cannot set aside the findings of the Commissioners on a question of fact if it was one to which they were entitled to come, notwithstanding that the court or another body of Commissioners might have reached a different conclusion on the same evidence, unless the court is satisfied that the inferences of fact could not reasonably have been drawn from the primary facts by any body of Commissioners who had properly directed themselves on the law.

1 [1956] AC 14, [1955] 3 All ER 48, 36 TC 207.

9.8 *Tax aspects*

9.9 In 1954, the Royal Commission on the Taxation of Profits and Income (the Radcliffe Commission) published its final report[1] which identified[2] six so-called 'badges of trade' as follows.

(1) **The subject matter of the realisation**

Whilst almost any form of property can be acquired to be dealt in, those forms of property, such as commodities or manufactured articles, which are normally the subject of trading are only very exceptionally the subject of investment. Again property which does not yield to its owner income or personal enjoyment merely by virtue of its ownership is more likely to have been acquired with the object of a deal than property that does.

(2) **Length of period of ownership**

Generally speaking property meant to be dealt in is realised within a short time after acquisition. There are many exceptions from this as the general rule.

(3) **The frequency or number of similar transactions by the same person**

If realisations of the same sort of property occur in succession over a period of years or there are several such realisations at about the same date, a presumption arises that there has been dealing in respect of each.

(4) **Supplementary work on or in connection with the property realised**

If the property is worked up in any way during the ownership so as to bring it into a more marketable condition; or if any special exertions are made to find or attract purchasers, such as the opening of an office or large-scale advertising, there is some evidence of dealing. For when there is an organised effort to obtain profit there is a source of taxable income. But if nothing at all is done, the suggestion tends the other way.

(5) **The circumstances that were responsible for the realisation**

There may be some explanation, such as a sudden emergency or opportunity calling for ready money, that negatives the idea that any plan of dealing prompted the original purchase.

(6) **Motive**

There are cases in which the purpose of the transaction of purchase and sale is clearly discernible. Motive is never irrelevant in any of these cases. What is desirable is that it should be realised clearly that it can be inferred from surrounding circumstances in the absence of direct evidence of the seller's intentions and even, if necessary, in the face of his own evidence.

1 Cmnd 9474.
2 At para 116.

9.10 These 'badges of trade' were restated, with helpful comments, by Sir Nicolas Browne-Wilkinson V-C in *Marson v Morton*,[1] which concerned the question of whether the sale of land, originally acquired as an investment but resold much sooner than was originally intended, amounted to an adventure in the nature of trade.

Like the Commissioners, I have been treated to an extensive survey of the authorities. But as far as I can see there is only one point which as a matter of law is clear, namely that a single, one-off transaction can be an adventure in the nature of trade. Beyond that I found it impossible to find any single statement of law which is applicable to all cases in all circumstances. I have been taken through the cases and invited to compare the facts in some cases with the facts in the case here before me. I fear that the General Commissioners may have become as confused by that process as I did. The purpose of authority is to find principle, not to seek analogies on the facts.

It is clear that the question whether or not there has been an adventure in the nature of trade depends on all the facts and circumstances of each particular case and depends on the interaction between the various factors that are present in any given case. The most that I have been able to detect from the reading of the authorities is that there are certain features or badges which may point to one conclusion rather than another. In relation to transactions such as this, that is to say a one-off deal with a view to making a capital profit, there do seem to be certain things which the authorities show have been looked at. For convenience I will refer to them in a moment but I would emphasise that the factors I am going to refer to are in no sense a comprehensive list of all relevant factors, nor is any one of them so far as I can see decisive in all cases. The most they can do is provide common sense guidance to the conclusion which is appropriate.

The matters which are apparently treated as a badge of trading are as follows:
(1) That the transaction in question was a one-off transaction. Although a one-off transaction is in law capable of being an adventure in the nature of trade, obviously the lack of repetition is a pointer which indicates there might not here be trade but something else.
(2) Is the transaction in question in some way related to the trade which the taxpayer otherwise carries on? For example, a one-off purchase of silver cutlery by a general dealer is much more likely to be a trade transaction than such a purchase by a retired colonel.
(3) The nature of the subject matter may be a valuable pointer. Was the transaction in a commodity of a kind which is normally the subject matter of trade and which can only be turned to advantage by realisation, such as referred to in the passage that the chairman quoted from *Reinhold*.[2] For example, a large bulk of whisky or toilet paper is essentially a subject matter of trade, not of enjoyment.
(4) In some cases attention has been paid to the way in which the transaction was carried through: was it carried through in a way typical of the trade in a commodity of that nature?
(5) What was the source of finance of the transaction? If the money was borrowed that is some pointer towards an intention to buy the item with a view to its resale in the short term: a fair pointer towards trade.
(6) Was the item which was purchased resold as it stood or was work done on it or relating to it for the purposes of resale? For example, the purchase of secondhand machinery which was repaired or improved before resale. If there was such work done, that is again a pointer towards the transaction being in the nature of trade.

147

9.10 *Tax aspects*

(7) Was the item purchased resold in one lot as it was bought, or was it broken down into saleable lots? If it was broken down it is again some indication that it was a trading transaction, the purpose being with a view to resale at profit by doing something in relation to the object bought.

(8) What were the purchaser's intentions as to resale at the time of purchase? If there was an intention to hold the object indefinitely, albeit with an intention to make a capital profit at the end of the day, that is a pointer towards a pure investment as opposed to a trading deal. On the other hand, if before the contract of purchase is made a contract for resale is already in place, that is a very strong pointer towards a trading deal rather than an investment. Similarly, an intention to resell in the short term rather than the long term is some indication against concluding that the transaction was by way of investment rather than by way of a deal. However, as far as I can see, this is in no sense decisive by itself.

(9) Did the item purchased either provide enjoyment for the purchaser (for example, a picture) or pride of possession or produce income pending resale? If it did, then that may indicate an intention to buy either for personal satisfaction or to invest for income yield, rather than do a deal purely for the purpose of making a profit on the turn. I will consider in a moment the question whether, if there is no income produced or pride of purchase pending resale, that is a strong pointer in favour of it being a trade rather than an investment.

I emphasise again that the matters I have mentioned are not a comprehensive list and no single item is in any way decisive. I believe that in order to reach a proper factual assessment in each case it is necessary to stand back, having looked at those matters, and look at the whole picture and ask the question – and for this purpose it is no bad thing to go back to the words of the Statute – was this an adventure in the nature of trade? In some cases perhaps more homely language might be appropriate by asking the question, was the taxpayer investing the money or was he doing a deal?

1   [1986] 1 WLR 1343, [1986] STC 463, 59 TC 381.
2   *IRC v Reinhold* 1953 SC 49, 34 TC 389.

9.11   In *Noddy Subsidiary Rights Co Ltd v IRC*[1] the taxpayer company was formed, among other things, to carry on and develop the business of exploiting and turning to account the fictitious character 'Noddy' or 'Little Noddy', to grant licences for use of this fictitious character by name or by pictorial representation or in the shape of dolls, toys, mechanical figures or other articles on royalty terms, to carry on business as proprietors of a licence from the respective owners of the literary and artistic copyright in the said fictitious character and to grant sub-licences on terms considered proper. Under the licence agreement from the two companies that owned, respectively, the literary and artistic copyright in the characters, no sub-licences were to be granted until the nature and form of the proposed exploitation had been approved by the two companies, and any authorised reproduction had to be closely based on actual copyright drawings, with examples of any proposed use being subject to approval by the taxpayer

148

company. This company granted licences to manufacturers in a standard form which required samples of licensed articles and containers and illustrated packing proposed to be submitted to it for approval before sale, and all advertising and publicity material to be similarly submitted for approval. It undertook to supply to the licensee at reasonable prices any pictures, photographs, sketches and artwork reasonably required. It employed as a general manager an assistant on the staff of an associated company, who was paid exclusively by the associated company. The manager worked at the office of one of the copyright-owning companies, and was assisted by a secretary and another girl on that company's staff. He gave half his time to the taxpayer company's work, visiting fairs to find items which would make promising 'Noddy' lines, and otherwise seeking out applications for licences, entertaining prospective customers at cocktail parties, dealing with applications, consulting on them with the 'Noddy' author, granting licences in appropriate cases (normally for a year only), discouraging applications or rejecting those not up to standard (at one stage over half were rejected), and watching the toy trade for infringements. There was much correspondence and many licences were granted. The Special Commissioner concluded that the taxpayer company was not carrying on a trade, but this was overturned by Pennycuick J, who concluded 'without hesitation' that the activities of the taxpayer company during the relevant years amounted to a trade:

> I have in mind in this connection the terms of the company's Memorandum, the fact that [the manager] spent half his working time managing the company's affairs, the fact that he actively sought out customers, that he exercised when dealing with the licences when granted, skill and labour of a continuous and variegated kind. Those activities seem to me to contain all the elements of a trade, and once it is accepted, as it now must be, that [the manager] was acting on behalf of the taxpayer company, it is, I think, irrelevant that he received his remuneration from some other source. The only respect in which it might be said that these activities do not contain the common elements of a trade is that the taxpayer company has no separate office or staff, but I do not think that that circumstance of itself is enough to prevent the activities from amounting to a trade. The activities admittedly go beyond investment in the ordinary sense...I can myself see no reason for denying to its activities the title of a trade and placing them in the residual category of Case VI, Schedule D.

1   [1967] 1 WLR 1, [1966] 3 All ER 459, 43 TC 458, .

9.12   The *Noddy* case was, however, distinguished by a Special Commissioner in the recent case of *British Olympic Association v Winter*.[1] The British Olympic Association is a company whose objects, among other things, are to encourage interest in the Olympic Games and to organise and coordinate British participation. As part of its fundraising to finance the sending of a British team to the Olympic Games, it licensed commercial sponsors to exploit its logo, licensed the manufacture of merchandise bearing the logo, and solicited donations. The Inland Revenue contended that the Association was carrying on a trade of exploiting its logo and granting the status of sponsor, but the Commissioner rejected that submission. He held that the test for determining whether or not a trade was being carried on was whether the operations involved in the venture were of the same kind, and carried on in the same way, as those which were characteristic of ordinary trading in the line of business in which the venture was made. Although some of the Association's activities appeared to be commercial in that a very commercial approach was adopted when dealing with commercial sponsors, many of its activities and functions were non-commercial. The sending of a team to the Games was partly financed by innumerable small gifts from the public. In addition, some sponsors were paying not only towards the sending of a team but to be associated with them to support the Association's other activities. The Association was not merely exploiting its logo. Its activities were far wider, and they were so intertwined as to form a melange. It was not possible to isolate the earning of the sponsorship income and this was not earned simply by the grant of the right of the use of the logo. On the facts, the Association's activities as a whole were uncommercial and did not constitute a trade.

1   [1995] STC (SCD) 85.

9.13   These cases illustrate the principle that, with merchandising as with any other undertaking, it is necessary to examine all the facts to ascertain whether the activities involved go beyond mere investment, and whether they are of a kind, and are carried on in a way which, taken as a whole and having regard to the so called 'badges of trade', is characteristic of trading.

Profession or vocation

9.14   The terms 'profession' and 'vocation' are not defined anywhere in tax legislation. The judicial definition of 'profession' most often quoted is that of Scrutton LJ in *IRC v Maxse*[1] where an author who published his own works was held to be carrying on both the profession of an author and the trade of publishing:

> I am very reluctant finally to propound a comprehensive definition. A set of facts not present to the mind of the judicial propounder, and not raised in the case before him, may immediately arise to confound his proposition. But it seems to me as at present advised that a 'profession' in the present use of language involves the idea of an occupation requiring either purely intellectual skill, or of any manual skill controlled, as in painting and sculpture or surgery, by the intellectual skill of the operator, as distinguished from an occupation which is substantially the production or sale or arrangements for the production or sale of commodities. The line of demarcation may vary from time to time. The word 'profession' used to be confined to the three learned professions, the Church, Medicine and Law. It has now, I think, a wider meaning.

1   [1919] 1 KB 647, 12 TC 41.

9.15   A journalist and editor has been held[1] to be carrying on a profession, as have an actress[2] and an entertainer,[3] but a photographer,[4] a dance band leader,[5] and a film production executive[6] have been held not to be.

1   In *IRC v Maxse*, supra; *Mason v Innes*, supra.

2 *Davies v Braithwaite* [1931] 2 KB 628, 18 TC 198; *Shiner v Lindblom* [1961] 1 WLR 248, [1960] 3 All ER 832, 39 TC 367.
3 *Radcliffe v IRC* (1956) 56 Taxation 612.
4 *Cecil v IRC* (1919) 36 TLR 164.
5 *Loss v IRC* [1945] 2 All ER 683.
6 *Asher v London Film Productions Ltd* [1944] KB 133.

9.16 'Vocation' has been described[1] as 'analogous to "calling", a word of wide signficance, meaning the way in which a man passes his life'. Authors[2] and dramatists[3] have been variously described as carrying on a vocation and as carrying on a profession.

1 By Denman J in *Partridge v Mallandaine* (1886) 18 QBD 276, 2 TC 179.
2 *Glasson v Rougier* [1944] 1 All ER 535, 26 TC 86; *Howson v Monsell* [1950] 2 All ER 1239n, 31 TC 529.
3 *Billam v Griffiths* (1941) 23 TC 757.

UK resident rights owner

THE PROFESSIONAL CREATOR

9.17 Once it is established that a person who creates material in which merchandising rights subsists, such as an author or illustrator, is resident in the United Kingdom,[1] and is carrying on a profession or vocation, such person will be liable to income tax under Schedule D, Case II in respect of the annual profits or gains arising or accruing to him from the profession or vocation, whether carried on in the United Kingdom or elsewhere.[2] For this purpose, all receipts from the profession or vocation in the relevant year of assessment will be taken into account, whether royalties or lump sums[3] or non-returnable advances,[4] and regardless of whether the rights have been licensed or assigned.[5] As Romer LJ stated in *MacKenzie v Arnold*:[6]

> An author may derive profit from the exercise of his skill and experience as a writer by receiving royalties from his books, by selling the copyrights of his books, or partly by doing the one and partly by doing the other. It seems to me that whichever way is adopted by the author, it has the similar characteristic of being a way of exploiting and bringing to the notice of the public, for the benefit of the author, his works, and the profit which comes to him from whichever of the ways he adopts is to be regarded as a profit or gain for the year of assessment in which he receives it, arising or accruing to him from his profession...

1 See para 9.63 et seq below.
2 ICTA 1988, s 18(1)(a) and (3). For overseas aspects, see paras 9.55–9.56 and 9.61–9.62 below.
3 See cases cited in footnote 2 to para 9.16 ante.
4 *IRC v Longmans Green & Co* (1932) 17 TC 272; *Taylor v Dawson* (1938) 22 TC 189. A returnable advance will be treated as a loan.
5 *Billam v Griffiths* ante and *MacKenzie v Arnold* (1952) 33 TC 363.
6 (1952) 33 TC 363.

BACKWARD SPREADING

9.18 Where an author,[1] assigns or licenses any interest in the copyright in a literary, dramatic, musical or artistic work, on the making of which

he has been engaged for a period of more than 12 months, he may, on
making a claim under section 534(1) of the Income and Corporation Taxes
Act 1988, spread his tax liability in respect of certain payments,[2] which
would otherwise all be included in the computation of his profits or gains
for a single year of assessment, backwards over two or three years of
assessment, depending on the duration of the period for which he was
engaged on the making of the work. If the author was engaged on the
making of the work for a period of more than 12, but not more than 24,
months, only one-half of the amount of any relevant payment will then be
treated as having become receivable on the date on which it actually
became receivable, and the remaining half will be treated as having become
receivable 12 months before that date. If the period for which the author
was engaged on the work exceeds 24 months, the effect of a claim under
Section 534 is that only one-third of the payment will then be treated as
having become receivable on the date on which it actually became
receivable, with one-third being treated as having become receivable 12
months and one-third 24 months before that date.

1   Including a joint author: ICTA 1988, s 534(7)(a).
2   Namely lump sum payments (including non-returnable advances on account of
    royalties) and any royalty payments which become receivable not more than two years
    after first publication of the work.

9.19   A claim under section 534(1) may be made any time not later than
seven years from 31 January next following the year of assessment in
which first publication occurs.[1]

1   ICTA 1988, s 534(7)(b). ICTA 1988, s 534(5) as amended by Finance Act 1994, ss 196,
    199(1) and (2)(a) and Sch 9, para 39. A work is first published on the first occasion
    when it, or a reproduction of it, is published, performed or exhibited.

9.20   Section 537 of the Income and Corporation Taxes Act 1988 extends
the provisions of section 534 to public lending right, and section 537A
contains identical provisions in relation to registered and unregistered
designs. Section 538 contains similar backward spreading provisions for
sums received by an artist by way of commission or fee for the creation of
any painting, sculpture or other work of art which he sells, where he was
engaged for a period of more than 12 months on the making of the work of
art, or in making a number of works of art, including the work, for an
exhibition.

FORWARD SPREADING

9.21   As an alternative to a claim under section 534, section 535 of the
Income and Corporation Taxes Act 1988 provides that, where an author[1]
of a literary, dramatic, musical or artistic work assigns or licenses for a
period of not less than two years any interest in the copyright in the work
in consideration of a lump sum payment, including a non-returnable
advance on account of royalties, which would otherwise be included in the
computation of his profits or gains for a single year of assessment, he may,
by making a claim under this section, spread the tax liability forward over
a number of years, depending on the length of the assignment or licence.

1   Including a joint author: ICTA 1988, s 535(11).

152

9.22 Where the copyright or interest is assigned or granted for a period of not less than six years, only one-sixth of the amount of the payment is then taxed as if it had become receivable on the date when the payment actually became receivable, with the remaining five-sixths being treated for income tax purposes as if it had become receivable in five equal instalments at yearly intervals thereafter.[1] Where the copyright or interest is assigned or granted for a period of less than six years, the payment may be spread forward in equal annual instalments over a correspondingly reduced period.[2]

1 ICTA, s 535(2).
2 ICTA, s 535(3).

9.23 If the author dies or otherwise permanently discontinues his profession or vocation, any instalment which, following a claim under section 535, would have been treated as becoming receivable after the date of death or permanent discontinuance, is treated as having become receivable on the date when the last instalment before the death or discontinuance was treated as having become receivable.[1] However, the author (in the case of a permanent discontinuance of his profession or vocation otherwise than on death) or his personal representatives (in the case of the author's death) may elect, within two years of the death or discontinuance, to have the tax recalculated on the basis that the relevant payment is treated as having become payable in equal annual instalments beginning with the date when the first instalment was treated as having become receivable and ending with the day before the death or discontinuance.[2]

1 ICTA 1988, s 535(4).
2 ICTA 1988, s 535(5) and (6).

9.24 Section 535 applies to public lending right in the same way as to copyright,[1] but there are no corresponding forward spreading provisions for payments in respect of designs or for the sale of works of art.

1 ICTA 1988, s 537.

9.25 A claim cannot be made under section 534 in respect of a payment if a prior claim has been made under section 535 in respect of that payment,[1] and vice versa.[2]

1 ICTA 1988, s 534(6).
2 ICTA 1988, s 535(9).

Cessation of profession

9.26 It may be very difficult for a person who has been carrying on a profession or vocation to persuade the Inland Revenue that he has ceased to do so during his lifetime. An author, for example, does not cease to carry on his profession or vocation merely because he has ceased active writing. In *MacKenzie v Arnold*,[1] the writer Compton MacKenzie was assessed to tax under Schedule D, Case II in 1943/44 and 1944/45 on lump sums received for the assignment of copyright in 20 books he had written between 1911 and 1930, while resident in Australia. It was held that he had been carrying on the profession of an author from 1907 onwards and, having become resident in the United Kingdom in 1930, had been correctly assessed on the lump sums received for the assignment.

1   For reference, see para 9.17, n 6, above.

9.27   The tax position on assigning copyright may be different where a person has not been carrying on a profession or vocation. In *Withers v Nethersole*,[1] Mrs Nethersole acquired from Rudyard Kipling in 1897 the exclusive right to dramatise his novel 'The Light that Failed'. The play was duly written, and Mrs Nethersole retained the copyright. In 1914, when the question of a film version arose, it was agreed that Kipling should control the film rights in both the novel and the play, and Mrs Nethersole assigned her copyright to Kipling for a one-third share of all sums he might receive. In 1939, Kipling's widow assigned the film rights to Paramount Pictures for £8,000, and Mrs Nethersole received her one-third share, namely £2,666. The Special Commissioners found that, at the material time, Mrs Nethersole was not carrying on the profession of a dramatist. However, they decided that the sum was of a revenue nature, and was liable to assessment under Schedule D, Case VI. The House of Lords disagreed, holding that the transaction was a sale of property with a limited life by a person who was not engaged in the trade or profession of dealing in such property and that, for income tax purposes, the proceeds of such a sale were in the nature of capital. At that time, they were, therefore, not taxable.[2] In the words of Viscount Simon:

> The taxpayer, under the relevant agreement, made a partial assignment of her copyright and ceased to be the owner of the portion assigned, receiving a sum of money in exchange. This amounts to a sale of property by a person who is not engaged in the trade or profession of dealing in such property, and the proceeds of such a sale are, for income tax purposes, a sum in the nature of untaxable capital and not in the nature of taxable revenue. .... Here we have the sale and transfer outright of an item of property which previously belonged to the taxpayer, not the licence to use it granted by its unchanged owner, and this does not give rise to annual profits or gains unless the sale takes place in the course of carrying on a trade or profession.

1   [1948] 1 All ER 400, 28 TC 501.
2   Capital sums received from the disposal of interests in copyright, otherwise than in the course of carrying on a trade profession or vocation, are now likely to be subject to capital gains tax. See para 9.131 et seq below.

9.28   Exceptionally, an author may be found to have ceased his profession or vocation even though he has retained his copyright, merely licensing publication rights to his publisher. In *Beare v Carter*,[1] a barrister, Dr AT Carter QC, had written one book, 'History of the English Courts', which was first published in 1899. Further editions were published in 1902, 1906, 1910 and 1927 and, when the fifth edition sold out in 1935, Dr Carter's publishers paid him £150 for a licence to publish the sixth edition. Dr Carter retained the copyright, and it was agreed that he was not carrying on a profession or vocation at the relevant time. The Inland Revenue sought to assess the £150 under Schedule D, Case VI, but the General Commissioners decided it was a capital receipt and their decision was upheld by MacNaghten J. *Beare v Carter* was, however, distinguished in *Glasson v Rougier*,[2] where MacNaghten J pointed out:

> The assessment in respect of Mrs Rougier is made under Schedule D Case II, which imposes the tax on profits from any 'profession' or 'vocation'. Dr Carter was assessed under Schedule D Case VI because there was no ground for saying that he was following any profession or vocation within the meaning of Case II. Mrs Rougier, on the other hand, is a well-known and talented authoress, and her profits, therefore, from that vocation fall to be assessed under Case II. In *Beare v Carter*, the General Commissioners had decided that the sum received by Dr Carter from the publishers of the one and only book which he had ever written was a payment in the nature of capital and not in the nature of income. This decision was upheld on the ground that the payment was made for the copyright of the book and was, therefore, to be regarded as a 'capital' payment. If Dr Carter had been assessed under Case II, and it had been established that he was following the vocation of an author, the decision would necessarily have been the other way, and the sum that he received from the publishers would have been part of the profits or emoluments gained by him from his vocation.

1   [1940] 2 KB 187, (1940) 23 TC 353.
2   For reference, see para 9.16, n 2 above.

POST CESSATION RECEIPTS

9.29   Until 1960, annual profits or gains arising or accruing from a profession or vocation were not subject to income tax if received in any year of assessment after the profession or vocation had been permanently discontinued. However, the law was changed following the House of Lords decisions in *Gospel v Purchase* and *Carson v Peter Cheyney's Executor*,[1] and provisions were introduced which subjected post-cessation receipts to tax under Schedule D, Case VI. These provisions can now be found in sections 103 to 110 of the Income and Corporation Taxes Act 1988 where, broadly speaking, sub-sections 103(1) and (2) provide that, following the permanent discontinuance of any trade, profession or vocation, tax is charged under Schedule D, Case VI on any sums received after the discontinuance, where such sums arose from the carrying on of the trade, profession or vocation during any period before the discontinuance and had not been brought into account in computing the profits or gains for any period before the discontinuance. Section 103(3), however, provides that section 103 does not apply to:

(a) sums received by a person beneficially entitled thereto who is not resident in the United Kingdom, or by a person acting on his behalf, which represent income arising directly or indirectly from a country or territory outside the United Kingdom; or

(b) a lump sum paid to the personal representatives of the author of a literary, dramatic, musical or artistic work as consideration for the assignment by them, wholly or partially, of the copyright in the work; or

(c) a lump sum paid to the personal representatives of the designer of a design in which design right subsists as consideration for the assignment by them, wholly or partially, of that right; or

(d) sums realised by the transfer of trading stock belonging to a trade at the discontinuance of the trade, or by the transfer of the work of a profession or vocation in progress at its discontinuance.

1 See para 9.40 below.

9.30 Section 105 of the Income and Corporation Taxes Act 1988 permits there to be deducted in computing the charge to tax on post-cessation receipts any loss, expense or debit (not arising directly or indirectly from the discontinuance itself) which would have been deductible for tax purposes if the trade, profession or vocation had not been discontinued, and any unrelieved capital allowance to which the person who carried on the trade, profession or vocation was entitled immediately before the discontinuance.[1]

1 For allowable expenses and capital allowances, see para 9.101 et seq below.

9.31 An election may be made under section 108 of the Income and Corporation Taxes Act 1988 to treat any sum received not later than six years after the date of discontinuance as having been received on that date. Such election must be made by the person by whom the trade, profession or vocation was carried on before the discontinuance, or by his personal representatives, within two years after the tax year in which the sum was received.

SECTION 775

9.32 The anti-avoidance provisions contained in section 775 of the Income and Corporation Taxes Act 1988 should be noted although, so far as the author is aware, there have been no reported cases on the section.[1] The section was originally directed towards the practice, which had developed during the 1960s, whereby an entertainer would transfer the rights to his services to a company in return for shares in the company, the object being to convert an income tax liability on his future earnings (which would be retained in the company) into a capital gains tax liability on the resulting increase in the value of his shares when they were eventually disposed of or the company liquidated. Since the rates of income tax and capital gains tax are now the same, the attraction of such schemes has substantially diminished.[2] Section 775 applies where:

(a) transactions or arrangements are effected or made to exploit the earning capacity of an individual in any occupation by putting some other person in a position to enjoy all or any part of the profits or gains or other income, or of the receipts, derived from the individual's activities in that occupation, or anything derived directly or indirectly from any such income or receipts; and

(b) as part of, or in connection with, or in consequence of, the transactions or arrangements, any capital amount is obtained by the individual for himself or for any other person; and

(c) the main object, or one of the main objects, of the transactions was the avoidance or reduction of liability to income tax.

1 A claim was made under the forerunner of s 775 in *IRC v Brackett* [1986] STC 521, but the assessments were discharged and the case decided on other grounds: see paras 9.83 and 9.86 below.
2 However, the rules for calculating profits for income tax purposes are still different from those for calculating chargeable gains for capital gains tax purposes and, in the case of individuals, the timing of the liability to pay is also different.

9.33 By virtue of section 775(2), the individual will be liable to income tax under Schedule D, Case VI on such capital amount.

9.34 For this purpose 'occupation' means activities of any of the kinds pursued in any profession or vocation[1] (irrespective of whether the individual is actually engaged in a profession or vocation or employment), and 'income' and 'receipts' include payments for any description of copyright, licence, franchise or other right deriving its value from the activities, including past activities, of the individual.[2] 'Capital amount' means any amount, in money or money's worth, which does not fall to be included in any computation of income for the purposes of the Tax Acts,[3] and an individual is deemed to obtain a capital amount for some other person where he has put the other person in a position to receive it by providing him with something of value derived, directly or indirectly, from the individual's activities in the occupation.[4]

1 But not activities of a kind pursued in a trade.
2 ICTA 1988, s 775(3).
3 ICTA 1988, s 777(13).
4 ICTA 1988, s 775(8).

9.35 Section 775 applies to any individual, whether resident in the United Kingdom or not, if his occupation is carried on wholly or partly in the United Kingdom.[1] However, the section does not apply to a capital amount obtained from the disposal of assets (including goodwill) of a profession or vocation, or of a share in a partnership which is carrying on a profession or vocation, or of shares in a company, insofar as the value of what is disposed of is attributable, at the time of disposal, to the value as a going concern of the profession, or of the company's business, unless such value is derived to a material extent from prospective income or receipts derived directly or indirectly from the individual's activities in the occupation and for which, when all capital amounts are disregarded, the individual will not have received full consideration, whether as a partner in a partnership or as an employee or otherwise.[2] References to a company's business include reference to the business of any other company in which it holds shares directly or indirectly.[3]

1 ICTA 1988, s 775(9).
2 ICTA 1988, s 775(5).
3 ICTA 1988, s 775(6).

THE AMATEUR CREATOR

9.36 It has been noted[1] that section 832(1) of the Income and Corporation Taxes Act 1988 defines 'trade' to include adventures or concerns in the nature of trade. However, the carrying on of a profession or vocation suggests some degree of continuity and, in the absence of any statutory extension of these terms to include 'adventures or concerns in the nature of a profession or vocation', it follows that a single or isolated transaction cannot of itself amount to the carrying on of a profession or vocation, the profits of which are taxable under Schedule D, Case II. The profits of such transactions may, however, be taxed under Schedule D, Case VI, which is charged 'in respect of any annual profits or gains not falling under any Case of Schedule D and not charged by virtue of Schedules A, C or E'.[2] As stated by Upjohn J in *Bradbury v Arnold*:[3]

> A contract for services may, and clearly does, form a matter for assessment under Case VI of Schedule D, and not the less so that the services are trivial or that they are to be rendered once and for all so that the remuneration may be regarded as a casual profit arising out of a single and isolated transaction.

1   See para 9.7 above.
2   ICTA 1988, s 18(3).
3   (1957) 37 TC 665 at p 669.

9.37 This principle is applicable to persons, such as authors or illustrators, who create material in which merchandising rights subsist, but who do not do so in the course of carrying on a profession or vocation. Thus, in *Hobbs v Hussey*,[1] a solicitor's clerk, who had never carried on the profession of an author, wrote his life story and sold the serial rights in it to a Sunday newspaper for a lump sum payment of £1,500. He contended that the payment was a capital payment for the purchase of property, namely the copyright in the series. It was held, however, that the true nature of the transaction was the performance of services, with the sale of the copyright being subsidiary. Accordingly, the £1,500, less expenses, represented annual profits or gains taxable under Schedule D, Case VI. As Lawrence J pointed out:

> Any sale of property where no concern in the nature of trade is carried on must result in the accretion of capital, and it is also true, in my opinion, that the performance of services, though they may involve some subsidiary sale of property (eg dentures sold by a dentist) are in their essence of a revenue nature, since they are the fruit of the individual's capacity, which may be regarded in a sense as his capital, but are not the capital itself. Does, then, the fact that the present transaction involved the sale of copyright in the appellant's series of articles constitute the profits therefrom capital, or is such sale merely subsidiary to what was in its essence a performance of services by the appellant? In my opinion, the true nature of the transaction was the performance of services. The appellant did not part with his notes or diaries or his reminiscences. He could republish the very articles themselves so long as they were not in serial form and, on the whole, I am of the opinion that the profits which he received were of a revenue nature and not the realisation of capital.

1   [1942] 1 KB 491, [1942] 1 All ER 445, 24 TC 153.

9.38 A similar conclusion was reached in *Housden v Marshall*,[1] where a well-known jockey agreed to make available 'reminiscences of his life and experiences on the turf', and to provide photographs and press cuttings, to a ghost writer. The writer produced a series of four articles, which were

published under his own name, and Mr Marshall was paid £750. In answer
to the question whether the payment should be treated as income for
providing services or capital for the sale of property, Harman J stated:

> This kind of case arises as a result of something emanating either from
> the famous...or from the infamous. Either category can produce money,
> particularly from the Sunday newspapers, because the public likes to
> read at its ease before the fireside sensational reminiscences of either
> of these two categories of persons. Strictly speaking, they are not
> usually reminiscences of those persons at all: they are written by what
> are called 'ghost' writers. The celebrated or notorious character
> communicates this or that to the 'ghost' and, as here, may allow his
> signature to be used to give an air of reality to an otherwise bold and
> unconvincing narrative. ... the taxpayer was called on to do very little
> of the things which he had undertaken to do. To use a vulgarism he
> merely had to 'vet' the product of the 'ghost' writer who also provided
> the pictorial background to illustrate it. So that the taxpayer did not
> do very much, but he did as much as he was called on to do, and he
> was paid the figure contracted for. What was he paid for? He was paid
> for making available his reminiscences and for producing certain
> documents if called on and, I think, for nothing else. ... The
> reminiscences were never his copyright: they were the copyright either
> of the man who wrote them (ie the 'ghost') or of the 'ghost's' employers.
> There was nothing for the taxpayer to grant. ... I do not think that he
> sold any publication rights in his reminiscenses. He had no
> reminiscences of which he could sell the rights. The reminiscenses
> which he communicated to the journalist were not his; he had no
> secrets to impart, his life was open. He was not selling anything of
> which he had the property like the copyright. He was not selling
> anything secret. He was merely talking to the journalist and allowing
> the journalist's write up to be put forward as his. ... Even though he
> did sell [the newspaper] something in which he had property, the right
> to use his name, that was a subsidiary matter in my view, and the
> major object and effect of the agreement was that he was paid a sum
> of money for services rendered.

1   [1958] 3 All ER 639, [1959] 1 WLR 1, 38 TC 233. See also *Alloway v Phillips* [1980] 3
     All ER 138, [1980] 1 WLR 888, 53 TC 372.

PERSONAL REPRESENTATIVES

9.39 Personal representatives of a deceased person, who created material
in which merchandising rights subsist, may receive income under contracts
exploiting such rights which were made by such person during his lifetime,
or they may enter into such contracts themselves after his death.

9.40 If the deceased person created the material in the course of carrying
on a profession or vocation, income received after his death from contracts
made during his lifetime to exploit such material retains the quality of
remuneration for professional services. However, since the source of the
income (the profession) has ceased, the payments cannot be taxed under
Schedule D, Case II. In *Stainers Executors v Purchase*[1] and in *Carson v
Peter Cheyney's Executor*,[2] the Inland Revenue sought to tax such sums

under Schedule D, Case III[3] or Case VI. It was held in both cases that remuneration for a deceased's person's professional activities, which would have been taxable under Schedule D, Case II during his lifetime, did not change their quality on his death so as to become taxable under Schedule D, Case III or Case VI. This meant at the time that the personal representatives could not be taxed on such receipts. These cases led to the passing of section 32 of the Finance Act 1960, which introduced the Schedule D, Case VI charge on post-cessation receipts, described in paragraphs 9.29–9.31 above. Accordingly, as regards continuing income from contracts made by the deceased in the course of his profession or vocation, personal representatives will be taxed in the same way as the deceased would have been if his profession or vocation had been permanently discontinued otherwise than by reason of his death.

1   [1952] AC 280, [1951] 2 All ER 1071, 32 TC 367.
2   [1959] AC 412, [1958] 3 All ER 573, 38 TC 240.
3   See para 9.48 et seq below.

9.41   It is, however, clear that the personal representatives cannot themselves carry on the deceased's profession or vocation, since they lack the requisite personal and intellectual connection with his work. Accordingly, receipts from contracts made by personal representatives after the deceased's death might be treated as trading income taxable under Schedule D, Case I, or as investment income taxable under Schedule D, Case III, or treated as a capital receipt from the disposal of property.

9.42   In *Earl Haig's Trustees v IRC*,[1] the Trustees of the late Field Marshall Earl Haig entered into an agreement with a biographer, the Right Honourable Alfred Duff Cooper, under which they agreed to make Earl Haig's First World War diaries available to Mr Duff Cooper, who was writing a biography of Earl Haig, in return for one half of all the profits resulting therefrom. Mr Duff Cooper received a non-returnable advance of £10,000 on account of 25% royalties from his publishers, and also received a further £10,000 from a Sunday newspaper for the serialisation rights. It was accepted that Mr Duff Cooper was taxable under Schedule D, Case II on his share of these sums but, having found as fact that the Trustees had not carried on any trade or adventure in the nature of a trade, either solely or jointly with Mr Duff Cooper, the Special Commissioners held that the sums received by the Trustees were remuneration for allowing Mr Duff Cooper use of the diaries and were properly assessable under Schedule D, Case VI. The Court of Session, in allowing the Trustees' appeal, held that the payments received by the Trustees were capital payments in return for the partial realisation of an asset, and so (before capital gains tax was introduced) were not taxable. In the words of Lord President Normand:

> It is well to recall that the appellants were Trustees who had a duty to realise the assets of the Estate for the benefit of the Trust. In the realisation they might confine themselves to a transaction which was clearly nothing more than a capital transaction, for example a simple out and out sale of the assets, but they might also, under the power of publication conferred on them by the Trust Deed, choose a means of realisation which would be using the assets in trade and for the

purpose of making trading profits. Here the appellants did neither: they did not sell their copyright out and out, and they did not carry on any trade or adventure. ... For reasons which commended themselves to the appellants and which we cannot question, they did not embark on selected publication or make a commercial agreement with a publisher for selected publication. What they did was to make a bargain with an author who intended to write a life of Lord Haig and in whose judgment of what the public interest required they were entitled to place confidence, and they allowed him the use of the material contained in the diaries. The result of the transaction is that to a large extent the publication value of the diaries is exhausted, because the author has, in fact, made full use of the material so far as the public interest permitted, though it may be that in future years further use of the diaries may be practicable and permissible. So far, there has been an alienation by the appellants of a large part of this particular asset in return for a sum ascertainable from the terms of the contract when Mr Duff Cooper's profits are ascertained. This seems to me to be a transaction as clearly resembling a realisation by sale as the circumstances allowed.

The *Earl Haig* case was distinguished in both *Hobbs v Hussey*[2] and *Housden v Marshall*,[3] in the first case because the sale of the right of access to the diaries was in no sense subsidiary to the performance of any services by the Trustees, and in the second case because, unlike Mr Marshall's reminiscences, the copyright in Earl Haig's diaries was property which the Trustees were entitled to sell.

1   (1939) 22 TC 725.
2   See para 9.37 above
3   See para 9.38 above.

BENEFICIARIES

9.43   Beneficiaries who inherit material in which merchandising rights subsist, will be in the same position as the personal representatives of the deceased creator, both as regards post-cessation receipts from contracts made by the creator during his lifetime, and as regards receipts from any further contracts which may be made by the beneficiaries after his death.

9.44   *Hume v Asquith*[1] concerned both types of receipts. Under his will, the late Sir James Barrie had bequeathed certain copyright interests in his works (other than 'Peter Pan', which he left to Great Ormond Street Hospital) to Lady Cynthia Asquith. Some of the books and plays were subject to existing publishing agreements. Subsequently, Lady Asquith assigned certain amateur dramatic rights to a US company for the territories of the USA and Canada, and to an English company for the rest of the world. She later assigned to her son the right to receive one half of her royalties, both under the existing publishing contracts and from the assignment of the amateur dramatic rights. Pennycuick J, in determining the son's appeal against assessments to income tax, distinguished between the different types of royalties as follows:
   (a) Royalties paid under the existing publishing agreements were not

taxable, following *Gospel v Purchase* and *Carson v Peter Cheyney's Executor*, because they derived from Sir James Barrie's profession, which was no longer being carried on as a result of his death. (Such royalties would, of course, now be taxed as post-cessation receipts under Schedule D, Case VI.) The Inland Revenue had argued that the *Gospel* and *Peter Cheyney* cases applied only to royalties received by a professional person or his personal representatives, and had no application to persons claiming under him, including legatees under his will. The judge held, however, that, where a professional author enters into a royalty contract, this represents merely the machinery whereby he collects the return for his professional activities and that, if this is the quality of the contract in the hands of the author and his personal representatives, there can be no change in its quality by reason of the fact that the benefit of the contract passes from the personal representatives to a beneficiary under a Will, or at a later stage from the beneficiary to someone in whose favour he disposes of it.

(b) The royalties paid by the English company for the assignment of amateur dramatic rights from Lady Asquith had been correctly held by the Special Commissioners to be 'annual payments payable wholly out of profits or gains brought into charge to tax' for the purposes of what is now section 348(1) of the Income and Corporation Taxes Act 1988. Under this section, the payments are treated as having been made after deduction of basic rate income tax, and the recipient cannot be held liable to pay the tax if it is has not, in fact, been deducted.[2]

(c) The royalties received from the US company were also 'annual payments' but, since the US company was not liable to UK tax on the profits or gains out of which they were paid, what is now section 349(1) of the Income and Corporation Taxes Act 1988 applied. Under this section, the payer is required, rather than entitled as under section 348(1), to deduct basic rate income tax from the payment[3] and he is also liable to be assessed to basic rate income tax on the payment or so much of it as is not made out of chargeable profits.[4] However, unlike with payments to which section 348(1) applies, the Inland Revenue has the option to assess the recipient of a payment to which section 349(1) applies instead of the payer.[5] The Inland Revenue's ability to make a direct assessment on the recipient where the payer had omitted to deduct the tax and pay it over to the Inland Revenue in full was not disputed, and such assessments had been properly made on the sum in this case.

1   [1969] 2 Ch 58, 45 TC 251.
2   For the position of the payer under ICTA 1988, s 348(1), see para 9.109 below
3   See para 9.112 below.
4   ICTA 1988, s 350(1).
5   *Grosvenor Place Estates Ltd v Roberts* [1961] Ch 148, 39 TC 433.

OTHER RIGHTS OWNERS

9.45   An owner of merchandising rights, other than the person who created the material in which such rights subsist or the personal representatives or beneficiaries of such a person, is likely to have acquired the rights either for exploitation as part of a trade, or to hold as an investment. To determine whether a trade is being carried on, as was found to be the case in *Noddy Subsidiary Rights Co Ltd v IRC*[1] and in *Jarvis v Curtis Brown Ltd*,[2] the activities of the rights owner must be reviewed in the light of the so-called 'badges of trade' described in paragraphs 9.9 and 9.10.

1   See para 9.11 above.
2   (1929) 14 TC 744.

9.46   The taxation of trading profits under Schedule D, Case I will follow normal principles, and there are no special rules where trading income is derived from the exploitation of merchandising rights.

9.47   Where the owner of merchandising rights is not carrying on a trade, profession or vocation, royalties received from the exploitation of such rights are likely to be treated as income of an investment, as in *IRC v Sangster*[1] and in *Asher v London Film Productions Ltd*.[2] Such income may be taxed under Schedule D, Case III if it is treated as an 'annual payment', or under Case V[3] if the rights are located overseas, or under Case VI.[4]

1   [1920] 1 KB 587.
2   [1944] KB 133.
3   As income arising from possessions out of the United Kingdom: see para 9.55 below.
4   ICTA 1988, s 18(3).

ANNUAL PAYMENTS

9.48   Section 18(3) of the Income and Corporation Taxes Act 1988 provides that tax is charged under Schedule D, Case III in respect of, among other things:

> ... any interest of money, whether yearly or otherwise, or any annuity *or other annual payment*, whether such payment is payable within or out of the United Kingdom, either as a charge on any property of the person paying the same by virtue of any deed or will or otherwise, or as a reservation out of it, or as a personal debt or obligation by virtue of any contract, or whether the same is received and payable half-yearly or at any shorter or more distant periods, but not including any payment chargeable under Schedule A.[1]

1   Tax is charged under Schedule A on the annual profits or gains of companies arising in respect of rents under leases of land in the United Kingdom, rent, charges and similar annual payments, and other receipts arising by virtue of ownership of estates or interests in land in the United Kingdom; and, in the case of individuals and trustees, on the annual profits or gains arising from any business carried on for the exploitation, as a source of rents or other receipts, of any estate, interest or rights in or over any land in the United Kingdom. See ICTA 1988, s 15 and FA 1995, s 39.

9.49   The meaning of 'other annual payment' has generated much case law, but is conveniently summarised in *Whitworth Park Coal Co Ltd v IRC*,[1] where the question arose as to whether certain revenue payments, made under section 22 of the Coal Industry Nationalisation Act 1946 as compensation to the company following the nationalisation of its colliery assets, should be taxed under Schedule D, Case III as 'annual payments' or under Schedule D, Case VI. The payments consisted firstly of a sum, payable in two instalments, representing compensation calculated by reference to the comparable ascertained revenues of the company attributable to activities for which the nationalised assets were used or owned, and secondly of a sum, described as 'interim income', which was equivalent to interest but was to be added to the amount of the compensation when finally determined and paid. It was held that the payments were assessable under Schedule D, Case VI: the interim income payments were equivalent to interest, but were not actually interest, and they were not 'annual payments' because they lacked the requisite quality of recurrence, while the compensation payments would have been 'annual payments' but were not within Schedule D, Case III as the relevant legislation at the time did not apply to payments by the Crown.[2] Jenkins LJ reviewed the relevant case law and summarised the requirements for a payment to come within the definition of 'other annual payment' as follows:

(a) The payment in question must be *eiusdem generis* with interest and annuities.[3]

(b) The payment must be made under some binding legal obligation, whether by virtue of a contract or by order of the court, as distinct from being a mere voluntary payment.[4]

(c) The payment must possess the essential quality of recurrence implied by the description 'annual'.[5] This is, however, broadly interpreted so that, for example, the fact that payments are made weekly, or are contingent and variable in amount, does not prevent them from being 'annual payments' if the instalments are capable of continuing over more than one year.

(d) The payments in question must be in the nature of a 'pure income' profit in the hands of the recipient.[6]

1 [1961] AC 31, [1959] 3 All ER 703, 38 TC 531.
2 This aspect was retrospectively reversed by s 39 of the Finance Act 1960. See now ICTA 1988, s 829(1).
3 *Earl Howe v IRC* [1919] 2 KB 336, 7 TC 289, where annual life assurance premiums were treated as instalments of purchase money for a capital sum payable on death [1918-19] All ER Rep 1088.
4 *Smith v Smith* [1923] P 191.
5 *Smith v Smith*, supra.
6 *Earl Howe v IRC* supra, and *Re Hanbury* (1939) 38 TC 588n.

9.50 The requirement for 'pure income profit' is particularly important because of the provisions relating to the deduction of basic rate income tax from 'annual payments' in sections 348 and 349 of the Income and Corporation Taxes Act 1988.[1] As Lord Greene MR explained in *Re Hanbury*:

There are two classes of annual payments which fall to be considered for income tax purposes. There is, first of all, that class of annual payment which the Acts regard and treat as being pure income profit of the recipient undiminished by any deduction. Payments of interest, payments of annuities, to take the ordinary simple case, are payments which are regarded as part of the income of the recipient, and the payer is entitled in estimating his total income to treat those payments as payments which go out of his income altogether. The class of annual payment which falls within that category is quite a limited one. In the other class there stand a number of payments, nonetheless annual, the very quality and nature of which make it impossible to treat them as part of the pure income profit of the recipient, the proper way of treating them being to treat them as an element to be taken into account in discovering what the profits of the recipient are.

In other words, royalties will be taxed under Schedule D, Case III if the full amount will be subject to income tax as 'pure income profit', without any deductions or expenses allowed to be deducted therefrom in computing the profits on which the tax is to be paid.

1   See paras 9.109–9.115 below.

9.51   The leading cases on the question of 'pure income profit' concern charities, since the right of a charity to recover the income tax deducted by the payer from payments made under a deed of covenant depends on whether the payments are 'annual payments', from which the tax should properly have been deducted. In particular, the question has arisen when the charities have agreed that certain benefits should be provided in return for the covenanted payments.

9.52   For example, in *IRC v National Book League*,[1] a charity provided club facilities to its members, including a reading room, drawing room, licensed bar and restaurant and other privileges. When it resolved to increase its membership subscriptions, it excluded from the increase those members who committed themselves to pay at the original rate under seven year covenants anticipating that, being a charity, it could substantially increase its income by recovering the income tax deemed to have been deducted from the covenanted payments. It was held that the League was not entitled to recover the tax, since the covenanted subscriptions were not 'pure income profit' and so could not be 'annual payments'. As Morris LJ explained:

> The question arises whether the payments can be said to be pure gifts to the charity. In the terms of a phrase which has been used, can the payments be said to be pure income profit in the hands of the charity? If the payments were made in such circumstances that the League was obliged to afford to the covenantors such amenities and such benefits of membership as would at any particular time be offered to all members, and if those amenities and benefits were appreciable and not negligible, then I do not think that the payments were pure income profit in the hands of the charity.

1   [1957] Ch 488, [1957] 2 All ER 644, 37 TC 455.

9.53   The *National Book League* case should, however, be contrasted with *Campbell v IRC*,[1] where the House of Lords affirmed the *National Book League* case on the basis of Morris LJ's judgment, but disapproved of suggestions from other judges (particularly Lord Evershed) in that case that payments could not be 'annual payments' if there were conditions or counter-stipulations attached to them. As Lord Donovan explained:

> It was said below that there cannot be an 'annual payment' within the meaning of Case III of Schedule D if the recipient has to 'give or do

anything in return for the payment'; or if there is a 'counter-benefit' to the covenantor; or if the covenantor should 'make conditions or stipulations'; or unless the payments are 'pure bounty'. These statements contradict the charging words of Case III of Schedule D itself which envisage that an annual payment may be payable 'by virtue of any contract'; and that, therefore, the recipient may have to give or do something in return for the payment, which will not in such circumstances be 'pure bounty' in his hands. An obvious example is the annuity purchased from an insurance company. ... Apart from the purchase of an annuity, instances are not lacking where the payer receives a counter-benefit or makes some counter-stipulation and yet the sum he pays is an annual payment within Case III in the hands of the recipient. For example, the right to use a secret process may be acquired, the purchaser agreeing to pay an annual sum during all the years of user: *Delage v Nugget Polish Co Ltd.*[2] An employee of a film company may give up all his existing rights to remuneration in return for a percentage of the takings of certain films: *Asher v London Film Productions Ltd.*[3] ... One must determine, in the light of all the relevant facts, whether the payment is a taxable receipt in the hands of the recipient without any deduction for expenses or the like. Where it is, in other words, 'pure income' or 'pure profit income' in his hands, as those expressions have been used in the decided cases. If so, it will be an annual payment under Case III. If, on the other hand, it is simply gross revenue in the recipient's hands, out of which a taxable income will emerge only after his outgoings have been deducted, then the payment is not such an annual payment.'

In other words, the question is not whether the payer receives any benefit in return for the payments, but whether the recipient of the payments incurs any costs or expenses in providing the benefits which would be deductible from the payments in computing his tax liability thereon. If not, the payments may be annual payments taxable under Schedule D, Case III; otherwise, unless the recipient is carrying on a trade profession or vocation, the payments are likely to be taxed under Schedule D, Case VI.

1   [1970] AC 77, [1968] 3 All ER 588, 45 TC 427.
2   (1905) 92 LT 682, 21 TLR 454.
3   [1944] KB 133, [1944] 1 All ER 77.

9.54 Lump sums received for the grant of merchandising rights cannot, of course, be 'annual payments' since they lack the requisite quality of recurrence. Lump sums received from the sale of rights held as an investment are likely to be treated as capital receipts.[1]

1   As in *Shiner v Lindblom* supra.

FOREIGN POSSESSIONS

9.55 Income arising from the exercise of merchandising rights overseas by a person who is resident in the United Kingdom but who is not carrying on a trade, profession or vocation in this country will be taxed under Schedule D, Case V as 'income arising from possessions out of the United Kingdom'.[1] 'Possessions' has been held[2] to include 'any form of property from which profit can be derived', although it will not include securities as income arising from securities out of the United Kingdom is taxed under Schedule D, Case IV.[3]

1   ICTA 1988, ss 18(3) and 65(3).
2   In *Singer v Williams* [1921] 1 AC 41, 7 TC 419.
3   ICTA 1988, s 18(3).

9.56   To all intents and purposes, Schedule D, Case V is similar to Schedule D, Case III except that, in the case of a person who satisfies the Board of Inland Revenue that he is not domiciled in the United Kingdom or that, being a Commonwealth citizen or a citizen of the Republic of Ireland, he is not ordinarily resident here, tax is charged only to the extent that the income is received in the United Kingdom.[1]

1   ICTA 1988, s 65(4) and (5).

9.57   A full description of the concept of 'domicile' is outside the scope of this work. This concept is not defined in tax legislation,[1] and its meaning is derived from general law. In summary, a child born legitimately takes as his 'domicile of origin' the domicile of his father on the day he is born.[2] Until his sixteenth birthday,[3] his domicile is dependent on his father's and, if the father's domicile changes during this period, he will acquire a 'domicile of dependence' which follows that of his father. Then, from his sixteenth birthday, he is capable of acquiring a 'domicile of choice' by settling in another country with the intention of living there permanently.[4]

1   Although a statutory extension of the general concept is applied for inheritance tax purposes. See para 9.153, n 1 below.
2   The domicile of origin of a posthumous or illegitimate child is his mother's domicile at his birth.
3   Or, in Scotland, fourteenth for a boy and twelfth for a girl.
4   *Winans v A-G* [1904] AC 287; *Udny v Udny* (1869) LR 1 Sc & Div 441.

9.58   Both these elements are necessary in order to acquire a domicile of choice. Thus, it is not possible to acquire a domicile of choice in a country without actually living there;[1] conversely, living in another country, even for a very long period of time, is not of itself sufficient in the absence of evidence of an intention to settle there permanently.[2,3]

1   *IRC v Duchess of Portland* [1982] Ch 314, [1982] STC 149.
2   *Winans v A-G* supra; *Buswell v IRC* [1974] 2 All ER 520, 49 TC 334; *IRC v Bullock* [1976] 3 All ER 353, [1976] STC 409, 51 TC 522.
3   Since 6 April 1996, an individual may be registered on the UK electoral roll as an overseas voter, and may vote in any election at which such registration entitles him to vote, without affecting his domicile status unless he wishes it to be taken into account; FA 1996, s 200.

9.59   A domicile of choice in another country will be lost if a person abandons his residence there or ceases to have the intention to reside there permanently; at that point, his domicile of origin revives unless and until he acquires a new domicile of choice.[1]

1   *Fielden v IRC* [1965] TR 221; *Re Fuld (No 3)* [1968] P 675, [1965] 3 All ER 776.

9.60   A company is domiciled in the country where it is registered.[1]

1   *Gasque v IRC* [1940] 2 KB 80, 23 TC 210.

9.61 *Tax aspects*

9.61 The general principle is that, subject to the provisions of any applicable double taxation treaty, a person who is resident in the United Kingdom for tax purposes will be liable to tax here on the profits of his trade, profession or vocation, whether carried on in the United Kingdom or elsewhere.[1] A person who is not tax resident here is liable to income tax on the annual profits or gains arising or accruing from any property whatever in the United Kingdom or from any trade, profession or vocation exercised here,[2] but a company which is not tax resident in the United Kingdom will not be liable to corporation tax unless it carries on a trade in the United Kingdom through a branch or agency here.[3] Such a company will be liable to corporation tax on any trading income arising through or from the branch or agency, on any income from property or rights used by, or held by or for, the branch or agency, and on chargeable gains accruing on the disposal of assets situated in the United Kingdom and used in or for the purposes of the trade, or acquired, used or held for the purposes of the branch or agency.[4] Credit will, however, be given for the basic rate income tax deducted at source from copyright and certain other royalties, as described in paras 9.116 to 9.123 below.[5] A non-resident company which does not trade in the United Kingdom through a branch or agency here will not be liable to corporation tax, but will be liable to basic rate income tax as so deducted at source.

1   ICTA 1988, s 18(1)(a)(ii).
2   ICTA 1988, s 18(1)(a)(iii).
3   ICTA 1988, s 11.
4   ICTA 1988, s 11(2).
5   ICTA 1988, s 11(3).

9.62 By concession the Inland Revenue will treat payments made by a person who is resident in an overseas country[1] to a person carrying on a trade in the United Kingdom as consideration 'for the use of, or for the privilege of using, in the overseas country, any copyright, patent, design, secret process or formula, trade mark or other like property' as income arising outside the United Kingdom for the purposes of tax credit,[2] even though the source of the payments might in strict law be in the United Kingdom, except to the extent that the payments represent consideration for services (other than merely incidental services) rendered in this country by the recipient to the payer.[3]

1   It is not sufficient that the taxpayer can establish he is not resident in the United Kingdom; he must be treated as tax resident in another country.
2   Whether allowed under ICTA 1988, s 790 or under the provisions of any applicable double tax treaty – see para 9.90 et seq below.
3   Inland Revenue Booklet IR1 (1992), paragraph B8.

RESIDENCE OF INDIVIDUALS

9.63 'Residence' has no statutory definition, and an individual's residence for tax purposes is a question of fact and degree, to be determined in accordance with the ordinary meaning of the word.[1] Inland Revenue practice is, however, set out in its booklet IR20 'Residents and Non-Residents – Liability to tax in the United Kingdom', of which the most recent edition was published in November 1993. This states[2] that an individual will be treated as resident in the United Kingdom in any tax year if he is here for 183 days or more in that year, or if he visits the United Kingdom regularly and after four tax years his visits during those years have averaged 91 days or more per tax year.

1   *Levene v IRC* [1928] AC 217, 13 TC 486.
2   See IR 20, para 3.3.

9.64   Section 336 of the Income and Corporation Taxes Act 1988 provides that a person is not treated as resident in the United Kingdom for tax purposes if he is here for some temporary purpose only, and not with any view or intent of establishing his residence here, and he has not actually resided in the United Kingdom at one time or several times for a period equal in the whole to six months in any year of assessment, but that if any such person resides here for such a period he shall be so chargeable for that year.

9.65   Section 334 of the Income and Corporation Taxes Act 1988 provides as follows:

> Every Commonwealth citizen or citizen of the Republic of Ireland–
> (a) shall, if his ordinary residence has been in the United Kingdom, be assessed and charged to income tax notwithstanding that at the time the assessment or charge is made he may have left the United Kingdom, if he has so left the United Kingdom for the purpose only of occasional residence abroad, and
> (b) shall be charged as a person actually residing in the United Kingdom upon the whole amount of his profits or gains, whether they arise from property in the United Kingdom or elsewhere, or from any allowance, annuity or stipend, or from any trade, profession, employment or vocation in the United Kingdom or elsewhere.

9.66   In *Levene v IRC*, a retired businessman, previously resident and ordinarily resident in the United Kingdom, left the country in 1919 and, for the following six years, had no fixed place of abode, staying in various overseas hotels but spending between four and five months in each year in the United Kingdom for the purpose of obtaining medical advice, visiting relatives, taking part in certain religious observances and dealing with his income tax affairs. It was held that he had gone to live abroad for the purpose of occasional residence only, and so remained resident in the United Kingdom throughout the period. As Viscount Sumner reasoned:[1]

> The evidence as a whole disclosed that Mr Levene continued to go to and fro during the years in question, leaving at the beginning of winter and coming back in summer, his home thus remaining as before. He changed his sky but not his home. On this I see no error in law in saying of each year that his purpose in leaving the United Kingdom was occasional residence abroad only. The occasion was the approach of an English winter and when with the promise of summer here that occasion passed away, back came Mr Levene to attend to the cause of interest, of friendship and of piety.

9.66 *Tax aspects*

1   [1928] AC 217 at page 227, 13 TC 486 at page 501.

9.67   Conversely, in *Reed v Clark*,[1] the pop musician Dave Clark left the United Kingdom and remained in the United States from 3 April 1978 to 2 May 1979 in order to avoid being taxed here in 1978 to 1979 on a substantial payment received from a record company during the previous tax year.[2] He continued to run his business from Los Angeles and, for most of the period, lived in a house there which had been rented by his company. In that case, although Nicholls J did not accept that, as a matter of law, residence abroad for an entire tax year can never be 'occasional' for the purposes of section 334, he considered on the facts that Mr Clark has been sufficiently settled in Los Angeles throughout his year of absence for this to be more than 'occasional residence abroad'. He said:

> ... it seems to me plain that a British resident's departure abroad for a period of a few weeks or months with the firm intention of returning at the end of the period to live here as before would be likely always to be for the purpose only of occasional residence. At the opposite end of the scale, it seems to me equally plain that the departure of such a resident abroad for a limited period of (say) three years would not necessarily be for the purpose only of occasional residence just because from the outset he had a firm intention of returning at the end of the period to live here as before; 'not necessarily' because all the circumstances would have to be considered. *Coombe's* case[3] is an example of this, where on the facts Captain Coombe's business and residential headquarters were permanently in New York throughout the three years. For my part, I think this latter conclusion is also true of residence abroad for just over one year in duration. The difference between these examples is one of degree, and there is an area in which different minds may reach different conclusions. In my view, a year is a long enough period for a person's purpose of living where he does to be capable of having a sufficient degree of continuity for it to be properly described as settled. Hence, depending on all the circumstances, the foreign country could be the place where, for that period, he would be ordinarily and not just occasionally resident.

1   [1986] Ch 1, [1985] STC 323, 58 TC 528.
2   Until 6 April 1994, ICTA 1988, s 60(1) provided that income tax was to be charged under Cases I and II of Schedule D on the full amount of the profits or gains of the year preceding the year of assessment. Since then, such tax has generally been charged on the profits or gains of the current year of assessment but, in the case of a trade, profession or vocation set up and commenced before 6 April 1994, the preceding year basis of assessment was replaced by the new current year basis, subject to the transitional provisions in Sch 20 to the Finance Act 1994, only with effect from the year 1996–1997.
3   *IRC v Combe* (1932) 17 TC 405.

9.68   It seems the crucial distinction between *Levene v IRC* and *Reed v Clark* was the establishment of a fixed place of abode overseas. This enabled Mr Clark successfully to contend that his residence abroad was more than 'occasional', even though he had the firm intention throughout to return to the United Kingdom soon after the end of one complete tax year abroad. On the other hand, the absence of any fixed place of abode tended to suggest that Mr Levene's residence abroad remained 'occasional' notwithstanding its much longer duration.

RESIDENCE OF COMPANIES

9.69 A company incorporated in the United Kingdom is treated as resident here, and nowhere else, for tax purposes.[1] A company incorporated in a country outside the United Kingdom is treated as resident for tax purposes in the country where its 'central management and control' is located.

1 Finance Act 1988, s 66(1).

9.70 The 'central management and control' test was enunciated by Lord Loreburn in *De Beers Consolidated Mines Ltd v Howe*:[1]

> In applying the conception of residence to a company, we ought, I think, to proceed as nearly as we can upon the analogy of an individual. A company cannot eat or sleep, but it can keep house and do business. We ought, therefore, to see where it really keeps house and does business. An individual may be of foreign nationality, and yet reside in the United Kingdom. So may a company. Otherwise it might have its chief seat of management and its centre of trade in England under the protection of English law, and yet escape the appropriate taxation by the simple expedient of being registered abroad and distributing its dividends abroad. ... A company resides for purposes of income tax where its real business is carried on. ... I regard that as the true rule, and the real business is carried on where the central management and control actually abides.

1 [1906] AC 455, 5 TC 198.

9.71 In the *De Beers* case, the head office of the company was formally at Kimberley, South Africa, and the general meetings had always been held there. The mining operations of the company were, of course, located in South Africa, and the profits were generated from the sale in South Africa of diamonds mined there. However, although some of the directors lived in South Africa, and board meetings were held at Kimberley as well as in London, it was established that the majority of the directors lived in England, and that the London board meetings exercised the real control over practically all the important business of the company except its mining operations. London, for example, controlled the negotiation of the contracts with the diamond syndicates, determined the policy on the disposal of diamonds and other assets, the working and development of mines, the application of profits, and the appointment of directors; and the majority of the directors meeting in London were able to control all questions of important expenditure. It was held by the House of Lords that the chief operation of the company was in fact controlled, managed and directed from London, where the 'head and seat and directing power of the affairs of the company' were located, and it followed that the company was resident within the United Kingdom for tax purposes.

9.72 It is often thought that the place where board meetings are held is conclusive as to where the central management and control is exercised. However, the place of central management and control is a question of fact, and the location of board meetings is only one pointer which needs to be considered. In *Unit Construction Co v Bullock*,[1] the Articles of

Association of three companies registered and carrying on business in East Africa recognised that management and control was in the hands of the directors, and expressly prohibited the holding of board meetings in the United Kingdom. The companies did not prosper, and the United Kingdom parent company decided to take over their management and control. There was no formal agreement with the subsidiaries but, thereafter, the parent company made all important decisions, and no further board meetings of the subsidiaries were held. The court decided that, while the company's Articles of Association stated what was to happen, they could not create an actual state of management and control, since this was a question of fact on the evidence. The subsidiaries were held to be resident in the United Kingdom for the relevant years.

1   [1960] AC 351, [1959] 3 All ER 831, 38 TC 712.

9.73 Inland Revenue Statement of Practice 1/90, published on 9 January 1990, sets out Inland Revenue practice in this area as follows:

In general the place of directors' meetings is significant only insofar as those meetings constitute the medium through which central management and control is exercised. If, for example, the directors of a company were engaged together actively in the UK in the complete running of a business which was wholly in the UK, the company would not be regarded as resident outside the UK merely because the directors held formal board meetings outside the UK. While it is possible to identify extreme situations in which central management and control plainly is, or is not, exercised by directors in formal meetings, the conclusion in any case is wholly one of fact depending on the relative weight to be given to various factors. Any attempt to lay down rigid guidelines would only be misleading.

Generally, however, where doubts arise about a particular company's residence status, the Inland Revenue adopt the following approach:
(i)   They first try to ascertain whether the directors of the company in fact exercise central management and control.
(ii) If so, they seek to determine where the directors exercise this central management and control (which is not necessarily where they meet).
(iii) In cases where the directors apparently do not exercise central management and control of the company, the Revenue then look to establish where and by whom it is exercised.

9.74 The Statement of Practice gives as an example of central management and control being exercised by a single individual the case where a chairman or managing director exercises powers formally conferred by the company's Articles and the other board members are little more than cyphers. An individual may also effectively control the company by reason of his dominant shareholding, or for some other reason. In such cases, the residence of the company is where the controlling individual exercises his powers.

9.75 It may be difficult to apply the 'central management and control' test where a subsidiary company and its parent operate in different territories. To a greater or lesser extent, the parent company will normally influence the actions of its subsidiary. The Statement of Practice indicates that, where the influence is exerted by the parent exercising its rights as a shareholder, for example in appointing and dismissing members of the board of the subsidiary or initiating or approving alterations to its financial structure, the Inland Revenue will not seek to argue that central management and control of the subsidiary is located where the parent company is resident. 'However, in cases where the parent usurps the functions of the board of the subsidiary (such as in *Unit Construction*) or where that board merely rubber stamps the parent company's decisions without giving them any independent consideration of its own, the Revenue draw the conclusion that the subsidiary has the same residence for tax purposes as its parent.' In particular, the Inland Revenue will have regard to the degree of autonomy which the directors of the subsidiary have in conducting the business of their company, and will take into account, among other things, the extent to which the directors of the subsidiary take decisions on their own authority as to investment, production, marketing and procurement without reference to the parent.[1]

1   In the recent Special Commissioners decision of *Untelrab Ltd v McGregor* and *Unigate Guernsey Ltd v McGregor* [1995] SWTI 1997 it was held that *Unit Construction* highlighted the very fine dividing line between a subsidiary being complaisant to do the will of the parent but actually functioning in giving effect to the parent's wishes (which would suggest the subsidiary was resident where its directors met), and a subsidiary whose board of directors did not function at all, even as a rubber stamp (which would suggest the subsidiary was resident where its parent was resident). The Commissioners thought it would be exceptional for a parent company to usurp control from its subsidiaries, rather than operating through their boards; although the board of a subsidiary might do what it was told to do, it did not follow that control and management lay elsewhere, so long as the board actually exercised its discretion, without being controlled by the parent, when deciding to do what it was told and would have refused to carry out any proposal which was improper or unreasonable. Finally, the Special Commissioners recalled that the burden of proving residence lay on the Crown (*Cesena Sulphur Co Ltd v Nicholson* (1876) ITC 88) and held that it had failed in this case to prove its contention that the subsidiaries' boards had merely rubber stamped decisions taken by the parent company in London and were not exercising central management and control.

9.76   The Statement of Practice concludes with the following warning:

In outlining factors relevant to the application of the case law test, this Statement assumes that they exist for genuine commercial reasons. Where, however, as may happen, it appears that a *major objective* underlying the existence of certain factors is the obtaining of tax benefits from residents or non-residents, the Revenue examine the facts particularly closely in order to see whether there has been an attempt to create the appearance of central management and control in a particular place without the reality.

NON-RESIDENTS TRADING IN THE UNITED KINGDOM

9.77   As indicated in paragraph 9.61, a person who is not tax resident in the United Kingdom is not liable to tax on the profits or gains of any trade, profession or vocation which is not exercised in this country, and a company which is not tax resident here cannot be liable to corporation tax unless it carries on a trade in the United Kingdom through a branch or agency here. Thus, it is necessary for both individuals and companies to decide whether trading etc is taking place in the United Kingdom. In the case of companies, it is also necessary to decide whether such trading is being carried on through a branch or agency here. In practice, the latter question is also important in the case of individuals because, in the absence of someone within the United Kingdom on whom an assessment can be raised, it may be difficult for the Inland Revenue to assess or collect the tax.

9.78 There has been a large number of cases on the distinction between trading *with* a country and trading *in* that country. In *Grainger and Son v Gough*,[1] a London wine merchant also acted as agent in Great Britain for the sale of wines and champagnes on behalf of Louis Roederer, whose chief place of business was in Reims, France. The agents sought orders in the name of Roederer and passed them on to him in Reims, where he exercised his discretion as to executing the orders. Roederer forwarded the wine direct to the customers in England, and invoiced them in his own name from Reims. Usually, the customers paid Roederer direct, although sometimes the agent collected the payments on his behalf. The agent was entitled to a commission on all orders received from Great Britain, if accepted by Roederer and executed. It was held that Roederer was not carrying on a trade in Great Britain through his London agent. As Lord Herschell explained:

> I think it clear that no contracts to sell wine were ever made by the appellants on behalf of Roederer. All that they did was to transmit to him the orders received, and until he had agreed to comply or complied with them there was no contract. ... Taking it to be the fact, as in my opinion it undoubtedly is, that contracts for the sale of wine are not made by Roederer in this country, and that the delivery by him to purchasers always takes place in France, it appears to me that the case differs widely from any that have hitherto been decided. In all previous cases, contracts have been habitually made in this country ... I think there is a broad distinction between trading with a country and carrying on a trade within a country. ... How does a wine merchant exercise his trade? I take it, by making or buying wine and selling it again, with a view to profit. If all that a merchant does in any particular country is to solicit orders, I do not think he can reasonably be said to exercise or carry on his trade in that country. What is done there is only ancillary to the exercise of his trade in the country where he buys or makes, stores and sells his goods.

1   [1896] AC 325, 3 TC 462.

9.79 By contrast, in the earlier case of *Pommery and Greno v Apthorpe*,[1] French wine merchants sold wine through English agents, who received orders from customers here and collected payment for wine sold here. The wine was supplied from stocks in England or, if the order was too large, direct from France. It was held that the French wine merchants were exercising a trade in the United Kingdom through the English agents, and that the profits of that trade were properly assessable on the agents regardless of where the wine was shipped from.

1   (1886) 2 TC 182.

9.80 It is often thought that whether a trade is being carried on in a country is determined by whether contracts are made in that country. Such thoughts may be based on cases such as *Erichsen v Last*,[1] which concerned a telegraph company established in Copenhagen. The company was not resident in the United Kingdom, but it had an agency and offices here to deal with calls received in this country using its wires. It had three lines in this country, two to Denmark and one to Norway. Payment was received here for messages sent from abroad and messages were sent abroad from here. In holding that the company was plainly exercising a trade in the United Kingdom and liable on the net profit derived from its receipts here, Brett LJ said:

> Wherever profitable contracts are habitually made in England by or for a foreigner with persons in England, because those persons are in England, to do something for or supply something to those persons, such foreigners are exercising a profitable trade in England, even though everything done or supplied by them in order to fulfil their part of the contract is done abroad. The profit arises to them from the contract which they made.

1   (1881) 8 QBD 414, 4 TC 422.

9.81 However, just as the location of board meetings is a relevant, but not necessarily conclusive, factor in determining the place where the central management and control of a company is exercised, the place where contracts are concluded is also no more than a factor, strongly indicative but not necessarily decisive. In *Greenwood v Smidth & Co*,[1] the respondents were a Danish firm resident in Copenhagen manufacturing and dealing in cement making and other similar machinery which they exported all over the world. They had an office in London in the charge of a qualified engineer who was their full-time employee. He received enquiries for machinery, sent to Denmark particulars of the work which the machinery was required to do and, when the machinery was supplied, he was available to give the English purchaser the benefit of his experience in erecting it. The contracts between the respondents and their customers were made in Copenhagen and the goods were shipped free by boat from Copenhagen. It was held that the place where a trade is exercised is the place where the transactions forming the alleged business are closed, in the case of a selling business by the sale of the commodity, and the profits thereby realised. The respondents were, therefore, exercising their trade in Denmark. However, the House of Lords approved the Court of Appeal judgment,[2] where Lord Sterndale MR said:

> There are indications in [*Grainger v Gough*] and other cases that it is sufficient to consider only where it is that the sale contracts are made which result in a profit. This is obviously a very important element in the enquiry, and if it is the only element the assessments are clearly bad. The contracts in this case were made abroad. But I am not prepared to hold that this test is decisive. I can imagine cases where the contract of resale is made abroad, and yet the manufacture of the goods, some negotiation of the terms, and complete execution of the contract takes place here under such circumstances that the trade was in truth exercised here. I think that the question is, where do the operations take place from which the profits in substance arise? To

my mind, there is no evidence in the present case of any other place than Denmark.

1   [1922] 1 AC 417, 8 TC 193.
2   [1921] 3 KB 583.

9.82   Similarly, in *Belfour v Mace,*[1] Italian silk manufacturers appointed a sole agent for the sale of their products in the United Kingdom, Canada and Australia. The agent solicited orders and transmitted them to Italy. The Italian manufacturers reserved the right to accept or reject the orders, and to fix prices. Acceptances were sent in duplicate to the agent, who forwarded one copy to the customer. Goods were then sent direct to the customer from Italy. The Italians had no stock or office in the United Kingdom, and no bank account here. Payments were made either direct to Italy or via the agent. The agent was entitled to a commission on net sales; he paid his own expenses and, whilst he was not responsible for bad debts, he earned no commission on them. He acted for non-competitive manufacturers, but the bulk of his work was done for the Italians. It was held as a matter of construction that no contracts were made until acceptance had been communicated to the English buyers; accordingly, the contracts were made in England, and the Italian manufacturers were exercising a trade in the United Kingdom. The agent was authorised to carry on a regular agency, and the profits of the Italian firm were correctly assessed on the agent. Lord Scrutton said:

> If you find a series of contracts made in England, it will be very difficult to escape liability for a trade exercised in England. In my view it is not impossible, but it would be very difficult. But it does not follow, in my view, that if you find a contract made abroad, there is necessarily no trade exercised in England. You may have, as the subject matter of the contract, work to be carried out in England by the foreign manufacturer, and the foreigner may carry out all the work in England and receive payment in England, and under these circumstances, in my view, it will not necessarily follow that because a contract is made abroad, the foreign merchant is not exercising a trade in England. I say that because there has been a tendency to argue that once you know where the contract is made, that settles the matter, once and for all, whether a trade is exercised in England or is not exercised in England. I do not think you can state the position in that absolute and clear cut way.

1   (1928) 13 TC 539.

9.83   The above quotation suggests that, where work is to be carried out in England, it is more likely that the trade will be found to be carried on here, notwithstanding that the contract, pursuant to which the work is done, was made abroad. In the words of Lord Sterndale MR in *Greenwood v Smidth & Co* quoted in paragraph 9.81 above, this is likely to be where 'the operations take place from which the profits in substance arise'. This is well illustrated by the more recent case of *IRC v Brackett,*[1] where a retired chartered surveyor resident in the United Kingdom entered into a contract of employment with a Jersey company, Drishane Investments Limited, the shares in which were owned by trustees of a Jersey settlement he had created for the benefit of the mother of his children. He was the company's only employee, and the company's only trade consisted of making his services as a property consultant available to clients. He was careful to refer all potential clients to the company, and to ensure that any contracts to supply his services to the clients were made by the company in Jersey. The Special Commissioners found as a fact that the company was trading in the United Kingdom, and this was accepted by Hoffmann J. In the words of the Special Commissioners:

> We find it impossible to say that the activities which the taxpayer conducts in this country as employee of Drishane are merely ancillary to a trade conducted by Drishane in Jersey. His activities constitute the essential operations of that trade and he represents its focal point. We have no evidence that Drishane through its officers resident in Jersey either seeks contracts or receives enquiries from potential clients otherwise than through the taxpayer. From start to finish, the client's contact is with the taxpayer in this country. ... The truth of the matter is that the arrangements whereby the taxpayer would render his services to clients in this country as an employee of Drishane, and contracts would be entered into in Jersey, were made for the specific purpose of transferring the trade to a non-resident person; but the operations which made up the trade of business consultant remained essentially the same. If we are to regard the place where the contracts are made as an important, but not necessarily the decisive, element, to be considered in deciding where a trade is carried on, we must reach the conclusion that Drishane's trade was carried on in this country. ... The commercial reality of the situation seems to us to require the whole extent of the operations to be looked at and not merely the place where the contracts are made. On that basis, we hold that Drishane was trading within the United Kingdom.

1   [1986] STC 521.

BRANCH OR AGENCY

9.84 Sections 78 and 79 of the Taxes Management Act 1970 provide as follows:

> 78(1).   A person not resident in the United Kingdom, whether a British subject or not, shall be assessable and chargeable to income tax in the name of ... any branch or agent, whether the branch or agent has the receipt of the profits or gains or not, in like manner and to the like amount as such non-resident person would be assessed and charged if he were resident in the United Kingdom and in the actual receipt of such profits or gains.

> 79.   A non-resident person shall be assessable and chargeable to income tax in respect of any profits or gains arising, whether directly or indirectly, through or from any branch or agency, and shall be so assessable and chargeable in the name of the branch or agent.

9.85 'Branch or agency' is defined, rather unhelpfully, both for the purposes of the Taxes Management Act 1970 and the Income and Corporation Taxes Act 1988, in section 118(1) of the former and section

834(1) of the latter as 'any factorship, agency, receivership, branch or management'. As with 'trade',[1] the statutory construction of 'branch or agency' is a question of law, but the primary facts, and the inferences to be drawn from those facts, are treated as questions of fact to be decided by the General or Special Commissioners. In practice, once a non-resident person is found to be carrying on a trade in the United Kingdom through the activities of a representative here, the representative is likely to be regarded as a 'branch or agency'. For example, in *Firestone Tyre & Rubber Co Ltd v Lewellin*,[2] the appellants were a subsidiary of Firestone Tyre & Rubber Co of Akron in the USA, which made and sold branded tyres throughout the world. By an agreement between the appellants and their US parent, the appellants were to fulfil from their premises in Brentford orders for the European market which had been obtained by the American company, to forward the goods ordered to the purchaser, and to give such instructions for payment of the price of the tyres as the American company should request. In consideration of these services, the American company undertook to pay to the appellants the cost price, as defined, of the tyres supplied plus 5%. In addition, however, the appellants fulfilled orders received direct from a number of exclusive distributors appointed by the US parent: provided these distributors appeared on the lists of authorised distributors supplied by the American company, the appellants executed orders which they received by post direct from them, delivering the tyres free alongside vessels at an English port and receiving payment in the United Kingdom. The House of Lords held that the appellants were properly assessed to income tax as agents for the American company, since the American company was exercising within the United Kingdom a trade of selling tyres to persons outside the United Kingdom, and was exercising the trade through the appellants as its agents. Lord Moreton said:

> The first stage is to determine whether the trade in selling tyres to persons outside the United Kingdom was exercised within the United Kingdom. I cannot doubt that it was so exercised ... Brentford were selling to distributors abroad under contracts made in the United Kingdom tyres manufactured by Brentford in the United Kingdom and delivering in the United Kingdom to the purchasers thereof against payment in the United Kingdom of the contract price; and, furthermore, were in fact effecting delivery of and receiving payment for such tyres in the United Kingdom. ...

> The next stage is to consider whether Akron was exercising the trade in question through Brentford as its agent ... this question must be answered in the affirmative ... the effect of the agreement and the course of the dealings between Akron and Brentford was to set up standing arrangements whereby Brentford agreed to hold goods of its own at the disposal of Akron and to sell the same on Akron's behalf to customers approved of by Akron and subject to terms imposed by Akron; and, further, to account to Akron for the proceeds of the sales less the cost of the goods sold plus 5%.

1   See para 9.7.
2   [1957] 1 All ER 561, [1957] 1 WLR 464, 37 TC 111.

9.86 It is clear from section 78(1) of the Taxes Management Act 1970 that a branch or agent can be assessed to tax on the profits or gains arising or accruing to a non-resident person through the activities of the branch or agent in the United Kingdom, whether or not the branch or agent is in receipt of such profits or gains. Moreover, it seems that an authority to conclude contracts in the name of the non-resident person is not an essential feature of a 'branch or agency'. Indeed, in *IRC v Brackett*, Hoffmann J remarked that 'wherever the contracts are made, I find it difficult to imagine how a non-resident company which carries on a trade with any degree of continuity in the United Kingdom can do so otherwise than through a "branch or agency" as defined in the Taxes Management Act 1970'.

9.87 In *IRC v Brackett*, the Special Commissioners found that the employee was an agent for Drishane:

> The intention is to bring within the charge to tax a foreign resident whose trade, though possibly centred abroad, includes operations conducted in this country through an establishment or permanent representative here. The taxpayer represents Drishane in this country and is in sole charge of the day to day conduct of the trading operations other than the formation of contracts. It is not straining language, in our opinion, to say that, by entrusting those operations to his care, Drishane has established at least a branch in this country. Alternatively, the taxpayer can properly be described as the manager of those operations, because he personifies them. ... The taxpayer is undoubtedly the personification of the branch or management of Drishane's business in this country and is, in our opinion, properly assessed as agent for Drishane on the authority of section 79.

9.88 In holding that there was evidence on which the Special Commissioners were entitled to find that the taxpayer constituted a 'branch or agency', Hoffmann J pointed out that the taxpayer was a United Kingdom resident and the sole United Kingdom resident by whom the company carried on its trade in the United Kingdom, adding that, for the purposes of section 79, he did not think that it was necessary that an agent should be a person who was empowered to enter into contractual relations on behalf of the non-resident company.

9.89 Section 78(2) provides, however, that a person who is not resident in the United Kingdom shall not, by virtue of section 78, be chargeable in the name of an agent in respect of profits or gains arising from investment transactions carried out by the agent in the ordinary course of carrying on a business of providing investment management services to a number of clients of whom the non-resident person is one, where the agent charges for his services at the agent's customary rate and is not connected[1] with the non-resident person. Similarly, section 82 of the Taxes Management Act 1970 provides that a non-resident person is not chargeable in the name of a broker or general commission agent where the agent is not authorised to carry on the regular agency[2] of the non-resident person, or where the agent executes sales or carries out transactions in the United Kingdom on behalf of the non-resident only with other non-residents. Where a broker or general commission agent acts regularly for the non-resident person, the profits or gains arising from sales or transactions carried out on his behalf cannot be assessed in the name of the agent if he is carrying on business as a bona fide independent agent in the United Kingdom, carries out the sales or transactions in the ordinary course of his business as such, and charges the non-resident person for such business at a rate not less than that customary in the class of business in question.

1   Within the meaning of s 839 of the Income and Corporation Taxes Act 1988.
2   In *Willson v Hooker* [1995] STC 1142, a solicitor was assessed to tax in respect of a gain made on the purchase and subsequent resale of some land by a non-resident company, for whom he acted. His appeal, based on the contention that he could not be carrying on a 'regular agency' as a result of acting in one single trading transaction, was dismissed by Vinelott J, who held that a 'regular agency' was one which was not casual or occasional. The solicitor was clearly not a casual or occasional agent, since all relevant transactions of the company in the UK during the relvant period had been carried out through him.

DOUBLE TAX TREATIES

9.90   It will be apparent that a non-resident person carrying on trading activities in the United Kingdom through a branch or agency here, or a non-resident individual carrying on a profession or vocation here, might be taxed twice on the profits or gains of such trade, profession or vocation if such profits or gains are taxed in his country of residence as well as in this country. Conversely, a resident of the United Kingdom might be taxed twice on profits or gains arising overseas, if such profits or gains are taxed overseas as well as in the United Kingdom. However, the United Kingdom has entered into a large number of double tax treaties which are intended to avoid such double taxation by providing that tax will be charged in only one of the two countries concerned, or that a credit or deduction will be allowed in one country in respect of tax charged in the other on the same income. Alternatively, unilateral relief may be available under section 790 of the Income and Corporation Taxes Act 1988, which allows foreign tax chargeable on income or chargeable gains to be allowed as a credit against the UK income or corporation tax liability on the same income or gains, thereby limiting the tax payable to the higher of that charged in the two jurisdictions.

9.91   Most current double tax treaties follow, to a greater or lesser extent, the form set out in a Model Tax Convention published by the Organisation for Economic Cooperation and Development, the latest version of which was published in 1992 and amended in March 1994. The following comments are based on the OECD Model Agreement, and should be treated with some caution as the actual treaty between the United Kingdom and the relevant overseas country may differ from the OECD Model Agreement. In particular, it should be noted that the double tax treaty between the United Kingdom and United States of America dated 31 December 1975[1] differs significantly from this Model Agreement.

1   SI 1980/568.

BUSINESS PROFITS

9.92   As regards business profits, Article 7 of the OECD Model Agreement provides that the profits of an enterprise carried on by a resident of one

Contracting State shall be taxable only in that State unless the enterprise carries on business in the other Contracting State through a 'permanent establishment' situated therein, in which case so much of the profit as is attributable to that permanent establishment may be taxed in the other State. The profits attributable to the permanent establishment will be those which the enterprise might be expected to make if it were a distinct and separate enterprise engaged in the same or similar activities under the same or similar conditions and dealing wholly independently with the enterprise of which it is a permanent establishment. Expenses incurred for the purposes of the permanent establishment, including executive and general administrative expenses so incurred in either country, are allowed as deductions in determining the profits of the permanent establishment.

PERMANENT ESTABLISHMENT

9.93 Article 5 of the OECD Model Agreement defines the term 'permanent establishment' to mean 'a fixed place of business through which the business of an enterprise is wholly or partly carried on'. The term expressly includes any place of management, branch, office, factory, workshop, mine, oil or gas well, quarry or other place of extraction of natural resources, and any building site or construction or installation project which lasts more than 12 months. However, the term is deemed not to include:
  (a) the use of facilities solely for the purpose of storage, display or delivery of goods or merchandise belonging to the enterprise;
  (b) the maintenance of a stock of goods or merchandise belonging to the enterprise solely for the purpose of storage, display or delivery;
  (c) the maintenance of a stock of goods or merchandise belonging to the enterprise solely for the purpose of processing by another enterprise;
  (d) the maintenance of a fixed place of business solely for the purpose of purchasing goods or merchandise, or of collecting information, for the enterprise;
  (e) the maintenance of a fixed place of business solely for the purpose of carrying on, for the enterprise, any other activity of a preparatory or auxiliary character; or
  (f) the maintenance of a fixed place of business solely for any combination of activities mentioned in (a) to (e) above, provided that the overall activity of the fixed place of business resulting from this combination is of a preparatory or auxiliary character.

9.94 Where an agent (other than a broker, general commission agent or other agent of independent status acting in the ordinary course of his business) has, and habitually exercises, in a Contracting State an authority to conclude contracts in the name of the enterprise, that enterprise is deemed to have a permanent establishment in that State in respect of any activities which the agent undertakes for the enterprise, unless they are limited to those mentioned in (a) to (f) of paragraph 9.93 above which, if exercised through a fixed place of business, would not make such fixed place of business a permanent establishment under the provisions of Article 5.

9.95 The fact that a company which is a resident of one Contracting State controls or is controlled by a company which is a resident of the other Contracting State, or which carries on business in that other State (whether through a permanent establishment or otherwise), does not of itself constitute either company a permanent establishment of the other.

PROFESSIONAL SERVICES

9.96 Article 14 of the OECD Model Agreement provides that income derived by a resident of one Contracting State in respect of independent personal services (which expressly include, among other things, independent scientific, literary, artistic, educational or teaching activities) shall be taxable only in that State unless he has a fixed base regularly available to him in the other Contracting State for the purpose of performing his activities. In the latter case so much of the income as is attributable to that fixed base may be taxed in the other State. Some treaties, including that between the United Kingdom and the United States of America, permit all income attributable to professional services performed in the other State to be taxed there if the individual is present in the other State for more than a specified number of days in the tax year concerned.

9.97 Many double tax treaties, however, follow the OECD Model Agreement in providing that, notwithstanding the provisions relating to professional services (and those relating to employment income), income derived by a resident of one Contracting State as an entertainer, such as a theatre, motion picture, radio or television artiste, or a musician, or as a sportsman, from his personal activities as such exercised in the other Contracting State, may be taxed in that other State, whether or not such income accrues to the entertainer or sportsman himself or to another person.

ROYALTIES

9.98 Double tax treaties will usually provide that royalties paid from a source within one country to a beneficial owner who is resident in another are taxable only in his country of residence or, alternatively, that the tax which may be charged[1] in the first country is limited to a specified percentage of the gross amount of the royalties. Nearly always, however, such treaties will follow the OECD Model Agreement in excluding these provisions in favour of the general provisions relating to business profits or professional services where the beneficial owner of the royalties carries on business in the country in which the royalties arise through the permanent establishment in that country, or performs professional services in that country from a fixed base situated there. In addition, double tax treaties will invariably provide that where, by reason of a special relationship between the payer and the beneficial owner, or between both of them and some other person, the amount of the royalties paid exceeds for whatever reason the amount which would have been agreed in the absence of such relationship, the royalty provisions in the treaty do not apply to the excess.

1   Usually by means of a withholding tax obligation imposed on the payer, as under ICTA 1988, ss 536–537B. See para 9.116 et seq below.

9.99 Article 12 of the OECD Model Agreement provides as follows:
1.   Royalties arising in a Contracting State and paid to a resident of the other Contracting State shall be taxable only in that other State if such resident is the beneficial owner of the royalties.
2.   The term 'royalties' as used in this article means payments of any kind received as a consideration for the use of, or the right to use, any copyright of literary, artistic or scientific work including cinematograph films, any patents, trade mark, design or model, plan, secret formula or process, or for information concerning industrial, commercial or scientific experience.
3.   The provisions of paragraph 1 shall not apply if the beneficial owner of the royalties, being a resident of a Contracting State, carries on business in the other Contracting State in which the royalties arise, through a permanent establishment situated therein, or performs in that other State independent personal services from a fixed base situated therein, and the right or property in respect of which the royalties are paid is effectively connected with such permanent establishment or fixed base. In such a case the provisions of Articles 7 or 14, as the case may be, shall apply.
4.   Where, by reason of a special relationship between the payer and the beneficial owner or between both of them and some other person, the amount of the royalties, having regard to the use, right or information for which they are paid, exceeds the amount which would have been agreed upon by the payer and the beneficial owner in the absence of such relationship, the provisions of this Article shall apply only to the last-mentioned amount. In such case, the excess part of the payments shall remain taxable according to the laws of each Contracting State, due regard being had to the other provisions of this Convention.

The licensee of merchandising rights

9.100 A person manufacturing and selling merchandise will almost certainly be carrying on a trade. The profits of that trade will be taxed under Schedule D, Case I according to the normal rules for computing trading profits. The income from sales of merchandise will clearly be receipts of the trade. In making payments to the owner of the merchandising rights, the trader will be concerned to know firstly whether such payments may be deducted from his trading receipts in computing the taxable profits of the trade, and secondly whether he is entitled or required to deduct tax from the payments.

TAX DEDUCTIBLE EXPENSES

9.101 The answer to the first question can be found in section 74 of the Income and Corporation Taxes Act 1988. This section sets out the general rules as to what deductions are *not* deductible. The first, and most important, is the general disallowance of any disbursements or expenses which are not 'wholly and exclusively laid out or expended for the purposes of the trade, profession or vocation'.[1]

1   ICTA 1988, s 74(1)(a).

9.102   There will not usually be a problem in establishing that payments made to the owner of merchandising rights pursuant to a licence which authorises the manufacture and sale of merchandise are paid 'wholly and exclusively' for the purposes of the trade of manufacturing and selling the merchandise. Problems may, however, arise if the sums paid represent:

    (a) capital expenditure;[1]
    (b) an annual payment payable out of the profits or gains of the trade.[2]

1   ICTA 1988, s 74(1)(f).
2   ICTA 1988, s 74(1)(m).

9.103   The purchase of merchandising rights, as distinct from the acquisition of a licence, is likely to be treated as capital expenditure, unless the trade includes dealing in such rights.

CAPITAL ALLOWANCES

9.104   Although capital expenditure is not generally deductible in computing the profits of a trade, capital allowances may be granted for expenditure on certain types of capital assets. Such allowances enable the expenditure to be written off for tax purposes against the profits of the trade over a prescribed period. This period is prescribed by statute, and any other basis of charging depreciation in the accounts of the trade is disallowed for tax purposes.

9.105   Capital allowances are available in respect of capital expenditure incurred on, among other things, industrial buildings and structures,[1] machinery and plant[2] (which is deemed to include computer software)[3] and the purchase of patent rights.[4] However, the only relevant form of merchandising rights on which capital expenditure may attract allowances, is likely to be know-how.[5] 'Know-how', for these purposes, is widely defined by section 533(7) of the Income and Corporation Taxes Act 1988 and includes, among other things, 'any industrial information and techniques likely to assist in the manufacture or processing of goods or materials'. Capital allowances are granted in respect of expenditure on acquiring know-how for use in a trade, if such expenditure is not otherwise deductible for tax purposes, at the rate of 25% per annum of the reducing balance of unrelieved expenditure.

1   Capital Allowances Act 1990, ss 1 to 21.
2   Capital Allowances Act 1990, ss 22 to 83.
3   Capital Allowances Act 1990, s 67A.
4   ICTA 1988, s 533.
5   ICTA 1988, ss 530 to 531.

9.106   The purchase of a trade mark for a lump sum should be disallowed as capital expenditure but, in practice, if the mark has a limited commercial life, the Inland Revenue may be willing to allow the acquisition cost to be written off over a period as deferred revenue expenditure.

9.107 Section 83 of the Income and Corporation Taxes Act 1988[1] expressly provides that, notwithstanding anything in section 74, a deduction is allowed in computing the profits or gains of a trade for any fees paid or expenses incurred in obtaining for the purposes of the trade the registration of a design or trade mark,[2] an extension of the period for which the right in a registered design subsists, or the renewal of registration of a trade mark.

1 This section contains the only reference to trade marks in the tax leglisation.
2 References to a trade mark include references to a service mark within the meaning of the Trade Marks (Amendment) Act 1984.

DEDUCTION OF TAX AT SOURCE

9.108 In a number of cases, a person making payments to the owner of merchandising rights may be required or permitted to deduct income tax at the basic rate from such payments.

ANNUAL PAYMENTS

9.109 It has been seen[1] that 'annual payments', payable out of the profits or gains of a trade, are disallowed as deductions in computing the profits of that trade by section 74(1)(m) of the Income and Corporation Taxes Act 1988. Instead, the payer is permitted to deduct income tax at the basic rate[2] from such payment under section 348(1) of the Income and Corporation Taxes Act 1988. This sub-section provides as follows:

> Subject to any provision to the contrary in the Income Tax Acts, where any annuity or other annual payment charged with tax under Case III of Schedule D, not being interest, is payable wholly out of profits or gains brought into charge to income tax:
> (a) the whole of the profits or gains shall be assessed and charged with income tax on the person liable to the annuity or other annual payment, without distinguishing the annuity or other annual payment; and
> (b) the person liable to make the payment, whether out of the profits or gains charged with income tax or out of any annual payment liable to deduction, or from which a deduction has been made, shall be entitled on making the payment to deduct and retain out of it a sum representing the amount of income tax[2] thereon; and
> (c) the person to whom the payment is made shall allow the deduction on receipt of the residue of the payment, and the person making the deduction shall be acquitted and discharged of so much money as is represented by the deduction, as if the sum had been actually paid; and
> (d) the deduction shall be treated as income tax paid by the person to whom the payment is made.

This means that, while the payer is not entitled to deduct the amount of the 'annual payment' when computing the profits of his trade, and will be taxed on the profits as if no such payment had been made, he is nevertheless permitted to deduct income tax at the basic rate from the payment. If the payer is an individual, he may then retain the tax so deducted, thereby obtaining effective relief at the basic rate for such payment. Higher rate relief is given against an individual's total income from all sources, including trading profits, in the relevant year by section 835(6)(b) of the Income and Corporation Taxes Act 1988.

1   Para 9.102 above.
2   ICTA 1988, s 4(1) provides that any provision of the Income Tax Acts requiring, permitting or assuming the deduction of income tax from any amount or treating income tax as having been deducted from or paid on any amount shall, subject to any provision to the contrary, be construed as referring to deduction or payment of income tax at the basic rate in force for the relevant year of assesment. For this purpose, s 4(2) provides that the relevant year of assessment shall be taken to be (except where otherwise provided) the year in which the amount becomes due where it is an amount payable wholly out of profits or gains brought into charge to tax and, in any other case, the year in which the amount is paid.

9.110   If the individual fails to deduct the tax, he will obtain no basic rate relief on the payment. The right to deduct tax under section 348 arises 'on making the payment', but it has been held that, if some payments are made without deduction of tax, such tax may be adjusted by deduction from later payments during the same tax year.[1] A failure to deduct cannot, however, be rectified after the end of the tax year in which the deduction should have been made.[2]

1   *Taylor v Taylor* [1938] 1 KB 320.
2   *Currie v Goold* (1817) 2 Madd 163; *Ex p Turner* (1864) 11 LT 352; *Re Hatch* [1919] 1 Ch 351.

9.111   Companies are able to deduct 'annual payments' as charges on income against their total profits from all sources, including trading profits, in the relevant year, after all other reliefs except group relief, pursuant to section 338 of the Income and Corporation Taxes Act 1988.

9.112   Where any 'annual payment' is not payable, or not wholly payable, out of profits or gains brought into charge to income tax, the person by or through whom the payment is made[1] is required by section 349(1) of the Income and Corporation Taxes Act 1988 to deduct from the payment a sum representing the amount of income tax at the basic rate thereon. This requirement applies, therefore, to all companies resident in the United Kingdom (since their profits or gains are brought into charge to corporation tax, not income tax), and to all individuals whose taxable profits do not exceed the amount of the payment. Such person is then required by section 350 of the Income and Corporation Taxes Act 1988 to deliver to the Inland Revenue an account of the payment. In the case of an individual, such account is required by section 350(1) to be delivered 'forthwith', although in practice it will be delivered with the annual tax return, and he is liable to be assessed and chargeable with income tax at the basic rate on the payment, or on so much thereof as is not made out of profits or gains brought into charge to income tax. In the case of a company, section 350(4) requires the account to be delivered in accordance with Schedule 16 to the Income and Corporation Taxes Act 1988, which provides for quarterly returns to be made, together with payment of the amount due, within 14 days from the end of the relevant quarter.

1   This includes an agent of the payer, such as his solicitor: *Rye & Eyre v IRC* [1935] AC 274, 19 TC 164.

9.113   Where an individual is required to deduct tax pursuant to section 349 from an annual payment made wholly and exclusively for the purposes of his trade, because the amount of his taxable profits were insufficient to cover the payment, section 387 of the Income and Corporation Taxes Act 1988 provides that the amount on which tax has been paid under section 350 may be treated as though it were a loss sustained in the trade. Following a claim under section 380, such losses are relieved against the individual's general income in the relevant year and, where this is insufficient to absorb the loss, the excess is carried forward to be set off against future profits of the same trade pursuant to section 385. A similar result is obtained under section 393(9) by companies whose charges on income include payments made wholly and exclusively for the purposes of the trade which exceed the total profits of the trade against which they are deductible in the relevant year.

9.114   Section 106 of the Taxes Management Act 1970 provides that a person who refuses to allow a deduction of income tax authorised by the Taxes Acts to be made out of any payment shall incur a penalty of £50, and that every agreement for payment of, among other things, annual payments in full without allowing any such deduction shall be void. However, it was held by the House of Lords in *IRC v Ferguson*[1] that an agreement to pay a sum 'free of income tax' means that the specified sum is net of any tax which should be deducted. In other words, the payer will be required to gross up the payment to such amount as will leave the payee with the specified sum after the basic rate income tax has been deducted.

1   [1970] AC 442, 46 TC 1.

9.115   It will be appreciated that the definition of 'annual payment' depends, among other things, on whether the payment constitutes 'pure income profit' in the hands of the payee.[1] This may cause the payer some difficulty, since his entitlement or obligation to deduct basic rate income tax at source when making any periodical payments[2] for merchandising rights will depend on how those payments are treated in the hands of the person to whom they are paid.

1   See para 9.50 et seq above.
2   Lump sum payments lack the requisite quality of recurrence to be 'annual payments': see para 9.54 above.

PAYMENTS TO OVERSEAS RIGHTS OWNERS

9.116   Sections 536, 537 and 537B of the Income and Corporation Taxes Act 1988 require income tax at the basic rate to be deducted under section 349(1) from any royalties or other periodic payments in respect of copyright, public lending rights, or rights in a design to an owner whose usual place of abode is outside the United Kingdom, whether or not payable out of profits or gains brought into charge to income tax.[1]

1   In the absence of any comparable provision for trade marks, there is no obligation to deduct tax from trademark payments unless they consititute 'annual payments'.

9.117 Where, however, payment is made through an agent resident in the United Kingdom and the agent is entitled as against the owner of the right to deduct any sum by way of commission for services rendered, the amount from which the tax must be deducted is the payment less the commission.[1]

1   ICTA 1988, ss 536(3) and 537B(3).

9.118 For this purpose, 'owner' includes a person who has assigned the rights but is entitled to receive periodical payments in respect thereof.[1] The provisions of sections 536, 537 and 537B do not, however, apply to copyright royalties, public lending right or other periodical payments in respect of copies of works, or to design royalties or other periodical payments in respect of articles, which are shown on a claim to have been exported from the United Kingdom for distribution outside the United Kingdom.[2]

1   ICTA 1988, s 536(2) and 537B(2)(b).
2   ICTA 1988, ss 536(2) and 537B(2)(c).

9.119 In *IRC v Longmans, Green & Co Ltd*[1] an English publisher bought exclusive English language translation and publication rights from the French author of 'Le silence de M. Clemenceau', and paid him a lump sum of FF500,000 for the right to sell 28,000 copies of the best edition after M. Clemenceau's death. Additional payments were due pro rata on further sales of the best edition, and a royalty on cheap editions but, in the event, only 7,000 copies of the best edition sold. It was held that the publishers had acquired a licence, and not a complete assignment, although the line between a partial assignment of copyright and a licence may be extremely fine. Finlay J said it would be odd if the licence fee was a capital payment in respect of the first 28,000 copies, with any further payments being royalty income. As he concluded:

> What they did was, so to speak, to quantify, fix a term for, the royalties in respect of 28,000 copies but, nevertheless, one can see from the Agreement itself that the sum was a sum in respect of royalties ... that there is a lump sum paid is not in any way decisive to show that this is not paid in respect of royalties ... it does not matter whether you have got a sum paid every year, or a sum paid every three years, or a sum paid once and for all: you have got to look at the substance of the thing and arrive at a conclusion as to whether in truth the sum paid was paid in respect of royalties.

It was held that the FF500,000 was clearly a payment of or on account of royalties, from which basic rate income tax should have been deducted under what is now section 536 of the Income and Corporation Taxes Act 1988.

1   (1932) 17 TC 272.

9.120 It appears that the provisions of section 536 do not apply to payments made to those who are authors by profession.[1] The Inland Revenue is believed to limit this interpretation to authors, although there seems no reason in principle why it should not apply to any other rights owner carrying on a profession or vocation whose usual place of abode is outside the United Kingdom, since the logic of the interpretation is that the source of the income is the profession, which is outside the United Kingdom.

1   See Parliamentary written answer of Mr Roy Jenkins, Chancellor of the Exchequer, on 10 November 1969 (Hansard, Volume 791, Col 31).

9.121   The obligation to deduct tax from royalties or other periodical payments made to residents of certain countries may also be excluded by the provisions of any applicable double tax treaty between the United Kingdom and those countries. Such a treaty may require the royalties to be paid without deduction of tax, or may require the deduction to be less than the basic rate of income tax.[1]

1   See para 9.98 et seq above.

9.122   In the case of countries whose double tax treaties with the United Kingdom follow the provisions of Article 12 of the OECD Model Agreement,[1] royalties may be paid to residents of those countries without deduction of tax, notwithstanding the provisions of sections 536, 537 or 537B of the Income and Corporation Taxes Act 1988. Many treaties, however, provide for tax to be deducted, albeit at a lesser rate than the basic rate of income tax, and it is essential to consult the text of any applicable Treaty as there may be other variations of wording.

1   See para 9.99 above.

9.123   If it appears to the Board of the Inland Revenue that any person entitled to any consideration or other amount taxable under section 775 (sale by individual of income derived from his personal activities)[1] is not resident in the United Kingdom, the Board may direct that section 349(1) shall apply to any payment forming part of that amount as if it were an annual payment charged with tax under Schedule D, Case III.

1   See para 9.32 above.

Non-resident entertainers and sportsmen

9.124   Sections 555 to 558 of the Income and Corporation Taxes Act 1988, and the Income Tax (Entertainers and Sportsmen) Regulations 1987[1] require basic rate income tax to be deducted from certain payments made to entertainers or sportsmen, or to third parties, in connection with certain activities in this country. The Inland Revenue appears to believe that these provisions will apply irrespective of the terms of any Double Tax Treaty.[2] By section 55(1) and (2), the provisions apply:
  (a) where a person who is an entertainer or sportsman of a prescribed description;
  (b) performs an activity of a prescribed description in the United Kingdom;
  (c) the person is not resident in the United Kingdom in the year of assessment in which the relevant activity is performed; and
  (d) a payment or transfer is made (to whichever person) which has a connection of a prescribed kind with the relevant activity.

9.125 *Tax aspects*

1   SI 1987/530.
2   See Inland Revenue Publication FEU50 at paragraph A8.

PRESCRIBED DESCRIPTION OF ENTERTAINER OR SPORTSMAN

9.125 The 'prescribed description' of 'entertainer or sportsman' is found in paragraph 2(1) of the Income Tax (Entertainers and Sportsmen) Regulations 1987, which defines 'entertainer' to mean 'any description of individuals (and whether performing alone or with others) who give performances in their character an individual, which is or may be made available to the public, or any section of the public, and whether for payment or not'.

PRESCRIBED DESCRIPTION OF ACTIVITY

9.126 A 'relevant activity' is defined by Regulation 6(2) as 'an activity performed in the United Kingdom by an entertainer in his character as entertainer on or in connection with a commercial occasion or event', including any appearance of the entertainer by way of or in connection with the promotion of any such occasion or event and any participation by the entertainer in or for sound recording, films, videos, radio, television or other similar transmissions (whether live or recorded). By Regulation 6(3), a 'commercial occasion or event' includes 'any description of occasion or event for which an entertainer (or other person) might receive or become entitled, for or by virtue of the entertainer's performance of the activity, to receive anything by way of cash or any other form of property, or which is designed to promote commercial sales or activity by advertising, the endorsement of goods or services, sponsorship, or other promotional means of any kind'.

RESIDENCE

9.127 It should be noted that the entertainer's residence in the year in which the payment is made is irrelevant, if this is not the same as the year in which the relevant activity is performed.

PAYMENT OR TRANSFER

9.128 By section 555(5) of the Income and Corporation Taxes Act 1988, 'payment' is defined to include a loan, and 'transfer' includes both a temporary transfer (as by way of loan) of something other than money and a transfer of any right. By Regulation 3(2) the payment or transfer has a connection of the 'prescribed kind' if it is made for, in respect of, or in any way derives either directly or indirectly from, the performance of a relevant activity. However, Regulation 3(3) excludes the following payments:
  (i) Any payment required by any other provision to be made under deduction of basic rate income tax.
  (ii) Any payment for the provision of services ancillary to the performance of a relevant activity, which is paid to a person who

is resident and ordinarily resident in the United Kingdom who is not connected with or an associate of the entertainer concerned, provided the amount or value of the payment does not exceed what would be reasonable for the provision of such services as between persons dealing with each other at arm's length.

(iii) Any payment made to an entertainer in respect of the proceeds of sale of records deriving from a recording made by him, where the payment is calculated by reference to such proceeds or payment on account of those proceeds.

9.129 In addition, Regulation 4(3) excludes payments which, together with any connected payments and connected transfers made to the entertainer or an associate or other person connected with him, do not exceed £1,000 in aggregate during a tax year.

9.130 Whilst it is clear that payments or transfers to an entertainer or sportsman otherwise than in connection with a 'commercial occasion or event', such as payments made for the right to reproduce his name or likeness on merchandise, will not of itself fall within these provisions, payments connected with personal appearances in the United Kingdom which are designed to promote the sale of such merchandise will do so. Difficulties may arise in practice in determining whether an appearance or other relevant activity is 'in connection with' a commercial occasion or event.

CAPITAL GAINS TAX

9.131 Capital gains tax[1] is charged in respect of chargeable gains (computed in accordance with the Taxation of Chargeable Gains Act 1992) accruing to a person on the disposal of assets[2] in a year of assessment during any part of which he is resident or ordinarily resident in the United Kingdom.[3] If he is not resident or ordinarily resident in the United Kingdom, but is carrying on a trade in the United Kingdom through a branch or agency here,[4] he will be liable to capital gains tax on the disposal of chargeable assets situated in the United Kingdom where these have been used in or for the purposes of the trade at or before the time when the capital gain accrued.[5] An individual resident or ordinarily resident, but not domiciled, in the United Kingdom is, however, not liable to capital gains tax in respect of gains accruing from the disposal of assets situated outside the United Kingdom, unless sums in respect of those gains are remitted to this country.[6]

1   Companies pay corporation tax in respect of chargeable gains: TCGA 1992, s 1(2) and see ICTA 1988, s 6.
2   TCGA 1992, s 1(1).
3   TCGA 1992, s 2(1).
4   For the meaning of 'branch or agency' see TCGA 1992, s 10(6) and para 9.84 et seq above.
5   TCGA 1982, s 10(1)(a). Or where the assets have been used or held for the purpose of the branch or agency at or before that time, or were acquired for use by or for the purposes of the branch or agency: TCGA 1992, s 10(1)(b).
6   TCGA 1992, s 12.

Assets

9.132 All forms of property, including incorporeal property generally, are treated as 'assets' for capital gains tax purposes, whether or not they are situated in the United Kingdom.[1] 'Property' is not itself defined in the 1992 Act, but may be understood to refer to anything capable of being owned and disposed of, or of otherwise being turned to account.[2] This includes goodwill,[3] the benefit of a royalty contract,[4] and all other forms of intellectual property likely to be relevant for the purposes of this work.

1   TCGA 1992, s 21.
2   In *O'Brien v Benson's Hosiery (Holdings) Ltd* [1980] AC 562; [1979] 3 All ER 652, 53 TC 241, it was held that rights of an employer under a service contract were 'assets' even though a right to personal services was not assignable and had no market value, because the employer was able to exact from the employee a substantial sum as a term of releasing him from his obligations to serve.
3   *Kirby v Thorn EMI plc* [1988] 2 All ER 947, [1988] 1 WLR 445, 60 TC 519.
4   *Rank Xerox Ltd v Lane* [1981] AC 629, [1979] 3 All ER 657, 53 TC 185.

9.133 The location of assets for capital gains tax purposes is governed by section 275 of the Taxation of Chargeable Gains Act 1992. As regards those assets likely to be relevant for the purposes of this work:
  (a) goodwill is situated where the relevant trade, business or profession is carried on;[1]
  (b) trademarks, service marks and registered designs are situated where they are registered, and rights or licences to use a trade mark, service mark or registered design are situated in the United Kingdom if they or any right derived from them are exercisable in the United Kingdom;[2]
  (c) copyright, design right and franchises, and rights or licences to use any copyright work or design in which design right subsists, are situated in the United Kingdom if they or any right derived from them are exercisable in the United Kingdom.[3]

1   TCGA 1992, s 275(g).
2   TCGA 1992, s 275(h).
3   TCGA 1992, s 275(j).

Disposals

9.134 'Disposal' is likewise not defined by the 1992 Act, although section 21(2) provides that references to a disposal of an asset include references to a part-disposal, and section 22(1) provides that there is a disposal of assets by their owner where any capital sum is derived from them notwithstanding that no asset is acquired by the person paying the capital sum. Section 22(1) refers in particular to capital sums received by way of compensation for any kind of damage or injury to assets, to capital sums received in return for forfeiture or surrender of rights or for refraining from exercising rights, and capital sums received as consideration for use or exploitation of assets. In principle, therefore, there will be a disposal for capital gains tax purposes if any sum is received in consideration of the assignment, or in respect of the grant of any licence, of merchandising rights, or by way of damages for infringement of any such rights.

9.135 Section 37(1) of the 1992 Act provides, however, that there shall be excluded from the consideration for a disposal of assets taken into account in the computation of a chargeable gain any money or money's worth charged to income tax as income of, or taken into account as a receipt in computing income or profits or gains or losses of, the person making the disposal for the purposes of the Income Tax Acts. Thus, where the assignor or licensor is carrying on a trade or profession, sums received for the assignment or licensing of merchandising rights are likely to be liable to income or corporation tax, rather than to capital gains tax.[1] If the owner of the rights holds them as an investment, the proceeds of an assignment are likely to be treated as a capital receipt,[2] not liable to income tax, and so may be liable to capital gains tax.

1   See para 9.17 above.
2   *Shiner v Lindblom* [1960] 3 All ER 832, [1961] 1 WLR 248, 39 TC 367.

VALUE ADDED TAX

9.136 Value Added Tax is charged on any supply of goods or services made in the United Kingdom, where it is a taxable supply made by a taxable person in the course or furtherance of any business carried on by him.[1]

1   Value Added Tax Act 1994, s 4(1).

9.137 'Supply' is defined, rather unhelpfully, to include all forms of supply, but excludes anything not done for a consideration.[1] However, section 5(2)(b) provides that anything which is not a supply of goods but is done for a consideration is a supply of services, and expressly mentions the granting, assignment or surrender of any right. Thus, it is clear that the assignment or licensing of merchandising rights for a consideration will amount to a supply of services.

1   VATA 1994, s 5(2)(a).

Taxable supplies

9.138 A 'taxable supply' is a supply of goods or services made in the United Kingdom other than an exempt supply.[1] 'Exempt supplies' are described in Schedule 9,[2] but none of the supplies described in that Schedule is likely to be relevant for the purposes of this work. Thus, the assignment or licensing of merchandising rights for a consideration will be a taxable supply if made in the United Kingdom.

1   VATA 1994, s 4(2).
2   See VATA 1994, s 31.

Taxable persons

9.139 A person is a 'taxable person' for Value Added Tax purposes while he is, or is required to be, registered under the Value Added Tax Act.[1] A person who makes taxable supplies but is not registered becomes liable to be registered at the end of any month, if the value[2] of his taxable supplies in the period of one year then ending has exceeded the registration limit,[3] or at any time if there are reasonable grounds for believing that the value of his taxable supplies in the period of 30 days beginning from that time will exceed that limit. A person does not, however, become liable to be registered by virtue of the value of his taxable supplies in the preceding year if he can satisfy the Commissioners of Customs & Excise that the value of his taxable supplies in the period of one year beginning at the time when he would otherwise become liable to be registered will not exceed a specified sum,[4] and a person who has become liable to be registered will cease to be so liable at any time after being registered if he can satisfy the Commissioners that the value of his taxable supplies in the period of one year then beginning will not exceed that sum.[5]

1 VATA 1994, s 3(1).
2 The general rule is that the value of a supply is the VAT-exclusive amount of the consideration, but see VATA 1994, s 19 and Sch 6.
3 The registration limit, with effect from 29 November 1995, is £76,000: Value Added Tax (Increase of Registration Limits) Order 1995, SI 1995/3037.
4 VATA 1994, Sch 1, para 1(3). With effect from 29 November 1995, the specified sum is £45,000: Value Added Tax (Increase of Registration Limits) Order 1995.
5 VATA 1994, Sch 1, para 4.

Business

9.140 'Business' is defined by section 94 to include any trade, profession or vocation, but bears a wider meaning than is borne by those terms for the purposes of income and corporation tax.[1] The European Community Sixth Council Directive of 17 May 1977 (77/388/EEC) defines a 'taxable person' to mean any person who independently carries out in any place any specified economic activity, whatever the purpose or results of that activity, and the specified economic activities comprise all activities of producers, traders and persons supplying services. The exploitation of tangible or intangible property for the purpose of obtaining income therefrom on a continuing basis is expressly mentioned in the Sixth Directive as an economic activity for this purpose.[2] It has been held[3] that it is necessary to consider the whole of a person's activities to determine whether they constitute a 'business' but that it is not necessary for them to be carried on with the object of making a profit, and that the word 'business' is wide enough to embrace any occupation or function actively pursued with reasonable continuity. However, the ordinary meaning of the word 'business' excludes any activity which is no more than an activity for pleasure and social enjoyment.[4] In the VAT Tribunal case of *Triangle Thoroughbreds*[5] the following factors were extracted from the decided cases as being relevant for the purpose of determining whether or not a particular activity constitutes a business, namely whether the activity:
>   (a) is a serious undertaking earnestly pursued;
>   (b) is an occupation or function actively pursued with reasonable or recognisable continuity;
>   (c) has a certain measure of substance as measured by the quarterly or annual value of taxable supplies made;

(d) is conducted in a regular manner and on sound and recognised business principles;

(e) is predominantly concerned with the making of taxable supplies to consumers for a consideration;

(f) involves the making of taxable supplies of a kind which are commonly made by those who seek to profit by them.

Accordingly, it is likely that a person dealing in merchandising rights for a consideration, particularly where this comprises royalties or other continuing payments, will be treated as carrying on a business for Value Added Tax purposes.

1   See paras 9.7–9.16 above.
2   Sixth Directive, Art 4.
3   In *Customs & Excise Comrs v Morrisons Academy Boarding Houses Association* [1978] STC 1.
4   *Customs & Excise Comrs v Lord Fisher* [1981] 2 All ER 147, [1981] STC 238.
5   MAN/90/470; quoted in *Strachan v Customs & Excise Comrs*, LON/91/2621Y.

Place of supply

9.141   The general rule is that a supply of services is treated as made in the country where the supplier belongs.[1] However, a supply of services comprising, among other things, the assignment or licensing of merchandising rights will be treated as made in the country where the recipient (ie, the assignee/licensee) belongs if the recipient:

(a) belongs in a country, other than the Isle of Man, which is not a Member State; or

(b) belongs in a Member State, other than the one in which the supplier belongs, and:

   (i) receives the supply for the purpose of a business[2] carried on by him;

   (ii) has been assigned a registration number by the Member State in which he belongs; and

   (iii) is not within the scope of the reverse charge described in paragraph 9.142.[3]

1   VATA 1994, s 7(10).
2   In *Diversified Agency Services Ltd v Customs & Excise Comrs* [1996] STC 398, a London advertising agency supplied advertising services to the Spanish Tourist Board, which had a London office and was registered for VAT both in Spain and in the UK. the advertising was mainly of tourist attractions in Spain to potential customers in the UK. The services were supplied to the head office in Madrid, but the Court held that art 16 of the 1992 Order did not apply because the promotion of tourism in Spain by a government body was not a 'business' for VAT purposes. Accordingly, the services supplied were not received by the Spanish Tourist Board for the purposes of a business carried on by it and since this rendered art 16 inapplicable, the general principle applied; the services were supplied in the UK, where the advertising agency belonged, and so were subject to UK VAT.
3   Value Added Tax (Place of Supply of Services) Order 1992, SI 1992/3121, art 16.

9.142   Where the supplier of services comprising the assignment or licensing of merchandising rights[1] belongs in a country other than the United Kingdom, and the recipient belongs in the United Kingdom, the supply will, if the services were supplied to the recipient for the purposes of any business carried on by him, be treated as taxable supplies made by the recipient in the United Kingdom in the course or furtherance of his business.[2] This means that the assignee/licensee must add UK VAT to the invoice he receives from the assignor/licensor. He will have to account for this to HM Customs & Excise as output tax but, assuming he makes only taxable supplies in the course of his business, will be entitled to a credit for input tax of the same amount.

1   Sch 5, para 1 of VATA 1994 refers to transfers and assignments of copyright, patents, licences, trademarks and similar rights. HM Customs & Excise regard this as including the grant of such rights: see Notice 741, para 9.10.
2   VATA 1994, s 8 and Sch 5, para 1.

9.143   Accordingly, the assignment or licensing of merchandising rights to a person who belongs outside the European Union will be outside the scope of Value Added Tax.[1] However, the supplier will still be entitled to credit for any input tax incurred on goods or services purchased for his business use in making the supplies.[2] Similarly, the supply will be outside the scope of UK Value Added Tax if the assignee/licensee belongs in a European Union country other than the United Kingdom or Isle of Man, is registered for VAT in the country where he belongs, and acquires the merchandising rights for the purposes of his registered business. (The assignee/licensee is likely to suffer a reverse charge under the equivalent of section 8 of the Value Added Tax Act 1994 in the country where he belongs.) If, however, the assignee/licensee is not registered in the country where he belongs, the supply will be treated as having been made in the United Kingdom, and will be subject to Value Added Tax at the standard rate.[3]

1   Before 1 January 1993, such supplies were zero rated under group 9, item 5 of Sch 5 to the Value Added Tax Act 1983.
2   VATA 1994, s 26(2)(b).
3   Before 1 January 1993, such a supply to a person belonging outside the United Kingdom was zero rated. See note 1 above.

9.144   The place where a supplier or recipient of services belongs is determined in accordance with the rules set out in section 9 of the Value Added Tax Act 1994. Except in the case of an individual receiving services otherwise than for business purposes (who is treated as belonging in whatever country he has his usual place of residence)[1] this will be the country where he has his only business establishment[2] or other fixed establishment or, if he has no such establishment, his usual place of residence; if he has such establishments in more than one country, he is treated as belonging in the country where the establishment of his which is most directly concerned with the supply is located.

1   In relation to a body corporate, 'usual place of residence' means the place where it is legally constituted.
2   A person carrying on a business through a branch or agency in any country is treated by VATA 1994, s 9(5)(a) as having a business establishment there, but this has recently been held by a VAT tribunal to be contrary to European Community law (see *WH Payne & Co*, para 9.145 below.

9.145   In the recent case of *WH Payne & Co v Customs & Excise Comrs*,[1] a firm of chartered accountants supplied accountancy, book-keeping and taxation services to various overseas companies which were incorporated, managed and controlled outside the European Union, but which owned property in the UK which was let and managed through letting agents and managing agents here. The firm contended its services (which related to the companies' UK tax liability on the rental income) were not supplied in the UK because the overseas companies did not belong in a Member State. The Commissioners argued that the companies had business establishments or fixed establishments in the UK, and that the firm's services were more directly used by those establishments than by the companies' business establishments or fixed establishments overseas. The Tribunal held that a person could have only one business establishment, which should be equated to a head office, headquarters or principal place of business. In this case, the companies' businesses were not run from the UK and they had no business establishments here. As regards fixed place of business, this denoted a place of certain minimum size where the human and technical resources necessary for receipt of the services were permanently present.[2] The properties were held not to be fixed establishments since they were the subject of the supplies, while the letting agents, managing agents and the firm itself were independent contractors. Accordingly, the companies did not have fixed establishments in the UK or, if they did, the firm's services were not supplied to them. The services related to the tax and accounting requirements of companies administered from overseas, and were both received and most directly used by their business establishments overseas. Accordingly, the companies belonged outside the European Union and not in the UK, so the firm's supplies were not made in the UK and were outside the scope of UK VAT.

1   LON/95/1436, [1995] SWTI 2024.
2   *G Berkholz v Finanzamt Hamburg-Mitte-Altstadt*: 168/84 [1985] 3 CMLR 667, ECJ.

Time of supply

9.146   A supply of services is generally treated for Value Added Tax purposes as taking place at the time when the services are performed.[1] Where, however, the whole amount of the consideration for a supply of services was not ascertainable at the time when the services were performed, and subsequently the use of those services by a person other than the supplier gives rise to the payment of additional consideration which is wholly or partly determined or payable periodically or from time to time or at the end of any period (for example a royalty related to the number of products manufactured or sold in the period), a further supply is treated as taking place each time a payment is received or a tax invoice is issued by the supplier, whichever is the earlier.[2, 3]

1   VATA 1994, s 6(3). The time of supply will be relevant for the purpose of determining, among other things, when the supplier must deliver a tax invoice, the VAT return in which the input or output tax attributable to the supply must be included and (in the event of a change in VAT rates) the rate which is applicable to the supply.
2   Value Added Tax Regulations 1995, SI 1995/2518, Reg 91.
3   In *BJ Rice & Associates v Customs & Excise Comrs* [1996] STC 581, a tax consultant invoiced a client for work done before he registered for VAT, but the invoice was not paid until after the registration had been completed. The Commissioners' view that, since the pre-registration invoice could not be a tax invoice the services should be treated as supplied when the payment was received, was upheld by the VAT Tribunal and the High Court but reversed by the Court of Appeal. It was held that the existence of a chargeable transaction had to be determined at the time of the actual supply.

Although s 6 (and Regulations made thereunder) contained deeming provisions to determine the amount to be charged and the time when the charge took effect, it was not itself a charging section and could not deem to be taxable a supply which was not taxable at the time it was actually made.

Compensation and damages

9.147 It is clear that compensation payments made pursuant to Court Orders, or to settlements embodied in Consent Orders, are outside the scope of Value Added Tax. However, HM Customs & Excise initially took the view that the discontinuance of an action, or the settlement of a claim without recourse to litigation, was a surrender of the right to sue, and thus a supply of services within section 5(2)(b) of the Value Added Tax Act 1994.[1] On this view, all payments made under out of Court settlements would generally be regarded as taxable.

1   See para 9.137 above.

9.148 This view forced taxpayers to go all the way through the courts without settlement or compromise in order to guarantee that any payment would not attract Value Added Tax. Following a VAT Tribunal decision[1] to the effect that settling a tort action did not involve any supply of services, HM Customs & Excise reviewed their policy on the VAT treatment of payments made under out of court settlements of disputes, after proceedings had been commenced by service of originating process (or by the appointment of an arbitrator). Press Notice 82/87 confirmed the revised view that, where such payments were in essence compensatory, and did not relate directly to supplies of goods or services, they were outside the scope of Value Added Tax, even if the settlement was expressed in terms that the payment was consideration for the plaintiff's agreement to abandon his rights to bring legal proceedings. However, payments would remain taxable if, and to the extent that, they were the consideration for specific taxable supplies by the plaintiff. By way of example, the Press Notice stated that, where the dispute concerned payment for an earlier supply, and the settlement confirmed a previously agreed price or a reduction to such price, the Value Added Tax should be adjusted, by means of a credit note, by reference to the price finally agreed. Similarly, where a copyright dispute was settled for a payment which both compensated for a past breach and also covered the future use of copyright material, the Press Notice stated that the former would be outside the scope of Value Added Tax while the latter would be taxable, and it was necessary to apportion the payment between the two.

1 *Whites Metal Co v Customs & Excise Comrs* (LON/86/686Z, No 2400).

9.149 In *Cooper Chasney Ltd v Customs & Excise Comrs*,[1] proceedings relating to the use of the name 'Infolink' were discontinued upon payment of an agreed sum to the plaintiff. The plaintiff, which had previously used the name 'Infolink' as a business name, reverted to its full corporate name, and expressly allowed the defendant to continue using this name. The settlement clearly went beyond past breaches and giving up the right to sue. Customs said that, in considering the taxability of a settlement payment, it would be necessary to look very carefully at the wording used by the parties in the settlement agreement or consent order.

1   LON/89/1409, No 4898, [1990] 3 CMLR 509.

9.150   It was considered by some that the *Cooper Chasney* case had cast doubt on the guidance contained in Press Notice 82/87 and, in order to resolve the ensuing confusion, representatives of the Law Society held a meeting with HM Customs & Excise on 23 October 1991 with a view to providing guidance to the profession. A note of this meeting was published in the Law Society's Gazette of 9 September 1992[1] and the material points relevant for the purposes of this work are as follows:

(a) The 1987 Press Notice was intended to apply only to genuine disputes. Giving up the 'right to sue' did not necessarily involve giving up any right as no-one had an intrinsic right to sue; instead, it amounted to a decision not to enforce an alleged wrong.

(b) Liquidated damages paid under contracts were outside the scope of Value Added Tax. Although not involving litigation, they were within the spirit of the Press Notice. If a contract contained provisions for damages for breach, this would generally be within the Press Notice, but if the plaintiff was giving up a separate right (eg the right to receive notice) this could be a taxable supply.

(c) The Press Notice only covered payments made after proceedings had been commenced but, if payments made before the commencement of proceedings would clearly not be within section 5(2)(b), Customs would similarly treat such payments as being outside the scope of Value Added Tax.

(d) In the case of 'involuntary supplies' (the example given was a dispute concerning right of light for which damages are awarded), damages in respect of past infringements would be outside the scope of Value Added Tax and, where a settlement covered both past infringements and also permission to continue in the future the conduct which gave rise to those infringements, Customs would accept a reasonable apportionment. Customs were still considering the difficult question of where the court required one party to give up a right (intellectual property rights were expressly mentioned in this connection) in return for a payment from the other party because, in exceptional cases, it could be argued that the court was merely deciding the level of consideration which was payable for granting the right. It was, however, thought that, in the majority of cases, the payment would be damages imposed upon the payer by the court and therefore outside the scope of Value Added Tax.

(e) Where litigation involved a supply on which Value Added Tax had already been accounted for (but the price not paid), if the result was a reduction in the price paid for the supply the supplier would need to issue a credit note; Customs would then credit him with the Value Added Tax for which he had already accounted, while the recipient would have to repay to Customs the Value Added Tax he had already recovered.

(f) Where a settlement involved cross supplies (other than the mere surrender of a right of action), Value Added Tax might be payable by each party, without netting off, according to the nature of the supply. This was because there might be consideration paid in return for a party agreeing to enter into an agreement.

(g) Interest does not increase the consideration for a supply, so interest on damages was outside the scope of Value Added Tax.

1 At page 32.

INHERITANCE TAX

9.151 Inheritance tax is charged on the value transferred by a 'chargeable transfer',[1] which is defined by sections 2(1) and 3(1) of the Inheritance Tax Act 1984 as a disposition, other than an exempt transfer, made by an individual, as a result of which the value of his estate immediately after the disposition is less than it would be but for the disposition, and the value transferred is the amount by which it is less.

1 Inheritance Tax Act 1984, s 1.

9.152 Any transfer of value made on or after 18 March 1986 which constitutes a gift to another individual, or into an accumulation and maintenance trust or a disabled trust (but not to a discretionary trust), which would otherwise be a chargeable transfer, is potentially an exempt transfer, and will become exempt if the individual survives the making of the gift by seven years.[1] Other exemptions are described in Part II of the Inheritance Tax Act 1984.

1 Inheritance Tax Act 1984, s 3A

9.153 Section 4(1) of the Inheritance Tax Act 1984 provides that, on the death of any person, tax shall be charged as if, immediately before his death, he had made a transfer of value and the value transferred by it had been equal to the value of his estate immediately before his death. By section 5(1), a person's estate is the aggregate of all the property to which he is beneficially entitled, other than excluded property. 'Excluded property' is described in section 6, and the most important category is property situated outside the United Kingdom of which the beneficial owner is an individual domiciled outside the United Kingdom.[1]

1 For a description of domicile at common law, see para 9.57 et seq above. In addition, s 267 of the Inheritance Tax Act 1984 provides that an individual who is not domiciled in the United Kingdom under the general law is nevertheless to be treated as so domiciled for inheritance tax purposes if he has been resident here for tax purposes in not less than 17 of the previous 20 years of assessment, or if he ceased to be domiciled here for general purposes less than three years ago.

9.154 The inheritance tax legislation makes no specific mention of merchandising rights or other forms of intellectual property, but rights to which a person is beneficially entitled will, of course, form part of his estate if they are not excluded property.

9.155 In *Redwood Music Ltd v B Feldman & Co*,[1] Robert Goff J said that 'copyright subsisting under the copyright legislation in this country is property situated in this country'.[2] It is apprehended that the same reasoning will apply to other forms of intellectual property for inheritance tax purposes.[3]

1   [1979] RPC 1.
2   See also *Curtis Brown Ltd v Jarvis* (1929) 14 TC 744.
3   Cf the location of assets provisions in TCGA 1992, s 275 for capital gains tax purposes: para 9.133 above.

9.156   Section 160 of the Inheritance Tax Act 1984 provides that, for inheritance tax purposes, the value of any property is the price it might reasonably be expected to fetch if sold in the open market at the relevant time. On 25 February 1983, the Financial Secretary to the Treasury, Nicholas Ridley MP, confirmed in a Parliamentary Answer that this applied to copyright[1] although, in practice, any such sale would be likely to be made on the basis of the discounted present value of the estimated future royalty income over a given number of years.

1   See Hansard, Volume 37, Col 570.

STAMP DUTY[1]

9.157   Stamp duty is payable on, among other things, the conveyance or transfer on sale of any property.[2] 'Property' is not defined in the Stamp Act 1891, but has been held[3] to refer to 'that which belongs to a person exclusive of others, and which could be the subject of bargain and sale to another'. This includes goodwill,[4] trademarks,[5] copyright,[6] and all other forms of intellectual property likely to be relevant for the purposes of this work, although know-how and show-how are not treated as 'property'[7] unless transferred as part of the goodwill of a business.[8]

1   S 110 of the Finance Act 1991 provides for the abolition of stamp duty where the property concerned is property other than land, an interest in the proceeds of the sale of land held on trust for sale, or a licence to occupy land. This Section is to come into force on the day appointed under s 111(1) of the Finance Act 1990 for the abolition of stamp duty on stocks, shares and other defined securities. This was intended to be the day when the Stock Exchange Taurus (Transfer and Automated Registration of Uncertificated Stock) Scheme came into force but, on 11 March 1993, the Stock Exchange announced that this scheme was being abandoned as unworkable. On 1 July 1993, the Securities Industry Task Force made recommendations for the introduction of a new scheme, to be known as 'Crest', an electronic book entry transfer system, within which stock will be dematerialised and which will provide delivery against payment. The position regarding abolition of stamp duty (otherwise than on land and property) remains under review, but Crest was introduced on 15 July 1996.
2   Stamp Act 1891, s 1 and Sch 1.
3   In *Potter v IRC* (1854) 10 Exch 147.
4   *Potter v IRC*, supra; *Troup v IRC* (1891) 7 TLR 610; *IRC v Muller and Co Margarine Ltd* [1901] AC 217, [1900-3] All ER Rep 413.
5   *Leather Cloth Co v American Leather Cloth Co* (1865) 11 HL Cas 523. S 20 of the Trade Marks Act 1994 provides that registered trade marks are personal property. Section 61 of the 1994 Act provides, however, that stamp duty shall not be chargeable on an instrument relating to a Community Trade Mark (defined in s 51) or an international trade mark (UK) (defined in s 53), or an application for any such mark, by reason only of the fact that such a mark has legal effect in the United Kingdom.
6   It was assumed, though not decided, in *Leather Cloth Co v American Leather Cloth Co* supra (a trade marks case) that copyright was 'property'. S 90(1) of the Copyright, Designs and Patents Act 1988 expressly provides that copyright is transmissible by assignment, by testamentary disposition or by operation of law, as personal or moveable property.

7   *Musker v English Electric Co Ltd* (1964) 41 TC 556 at 585.
8   *Re Keene* [1922] 2 Ch 475, [1922] All ER Rep 258.

9.158 Section 59(1) of the 1891 Act provides that any contract or agreement for the sale of any equitable estate or interest in any property whatsoever, or for the sale of any estate or interest in any property (with some non-relevant exceptions) situate in the United Kingdom shall be charged with the same duty as if it were an actual conveyance on sale of the estate, interest or property contracted or agreed to be sold, and section 62 provides that every instrument, and every decree or order of any court or of any commissioners, whereby any property is transferred to or vested in any person on any occasion, other than a sale or mortgage, is also to be charged with duty as a conveyance or transfer of property.

9.159 It is clear that an assignment of merchandising rights will amount to a transfer of property. A grant of an exclusive licence (even if restricted as to period or territory, or limited to particular forms of exploitation) will also be treated as a transfer of property,[1] unless the instrument contains a power of revocation (for example, if either party can terminate the licence by notice, or if the licensor can terminate the licence for non-use).[2] Non-exclusive licences, however, do not transfer property, and are not treated as conveyances on sale.[3]

1   *Smelting Corpn of Australia v IRC* [1897] 1 QB 175; cf *George Wimpey & Co Ltd v IRC* [1975] 1 WLR 995.
2   See *Sargent and Sims on Stamp Duties* (9th edn) page 122.
3   *Thames Conservators v IRC* (1886) 18 QBD 279.

Rate of duty

9.160 Stamp duty is payable on conveyances on sale on an ad valorem basis, the current rate being, in the case of all forms of property relevant to this work, 1% of the amount or value of the consideration for the sale.[1] There are exemptions in the case of, among other things, transfers in favour of a charity,[2] gifts or other transfers between associated companies[3] and transfers falling within the Stamp Duty (Exempt Instruments) Regulations 1987.[4]

1   No ad valorem duty is payable if it can be certified that the amount or value of the consideration does not exceed £60,000: Finance Act 1963, s 55(1)(a), as amended by Finance Act 1984, s 109 and Finance Act 1993, s 201.
2   Finance Act 1982, s 129.
3   Finance Act 1930, s 42, as amended by Finance Act 1967, s 27 and Finance Act 1995, s 149.
4   SI 1987/516.

Ascertainment of consideration

9.161 For stamp duty purposes, the consideration includes any lump sum, and any periodic payments which can be ascertained from the face of the transfer document as being payable over a definite period not exceeding 20 years.[1]

1   Stamp Act 1891, s 56(1). It appears this period can be reckoned from the date of the
first payment provided for in the document, even if later than the date of the document,
although s 56(2) provides that, where periodic payments can be ascertained from the
face of the document as being payable over a definite period exceeding 20 years or in
perpetuity, or for any indefinite period not terminable with life, ad valorem duty will
be charged on the total amount payable during the period of 20 years from the date of
the document. If the periodic payments are payable during any life or lives, the duty
is charged on the amount which can be ascertained from the document as being payable
during the period of 12 years from the date of the document: s 56(3).

9.162   Periodic payments, the amount of which cannot be ascertained
from the face of the document (for example royalties related to the number
of products manufactured or sold, with no minimum or maximum royalties)
cannot be brought into account as part of the consideration when
determining the amount of ad valorem stamp duty. If, however, the
document provides for a cap on the amount of the periodic payments which
can become payable during the relevant period, the ad valorem duty will
be charged on the capped total amount; if there is no cap, but the total
amount payable during the relevant period is subject to a guaranteed
minimum amount, the duty will be charged on such minimum amount.[1]

1   *Underground Electric Railways Co of London Ltd v IRC* [1906] AC 21; *Independent
Television Authority v IRC* [1961] AC 427.

9.163   If a definite total amount, or a definite maximum or minimum
amount, can be ascertained from the face of the document as being payable
over the relevant period, stamp duty will be charged on this amount, with
no discount to reflect the fact that it will be payable over a period.[1] It must
be assumed that all payments will be made in accordance with the terms
of the document, no allowance being made for the possibility of default.[2]
If no definite amount of consideration is ascertainable from the face of the
document, it cannot be liable to *ad valorem* stamp duty.

1   *Hotung v Collector of Stamp Revenue* [1965] AC 766, [1965] 2 WLR 546.
2   *Western United Investment Co Ltd v IRC* [1958] Ch 392, [1958] 1 All ER 257.

9.164   Where the consideration payable for a transfer of merchandising
rights is subject to Value Added Tax, it appears that the consideration for
stamp duty purposes will be the VAT-inclusive amount. Conversely,
however, the stamp duty will not form part of the consideration for Value
Added Tax purposes.[1]

1   See Inland Revenue Statement of Practice SP 11/91.

Payment of duty

9.165   Where a document is liable to ad valorem stamp duty, the duty
must generally be paid within 30 days after execution of the document or,
if it was executed outside the United Kingdom, within 30 days after it was
first brought into the United Kingdom.[1] Unstamped or insufficiently
stamped documents may be stamped late, on payment of the unpaid duty
and a penalty of £10 and also, by way of further penalty where the unpaid
duty exceeds £10, of interest on the unpaid duty at the rate of 5% per
annum from the date the document was first executed up to the time when

the amount of interest is equal to the unpaid duty.[2] The consequence of failing to stamp a document which is liable to ad valorem stamp duty, or of failing to stamp it sufficiently, is that, until it has been duly stamped, it cannot be used as evidence, except in criminal proceedings, in any court, or before any arbitrator or referee, in any part of the United Kingdom.[3] Where an assignee or exclusive licensee of merchandising rights needs to rely on the assignment or exclusive licence to prove his title in any infringement action, therefore, he will be unable to do so until any deficiency in the stamping of the document has been cured, and any applicable penalties paid.[4]

1   Stamp Act 1891, s 15(2)(a).
2   Stamp Act 1891, s 15(1).
3   Stamp Act 1891, s 14. For an interesting recent example, see *Re Brown & Root, McDermott Fabricators Ltd's Application* [1996] STC 483. A company bought four patents for a lump sum, but the assignment was returned unregistered by the Patent Office because it was unstamped. A second assignment was prepared which apportioned the consideration between the four patents, and this was duly stamped and registered. In subsequent proceedings alleging patent infringement, the defendants applied to rectify the patent register by removing reference to the second assignment, arguing that, although not admissible in evidence, the first assignment was legally effective and secondary evidence of its existence and terms could be adduced to prove the second assignment was a nullity. It was held that, although s 14 did not make the first assignment a nullity, it could not be used in evidence against a company and, without such evidence, the second assignment could not be proved to be a nullity.
4   In proceedings for infringement of copyright, the statutory presumptions in s 104 of the Copyright, Designs and Patents Act 1988 may assist the author of a literary, dramatic, musical or artistic work, but will not assist other persons.

Certificates of value

9.166   The threshold for ad valorem stamp duty for conveyances on the sale of property (including intellectual property), where the amount does not exceed £60,000 applies if the instrument effecting the conveyance is certified in accordance with the statutory requirements.[1] A precedent for such a certificate is given in Precedent 3, clause 10.

1   Finance Act 1958, s 34(4); Finance Act 1963, s 55(1).

Part C

Policing merchandising rights

Chapter 10

Introduction

10.1 It goes without saying that a merchandiser must at all times be alert both to secure and to police his rights. This may involve, amongst other things, employing agents to track down the source of infringing goods. If the goods originate overseas, it may be worthwhile taking action in the relevant jurisdiction. Consideration of this latter course is beyond the scope of this book, however. The focus of this section is the steps which may be taken in this country to stop piracy, ie for these purposes England and Wales.[1] The possibility of suing in other member states of the Brussels Convention (as amended), on the other hand should not be overlooked. In particular, under Article 24, provisional relief can be sought in any member state.[2]

1   It is to be noted that the effect of the Civil Jurisdiction and Judgments Act 1982, s 16 is that the Scottish and Northern Irish courts may in practice be an option. S 16 imposes a similar regime between the domestic tribunals, as the Brussels Convention does between the tribunals of the member states of the Convention.
2   A detailed analysis of the provisions of the Convention is given in *The Patents County Court* by Adams and Thomas, Intellectual Property Institute 1995.

10.2 When piracy is discovered, the merchandiser must plan his line of attack. He is after all in business to maximise the profits to be gained from exploiting his rights. Consequently, at the outset, he should decide what for him would be the most beneficial outcome of his attack. Usually it will simply be to stop the offending activity, and if possible to obtain damages. In some cases, however, the objective may be to license the offender on the most advantageous terms possible. In such a case there may be merit in the strategy of a delayed ambush. An infringer whose investment is high is likely to be more worried by the threat of action than if it is small because his activities are just commencing. It may also be felt desirable to delay in order that the reputation of the property can be more firmly established. The danger of delay is that it may deprive a plaintiff of equitable relief on the ground that he has acquiesced in the defendants' activities. In *Electrolux Ltd v Electrix Ltd*,[1] however, it was held that where the plaintiffs had deliberately delayed in order to strengthen their position by using their trade mark, they were nevertheless entitled to relief. In *H P Bulmer Ltd v J Bollinger SA*,[2] Goff LJ citing inter alia this case said:

> It seems to me, therefore, that the true test whether equitable relief should be withheld in the case of a continuing legal wrong on the ground of delay by the plaintiff in enforcing his rights is that the facts must be such that the owner of the legal right has done something

beyond mere delay to encourage the wrongdoer to believe that he does not intend to rely on his strict legal right, and the wrongdoer must have acted to his prejudice in that belief.

1   (1954) 71 RPC 23.
2   [1978] RPC 79 at 136.

10.3 Delay will always prejudice a party's chances of obtaining interlocutory relief: even quite a short delay.

10.4 Whatever the object in view, it is obviously important at the outset to establish what intellectual property rights exist,[1] and equally to establish who owns them. The most troublesome area in this respect is copyright. It should be noted that the 1988 Act contains no direct equivalent to section 20(1) of the Copyright Act 1956 which presumed copyright to subsist if the defendant did not put the matter in issue.[2]

1   Alleging that rights exist when they do not may give rise to an action for trade libel or malicious falsehood if made to customers of the 'infringer'. See also 'threats action' under Patents Act 1977, s 70; Designs Act 1949, s 26; Copyright Designs and Patents Act 1988, s 253 (design right); Trade Marks Act 1994, s 21.
2   Though note ss 104-106 of the 1988 Act.

10.5 Since *American Cyanamid Co v Ethicon Ltd*[1] a plaintiff seeking interlocutory relief has merely had to show an arguable case, not a strong *prima facie* case. Thus he is unlikely to be put to strict proof of ownership anyway. He may thus be in a better position at an interlocutory stage, than at a later stage in the proceedings, when defects in his title may be exposed.

1   See para 11.1.

10.6 Whilst an interlocutory injunction will commonly be the first line of attack, and the most satisfactory, other possibilities should not be overlooked. In the first place, it is to be remembered that interlocutory injunctions are granted and refused on the balance of convenience. It is certainly true that, whatever the merits of the case, a plaintiff who has applied for and been refused an interlocutory injunction, is in a weakened position vis-à-vis the alleged infringer. The possibility of using Order 14 procedure to obtain summary judgment should not be overlooked therefore. This is used where there is no arguable defence to the plaintiff's claim, and has the advantage of leading rapidly to a final disposal of the action. Order 14 is inherently less suitable for passing off actions, but it can on occasion be used.

10.7 In many cases, the source of the pirated goods may be unclear. In such cases, the *Anton Piller* procedure is of great utility. This may be used to obtain evidence of acts of piracy, and, when coupled with orders requiring the revelation of the distribution network, to trace them to their source. Since those who indulge in piracy are frequently fairly mobile, the *Mareva* injunction to prevent assets being removed from the country, is also a useful device. There is also an informal seizure procedure which can be used against street vendors and the like in section 100 of the 1988 Act.

10.8 Where pirated goods are being imported, and a trade mark proprietor has knowledge of this, notice may be given to the Customs & Excise under section 89 of the Trade Marks Act 1994.

10.9 Where the manufacturer of the goods is known, and the object of the exercise is to sell a licence at the end of the day, obviously that person will be the target of attack. If, however, the object is simply to stop the pirate activities, it may be more effective to hit those further down the distribution chain (even when the source of the goods is known), the idea being that small retailers etc are unlikely to fight back, and interlocutory relief may more readily be obtained against them. The result of obtaining such relief can be to strengthen the plaintiff's hand in dealing with those further up the chain, and possibly to frighten them off altogether.

10.10 Whatever the plan of attack, it goes without saying that the case should be properly prepared. Passing off actions in particular require careful assembling of evidence. A plaintiff who loses a poorly prepared case against the principal culprit is estopped from litigating the issue again against the same party,[1] and has thus weakened his position disastrously.

1   See Cornish *Intellectual Property* (2nd edn, 1989) Sweet & Maxwell, para 2.039 et seq.

10.11 Finally, it need scarcely be added that any legal proceedings should be instituted in the name of the right plaintiff. An exclusive licensee of copyright has, except against the copyright owner, the same rights and remedies in respect of matter occurring after the grant of the licence as if the licence had been an assignment.[1] A difficulty which occasionally arises is that an exclusive UK licensee has in turn purported to grant an exclusive UK licence. Who then is the 'exclusive licensee' for the purposes of the 1988 Act? A crucial definition is that contained in section 92(1) of the 1988 Act:

'... "exclusive licence" means a licence in writing signed by or on behalf of the copyright owner authorising the licensee *to the exclusion of all other persons*, [emphasis supplied] including the person granting the licence, to exercise a right which would otherwise be exercisable exclusively by the copyright owner.'

This provision clearly contemplates the grant of a licence by an agent, hence the use of the words 'person', and 'by or on behalf of'. In the absence of an agency agreement permitting the exclusive licensee to appoint 'sub-licensees' what is the position? Non-revocable exclusive licences are treated as conveyances on sale for the purposes of stamp duty,[2] but tax law generally is concerned with economic effects, not technical legal questions of proprietorship, so that treating tax law as analogous is dangerous.

1   Copyright, Designs and Patents Act 1988, s 101(1).
2   *Sergeant and Sims on Stamp Duties*, 9th edn, p 122 – see para 9.156 et seq.

10.12 The reason for section 101 of the 1988 Act conferring rights on an exclusive licensee are practical: an exclusive licensee is obviously more concerned with infringements in a territory than a copyright owner, whose concern will depend upon its personal interest conferred by the contractual licence, which may be greater or lesser according to the terms of the licence.

10.12 *Introduction*

An exclusive licence, might, for example, have been granted in return for a once and for all payment. These considerations do not apply between an exclusive licensee and a 'sub-licensee' for the obvious reason that there can only be one exclusive licence of rights, namely that granted by the copyright owner, to the exclusive licensee licensed by it. The rights of a 'sub-licensee' are purely a matter of contract between the exclusive licensee and the 'sub-licensee'.

10.13 This conclusion is supported by the interpretation placed on section 19 of the 1956 Act, which was the equivalent of section 101. As the previous edition of Copinger stated:

> Whilst it is clear that section 19 applies to the first exclusive licence granted by the owner of the copyright, it may not apply to exclusive sublicences granted by the exclusive licensee unless the exclusive sublicensee is deemed to be the owner of the copyright for the purposes of such licence.

10.14 *CBS United Kingdom Ltd v Charmdale Record Distributors Ltd*[1] is cited for this proposition. That case confirms the proposition stated above that the rights of an exclusive licensee are not proprietary. Section 101, like its predecessor, is purely procedural.

1   [1981] Ch 91.

10.15 In short, so far as the 1988 Act is concerned, the only persons who are relevant are the copyright owner, and *its* exclusive licensee. Section 92(1) makes sense read in this context, for it provides that an exclusive licence is a licence signed 'by or on behalf of the copyright owner'.

10.16 In the case of registered trade marks, the proprietor is the person entitled to bring an action for infringement. A licensee of the marks may call upon the proprietor to take proceedings for infringement, and if the proprietor refuses to do so within two months, the licensee can institute proceedings in his own name.[1] However, an exclusive licence may provide that the licensee shall have, to such extent as may be provided by the licence, the same rights and remedies as if the licence had been an assignment.[2]

1   Trade Marks Act 1994, s 30.
2   S 31(1).

10.17 The right to bring an action for passing off depends upon the ownership of the goodwill allegedly damaged.

10.18 In the case of registered designs being the property right sued on, the proprietor is the proper plaintiff. The Registered Designs Act 1949 expressly recognises the power to license, but merely provides that any equities in respect of the design may be enforced in a like manner as in respect of any other personal property.[1] It would not appear therefore that an exclusive licensee can sue without joining the proprietor, save for interlocutory relief.[2]

1   S 19(4).

2   *Roban Jig and Tool Co v Taylor* [1979] FSR 130.

10.19   An equitable title will support the grant of an interlocutory injunction,[1] but for final relief, the legal owner must be joined.

1   See *Roban Jig and Tool Co v Taylor* [1979] FSR 130.

Chapter 11

Civil remedies

INJUNCTIONS

Interlocutory (or interim) injunctions

11.1 Obviously, since the need for speed is the whole point of this remedy, it will be refused to a person who has delayed without good reason after discovering the infringement.[1] The plaintiff must give an undertaking to make good any damage suffered by the defendant should he fail at the trial, as a condition of obtaining interlocutory relief.[2] The circumstances in which the discretion to issue an injunction will be exercised were clarified by the House of Lords in *American Cyanamid Co v Ethicon Ltd*:[3]

    (1) there must be a serious question to be tried;

    (2) thereafter the court should not try to assess the merits of the plaintiff and defendant's respective cases, but should turn to the balance of convenience in granting or refusing the injunction.

If it appears that damages will be an adequate compensation for the plaintiff (and the defendant will be able to pay them), then an injunction should be refused. If they will not be, it must be decided whether damages would be an adequate compensation to the defendant under the plaintiff's undertaking to pay them. Where there is doubt about the adequacy of damages the court may have regard to other factors which may affect the balance of convenience eg it is advisable to preserve the *status quo*. As a last resort, the court may take account of the strengths of the parties' respective cases as revealed by the evidence. The object of approaching the matter in this way is to obviate as far as possible a pre-trial of issues which will have to be resolved at a later date. In *Series 5 Software Ltd v Clarke*[4] Laddie J embarked on a detailed analysis of the law both before and after *American Cyanamid*. He concluded that the following matters should be borne in mind by a court in considering whether or not to grant interlocutory relief:

    (1) The grant of an interlocutory injunction is a matter of discretion and depends on all the facts of the case.

    (2) There are no fixed rules as to when an injunction should or should not be granted. The relief must be kept flexible.

    (3) Because of the practice adopted on the hearing of applications for interlocutory relief, the court should rarely attempt to resolve complex issues of disputed fact or law.

    (4) Major factors the court can bear in mind are

        (a) the extent to which damages are likely to be an adequate remedy for each party and the ability of the other party to pay,

(b) the balance of convenience,

(c) the maintenance of the status quo, and

(d) any clear view the court may reach as to the relative strength of the parties' cases.

Most practitioners have welcomed this clarification of the law, and in particular the statement that the relative strengths of the parties' cases is a relevant consideration.

1   *Versil Ltd v Cork Insulation & Asbestos Co Ltd* [1966] RPC 76; *Carroll v Tomado Ltd* [1971] RPC 401.
2   See eg *Harman Pictures NV v Osborne* [1967] 2 All ER 324.
3   [1975] AC 396.
4   [1996] 1 All ER 853.

11.2   In many cases in the merchandising context, the grant of an interlocutory injunction will effectively determine the final outcome, as the defendant will not be interested in recommencing trading under styles he has had to discontinue using for many months. This will often justify a closer look at the merits of a case. The fundamental principle is that the court will act so as to cause the least injustice if it should turn out that it made the wrong decision.

11.3   Delivery up can be ordered at an interlocutory stage. This is discussed below. An interlocutory injunction should say exactly what it is that is restrained.

Final injunctions

11.4   The award of a final injunction is also discretionary, but in the case of proven infringement or passing off it will generally be granted.

11.5   The general rule is that an injunction will not be awarded where damages are an adequate remedy, however in the case of most infringements and passing off, they are not an adequate remedy. A court may however also refuse an injunction if the defendant can satisfy it that there is no chance of the tort being repeated.

DELIVERY UP

11.6   The court may order the offending articles to be delivered up to it,[1] or destroyed. The option should always be pleaded and supported by an affidavit. If it is possible to salvage valuable material from the articles, the court may permit this to be done.[2] This can be ordered at an interlocutory stage provided that there is a high degree of assurance that the plaintiff will be able to establish entitlement at the trial.[3]

1   Patents Act 1977, s 61(1); Copyright, Designs and Patents Act 1988, s 99; Trade Marks Act 1994, s 16. Also under RSC Ord 29,r 2A – Torts (Interference with Goods) Act 1977. In the case of registered designs there is no specific provision in the Act, but the court may order delivery up under its inherent powers to grant equitable relief.
2   *Peter Pan Manufacturing Corpn v Corsets Silhouette Ltd* [1963] 3 All ER 402.
3   *Nottingham Building Society v Eurodynamics Systems plc* [1993] FSR 468.

11.7 It is advisable to include in the pleading two claims for delivery up:
  (1) for delivery up of articles which the plaintiff wishes to keep and sell;
  (2) for delivery up of things for destruction.[1]

1   Destruction is ordered upon oath verified by affidavit.

11.8 Delivery up can include articles specifically designed or adapted for making copies of a copyright work, if the owner knew or has reason to believe that it had been used for making infringing copies. In *Swintex v Horsburgh*,[1] moulds had been used to make goods which infringed copyright. The defendants when they learned of the plaintiff's claim, modified them so that it could no longer be said that they were being used to produce infringing copies. It was held that the effect of section 18 of the 1956 Act was that the plaintiff was the owner of the moulds, and the subsequent modification could not alter that fact (indeed arguably it was itself a conversion entitling the plaintiff to damages, though that point was not taken). Accordingly, delivery up of the moulds, though not of the moulding machine, was ordered, there being no evidence of the defendant's financial substance to meet a claim for damages based on a royalty for use of the moulds. There is no equivalent to section 18 in the 1988 Act, accordingly, it would now simply be a question of the state of the defendant's knowledge at the time the infringing copies were made whether or not the plates were liable to be delivered up.

1   Unreported, 8 May 1984.

11.9 Where it is impossible to separate the whole from the infringing parts, the court may order the whole to be delivered up,[1] or give the defendant the option to sever the infringing parts.[2]

1   *Stevens v Wildy* (1850) 19 LJ Ch 190.
2   *Nichols Advanced Vehicle Systems Inc v Rees and Oliver* [1979] RPC 127 at 141.

DAMAGES

11.10 The basic rule is that damages are compensatory only ie they should as far as possible put the plaintiff in the position he would have been in had the tort not been committed. This can include a sum in appropriate cases for injury to the plaintiff's feelings or reputation. This may be so where there is copyright infringement,[1] and possibly also is the case where other intellectual property rights are infringed. This is obviously something to bear in mind, particularly in relation to some aspects of personality merchandising.

1   *Sutherland Publishing Co Ltd v Caxton Publishing Co Ltd* [1936] Ch 323 at 336.

11.11 The case of *Catnic Components Ltd v Hill & Smith Ltd*[1] provides useful guidance on the computation of damages. The case involved a patent infringement, but its principles are applicable to copyright infringement damages, but, in the nature of things, less directly applicable to trade mark infringements. It was held that 'fair' damages should be assessed as a 'jury' question, liberally so as to compensate the plaintiffs for the direct and natural consequences of each infringing sale, and disregarding the fact that (in the circumstances of that case) the defendants could have sold non-infringing goods instead. On the facts of the case, it was proper to assume (unless the defendant showed otherwise) that the plaintiff would have made those sales effected by the defendants of the infringing articles. A proper notional royalty rate was that which a potential licensee not yet in the market would pay. In *Gerber Garment Technology v Lectra Systems*[2] it was held that a reasonable royalty should represent consequential gains to the infringer. This would appear to be the appropriate measure of compensation in most merchandising cases, including trade mark infringements, whether or not the infringer is competing with the licensees, or (as will often be the case) is opening up new markets. Where, however, in the case of trade mark infringements, including passing off, there is damage to the reputation of the merchandiser, to confine damages to a reasonable royalty will be inappropriate, and a sum should be included to reflect damage to reputation.[3]

1   [1983] FSR 512.
2   [1995] RPC 383.
3   Many trade mark infringements are, however, as noted in the text above, the equivalents of copyright infringements in the case of trade marks, but where the mark is the well known mark of a merchandiser, or a mark which is not a well known mark in the technical sense, but nevertheless a famous one, there is a potential damage to the merchandiser's reputation.

11.12   It has been established in other cases that damages can include a sum to compensate the plaintiff for being forestalled from exploiting markets he might otherwise have been able to exploit.[1] The measure in this case will be based on an estimate of the plaintiff's lost profit.

1   Eg *Khawam & Co v Chellaram & Sons (Nigeria) Ltd* [1964] 1 All ER 945, [1964] RPC 337.

11.13   It was also held in *Catnic* that the plaintiffs were entitled to simple interest (not compound interest) at 2% over the clearing bank base rate, since this was a rate which a company of the plaintiff's size and standing might be expected to pay to borrow the money.

11.14   It was further held that in the absence of any authority that exemplary damages had been awarded for the infringement of a patent prior to the decision in *Rookes v Barnard*,[1] a claim for exemplary damages was not open to the plaintiffs. This would also appear to be the position in trade mark infringement and passing off. In the case of copyright infringement, section 97(2) of the 1988 Act provides that in addition to all other material considerations, the court may have regard to the flagrancy of the infringement.

1   [1964] AC 1129.

11.15   In the case of primary copyright infringements, no damages are payable during a period in which the defendant acted innocently,[1] ie acted without knowing any right existed, rather than in the belief that the activities concerned did not infringe a known right. The scope of this provision is presumably as limited as was that of its predecessor,[2] and it is unlikely that it would avail a defendant very often in merchandising

11.15 *Civil remedies*

cases. In the case of trade mark infringement and passing-off, the position is possibly the same.[3]

1   Copyright, Designs and Patents Act 1988, s 97(1).
2   Copyright, Designs and Patents Act 1988, s 22.
3   *Draper v Trist* [1939] 3 All ER 513; *Henderson v Radio Corpn Ltd* [1969] RPC 218 at 229 (NSW). Also in the case of designs – Registered Designs Act 1949, s 9(1).

11.16   In the case of secondary infringements of copyright by unlicensed importers it is a requirement that the importer knew, or had reason to believe, the copy infringed UK copyright, accordingly, it is a defence if the importer can show that he had no such knowledge.[1] Dealings after notice are infringements, of course.

1   Copyright, Designs and Patents Act 1988, s 22.

ACCOUNT OF PROFITS

11.17   A successful plaintiff in an infringement or passing off action is entitled to damages as of right. The court, however, may in exercise of its equitable jurisdiction, order the defendant to account to the plaintiff for the profits made from the infringing activities. A plaintiff cannot both have damages and an account: he must elect. In the important case of *Island Records v Tring*[1] it was held that the plaintiff need not elect until after discovery has been made in order to enable the plaintiff to make an informed choice. An account is not a common form of relief because the taking of an account is complicated and expensive. The plaintiff is entitled to the whole profit on each infringing article sold[2] – which may exceed the measure of damages on a notional licence computation. Thus, if, for example, the plaintiff would have been unable to satisfy the market demand which the infringer has met, an account of profits would be the better option. Furthermore, a copyright infringer who has acted innocently is excused payment of damages.[3] He can nevertheless be ordered to account to the plaintiffs for the profits made during the relevant period.[4] However, the remedy being discretionary may be refused on the ground that the defendant acted innocently.[5] It is unclear whether a person against whom an account of profits is ordered is entitled to deduct the capital cost of the infringing articles. The profits made in disposing of them would have been arrived at by deducting such cost, and accordingly the cost ought in principle to be deductible, but there seems to be no authority on the point. The fact that the amount recoverable under an account is greater than the damages recoverable is not, in principle, a reason for refusing the order, which is based on the proposition that a defendant should not profit from his wrong. On the other hand, unreasonable delay, and the like, which would bar a plaintiff from other equitable remedies, is a ground for a court exercising its discretion against ordering an account.

1   [1995] 3 All ER 444.
2   *Peter Pan Manufacturing Corpn v Corsets Silhouette Ltd* [1963] 3 All ER 402.
3   See Copyright, Designs and Patents Act 1988, s 97(1).
4   Copyright, Designs and Patents Act 1988, s 96(2). S 97(1) only restricts the plaintiff's right to damages.
5   *Edelsten v Edelsten* (1863) 1 De GJ & S 185; *Gillette UK Ltd v Edenwest Ltd* [1994] RPC 279.

216

PRESERVATION OF EVIDENCE
Introduction

11.18 The equitable procedure for the preservation of evidence is of great importance especially in the form known as an *Anton Piller* order. This form of order is used to enable a plaintiff to seize the evidence of infringement before the defendant has had an opportunity to dispose of it. Discovery can also be used, whether or not in conjunction with an *Anton Piller* order, to make a person currently in possession of infringing goods, disclose his supplier, or disclose information leading to the identification of the tortfeasor.[1] In *Norwich Pharmacal v Customs & Excise Comrs*[2] it was held that disclosure could also be ordered against the Commissioners of Customs & Excise to compel them to disclose the names of the importers of a patented drug. This is an important decision because under section 28 of the Customs and Excise Act 1952 the importers had to fill in a form of entry giving their names and a description of the goods.[3] This information was formerly, and still is, regarded as confidential, but this case establishes that this confidentiality can be overridden by a court order.

1   *British Steel Corpn v Granada Television Ltd* [1981] AC 1096.
2   [1974] AC 133.
3   The equivalent provision is now to be found in the Customs and Excise Management Act 1979, s 37.

Anton Piller orders

11.19 The *Anton Piller* procedure to preserve evidence is of considerable practical importance. The principal use of the procedure is to enable the plaintiff to preserve evidence of infringement before the defendant has had an opportunity to destroy, conceal or dispose of it. Under the procedure the plaintiff is permitted to apply *ex parte in camera* to the High Court (generally the Chancery Division), without notice to the defendant, for an order that he be permitted to inspect the defendant's premises and seize copy or photograph material which may be used as evidence in the infringement or passing off action. The defendant can also be ordered to keep infringing stock or incriminating papers, or give information. The procedure exists under the powers conferred on the Court by RSC Order 29, rule 2 and the court's inherent jurisdiction to make an order for the preservation or detention of the subject matter or an action and documents relating thereto. The standard forms for use in *Anton Piller* applications are set out in Annex 1 to the *Practice Direction* of 28 July 1994.[1]

1   [1994] 1 WLR 1233. For the form of the order see Atkins Court Forms, Vol 30, Form 25.

11.20 An *Anton Piller* order can contain the following provisions:
  (1) an injunction against trading or dealing in the infringing goods;
  (2) an injunction to prevent their destruction or disposal;
  (3) an injunction (limited in time) to prevent the defendant informing third parties, other than his lawyers, of the existence of the proceedings;
  (4) an order that the defendant permit the plaintiff's solicitor[1] and a

11.20 *Civil remedies*

limited number of other people (usually no more than four) to enter and search the premises;
(5) an order that the defendant deliver up the infringing goods, and (sometimes), documents etc to the person serving the order and that the goods be held in the safe custody of the plaintiff's solicitors;
(6) an order that the defendant disclose the names of his suppliers;
(7) an order that the defendant file an affidavit within a specified time (usually four days) setting out the required information;
(8) a provision that the defendant be at liberty to discharge the order upon giving 24 hours' notice.

The order must have a return date.

1   See below as to execution of order.

The hurdles to be overcome

11.21 To obtain an order the plaintiff must:
(1) show that he has an extremely strong prima facie case;
(2) show that the potential or actual damage to him is very serious;
(3) provide clear evidence as to the defendant's possession of the goods etc; and
(4) show that there is a real possibility that such goods etc will be destroyed or disappear before an inter partes application can be made.

The plaintiff must make full disclosure of all the facts known to him and must give an undertaking as to possible damages having to be paid to the defendant. The procedure being in effect (though not in theory) a search warrant has obvious potential for abuse. It could, for example, be used to obtain information about the legitimate activities of a trade rival. For these reasons the courts are concerned to ensure that applications are genuine. In the important case of *Universal Thermosensors Ltd v Hibben*[1] Nicholls V-C laid down guidelines for the execution of the order. Subsequently, a *Practice Direction* was promulgated on 28 July 1994.[2] This provides as follows:

(1) (a) As suggested in *Universal Thermosensors Ltd v Hibben*[3] the specimen order provides for it to be served by a supervising solicitor and carried out in his presence and under his supervision. The supervising solicitor should be an experienced solicitor, having some familiarity with the operation of *Anton Piller* orders, who is not a member or employee of the firm acting for the applicant. The evidence in support of the application should include the identity and experience of the proposed supervising solicitor.
(b) If in any particular case the judge does not think it appropriate to provide for the order to be served by a supervising solicitor, his reason should be expressed in the order itself.
(2) Where the premises are likely to be occupied by an unaccompanied woman and the supervising solicitor is a man, at least one of the persons attending on the service of the order should be a woman.
(3) Where the nature of the items removed under the order makes this appropriate, the applicant should be required to insure them.
(4) The applicant should undertake not to inform any third party of the proceedings until after the return date.

218

(5) In future, application in the Queen's Bench Division will no longer be heard by the judge in chambers. In both Chancery and Queen's Bench Divisions, whenever practicable, applications will be listed before a judge in such a manner as to ensure that he has sufficient time to read and consider the papers in advance.

(6) On circuit, application will be listed before a High Court judge or a circuit judge, sitting as a judge of the High Court specially designated by the presiding judge to hear such applications.

1 [1992] 1 WLR 840.
2 [1994] 1 WLR 1233.
3 [1992] 1 WLR 840 at 861.

11.22 Where practical papers to be used on the application should be lodged with the judge at least two hours before the hearing.[1] An application for an order can be made before the writ has been issued, on undertakings to issue the writ forthwith. For obvious reasons, the application will usually be made before any writ has been served. Affidavits in support of the application should:

(1) demonstrate that the requirements for an order set out in paragraph (a) above are satisfied;

(2) satisfy the duty of full disclosure; and,

(3) provide the material to enable the court to strike a balance between the plaintiff's need that the remedies allowed by the civil law for the breach of his rights should be attainable, and the requirement of justice that a defendant should not be deprived of his property without being heard.[2]

In very urgent cases, orders have been obtained even without the affidavit evidence. A reported example of this is *WEA Records v Visions Channel 4 Ltd*[3] where counsel appeared armed only with a draft writ and instructions as to the nature and results of the plaintiff's enquiries. Counsel was not even in possession of unsworn affidavits. It is important to emphasise that the plaintiff must be able to satisfy the court that each of the conditions above is complied with. In particular, it should not be forgotten that the plaintiff must show the likelihood of very serious damage. A strong *prima facie* case, combined with evidence that the relevant goods, or whatever, are in the defendant's possession, is not enough. When the courts indulge in periodic crack-downs on *Anton Piller* orders, this is the aspect upon which they tend to concentrate.[4]

1 *Practice Direction* (28 July 1994) [1994] 1 WLR 1233.
2 *Columbia Picture Industries v Robinson* [1987] Ch 38 at 76 per Scott J. See also *Lock International plc v Beswick* [1989] 1 WLR 1268.
3 [1983] 2 All ER 589.
4 It should also be noted that in November 1992 the Lord Chancellor's Department produced a Consultation Paper. Its brief from the Judges' Committee, which had made a number of recommendations, was to consider and report on the practical operation of *Anton Piller* orders. The recommendations made by the Judges' Committee included laying down the basis for these orders by primary legislation. At the time of writing, no legislation has been promulgated, however, the *Practice Direction* of 28 July 1994 [1994] 1 WLR 1233 has been promulgated. The terms of this are set out above.

11.23 An applicant should be required, in an appropriate case, to support his cross-undertaking in damages by a payment into court or the provision of a bond by an insurance company. Alternatively, the judge may order

11.23 *Civil remedies*

payment by way of such security to the applicant's solicitor as an officer of the court pending further order.[1]

1   *Practice Direction* (28 July 1994) [1994] 1 WLR 1233.

11.24   So far as practicable, any application for the discharge or variation of the order should be dealt with effectively on the return date.[1]

1   *Practice Direction* (28 July 1994) [1994] 1 WLR 1233.

COMPLIANCE WITH THE ORDER

11.25   The terms of the order must be complied with by both parties. If the defendant refuses immediate entry to the premises, or otherwise fails to comply with the terms of the order, he risks contempt proceedings. This is the case even if there has been a material non-disclosure by the plaintiff, or a party is at risk of violence for disclosure.[1] The order in such a case is not void *ab initio*. The only circumstances in which a defendant may safely ignore an order are when it is being served otherwise than in accordance with its own terms. The solicitor executing the order is not however permitted to enter any premises forcibly. The court has no power to make such an order.[2] If it is apprehended that a breach of the peace may occur, it is advisable to inform the police. The police presence must not however be oppressive.[3] It is possible to ask the court to make express provision for a police presence in the order.[4]

1   *Coca-Cola v Gilbey* [1996] FSR 23.
2   *Anton Piller KG v Manufacturing Processes Ltd* [1976] Ch 55 at 60.
3   *ITC Film Distributors v Video Exchange Ltd* [1982] Ch 431.
4   *Nestez v Arabic Centre* (11 March 1988, unreported).

PROPERTY INCLUDED IN THE ORDER

11.26   In appropriate cases, the court may allow not only infringing material to be removed, but also goods bought with the proceeds of the sale of infringing articles.

USE OF EVIDENCE FOR OTHER PROCEEDINGS

11.27   The *Anton Piller*'s primary function is to enable the plaintiff to preserve evidence, both for the purposes of the action against the particular defendant, and for the purposes of establishing the chain of supply. Although the use of evidence obtained on discovery for a purpose other than the action for which discovery was granted can be a contempt of court, evidence obtained under the *Anton Piller* procedure is exempt from this rule.[1] However, if a different plaintiff is to be involved in subsequent proceedings, eg because the evidence obtained revealed breaches of copyright or trade marks owned separately, then leave of the court must be obtained. The circumstances in which leave may be given were dealt with at length by Laddie J in *Cobra Golf Inc v Rata*.[2]

1   *Sony Corpn v Anand* [1981] FSR 398.
2   (19 March 1996, unreported).

11.28 If during an *Anton Piller* 'raid' other counterfeit goods come to light than those covered by the order, a further order can be obtained in respect of those goods.[1]

1   *Sony Corpn v Time Electronics* [1981] 3 All ER 376.

DISCHARGE OF ORDER

11.29 If an *Anton Piller* order is discharged on the return date, the judge should always consider whether it is appropriate that he should assess damages at once and direct immediate payment by the applicant.[1]

1   *Practice Direction* (28 July 1994) [1994] 1 WLR 1233.

SEIZURE UNDER S 100 OF THE COPYRIGHT, DESIGNS AND PATENTS ACT 1988

11.30 The *Anton Piller* procedure is of no value against transient street traders, because they will have moved on before the order can be obtained and executed. Accordingly, the 1988 Act provides that where an infringing copy of a work is found exposed for sale or hire, in respect of which the copyright owner would be entitled to apply for delivery up,[1] it may be seized by the rights owner. The conditions under which this may be done are as follows.

(1) Prior notice of the time and place of seizure must be given to the local police station.
(2) No force must be used.
(3) There must be left at the place where the work was seized, particulars of the person by whom or with whose authority the seizure is made notice in the prescribed form containing the prescribed particulars as to the person by whom or on whose authority the seizure was made and the grounds on which it was made.

Seizure can be made on premises to which the public has access, such as underground stations, but not at a person's permanent or regular place of business.

1   Under s 99.

MAREVA INJUNCTIONS

Introduction

11.31 The court has power to freeze the defendant's assets where there is evidence that those assets may be dissipated, or removed from the jurisdiction, before judgment can be enforced. This jurisdiction is derived from the discretionary power conferred by section 37 of the Supreme Court Act 1981. The principle may be stated as follows: where a plaintiff can show a good arguable claim to be entitled to money from a defendant who has assets within the jurisdiction, and there is a real risk that the defendant will remove those assets from the jurisdiction, or dispose of them within the jurisdiction so as to render them unavailable or untraceable, the court may grant an injunction to restrain the defendant from disposing of the assets or removing them from the jurisdiction until judgment in the action or further order.

11.32 It is possible to combine an application for an *Anton Piller* order with an application for a *Mareva* injunction.

Procedure

11.33 The basic procedure for *Mareva* applications is similar to that for other interlocutory applications. For obvious reasons, the application is *ex parte in camera* in the Chancery Division. The *Practice Direction* of 28 July 1994 also covers *Mareva* injunctions.[1] Where practical papers to be used on the application should be lodged with the judge at least two hours before the hearing.[2] An applicant should be required, in an appropriate case, to support his cross-undertaking in damages by a payment into court or the provision of a bond by an insurance company. Alternatively, the judge may order payment by way of such security to the applicant's solicitor as an officer of the court pending further order.[3]

1   [1994] 1 WLR 1233.
2   Ibid.
3   Ibid.

11.34 So far as practicable, any application for the discharge or variation of the order should be dealt with effectively on the return date.[1]

1   *Practice Direction* (28 July 1994) [1994] 1 WLR 1233.

Hurdles to be overcome

11.35 The plaintiff must show:
(a) a cause of action justiciable in England and Wales;
(b) a good arguable case (though it need not be so strong as to warrant summary judgment under RSC Order 14). It must appear likely that the plaintiff will recover judgment against the defendant for a certain or approximate sum;[1]
(c) that the defendant has assets within the jurisdiction. *Prima facie* evidence suffices, since in the nature of things, it will not usually be easy to specify exactly what assets exist in this country in the case of the sort of defendant against whom a *Mareva* injunction needs to be obtained;
(d) that there is a real risk of removal or disposal of the assets. The order can extend to assets likely to be disposed of within this jurisdiction;[2]

1   [1982] QB 558.
2   Ibid.

Property included in the order

11.36 The Court of Appeal has provided the following guidelines:[1]

(1) There should be clear evidence that a defendant was likely, unless restrained by order, to dispose of his chattels in order to deprive the plaintiff of the fruits of any judgment he might obtain. Moreover, the court should be slow to order the delivery up of the defendant's property unless there was evidence or inference that the defendant had acquired the property as a result of his alleged wrongdoing.

(2) No order should be made for delivery up of a defendant's wearing apparel, bedding, furnishings, tools of his trade, farm implements, livestock or any machines (including vehicles) or other goods such as materials or stock in trade, which is likely to be used in a lawful business. Sometimes, however, furnishing might consist of *objets d'art* of great value and if the evidence was clear that they were bought for the purposes of frustrating judgment creditors, they could be included in an order.

(3) All orders should specify clearly what chattels or classes of chattels were to be delivered up. A plaintiff's inability to identify what he wants to be delivered up and why is an indication that no order should be made.

(4) The orders must not authorise the plaintiff to enter on or to seize the defendant's property save by permission of the defendant.

(5) No order should be made for delivery up to anyone other than the plaintiff's solicitor or a receiver appointed by the High Court. The court should appoint a receiver to take possession of the chattels unless satisfied that the plaintiff's solicitor has, or can arrange, suitable safe custody for what was delivered to him.

(6) The court should follow the guidelines set out in *Z Ltd v A-Z and AA-LL*[2] in so far as they were applicable to chattels in the possession, custody or control of third parties.

(7) Provision should always be made for liberty to apply to stay, vary or discharge the order.

1   *CBS (UK) Ltd v Lambert* [1983] Ch 37.
2   [1982] QB 558.

11.37   The court pointed out that guidelines are guidelines, not rules of court, and the spirit of them and not the letter should be kept in mind.

The application

11.38   As in the case of *Anton Piller* proceedings, where practical papers to be used on the application should be lodged with the judge at least two hours before the hearing.[1] An applicant should be required, in an appropriate case, to support his cross-undertaking in damages by a payment into court or the provision of a bond by an insurance company. Alternatively, the judge may order payment by way of such security to the applicant's solicitor as an officer of the court pending further order.[2]

1   *Practice Direction* (28 July 1994) [1994] 1 WLR 1233.
2   Ibid.

RSC ORDER 14

Introduction

11.39 The great advantage of Order 14 procedure is that it leads expeditiously to a final disposal of the dispute between the parties. Not only can the plaintiff obtain an injunction, but can also obtain such other relief as may be appropriate. The procedure is only appropriate in clear cases, where the facts supporting the plaintiff's complaint are clear. If they are clear, the court should not be reluctant to decide any difficult points of law which they raise. The procedure, where appropriate, offers considerable advantages therefore over interlocutory applications. Moreover, because the injunction is final, there is no cross-undertaking in damages, and no question of an injunction being refused on the balance of convenience, which is one of the most important considerations affecting the granting or refusal of interlocutory injunctions. A further consideration to be borne in mind is that where an Order 14 application has been successfully resisted, the plaintiff will at least have had the benefit of forcing the defendant to nail his colours to the mast at an early stage.

11.40 Order 14 applications are of great value in enforcing, where necessary, agreements to settle proceedings, provided the agreement has been satisfactorily drafted.

Procedural requirements

11.41
- (a) the Statement of Claim must be served (usually this is indorsed on the writ);
- (b) the defendant must have filed an acknowledgement of service indicating an intention to defend;
- (c) the summons, a copy of the affidavit in support and of any exhibits referred to therein must be served on the defendant not less than ten clear days before the return day;
- (d) if an injunction or other relief that cannot be granted by the master is sought, then the application may be heard before a judge in chambers;
- (e) the affidavit in support of the application must verify the facts pleaded in the Statement of Claim, and must contain a statement of the deponent's belief that there is no defence to the claim or part thereof in respect of which the application is made, except as to the amount of damages claimed.

Chapter 12

Criminal and regulatory protection of a name or character

Introduction

12.1 In addition to the civil actions and remedies considered in the previous chapters, there is some criminal and regulatory protection for a merchandiser. This could be especially important where an action for copyright or trade mark infringement is unavailable. Personalities, for example, may be afforded some protection against the unauthorised use of their names, through the Trade Descriptions Act 1968 and the Codes of Advertising Practice.

12.2 Where copyright or trade mark protection exists, customs law provides a useful way of preventing the importation of offending goods, when the merchandiser has advance warning of the consignment.

TRADE DESCRIPTIONS ACT 1968

12.3 There are two offences under this Act which are relevant for present purposes: (a) applying a false trade description to goods;[1] (b) supplying goods to which a false trade description has been applied.[2] Thus both the application of a label which suggests that they are genuine to counterfeit goods, of itself is an offence, as is the later supply of those goods to customers. Moreover the use of a name so as to imply that goods are approved by a person when they are not, can amount to a false trade description.[3] Section 2(1)(g) defines 'trade description' to include 'approval by any person or conformity with a type approved by any person'. Section 3(4) defines a 'false trade description' as including 'A false indication, or anything likely to be taken as an indication which would be false, that any goods comply with a standard specified or recognised by any person or implied by the approval of any person shall be deemed to be a false trade description, if there is no such person or no standard so specified, recognised or implied'. The equivalent provision relating to services is section 14(1)(iv) which provides that it is an offence to make a statement knowingly or recklessly which is false as to 'the examination, approval or evaluation by any person of any services, accommodation or facilities so provided'.

12.3 *Criminal and regulatory protection of a name or character*

1 S 1(1)(a).
2 S 1(1)(b).
3 Trade Descriptions Act 1968, ss 1, 2(1)(g) and 3(4).

12.4 The enforcing authorities under the Act are the local Trading Standards authorities.[1] The time limit for prosecution is three years.[2] If the local authority refuses to act, representations may be made to the Secretary of State for Trade and Industry.[3] There is no reason in principle why a private prosecution should not be brought. Some magistrates' courts are less willing than others to entertain this, however. The penalty on summary conviction is a fine not exceeding the prescribed sum.[4] There is no limit to the fine which can be imposed on indictment, and up to two years' imprisonment can be ordered either in addition, or instead of, a fine.[5]

1 Ibid, s 26.
2 Ibid, s 19.
3 Ibid, s 26(3).
4 Trade Descriptions Act 1968, s 18(a) as amended by the Criminal Law Act 1977 and the Magistrates' Courts Act 1980. The prescribed sum is currently £5,000 – Magistrates' Courts Act 1980, s 39(2).
5 Ibid, s 18(b).

12.5 Could the Trade Descriptions Act 1968 apply to prevent the use of a fictional name of a character used in eg a TV series, as well as a celebrity name? It is submitted that in a situation such as the *Kojak* case,[1] it might (though on the actual facts of that case one would not wish to press the argument too far). After all, the whole point of marketing 'Kojakpops' was that the fictional character 'Kojak' sucked lollipops in the television series. A reasonable inference for a member of the public to make would be that the lollipops bearing his name were the same as those he sucked in the television series. Were Kojak represented as recommending hair shampoo, however, the situation would be more difficult (to say the least).[2] Any application of the Act would have to depend upon the fact that people frequently do not distinguish the fictional character from the actor playing him or her. To such persons, the fictional character is 'real'. Whether or not the law should take account of such gullibility is another matter, though it is perhaps not so unreasonable to suppose that the actor (as a real person) is endorsing the product bearing his fictional name.

1 *Tavenor Rutledge Ltd v Trexapalm Ltd* [1975] FSR 479, para 4.7 above.
2 The character in question was bald.

12.6 Under section 2(1)(i) of the 1968 Act 'trade description' is defined to include statements as to the person by whom goods are manufactured, produced, processed or reconditioned. Falsely applying a trade mark is an offence under the Act,[1] as is the supply of the goods bearing it.[2] In 1981 and 1982 Mid-Glamorgan County Council successfully prosecuted three market traders and three wholesalers under this section for selling counterfeit 'Hoover' spares.[3]

1 S 1(1)(a). See *Stone v Burn* [1911] 1 KB 927 (under the Merchandise Marks Acts 1926-1953); *Roberts v Severn Petroleum and Trading Co Ltd* [1981] RTR 312.
2 S 1(1)(b).
3 O'Keefe *Trade Descriptions*, Vol 1, 67.1 (now *Butterworths Trading and Consumer Law*).

12.7   It is a defence to a charge under the Act for the defendant to show that the commission of the offence was due to a mistake or to reliance on information supplied to him or to the act or default of another person, an accident or some other cause beyond his control.[1] It is also a defence for the defendant to show that he took all reasonable precautions and exercised all due diligence to avoid the commission of an offence by himself or any person under his control.[2] Thus, innocent dealers in counterfeit goods might be able to bring themselves within either of these provisions.

1   S 24(1)(a).
2   S 24(1)(b).

CONTROL OF MISLEADING ADVERTISEMENTS REGULATIONS AND CODES OF ADVERTISING PRACTICE

12.8   The Control of Misleading Advertisements Regulations[1] could apply to advertisements suggesting sponsorship or endorsement of goods, where none in fact exists. The definition of a misleading advertisement is very wide:

'For the purposes of these rRegulations an advertisement is misleading if in any way, including its presentation, it deceives or is likely to deceive the persons to whom it is addressed or whom it reaches and if, by reason of its deceptive nature, it is likely to affect their economic behaviour or, for those reasons injures or is likely to affect to injure a competitor of the person whose interests the advertisement seeks to promote.'[2]

1   SI 1988/915.
2   Reg 2(2).

12.9   Advertising goods as genuine which are, in fact, counterfeit, would appear to contravene the regulations. The procedure under the regulations is initiated by complaint to the Director General of Fair Trading, who may take action through the courts seeking an injunction.[1] He also has powers under the regulations to obtain information.[2] Complaints can also be made to the IBA and the Cable Authority.[3]

1   Reg 4.
2   Reg 5.
3   Regs 8 and 10.

12.10   Advertising the fact that goods or services are approved by a celebrity if they are not, almost certainly infringes the Codes of Practice of the Advertising Association and the Independent Broadcasting Authority which monitors television and radio advertising.

12.11   The object of the British Code of Advertising Practice is to ensure that advertisements are legal, decent, honest and truthful, framed with a sense of responsibility to the consumer and conform to the principles of fair competition as generally accepted in business. The Code is a self-regulating system supervised by the Advertising Standards Association

(ASA). The chairman is appointed from outside the advertising industry and about half of its members have no connection with advertising. The day to day administration of the Code is the responsibility of the Code of Advertising Practice (CAP) Committee and the CAP/ASA Secretariat.

12.12   Complaints are investigated by the Secretariat, which reports to ASA. The ASA publishes details of the complaints when they have been upheld, and the names of the advertisers involved. The media adherents of the Code have undertaken not to publish any advertisement found to be in breach of the Code, nor will they accept advertisements from agencies which defy the ASA's authority. Obviously this is one of the principal sanctions.

12.13   Paragraph 17 of the Code provides as follows:

PROTECTION OF PRIVACY AND EXPLOITATION OF THE INDIVIDUAL

17.1 1. Except in the circumstances noted in 17.2 to 17.5 below, advertisements should not portray or refer to any living persons, in whatever form or by whatever means, unless their express prior permission has been obtained.

2. 'Refer' in the preceding sub-paragraph embraces reference to a person's possessions, house etc, in any manner which unambiguously identifies their owner to prospective readers of the advertisement.

17.2 The circumstances in which a reference or portrayal may be acceptable in the absence of prior permission, are the following:
   – generally, when the advertisement contains nothing which is inconsistent, or likely to be seen as inconsistent, with the position of the person to whom reference is made, and when it does not abrogate his right to enjoy a reasonable degree of privacy;
   – in the special case of advertisements the purpose of which is to promote a product such as a book or film, when the person concerned is the subject of that book, film etc.

A complaint from a person falling within either of these exclusions is none the less offensive, harmful or humiliating, will be weighed by ASA or CAP when deciding whether the adveriement concerned is within the spirit of the Code.

The applicability of these two exceptions to the general rule is further considered in sub-paragraphs 17.3 to 17.5 below.

17.3 It follows from the above that complaints from those who occupy positions or exercise trades or professions which necessarily entail a high degree of public exposure, such as actors, sportsmen and politicians, can be entertained only
   – when it can reasonably be argued that the advertisement concerned suggests some commercial involvement on their part which is of a kind likely to be generally perceived as inconsisitent with their status or position; or
   – when the effect of the advertisement is to substantially diminish or to abrogate their right to control the circumstances or terms upon which they may exploit their name, likeness or reputation on a commercial basis.

17.4 The use of crowd or background shots, which individuals or their possessions, houses etc are recognisable, is not regarded under the Code as inconsistent with the right of such individuals to enjoy a reasonable degree of privacy, provided that there is nothing in the depiction which is defamatory, offensive or humiliating. Advertisers should be ready to withdraw any advertisement in respect of which they recive a reasonable objection on such grounds from a person affected.

17.5 [*Advertisements in which reference may properly be made to members of the Royal Family*]

17.6 It is not regarded as contrary to the principle set out in 17.1 above for unsolicited advertising material to be addressed to a consumer personally.

17.7 References to individuals with whom the advertiser is personally acquainted, and which he has no reason to suppose will be resented, are not regarded as infringements of privacy of such individuals, but should be withdrawn if any reasonable objection is received.

17.8 [*Avoidance of unnecessary offence to the susceptibilities of those connected with deceased persons*]

12.14   The address of the Advertising Standards Authority is:

Brook House,
Torrington Place,
London WC1E 7HJ

12.15   Television and radio advertising is monitored by the Independent Television Commission.[1] Standards and practice are set out in the ITC Code and are similar to those contained in the Code of Advertising Practice. Paragraph 15 of the Code provides:

Individual living persons must not be portrayed or referred to in advertisements without their permission except in circumstances approved by the Commission.

1   Broadcasting Act 1990.

12.16   The address of the Independent Television Commission is:

Advertising and Sponsorship Division,
Independent Television Commission,
Foley Street,
London W1P 7LB

DECEPTION

12.17   If it can be established that persons have been induced to buy goods on the strength of a representation that the goods are approved by a person when they are not, it would appear that the representor could be convicted of the offence of deception.[1] It is not even clear that the lie has to be shown actually to have induced any particular purchaser to buy the goods. In *R* *v Sullivan*,[2] the defendant was convicted simply for advertising himself as the 'actual maker' of dartboards.

1   Theft Act 1968, s 15.
2   (1945) 30 Cr App Rep 132. See however *R v Laverty* [1970] 3 All ER 432 at 434.

12.18   The existence of this offence is more of academic than practical interest, however, for in the above case, as in the case where the representation implies an indication as to the person by whom the goods were manufactured, it is more probable that proceedings would be instituted under the Trade Descriptions Act 1968 discussed at paragraph 12.3 et seq above.

CUSTOMS LAW

12.19   Where a false trade description is applied to goods outside the UK, and the false indication, or one of the false indications, given, or likely to be taken as given, is an indication of the place of manufacture, production, processing or reconditioning of the goods, their importation may be prevented.[1] Simlarly, the importation of goods bearing infringing trade marks[2] or goods which infringe copyright,[3] may be prevented by the customs authorities. In the case of trade marks the proprietor may give notice to the Commissioners of Customs & Excise in the prescribed form.[4] In the case of copyright material, the owner may again give notice to the Commissioners.[5] The person making this request may have to give an indemnity to the Commissioners against the consequences of wrongful seizure. There are no similar provisions dealing with goods infringing other branches of the law which may be involved in merchandising. Moreover, it would seem that the Customs have no power to prevent goods bearing other statements contrary to the provisions of the Trade Descriptions Act 1968,[6] eg a false statement that they are endorsed by a person. The only restriction imposed by that Act is on the importation of goods bearing a false indication of origin.[7]

1   Trade Descriptions Act 1968, s 16.
2   Trade Marks Act 1994, s 89.
3   Copyright, Designs and Patents Act 1988, s 111.
4   Trade Marks (Customs) Regulations 1994, SI 1994/2625, Schedule.
5   Copyright (Customs) Regulations 1989, SI 1989/1178.
6   See para 12.3 et seq above.
7   S 16.

COPYRIGHT, DESIGNS AND PATENTS ACT 1988

12.20   Section 107 of the Copyright, Designs and Patents Act 1988 consolidates, with amendments, the offences created by section 21 of the Copyright Act 1956, as well as the 'video piracy' offences created by the Copyright Act 1956 (Amendment) Act 1982 and the Copyright (Amendment) Act 1983. Section 107 covers all copyright works with in the 1988 Act. The offences created by the Act broadly relate to 'making or dealing' in an article which the defendant knows or has reason to believe is an infringing copy. Section 109 permits the police to apply for a search warrant when it is believed that an offence under section 107 has been or is about to be committed and that evidence of this is in those premises. The warrant will be issued by a justice of the peace.

CONSPIRACY

12.21   An offence of conspiracy to defraud at common law would be committed where two or more persons combine to infringe property rights, including intellectual property.[1]

1   See eg *Scott v Metropolitan Police Comr* [1975] AC 819.

Section II

Other jurisdictions

Introduction

The choice of the jurisdictions represented here was made for the following reasons. Australia, whilst in many respects similar to England and Wales, has begun to develop some interesting new concepts which are of importance in the merchandising context, notably in relation to passing off and under the Trade Descriptions Act 1974. Similarly, Canada, but in this case the most interesting developments are in relation to personality merchandising. The United States is the third representative of the common law family of jurisdictions, and is included both because of its importance, and because of the many differences between US law and that of other common law countries. France and Germany each represent different strands in the civil law tradition; it tends to be the case that in that family of jurisdictions, states have modelled their laws on those of one or the other of these two. A further distinction between the countries chosen is between unitary and federal jurisdictions. France, like England and Wales, is unitary; the remaining jurisdictions included here are federal.

Chapter 13

Australia[1]

INTRODUCTION

13.1 Australian law corresponds quite closely to UK law with regard to trade marks, designs and copyrights, to the extent that they are the principal sources of protection involved in character merchandising. However, with regard to personality merchandising, it probably affords more extensive protection.

1　I would like to thank Professor Jim Lahore and Professor Sam Ricketson for their help with this Chapter. Needless to say, responsibility for errors and omissions is mine.

13.2 The situation as to the courts having jurisdiction in the field used to be complicated, there being distinctions not only between the different statutory rights, but between those and the common law rights. As a result of the Cross Vesting Act 1987, however, the jurisdiction of State and Territorial Supreme Courts in respect of these matters is cross vested in the Federal Court of Australia, and vice versa.

THE RIGHTS EXISTING UNDER AUSTRALIAN LAW

Copyright

13.3 Essentially the situation is quite close to that under UK law. So far as the substantive law is concerned, the 1968 Act closely follows the UK Copyright Act of 1956. Cartoon characters and sculptures are 'drawings' or 'paintings' within the definition of 'artistic works' contained in section 10(1), and infringement of artistic works includes making three-dimensional reproductions of them in the form of such objects as dolls.[1] Reproduction can be direct, or indirect. Thus dolls made from other dolls, and toys made from the drawings will infringe the copyright in the drawings.[2]

1　Ibid, ss 21(3), 31(1).
2　See Ricketson *Law of Intellectual Property* Law Book Company 1984 [9.25].

13.4 The owner of the copyright in a work is *prima facie* the author, but there is an equivalent exception to that contained in the UK Act for works created by employees in the course of their employment.[1]

1　S 35(6).

13.5 *Australia*

13.5 Copyright subsists from the time a work is created, and expires 50 years from the end of the calendar year in which the author died.[1] Copyright in a literary, dramatic or musical work, not published, publicly performed or broadcast during the author's lifetime expires 50 years after the end of the calendar year in which the first of these events occurs.[2] Copyright protection ceases when an artistic work is applied as an industrial design. It ceases on the day on which articles made to the design are first sold, let for hire, or offered or exposed for sale or hire,[3] unless registration of the design has been applied for and refused.[4] Thereafter, it is not an infringement of the copyright in a work to reproduce the design. It is likely that as in UK law, a name as such will not be treated as a literary work within section 10(1) of the Act.[5]

1   S 33(2).
2   S 33(3) and (5).
3   S 77(2).
4   S 77(3).
5   *Exxon Corpn v Exxon Insurance Consultants* [1982] Ch 119 – see Lahore *Intellectual Property Law in Australia, Copyright Law*, Butterworths (loose leaf), para 2.3.20.

13.6 In relation to photographs, the 'author' is the person who took the photograph,[1] thus the position is the same as under the 1988 UK Act.[2] On the other hand, stills from photographic films are excluded from the definition of 'photographs'.[3] This same exclusion was to be found in section 48 of the UK Act of 1956, but in *Spelling Goldberg Productions Inc v BPC Publishing Ltd*[4] the English court concluded that reproduction of a single frame infringed cinematic copyright. The definition of 'copyright' contained in section 10(1) is not, however, the same as that contained in the old UK Act, and it would appear that a copy could not comprise a single frame.[5] Both the images and the sound track of a film are subject to cinematic copyright as under the previous UK law.[6] It is important to note that the owner of the copyright in a film, as under UK law, is the 'maker' ie the person by whom the arrangements necessary for making the film were undertaken.[7]

1   S 10(1).
2   Under previous UK law, where a photograph, painting or drawing was commissioned for money or money's worth the owner of the copyright was the commissioner – 1956 Act, s 4(3).
3   In s 10(1).
4   [1981] RPC 283.
5   Lahore, op cit, para 2.3.110.
6   S 10(1). As to the previous UK law see Copyright Act 1956, s 13.
7   S 22(4)(a) and (b).

13.7 Artistic works such as drawings are protected whether or not the work is of artistic quality[1] (as under UK law). On the other hand, if the property relied on is not a drawing (which as explained above can be infringed by a three-dimensional reproduction such as a doll), but the three-dimensional object itself, it must qualify as a work of artistic quality. In the English case of *George Hensher v Restawhile Upholstery*[2] the House of Lords held that a commercial suite of furniture was not a work of artistic craftsmanship, and in the Victorian decision in *Cuisenaire v Reed*[3] Pape J found it impossible to say that a box of rods of varying length was a work of artistic craftsmanship. No special skill was needed to cut the wood into different lengths and to colour them in various colours. Although the exact ratio of the *Hensher* case is difficult to determine, it does seem likely on the basis of these cases that many merchandised properties would fail to qualify as works of artistic craftsmanship, so that a merchandiser who is unable to rely on a drawing, or the like, will be in difficulties.

1   S 10(1).
2   [1976] AC 64, [1975] RPC 31.
3   [1963] VR 719.

13.8 The right to object to false attribution is recognised by Australian law,[1] including the right of an author to object to an altered work being attributed to him or her.[2] But other moral rights are not recognised.[3]

1   Ss 190-192.
2   S 191.
3   Lahore *Copyright Law* 4.15.455.

13.9 Where an industrial design is registered, it is not infringement of the copyright in the design to reproduce the design by applying it to an article.[1]

1   S 75.

Registered designs

13.10 A registrable design is defined as meaning:[1]

> ... features of shape, configuration, pattern or ornamentation applicable to an article, being features that, in the finished article, can be judged by the eye, but does not include a method or principle of construction.

This is, in effect, virtually identical to the definition contained in section 1(3) of the UK 1949 Act.[2] In consequence, the comments made in the principal Report where UK designs law is dealt with, are applicable here.

1   Designs Act 1906 (Cth), s 4(1).
2   And, for present purposes the definition replacing s 1(3) contained in s 265 of the UK 1988 Act.

13.11 The Australian Law Reform Commission has made an extensive study of this area, and has made a number of suggestions for reform.[1]

1   Discussion Paper No 58, August 1994.

Passing off

13.12 As in the UK, the action of passing off is the standard remedy for protecting unregistered marks. The basis of the tort is similarly a misrepresentation calculated to damage the plaintiff's goodwill, though unlike the situation in England and Wales,[1] it would appear that a reputation can suffice. That the basis of the tort is misrepresentation, rather than misappropriation, is clearly established by the case of *ConAgra*

13.12 *Australia*

Inc v McCain Foods (Aust) Pty Ltd.[2] In this case the appellants manufactured and sold in the USA a range of frozen food products under the name 'Healthy Choice'. The respondent commenced selling a similar range of products in Australia using the same trade name and a similar get-up and packaging. The court held that it was not necessary in order to succeed in passing off that the plaintiff should have a place of business or a business presence within the jurisdiction; it is sufficient if the plaintiff's goods have a reputation in the jurisdiction among persons, whether residents or otherwise, of a sufficient degree to establish that there is a likelihood of deception among consumers and potential consumers and of damage to the plaintiff's reputation. However, on the facts of the case the appellants failed, because they had not established that there was a substantial proportion of persons in Australia who were aware of their product.

1 See the discussion of *Budweiser* at para 4.24 above.
2 (1992) 106 ALR 465.

13.13 Otherwise, in general, what was said in relation to the use of passing off in merchandising cases in England and Wales, is applicable to the Australian context, though there are differences which need to be noted. These are dealt with below.

13.14 Arguably, the doubts about the possibility of licensing unregistered trade marks, which were expressed in *Star Industrial v Yap Kwee Kor*[1] were inconsistent with the Privy Council decision in *JH Coles v Need*[2] which was an Australian case. This latter case, incidentally, also supported the view that where unregistered marks were licensed in circumstances where proper quality control is exercised, the goodwill accrued to the licensor. At all events, any surviving doubts seem to have been put to rest by *Kettle Chip Co Pty Ltd v Apand Pty Ltd.*[3] In this case the applicant had begun in 1989 to market distinctive potato chips under the trade name 'Kettle Chip'. No product of this kind had previously been marketed in Australia. It also licensed two other companies to produce and sell the product. In 1990 the respondent had begun to market a similar product under the name 'Country Kettle'. It was held that there was sufficient similarity between the packaging of the two products as to create a likelihood of confusion in the mind of the ordinary consumer. It was also held that passing off can be based on a shared reputation. It does not follow that an applicant who has obtained an exclusive right to make and vend articles under a particular name, mark or get-up will have lost that right because he has licensed another trader to market some of the articles made by him under circumstances which have led a limited section only of the public to conclude that the other trader was entitled to use the name etc. It is not necessary that *all* consumers associate the name etc with the applicant alone. The association by a significant number of consumers is sufficient.[4]

1 [1976] FSR 256.
2 [1934] AC 82.
3 (1993) FCR 152.
4 As well as *J H Coles Pty Ltd v Need*, the following cases were cited and discussed: *ConAgra* (above); *Dodds Family Investments Pty Ltd v Lane Industries Pty Ltd* (1993) 26 IPR 261; *Erven Warnick BV v Townend* (see para 4.4 above). *Re Wood's Trade Mark* (1886) 32 Ch D 247 was distinguished.

13.15 Australian courts showed themselves more ready to adjust to character merchandising than the English courts, although as we have seen[1] the interlocutory decision in the English case of *Mirage Studios v Counter-Feat Clothing Co Ltd*[2] adds weight to the view that English judges are increasingly coming to terms with the practice, and have moved a long way from the views expressed by Walton J in *Tavenor Rutledge v Trexapalm Ltd*[3] that we were miles away from reaching the point where a member of the public seeing a well known name from a TV series or the like attached to a product, will say to himself 'This must have been licensed by [the owners of the series]' and 'that is a guarantee of its quality'. In expressing these views, Walton J was responding to the argument that using the name of the hero of a TV series in relation to goods (lollipops), entailed a misrepresentation that they had been approved by the proprietors of the series. There would only be such a misrepresentation if the public were generally aware of the practice of merchandising. By contrast, in the New South Wales case of *Children's Television Workshop Inc v Woolworths (NSW) Ltd*[4] the defendants were restrained from marketing plush toys representing characters in the plaintiff's television series 'Sesame Street'. Helsham CJ was satisfied that there was an association in the minds of the public between the first plaintiffs as producers of the TV series and representations of its character in any form.

1   Para 4.13 above.
2   [1991] FSR 145.
3   [1977] RPC 275. See also *IPC Magazines Ltd v Black and White Music Corpn* [1983] FSR 348; *Stringfellow v McCain Foods (GB) Ltd* [1984] RPC 501.
4   [1981] 1 NSWLR 273.

13.16 Australian law has also gone rather faster than English law in developing the tort of passing off in a way which is of special relevance to *personality* merchandising. It must be emphasised, however, as noted at the beginning of this section, that these developments, although examples of what is generally regarded as unfair competition, do not amount to a tort of unfair competition in the sense of misappropriation.[1] The clear implication of the Privy Council decision in *Cadbury Schweppes Pty Ltd v Pub Squash Co Pty Ltd*[2] is that there is no such tort at the present time. One reason for this, as I have suggested elsewhere,[3] is the need in adversarial procedure to have rather specific targets to which pleadings and evidence can be directed. Another is that many cases start with an application for an interlocutory injunction against the alleged infringer. In deciding whether or not to grant such an injunction, the judge does not have to decide finally whether or not there is an infringement, merely that there is a serious question to be tried.[4] This question is easier to answer where there is a fairly sharply defined tort involved, such as passing off. Nevertheless, the extended action of passing off as it has developed in Australia may afford more protection to personality merchandising operations than did English law until recently. As explained in paragraph 13.26. below, the developments at a Federal level, which until recently looked interesting in this respect, seem to have been checked for the present by the *ConAgra* case.[5]

1   Lahore op cit *Patents Trade Marks and Designs*, Vol 2, para 5.3.001.
2   (1980) 32 ALR 387 (on appeal from the Supreme Court of New South Wales).
3   Adams [1994] 8 EIPR 259.

4   *American Cyanamid Co v Ethicon Ltd* [1975] AC 396. This is the leading case laying down the criteria to be satisfied for the granting of an interlocutory injunction.
5   See para 13.12 above.

13.17   Australian law relaxed the 'common field of activity' requirement, which was a serious inhibition to the value of passing off in personality merchandising cases, earlier than English law. In *Henderson v Radio Corpn Pty Ltd*[1] the plaintiffs were famous ballroom dancers. Without their permission, the defendants manufactured and marketed records of ballroom dance music in a sleeve bearing a photograph of the plaintiffs. The Full Court of the Supreme Court of New South Wales affirmed the first instance judges' decision to grant the plaintiffs an injunction. In doing so they criticised the 'common field of activity' rule which apparently underpinned the English decision in *McCulloch v Lewis A May (Produce Distributors) Ltd*.[2] Although English law has abandoned the 'common field of activity' rule (if it ever really adopted it), it may be that where the fields of activity of the plaintiff and defendant are different, English judges are likely to require clearer evidence that the defendant's activities are likely to damage the plaintiff's goodwill. *Henderson* was followed in Victoria in *Totalizator Agency Board v Turf News Pty Ltd*.[3] It was also applied in *Children's Television Workshop Inc v Woolworths (NSW) Ltd*[4] mentioned above.

1   (1960) SRNSW 576.
2   [1947] 2 All ER 845 – see para 4.16 above.
3   [1967] VR 605 – involving the use of a trade name in another context.
4   [1981] 1 NSWLR 273.

13.18   It would appear that the action of passing off now extends to enjoin any deceptive connection or association between the defendant's business and the plaintiffs or their business induced by the defendant's misrepresentation.[1] It also extends beyond the protection of trading goodwill, to the promotional exploitation of a name, personality or reputation.[2] It protects the plaintiff's relationship with lines of business other than those actually engaged in by the plaintiff at the time.[3] The defendant does not necessarily, therefore, have to represent his goods as being those of the plaintiff, it suffices that he makes a representation which links him with the plaintiff or his goods. The public may well be aware that the goods in question are the defendant's, but they are deceived into thinking that the plaintiff is associated with them.[4] This view can be supported from some recent cases. In *Shoshana Pty Ltd v 10th Cantanae Pty Ltd*[5] a well known TV personality, Sue Smith, objected to the use of her name in advertisements for a video recorder. The advertisement depicted a young woman with the caption 'Sue Smith took total control of her video recorder'. Although the majority concluded that the use of a common name, such as 'Sue Smith', in conjunction with a picture of a person who clearly was not the TV personality, would not mislead members of the public into associating the plaintiff with the advertisement, both Wilcox and Gummow JJ agreed that protection in passing off should be granted where the representation of a defendant held out an association or approval of a product by the plaintiff where none had in fact been sanctioned. In *Paul Hogan v Koala Dundee Pty Ltd*[6] the plaintiff was the actor Paul Hogan, player of the well-known film character 'Crocodile Dundee'. The defendants owned several shops which they called 'Dundee

County', and used on signs inside and outside those shops, and on T-shirts, shopping bags and clothing tags, an image showing the upper half of a koala bear dressed in the manner associated with the character Crocodile Dundee. Pincus J held that the holding out of an association between the Crocodile Dundee character and the defendant's shops and goods was a sufficient misrepresentation. The same plaintiff also succeeded in *Paul Hogan v Pacific Dunlop*.[7] In that case a famous scene from the film was adapted to advertise the defendant's shoes. The first instance judge, Gummow J held that it was generally recognised that Paul Hogan made a practice of licensing his name, so that the public would be deceived into thinking that approval or licence had been given when it had not. In this respect the decision is arguably narrower than that of Pincus J in the *Koala Dundee* case, in that for Pincus J it appeared to be sufficient that the respondents had held out that they had an association with a well-known public figure. This decision was upheld on appeal by the Full Federal Court. As one commentator has said,[8] these cases are significant in that they confirm the recognition given to character merchandising in earlier cases such as *Henderson v Radio Corpn*. Furthermore, whilst misrepresentation still remains of the essence in passing off actions of this kind, these cases demonstrate a flexible and expansive approach to the kind of misrepresentation that will suffice for the purposes of liability. In short, it has been judicially accepted by the Full Federal Court that the possessors of well-known names and images control carefully the use that may be made of those names and images, with the consequence that any unauthorised use will almost inevitably involve an actionable misrepresentation. It would appear likely, therefore, that the earlier case of *Wickham v Associated Pool Builders*,[9] in which the first instance judge came close to resuscitating the common field of activity test, was wrongly decided, though another earlier case in which the plaintiff also lost was probably correctly decided on its facts.[10]

1 Murumba *The Commercial Exploitation of Personality*, Law Book Co 1986 p 63.
2 The position under English law may now be similar – see *Stringfellow v McCain Foods* (above); *Mirage Studios v Counter-Feat Clothing Co Ltd* (above). Though a mere reputation per se is not protected – see *Anheuser-Busch Inc v Budejovicky Budvar Narodni Podnik* [1984] FSR 413.
3 Murumba, op cit, p 63.
4 Ibid, p 65.
5 (1987) 18 FCR 285.
6 (1988) AIPC 90-291.
7 (1988) AIPC 90-578.
8 Ricketson (1990) 1 Intellectual Property Journal 191, 196.
9 (1988) 12 IPR 567.
10 *Honey v Australian Airlines* (1989) 14 IPR 264.

13.19 Two types of case will still fall outside of this extended action of passing off, however: (1) where the plaintiff is a public figure, but the defendant's activities are likely to lead neither to confusion nor deception; (2) where the plaintiff is simply a private individual with no previous goodwill or reputation.[1] Thus if the defendant were to use in relation to his product a favourable remark made by the plaintiff in private, there would be no confusion of deception, and passing off would not lie.[2] The English case of *Harrison and Starkey v Polydor Ltd*[3] is an example of the first exception. In that case two members of the Beatles pop group were unable to restrain the use of their actual words recorded by a journalist in various interviews, on a set of records the defendants proposed to issue.[4] There was no deception, and Walton J expressly distinguished the *Henderson* case on this basis. Again, the remedy of passing off is available only to those engaged in some kind of business activity. It will not be available therefore to a private individual whose name is used in association with goods. As one writer has observed 'John Citizen can be pressed into unwilling service for a toothpaste but not John Well-Known'.[5] Of course, other remedies may be available such as defamation if this is what the defendant's activities amount to.

1   Murumba, op cit, p 66.
2   Report on the Law of Privacy by WL Morison, New South Wales Parl Paper No 170 17-18.
3   [1977] FSR 1.
4   Under the Copyright, Designs and Patents Act 1988, the speaker of recorded words now enjoys copyright in the UK.
5   Gummow (1974) 7 Sydney LR 224, 226.

13.20   A plaintiff who succeeds in a passing off case is entitled to damages covering diminution of the licensing right by the discouragement of potential licensees, and the harm to a reputation which the marketing of inferior merchandise by the defendant has caused. In the *Children's Television Workshop* case Helsham CJ said that the plaintiff was not required to point to a particular loss, to quantify a diminution in licence royalties, or to demonstrate that it could not negotiate a licence on such favourable terms as it otherwise might. The mere presence of unlicensed goods on the same market as the plaintiff's and the deception as to their authenticity, led properly to an inference that the plaintiff's business was bound to be adversely affected in some way.[1] Similarly, in the *Mirage Studios* case the Vice-Chancellor observed that the plaintiffs would not only lose royalties, but the defendant's inferior goods would damage the plaintiff's licensing right.

1   At p 195.

Registered trade marks

13.21   From 1 January 1996 the Trade Marks Act 1955 has been replaced by the Trade Marks Act 1994. This, in essence, brings Australian law into line with the new UK law. Section 16 provides that a 'trade mark' is

'a sign used, or intended to be used, to distinguish goods or services dealt with or provided in the course of trade by a person from goods or services so provided or dealt with by any other person.'

Therefore, marks are registrable both for goods and services.[1] Any mark which can be represented in writing is registrable, unless excluded on one or more of the grounds for rejection set out in Division 2 of the Act. 'Writing' includes any mode of representing or reproducing works, figures, drawings or symbols in a visible form. This is in effect equivalent to the requirement of the UK Act that the sign can be represented graphically, and it would appear that a similar range of signs is, in principle, registrable to that which is registrable in the UK. The exclusions from registration are also similar:

(1) marks consisting wholly or principally of the shape of goods, if the shape is possessed because of the nature of the goods, or is necessary if a particular technical result is to be obtained;[2]

(2) marks not capable of distinguishing the applicant's goods or services – in deciding which question distinctiveness acquired by use can inter alia be taken into account;[3]

(3) marks consisting wholly or principally of signs designating quality;[4]

(4) scandalous marks;[5]

(5) marks consisting wholly or principally of the name etc of a person, unless the applicant provides evidence of that person's consent;[6]

(6) marks which are the same as, or substantially identical with, or deceptively similar to, an earlier registered mark,[7] and registration is sought for the same, or same kind of goods or services, to which the earlier registration relates.[8]

1 S 18 – it should be noted that this was the position before the coming into force of the 1994 Act.
2 S 39.
3 S 40.
4 S 41.
5 S 42.
6 S 43.
7 Or a mark already applied for.
8 S 44.

13.22 As in the case of the 1994 UK Act, the Act states that a registered trade mark is personal property,[1] and following from that proposition, it is provided that a trade mark is assignable or transmissible with or without the goodwill of the business concerned.[2] As in the UK, applications are assignable or transmissible.[3] Again, as in the UK, in consequence, the restrictions on licensing have disappeared. There is no equivalent of section 74(4) which contained a similar prohibition on 'trafficking' to that contained in section 28(6) of the 1938 UK Act. Provision for the registration of licensees as users has been retained[4] and there is also provision for the voluntary recording of interests in marks,[5] though, needless to say, recordal does not prove the existence of the right.[6]

1 S 20.
2 S 106.
3 S 108.
4 S 113 et seq.
5 S 121 et seq.
6 S 125.

Defamation

13.23 The Australian law of defamation follows the English model, rather than the US one, and consequently what was said in paragraphs 5.8 and 5.9 above about English law is applicable.

Invasion of privacy

13.24 As in England, no general right of privacy has yet been recognised in Australia.[1]

13.24 *Australia*

1   Murumba, op cit, p 86.

The Unfair Publications Bill

13.25 This Bill followed the Australian Law Reform Commission report 'Unfair Publication: Defamation and Privacy'.[1] Its passage has been held up, inter alia, because of doubts as to whether the Commonwealth Parliament has the powers to legislate in these fields. Clause 23 of the Bill provides:

> A person whose name, identity, reputation or likeness is appropriated has a right of action against the person who appropriated his name, identity or likeness and against each person who, knowing of the appropriation, has used the appropriation for his own benefit or to the detriment of the first-named person.

Clause 22 sets out the conduct which will amount to appropriation:

> For the purposes of this Part but subject to sub-section (2), a person shall be regarded as having appropriated the name, identity or likeness of another person if he, with intent to exploit for his own benefit, the name, identity, reputation or likeness of that other person and without the consent of that other person, publishes matter containing the name, identity or likeness of that other person -
> (a) in advertising or promoting the sale, leasing or use of property or the supply of services;
> ...
> (2) The publication of mere information or comment about a person shall not be regarded as appropriation of the name, identity, reputation or likeness of that person.

If this Bill ever becomes law, it will provide considerable protection in personality merchandising operations. The remedies available to plaintiffs will include damages, injunctions and an account of any profits made by the defendant in consequence of the appropriation.[2] In assessing damages injury to the health, social or financial position of the plaintiff, or his distress, annoyance or embarrassment can be taken into account.[3]

1   Report No 11, 1979.
2   Cl 25.
3   Cl 29(1)(b).

The Trade Practices Act 1974

13.26 This is in certain respects similar to the UK Trade Descriptions Act 1968 dealt with in the principal Report, but it has significant differences. Section 52 provides:

> (1) A corporation shall not, in trade or commerce, engage in conduct that is misleading or deceptive or is likely to mislead or deceive.
> (2) Nothing in the succeeding provisions of this Division shall be taken as limiting by implication the generality of sub-section (1).

246

Unlike the Trade Descriptions Act, infringement of these provisions gives rise to civil remedies including injunctions,[1] damages[2] and others.[3] Furthermore, according to section 53:

> 'A corporation shall not, in trade or commerce, in connection with the supply or possible supply of goods or services or in connection with the promotion by any means of the supply or use of goods or services –
> (c) represent that goods or services have sponsorship, approval ... they do not have;
> (d) represent that the corporation has a sponsorship, approval or affiliation it does not have.'

Although, for constitutional reasons, the Act by its terms is limited to the activities of corporations, it is made applicable to the activities of non-corporate bodies if the use of postal, telegraphic or telephonic services, or a radio or television broadcast is involved.[4]

1   S 80.
2   S 82.
3   S 87.
4   S 6(3).

13.27   This is a consumer protection measure like the Trade Descriptions Act providing public law sanctions for infringements of its provisions, but it has been held to confer private rights of action on individual personalities. The effect of this is to create proprietary rights in personal reputations. The Act also provides remedies which are similar to those available under the tort of passing off,[1] but at a Federal level.

1   *Hornsby Building Information Centre Pty Ltd v Sydney Building Information Centre Ltd* (1978) 18 ALR 639; *Prince Manufacturing Inc v ABAC Corpn Australia Pty Ltd* (1984) 57 ALR 159.

13.28   An example of the use of the Act in personality merchandising is provided by the case of *Hutchence (trading as INXS) v South Sea Bubble Co Pty Ltd*[1] where it was held that the unauthorised sale of T-shirts bearing the indicia of a pop group, INXS contravened sections 52 and 53 and amounted to passing off, even though the shirts bore a disclaimer of any authorisation from the group. As noted in paragraph 3.52 above, such use might not infringe a registered trade mark, and under English common law, it almost certainly would not amount to passing off. Also, unlike the common law tort, the remedies provided by the Act do not require actual damage to the plaintiff's goodwill, or the likelihood of it, to be shown. Moreover, section 53 in effect protects a plaintiff against the foreclosure of the possibilities of sponsorship which his reputation gives him. The section was, for example, used by those acting on behalf of the rock singer Bruce Springsteen to enjoin a number of companies which had produced unauthorised merchandise bearing his name in anticipation of his tour of Australia.[2] It is not clear, however, whether the Act might assist a non-celebrity in the situation mentioned above.

1   (1986) ATPR 47,369.
2   Murumba, op cit, pp 122 -4.

13.29 The possibility that a remedy for unfair competition based on misappropriation might develop out of these provisions seems for the present to have been put an end to by the *ConAgra* case, disussed above.[1] Although the activities of the respondent amounted essentially to a misappropriation of the appellants' marketing style, the court held that the failure of the appellants to establish a reputation in Australia for the purposes of the law of passing off caused it to fail also in its case of contravention of Part V of the Trade Practices Act.

1   Para 13.12.

Chapter 14

Canada[1]

Introduction

14.1 The laws relating to copyright, designs and trade marks are Federal, and the Federal courts have jurisdiction in disputes relating to these matters. There is also a statutory action of passing off contained in the Trade Marks Act. Although the constitutionality of this was doubted, these doubts now seem to be removed. There are also certain criminal offences provided for in the Criminal Code over which the Federal courts have jurisdiction. Subject to this, passing off, defamation and the newer tort of appropriation of personality are matters for the provincial courts. Some provinces also have specific statutes dealing with invasion of privacy which are relevant in personality merchandising.

1   I would like to thank Sylvana Conte, associate in the law firm of Goodman, Phillips & Vineberg, Montréal, for reading through this section, and for her helpful comments and suggestions. Needless to say, responsibility for errors and omissions is mine.

COPYRIGHT

14.2 Generally speaking, for present purposes, the Canadian law of copyright resembles that of the UK and Australia. As in those jurisdictions, originality entails only a requirement that the work should not have been copied.[1] Similarly, it is clear that copyright protects the form of ideas, and not ideas themselves. Consequently, copyright law can prevent only the use or reproduction of the material form or expression of a character, and not its name or personality. In *Paramount Pictures Corpn v Howley*[2] the plaintiff was able to prevent the poster used to promote the film 'Crocodile Dundee' from being used by the defendants to promote a line of sportswear.[3] By contrast, the use of a character's name by itself cannot be restrained under copyright law,[4] unless the name identifies a well-known copyright character, when copyright in the character associated with the name might be recognised. The character must be sufficiently clearly delineated in the work subject to copyright that it becomes widely known and recognised. The less developed the character, the less it is subject to copyright. In this respect, Canadian law follows that of the USA.[5]

1   *Canadian Admiral Corpn v Rediffusion Inc* (1954) 20 CPR 75 at 90 citing *University of London Press Ltd v University Tutorial Press Ltd* [1916] 2 Ch 601 at 609.
2   (1991) 1 DCIPL 298.

249

3 A claim in passing off also succeeded – see below.
4 *King Features Syndicate v Lechter* (1950) 12 CPR 60.
5 *Preston v 20th Century Fox* (1990) 38 FTR 183 citing Learned Hand J in *Nichols v Universal Pictures* 45 F 2d 119 (1930).

14.3 Subject to section 46(1) of the Copyright Act, the reproduction in two or three dimensions of a cartoon character will infringe the copyright in the drawing,[1] and copying a work is an infringement whether it is direct, or indirect.[2] Section 46(1) bars any copyright claim in respect of designs capable of being registered under the Industrial Designs Act. This section has, however, been interpreted restrictively, because the courts have recognised the need to protect merchandising rights.[3]

1 *King Features Syndicate v Lechter* (above); *California Raisin Advisory Board v 132832 Canada Inc* (1988) 19 CIPR 153; *Preston v 20th Century Fox Canada Ltd* (above).
2 *King Features Syndicate v O and M Kleeman Ltd* [1941] AC 417, [1941] 2 All ER 403.
3 See on the equivalent provision in the previous Act: *Cuisinair v Southwest Imports* [1969] SCR 208; *Universal City Studios Inc v Zellers Inc* (1983) 73 CPR (2d) 1 (Fed TD); *Royal Doulton Tableware Ltd v Cassidys Ltd* (unreported Fed TD) June 29, 1984.

14.4 Copyright generally vests in the author of a work,[1] but works created by employees in the course of their employment belong to their employers.[2] Subject to any contract of employment, or any agreement to the contrary, the owner of a photograph, however, is the owner of the negative.[3] This, it will be appreciated, is different from the position under current UK law. However, the comments made about the special situation which prevails in the music industry in the UK in relation to the merchandising of 'pop stars' is equally applicable to the situation in Canada.

1 Copyright Act 1985, s 13(1).
2 Ibid, s 13(3).
3 Copyright Act 1985, s 10.

14.5 The author of a work has, subject to certain limitations, the right to the integrity of a work, the right where it is reasonable in the circumstances to be associated with a work by name or to remain anonymous.[1] The author's right to integrity is infringed, inter alia, if the author's honour or reputation is prejudiced by the use of a work in connection with a product.[2] Thus in *Snow v Eaton Centre Ltd*[3] an injunction was granted to the plaintiff to whose geese sculptures Christmas bows had been added. Canadian law also recognises a right to claim paternity of a work.

1 Ibid, s 14(1).
2 Ibid, s 28(2)(1).
3 (1982) 70 CPR (2d) 105 (Ontario SC).

14.6 The term of copyright is generally the life of the author plus 50 years,[1] but works unpublished at the author's death continue to enjoy copyright for 50 years after their publication, performance or delivery to the public.[2] No suit may be brought for copyright or moral right infringement where a design in which copyright subsists is applied to more than 50 useful articles,[3] though only in respect of articles in respect of which the design is used.[4]

1 Ibid, s 6.

2 Ibid, s 7.
3 Ie articles having a function other than as mere carriers of artistic matter - Copyright Amendment Act 1988, s 11.
4 Ibid, s 11.

14.7 The question has been raised as to whether or not there is a defence to an infringement action based on the entrenchment of freedom of expression in section 2(b) of the Charter of Human Rights and Freedoms. In *R v James Lorimer & Co*[1] the court rejected this defence, and one based on public interest.

1 (1984) IFC 1065, 1079.

REGISTERED DESIGNS

14.8 Designs are registrable under the provision of the Industrial Designs Act.[1] A design or industrial design means features of shape, configuration, pattern, or ornament, and any combination of these features, that in the finished article appeal to or are judged solely by the eye.[2] This definition is quite close to the definition contained in the UK Registered Designs Act 1949 (as amended). It is, in fact, derived from English case law.[3] The design applied for must not resemble any other design already registered. The design must be original in fact, and not merely as applied to a particular article, where it has previously been applied to an analogous article.[4] Subject to the above, what was said about UK law in paragraph 1.86 et seq is in general applicable to Canada.

1 RSC 1985, c I–9.
2 Copyright Amendment Act 1988, s 18 amending s 2 of the Industrial Designs Act. This corresponds to the definition which had emerged from the case law – see Goldsmith 'Trade Marks and Industrial Designs' 1982, para 414, citing, inter alia *Clatworthy & Son Ltd v Dale Display Fixtures Ltd* [1929] SCR 429 at 431, [1929] 3 DLR 11; *Kaufman Rubber Co Ltd v Miner Rubber Co Ltd* [1926] Ex CR 26.
3 *Re Clarke's Design* [1896] 2 Ch 38 at 43; *Kestos Ltd v Kempat Ltd* (1935) 53 RPC 139 at 152 – see cases cited in note above.
4 *Clatworthy & Son Ltd v Dale Display Fixtures Ltd* [1929] SCR 429; [1929] 3 DLR 11.

STATUTORY PASSING OFF

14.9 Section 7(b) of the Trade Marks Act provides that no person shall:

'direct public attention to his wares, services or business in such a way as to cause or be likely to cause confusion in Canada, at the time he commenced so to direct attention to them, between his wares, services or business and the wares, services or business of another.'

This provision places in statutory form the common law prohibition of certain acts which amount to passing off. However, in *Seiko Time Canada Ltd v Consumers Distribution Co Ltd*[1] the Ontario Court held this provision of the Act, amongst others regulating unfair competition, to be unconstitutional. The Federal Court also held that these provisions could not be used to support an action based solely on passing off.[2] The Federal Court of Appeal reviewed the conflicting jurisprudence in *Asbjorn Horgard A/S v Gibbs/Nortac Industries Ltd*.[3] It held that section 7(b) was intra vires in so far as it might be said to round out the regulatory schemes prescribed by Parliament in the exercise of legislative power in relation to patents, copyrights, trade marks and trade names. It creates a civil remedy in relation to trade marks, whether or not they are registered. Remedies in relation to unregistered marks in this way are brought within the competence of the Federal courts.[4]

1   (1980) 29 OR (2d) 221 at 231-45.
2   *Motel 6 Inc v No 6 Motel Ltd* [1982] 1 FC 638 at 661-76.
3   (1987) 14 CPR (3d) 314.
4   *75490 Manitoba Ltd v Meditables Inc* (1989) 26 CIPR 16.

14.10   The statutory tort may be wider in scope than the common law one.[1] The ingredients of the statutory tort are: (1) a false or misleading statement; (2) made by a competitor; (3) that tends to discredit the business, wares, or services of the complainant.[2] Confusion leading to public deception is the key element. Coincidence of wares or services, or even that they occupy the same general class is not required.[3] The action co-exists with state laws of passing off, but is clearly not subject to the 'common field of activity' rule, which, as noted below, appears to retain more life in Canada than in England or Australia. This is of particular importance in the case of character merchandising. No action will lie under this section where the parties do not trade in the same area of the country.[4] Passing off is also an offence under the Criminal Code.[5]

1   *Hughes on Trade Marks*, Butterworths, 1984, para 70.
2   Ibid, para 70.
3   Ibid, para 71.
4   *Molson Breweries v Moosehead Breweries* (1990) 31 CPR (3d) 546.
5   RSC 1985, c C-46, s 408.

COMMON LAW PASSING OFF

14.11   The ingredients of the common law tort are that:
  (1) the plaintiff's wares (or services) enjoy a reputation;
  (2) the defendant has misrepresented its wares (or services) as those of the plaintiff;
  (3) there is actual confusion or a likelihood of confusion in the public's mind between the wares (or services) of the plaintiff and defendant;
  (4) that the plaintiff has suffered damage as a result.[1]

This definition is not dissimilar to that applied by the English and Australian courts, however, it is a requirement that a common field of activity be established between the activities of the plaintiff and the defendant.[2] This requirement has had an important effect on the development of the tort of defamation into a new tort of appropriation of personality. This is discussed below. In *Paramount Pictures v Howley*,[3] however, which was discussed above in relation to copyright, the plaintiff also succeeded in passing off on the basis that the business of licensing the name of 'Crocodile Dundee' would be adversely affected by the defendant's activities, and that stores purchasing the defendant's goods would erroneously assume that the defendant had been licensed by the plaintiff.

1   Hughes, op cit, para 76.
2   Ibid, para 76.
3   (1991) 1 DCIPL 298.

14.12   Québec requires special consideration. The Treaty of Paris 1763 did not deal with the law of property and civil law. By English common law at the time, a change of political allegiance did not affect the private law. Accordingly, French customary law continued in force. This situation was unaffected by the Union Act 1840. In 1857 Commissioners were appointed to effect a codification. Their work resulted in the Civil Code of Lower Canada of 1866 which remained in force until 1 January 1994 when the Civil Code of Québec came into force. This Code contains in Article 1457 an equivalent of the former Article 1053 of the Civil Code of Lower Canada, which in turn was an equivalent of Article 1382 of the French Civil Code which is discussed in Chapter 15 as a source of protection for trade names in France.[1] Article 1457 provides

> Every person has a duty to abide by the rules of conduct which lie upon him, according to the circumstances, usage or law, so as not to cause injury to another.
> Where he is endowed with reason and fails in this duty, he is responsible for any injury he causes to another person and is liable to reparation for the injury, whether it be bodily, moral or material in nature.
> He is also liable, in certain cases, to reparation for injury caused to another by the act or fault of another person or by the act of things in his custody.

This provision, as well as sections 4 and 5 of the Québec Charter of Human Rights and Freedoms,[2] is employed to prevent a person's name, image or personality from being used for commercial purposes without his knowledge or consent. In general, the case law relies heavily on French jurisprudence and appears to be developing along the lines discussed in Chapter 15.

1   Art 1053 provides 'Toute personne capable de discerner le bien du mal, est responsable du dommage causé par sa faute à autrui, soit par son fait, soit par imprudence, négligence ou inhabileté'.
    Art 1382 provides 'Tout fait quelconque de l'homme, qui cause à autrui un dommage, oblige celui par la faute duquel il est arrivé, à le réparer'.
2   RSQ cC 12.

14.13   Article 1053 encompasses various forms of delicts including passing off, appropriation of personality, libel or defamation of character, and violations of sections 4 and 5 of the Québec Charter of Human Rights and Freedoms.

14.14   Passing off is clearly accepted under Article 1053 as 'Le délit de substitution ou la concurrence déloyale'.[1] In *Theriault v Association*

Montréalaise d'Action Récréative et Culturelle[2] the plaintiffs were comedians. The defendants utilised expressions made popular by, and associated with, the plaintiffs' comic routine in a jingle promoting their amusement park. The court held that the plaintiffs had a right, albeit uncertain, to the exclusive use of expressions or words which had acquired a secondary meaning and become synonymous with their comic routine.[3] The court declined to grant an injunction, however, on the ground that the balance of convenience weighed with the defendant, and damages would be an adequate remedy. As with other Canadian jurisdictions, the Québec courts apply a restrictive common field of activity requirement.

1   *TV Guide Inc/TV Hebdo Inc v Publications La Semaine Inc* (1984) 9 CPR (3d) 368.
2   (1984) CS 946.
3   The court considered the following factors when examining the passing off claim: 1) the distinctiveness of the plaintiff's expressions; 2) the common nature of the parties' fields of activity with respect to the similarity of the audience; and, 3) the likelihood of confusion.

TRADE MARKS

14.15   Registered trade marks are governed by the Trade Marks Act 1952-1953 (as amended).[1] As in the UK and Australian systems, marks as applied for are examined as to registrability, and published for opposition by any interested party. Registration confers the exclusive right to use the mark for the goods or services in respect of which it is registered, throughout Canada.[2] Section 2 of the English language text defines a 'trade-mark' as:

'(a)   a mark that is used by a person for the purpose of distinguishing or so as to distinguish wares or services manufactured, sold, leased, hired or performed by him from those manufactured, sold, leased, hired or performed by others,
(b)   a distinguishing guise, or
(c)   a proposed trade-mark.'

Except that the Act does not divide the Register into Parts A and Part B, the system has a family resemblance to the system in operation in Australia, and in operation in the UK under the 1938 Act.[3]

1   Consolidated as RSC 1985, c T-13. The most recent amendments are those made by SC 1993, c 15 s 64.
2   Ibid, s 19.
3   Now repealed – see Chapter 3.

14.16   Merchandisers usually seek a wide range of registrations, in the hope of finding licensees who are prepared to use the mark on the relevant goods. Under the former UK law[1] this could be held to amount to 'trafficking' contrary to section 28(6)[2] or evidence of a lack of a *bona fide* intention to use.[3] The Canadian Act has no equivalent of section 28(6), however section 30(e) of the Canadian Act provides the applicant must file:

'In the case of a proposed trade-mark a statement that the applicant, by itself or through a licensee, intends to use the mark in Canada.'

This, of course, could provide a ground for refusing registration where a merchandiser seeks to register the names of a character for a wide variety of goods.[4]

1   Ie the Trade Marks Act 1938.
2   *Re American Greetings Corpn 'Holly Hobbie' Trade Mark* [1984] FSR 199, and see subsequent Registry Guidelines of August 1984.
3   Trade Marks Act 1938, s 68(1), *'Pussy Galore' Trade Mark* [1967] RPC 265.
4   See eg *Bacardi & Co v Jack Spratt Manufacturing* (1984) 1 CPR (3d) 122.

14.17   Unlike the situation under English law, in Canada the licensing of unregistered trade marks, and of trade marks outside the statutory system is prohibited and will cause a mark to lose its validity.[1] Subject to certain exceptions which are unimportant for present purposes, licensing can therefore only take place subject to the control of the Registrar pursuant to section 50. Under these provisions licensing to registered users is a 'permitted use'.

1   *Cliff McKay Ltd v CBC* (1957) 17 Fox Pat C 64 (Reg); but see *Munn & Steele Inc v Siscoe Vermiculite Mines* (1957) 17 Fox Pat C 55; ibid, [1959] Ex CR 455; and see *Sarco Canada Ltd v Sarco Co* [1968] 2 Ex CR 537; *WJ Hughes & Sons Ltd v Morawiec* (1977) 44 Fox Pat C 88 (Ex Ct).

14.18   Marks which are registrable are defined negatively by section 12:

(1)   Subject to section 13, a trade mark is registrable if it is not
   (a)   a word that is primarily merely the name or the surname of an individual who is living or has died within the preceding 30 years;
   (b)   whether depicted, written or sounded, either clearly descriptive or deceptively mis-descriptive in the English or French language of the character or quality of the wares or services in association with which it is used or proposed to be used or of the conditions of or the persons employed in their production or of their place of origin;
   (c)   the name in any language of any of the wares or services in connection with which it is used or proposed to be used;
   (d)   confusing with a registered trade-mark; or
   (e)   a mark of which the adoption is prohibited by section 9 or 10.[1]

1   S 9 prohibits the registration of trade-marks inter alia resembling Royal coats of arms, national emblems and the insignia of certain international bodies. S 10 prohibits the registration of marks which by ordinary commercial usage designate the kind, quality, quantity, destination, value, place of origin or date of production of any wares or services.

14.19   The restriction contained in section 12(1)(a) on the registration of surnames as marks is apparently more stringent than the equivalent UK former provision which merely prohibited the registration in Part A of words which were in their ordinary signification surnames.[1] Moreover, the registration of names is contrary to the Competition Act.[2] This would limit the possibility of using registered trade marks in personality merchandising. However, it would appear that in practice the two systems are somewhat similar. Rare names may be registrable,[3] and the Registry do not appear to operate any de minimis guidelines. Moreover, names unregistrable under the above provisions may be registered on proof of a secondary meaning under section 12(2).[4] Thus it is clear that celebrities' names, stage names and logos acquire a secondary meaning and may be registered in association with their services.[5] The same thing applies to fictional characters' names.[6] Descriptive names may similarly be registered on evidence of distinctiveness.[7]

1   1938 Act, s 9(1)(d). The Registry guidelines as to the de minimis criteria for registration in Parts A and B respectively could be found in the former Work Manual para 9.231 et seq.
2   S 26(1)(b) – see *Virginia Dare Ltd v Comr of Patents* [1938] Ex CR 172, [1938] 2 DLR 617.
3   *Re Horlick's Trade Mark* (1917) 64 SCR 466.
4   *Love v Latimer* (1900) 32 OR 231; *Templeton v Wallace* (1900) 4 Terr LR 240; *Re Holt & Co's Trade Mark* [1896] 1 Ch 711.
5   *Dower v Boatner* (1963) 41 CPR 216; *Musidor BV v Jabuna Proprietary Ltd* (1987) 15 CIPR 6; *Gretzky v Fortin* (1989) 24 CIPR 136.
6   *D C Comics Inc v Canada's Wonderland Ltd* (1991) 1 DICPL 142 - registration of a sign for an amusement park ride refused, inter alia, because of possibility of confusion with Batman comic character; *Henson Associates Inc v 119201 Canada Inc* (1987) 15 CPR (3d) 285 registration of 'Miss Piggy' successfully opposed.
7   *Virginia Dare Ltd v Comr of Patents* [1938] Ex CR 172, [1938] 2 DLR 617; *Moore Dry Kiln Co v United States Natural Resources Inc* (1975) 30 CPR (2d) 40.

14.20   Section 9(1)(k) prohibits registration of any matter that may falsely suggest a connection with any living individual, and section 9(1)(l) prohibits the registration of the portrait or signature of any individual who is living, or who has died within the preceding 30 years. These provisions can be used both as a ground of opposition,[1] and as a ground for injunctive relief.[2]

1   *Carson v Reynolds* (1980) 49 CPR (2d) 57 (FCTD).
2   *Baron Philippe de Rothschild SA v La Case de Havana* (1987) 19 CPR (3d) 114.

14.21   Forging a trade mark is a criminal offence.[1]

1   Criminal Code, s 407.

14.22   The question has been raised in relation to trade mark infringement as to whether section 2(b) of the Charter of Human Rights and Freedoms affords a defence. In *Source Perrier SA v Fira-Less Marketing Co*[1] Dubé J commented that the most liberal interpretation of freedom of expression does not embrace the freedom to depreciate the goodwill of registered trade marks, nor to impugn the business integrity of the owner.

1   [1983] 2 FC 18, 67.

14.23   The Trade Mark Act is a powerful weapon for preventing the unauthorised merchandising of a person's persona or identifying insignia.[1]

1   Robert G Howell 'Character Merchandising the Marketing Potential Attaching to a Name, Image, Persona or Copyright Work' (1991) 6 IPJ 1215.

DEFAMATION

14.24   It will be evident from the discussion of the law of defamation in both the UK and Australia that it is of limited value in personality merchandising. The tort requires not only a falsehood, but a depreciation of the value or worth of the plaintiff in the eyes of the public. In the Manitoba decision in *Mazatti v Acme Products Ltd*,[1] however, it was held that a person whose name or likeness had been commercially appropriated might have a cause of action, whether he was a public figure or an ordinary citizen. In the later Ontario case of *Krouse v Chrysler Canada Ltd*[2] the defendants had devised, and distributed for advertising purposes, a device to help television viewers to identify professional football players. It featured an action photograph of the plaintiff which had been reproduced without his permission. The Ontario Court of Appeal, following the English decision of *McCulloch v Lewis A May (Produce Distributors) Ltd*[3] held that the complaint of passing off failed as there was no common field of business activity in which both parties to the action operated, and 'the buying public would not buy the products of the appellant on the assumption that they had been designed or manufactured by the respondent'.[4] A complaint based on appropriation of personality was also dismissed: if such a tort existed in Ontario, the defendant had not committed it since the trading advantage sought by the defendant was with the game of football, rather than with the plaintiff's personality. Nevertheless, the court held that the common law did 'contemplate a concept in the law of torts which may be broadly classified as appropriation of one's personality'. It drew support for this view, rather surprisingly, from the English defamation case of *Tolley v J S Fry & Sons Ltd*,[5] which was discussed at paragraph 5.8. It said:

> '*Tolley v J S Fry & Sons Ltd* although based in the law of libel does in the end protect a public athlete figure from invasion of or aggression against his status as an athlete by commercial interests for their gain.'[6]

1 [1930] 4 DLR 601.
2 (1973) 40 DLR (3d) 15.
3 [1947] 2 All ER 845 – discussed at para 4.16.
4 (1973) 40 DLR (3d) 15 at 25-26.
5 [1930] 1 KB 467.
6 Ibid at p 27.

APPROPRIATION OF PERSONALITY

14.25 A more defensible ground for this view would be to base it on the existence of a tort of appropriation of the plaintiff's personality. The Ontario High Court eventually reached this position in *Athans v Canadian Adventure Camps*.[1] The plaintiff was a well-known professional waterskier. He used his name and an action photograph of himself (which he described as his 'trade mark') to promote various items of waterskiing equipment. The defendants had used a graphic representation identifiable with this photograph to promote their summer camp. Again, a complaint of passing off was dismissed because of the lack of a common field of activity between the parties. The judge, Henry J, went on, however, to formulate a new tort of appropriation of personality. He said:

> I turn to the second head of claim, namely, wrongful appropriation of the plaintiff's personality. I say at once that, on the balance of recent authority, it is clear that Mr Athans has a proprietary right in the exclusive marketing for gain of his personality, image and name, and

that the law entitles him to protect that right, if it is invaded: see *Krouse v Chrysler Canada Ltd*. If a case for wrongful invasion of this right is made out, then the plaintiff is entitled, in appropriate circumstances, to an injunction and to damages if proved. It is only in recent years that the concept of appropriation of personality has moved from its place in the tort of defamation, as exemplified by *Tolley v J S Fry & Sons Ltd* to a more broadly based common law tort.[2]

In order to succeed in this action the plaintiff must establish 1) that the public is likely to identify him; 2) that the usurpation or culpable taking of his identity is tantamount to the exploitation by the defendant of the celebrity's reputation (by suggesting the celebrity's endorsement of the product in question). It is closely related to the 'right of publicity' developed in some US jurisdictions. In fact, it does not appear to be very far removed from the tort of passing off as it has developed in England and Australia. Arguably, the court has been led into error by a misunderstanding of the English law of passing off (the court in *Krouse* actually believed that *McCulloch* was a House of Lords decision, whereas it was in fact a first instance decision). As Russell LJ observed in *Annabel's (Berkeley Square) Ltd v Schock*[3] the question of whether there was an overlap between the respective field of activity of the plaintiff and the defendant was 'simply a question which is involved in the ultimate decision whether there is likely to be confusion'.[4] It is quite possible at the present day that both the English courts and the Australian courts faced with the fact situation in *Athans* might conclude that the defendant's activities amounted to passing off. It seems reasonably clear that in evaluating the evidence, in order to decide whether there is a likelihood of the public being deceived, judges in these jurisdictions pay rather less attention to the common field of activity question than they once did.[5] It may be that it was excessive concern with the common field of activity question which led Henry J to conclude that no one was likely to be deceived by the defendant's activities. This finding of fact would, of course, be fatal to the plaintiff succeeding in a passing off action, but equally it should have been fatal to the plaintiff succeeding in the tort of appropriation of personality. Indeed, the judge concluded that on the evidence the defendant's activities did not amount to a wrongful appropriation of the plaintiff's personality as such. He went on to hold, however, that:

> 'The commercial use of [the plaintiff's] representational image by the defendants without his consent constituted an invasion and *pro tanto* an impairment of his exclusive right to market his personality.'[6]

He held that this constituted an aspect of the tort of appropriation of personality. He also observed that this unauthorised use might be regarded as falling within the general field of infringement of unregistered trade marks and copyright. The latter would be consistent with both UK law and Australian law, however, to the extent that unregistered trade marks are protected only through the action for passing off, the observation about infringement of unregistered trade marks is unsustainable in the light of the judge's finding that there was no likelihood of deception.

1   (1977) 80 DLR (3d) 583.
2   Ibid at p 592.

3 [1972] FSR 261.
4 Ibid at p 261.
5 Compare the English case of *Wombles Ltd v Wombles Skips Ltd* [1977] RPC 99 with the more recent English case of *Lego Systems A / S v Lego M Lemelstrich* [1983] FSR 155 – see para 4.18 above.
6 Ibid at p 595.

14.26 The state of confusion about this new tort[1] seems to be due to the lack of distinction between the misappropriation of personality element in it, and the misrepresentation element in passing off. It has been suggested that the element of endorsement in passing off is necessary to show public confusion as to the celebrity's endorsement of the product, while in the tort of appropriation the element of endorsement goes to the requirement of the exploitation or taking of the celebrity's identity without his or her consent.[2]

1 See *Dowell v Mengen Institute* (1983) 72 CPR (2d) 238 per Hughes J.
2 Robert G Howell 'Common Law Appropriation of Personality Tort' (1986) IPJ 149.

14.27 The decision in *Athans* has therefore left some uncertainty as to the exact ambit of the new tort, the existence of which was also recognised in the later Ontario case of *Heath v Weist-Barron School of Television Canada Ltd*[1] which involved the use of a young professional actor's photograph and identity without permission, and in the British Columbia case of *Joseph v Daniels*.[2] A number of questions about the tort remain to be answered. Would it be committed in the following circumstances:[3]

(1) if the photograph or other indicia had not been used in such a way that it was singularly distinctive of the plaintiff's activities (in *Athans* the photograph in question was one of the most famous in the world);

(2) if it had not been used by the plaintiff as a trade mark for his or her activities;

(3) if the plaintiff had not at the time of the action commercially exploited his or her personality;

(4) if the plaintiff were precluded from exploiting his or her personality commercially eg by having to preserve his or her status as an amateur;

(5) if the plaintiff were an ordinary private citizen with no public reputation.

1 (1982) 62 CPR (2d) 92.
2 (1986) 11 CPR (3d) 544.
3 Murumba, op cit, p 85.

14.28 Until these uncertainties are resolved, it is impossible to say how far the new tort goes beyond the extended tort of passing off as it exists in England and Australia.

14.29 Québec recognises a proprietary right in a personality, but limited to rights having an economic value. It also recognises a personal, moral, right which is extra-patrimonial and protects an individual's dignity, honour and reputation.[1] In *Déschamps v Renault Canada Ltée*[2] Rothman J granted an injunction to two well known entertainers to restrain the defendants from using their photographs in association with a Renault car. He said:

'... the names and likenesses of petitioners involved property rights which they are free to exploit commercially or to refrain from doing so and equally free to decide the conditions under which such exploitation shall take place ... it is clear from the evidence that their names and likenesses have a real commercial value capable of being translated into money terms. Specific proof was made as to the remuneration paid to the petitioners for their publicity services by various distributors of commercial products and services. Moreover, in this day and age, it would be hard for any court not to take judicial notice of how common it is for film stars and other public figures to lend their names and talent to commercial promotion.

... now if the right of commercial exploitation of a film star's name and image is a property right, a real right in property which is capable of yielding a financial return then it cannot be appropriated or used by anyone without the consent of its owner.'

This case relied heavily on *Krouse* discussed above. However, in assimilating the right to a person's personality to a property right, the court went further. Thus it said that there was no need for a culpable taking, as ownership is absolute, and appropriation is a fault whether innocent or not.[3] Nevertheless, not every appropriation is delictual. The public interest can override private rights eg for the reporting of news, or making a documentary.[4]

1 See *Rebeiro v Shawnigan Chemicals* (1969) Ltd (1973) SC 389 where the plaintiff was awarded C$300 moral damages following the unathorised publication of his photograph doing manual work during a summer vacation. The plaintiff was a school teacher, and had no reputation of commercial worth. The court, following French jurisprudence, awarded damages for humiliation. The right to privacy not only protected the reputation of an individual, but also his dignity. See also *Cohen v Queenswear International* (1989) RRA 570.
2 (1977) 18 C de D 937 (Mtl SC).
3 Ibid, p 941.
4 *Fields v United Amusement Corpn* (1971) SC 283. Whilst the facts of this case did not warrant the granting of an injunction, the court implicitly recognised the protection of a person's reputation against unauthorised use of their photograph. See 'Publicity exploitation of celebrities: Protection of a star's style in Québec Civil Law' (1991) 32 C de D 301.

14.30 Québec jurisprudence encourages the extension of the right of a person to their personality from a limited proprietary one to a fundamental right to a personality as an individual. This protects individuals whether they are celebrities or not.[1] In *Fondation Le Corbusier v Société en commandité Manoir Le Corbusier*[2] Lemieux J relied heavily on French case law and doctrine in holding that the plaintiffs were entitled to enjoin the defendant from using the pseudonym of its benefactor after his death without authorisation. The pseudonym was held to be the property of its bearer and passed to his heirs. A mixed right of property and personality, and thus both economic and moral damages, resulted from its unauthorised use. The court also held that the use of a pseudonym was no less a fault than the unauthorised use by others of a real name.

1 Patrick H Glenn 'Civil Responsibility – the Right to Privacy in Québec – recent cases' (1974) Canadian Bar Review 297; Patrick A Molinari 'Le Droit de la Personne sur son Image en Droit Québécois et Français' (1977) RJT 95; Art 1053 of the Civil Code of Lower Canada and Art 1457 of the new Québec Civil Code.

2   [1991] RJQ 2864, JE 91-1633 Mtl SC.

14.31 Although this area has yet to be developed, there have been two cases suggesting that this action might be used in the case of character merchandising. In both a motion for an interlocutory injunction was denied to prevent characters from a TV series being impersonated in commercials without authorisation. The reason for refusing injunctive relief was, however, because the courts considered that damages would be an adequate remedy.[1]

1   *Productions Lance & Compte Inc v Corpn des Concessionnaires General Motors du Montréal Métropolitain* (1988) 18 CIPR 45, JE 88-931 QSC; *Productions OP Inc v Groupe Morrow Inc* (1988) 18 CIPR 34.

PRIVACY

14.32 A number of provinces have enacted privacy laws. Thus the Privacy Act of British Columbia[1] makes it an actionable tort to violate the privacy of a person, including the use of the name or portrait of another, without consent, with intent to exploit the name or replica of that person in an advertisement or promotion. There are exceptions for the use of a person's name or portrait in relation to such matters as reporting current affairs. The Privacy Acts of Saskatchewan,[2] Manitoba[3] and Newfoundland[4] make it an actionable tort to violate the privacy of a person, for the purposes of advertising or promoting the sale of, or any other trading in any property or services, or for any other purposes of gain or advantage to the user if, in the course of the use, the person is identified or identifiable and the user intended such exploitation.[5]

1   RSBC 1979, c 336, ss 1 and 3.
2   RSS 1978, c P-24, ss 2 and 3 as amended.
3   RSM 1987, c P-125, ss 2 and 3.
4   SN 1981, c 6, ss 3 and 4.
5   See Hughes, op cit, para 81.

14.33 The statutory rights are limited to living persons, and are considered personal. In principal, therefore, they cannot be licensed or assigned. However, the basic common law principle that a licence is simply a right to do that which is otherwise unlawful[1] would appear at least to enable at least a first sale of licensing rights. The elements of the tort are similar to those of the tort of appropriation, that is, the identifiability of the celebrity or individual, as well as the intention to exploit his name or reputation are required. There is little authority on the tort. In *Joseph v Daniels*[2] a photograph of the plaintiff's torso was used by the defendant beyond the scope of a modelling contract. The Court of Appeal upheld the breach of contract argument, but did not apply section 3(1) of the Manitoba Privacy Act because of the absence of the plaintiff's face and the fact that he was not, therefore, recognisable to the public.

1   *Federal Comr of Taxation v United Aircraft Corpn* (1943) 68 CLR 525.
2   (1986) 11 CPR (3d) 544.

14.34 Many Canadian writers speculate that these statutes could pre-

14.34 *Canada*

empt the development of a common law tort. This view is supported by the case of *Seneca College of Applied Arts & Technology v Bhadauria*[1] where the Supreme Court of Canada prohibited the creation of a common law tort of discrimination in provinces which had statutory protection against discrimination. However, a possible difference from the Privacy Acts is that most of them contain an express provision that the victim has other rights and remedies available to him or her.

1   (1981) 2 SCR 181.

14.35 There is some disagreement as to whether or not these statutes would help a celebrity in any case. Would an invasion of privacy be suffered by the use of a celebrity's name? It has been argued that commercial appropriation should find no remedy in privacy law since a celebrity possesses a public reputation.[1] On the other hand, it has been argued that there is no indication that the Privacy Acts did not intend to protect the 'anonymous and the famous, the infant and the politician, the housewife and the film star'.[2]

1   D Gibson 'Aspects of Privacy Law', Butterworth & Co, Toronto (1980), p 345.
2   David Vaver '"What's mine is not yours": Commercial Appropriation of Personality under the Privacy Acts of British Columbia, Manitoba, and Saskatchewan' (1981) U Br Col LR 241, 256.

14.36 Québec has also enacted a privacy law, the Charter of Human Rights and Freedoms.[1] Sections 4 and 5 of this provide as follows:

Every person has a right to the safeguard of his dignity, honour and reputation.

Every person has a right to respect for his private life.

Section 49 of the Charter provides for exemplary or punitive damages for any infringement of the Charter and these damages are added to the damages actually incurred by a plaintiff in a delictual or passing off action.

1   RSQ, c C-12.

14.37 In *Cohen v Queenswear International Ltd*[1] Bishop J of the Superior Court held:

The right to safeguard one's dignity and to respect one's private life must include the right to prevent photos of one's semi-naked body from being displayed in public for commercial use without one's consent.[2]

The Civil Code of Québec has now codified some interesting articles relating to the rights to the respect of a person's name, reputation and privacy. Articles 35, 36 and 56 provide:

Every person has a patrimony. The patrimony may be divided or appropriated to a purpose, but only to the extent provided by law.

Every person has a right to the respect of his reputation and privacy. No one may invade the privacy of a person without the consent of the person or his heirs unless authorised by law.

The following acts, in particular, may be considered as invasions of the privacty of a person:

[...]

appropriating of using his image or voice while he is in private premises;

[...]

using his name, image, likeness or voice for a purpose other than the legitimate information of the public;

[...]

A person who uses a name other than his own is liable for any resulting confusion or damage. The holder of a name as well as his spouse or close relatives may object to such use and demand redress for the damage caused.

In addition, Article 458 and 909 specifically classify intellectual rights as proprietary rights. These state:

Intellectual and industrial property rights are private property, but all fruits and income arising from them and collected or fallen due during the regime are [acquests].

Property that produces fruits and revenues, property appropriated for the service or operation of an enterprise, shares of the capital stock or common shares of a legal person or partnership, the reinvestment of the fruits and revenues, the price for any disposal of capital or its reinvestment, and the expropriation or insurance indemnities in replacement of capital, are capital.

Capital also includes rights of intellectual or industrial property except sums derived therefrom without alienation of the rights, bonds and other loan certificates payable in cash and rights the exercise of which tends to increase the capital, such as the right to subscribe to securities of a legal person, limited partnership or trust.

There is no case law as yet on the interpretation of these provisions, but they may eventually be utilised to protect celebrities and non-celebrities against the exploitation of their name, voice and image.

1   (1989) RRA 570.
2   At p 578.

COMPETITION ACT[1]

14.38   This Act has resemblances to the UK Trade Descriptions Act 1968 and its Australian equivalent. Like the former, and unlike the latter it imposes only criminal sanctions; it does not confer any civil remedy. It makes it a criminal offence to represent to the public that a person has tested a product or to publish a testimonial unless such representation or testimonial has been previously published by that person, including the name or portrait of another unless such a representation or testimonial has been previously published by that person or that person's approval has been given.[2]

1   RSC 1985, c C-34, s 53.
2   Hughes, op cit, para 81.

Chapter 15

France[1]

Introduction

15.1   French law offers extensive and effective protection to characters and personalities through a variety of actions, even though there is no specific regulation dealing with character merchandising.

1   By Jacques Mazaltov

15.2   Characters are protected by the law of copyright, trade mark law, (if the character is registered as a trade mark), and the action for unfair competition. Such protection is reinforced by criminal penalties. The principal form of protection for personalities is through the registration of trade marks, and through the law of unfair competition.

COPYRIGHT
Protection of intellectual works in France

APPLICABLE TEXTS

15.3   Copyright is governed by the Intellectual Property Code, as enacted by the Act of 1 July 1992 (Articles L 111-1 to L 335-10, R 111-1 to R 335-1). France is a party to the Berne Copyright Convention and the Universal Copyright Convention.

LEGAL DEFINITION OF INTELLECTUAL WORKS

15.4   The Code does not provide a comprehensive and definitive definition of an intellectual work. Article L 112-2 provides a *non-exhaustive* list of works which are to be considered as intellectual works and thus subject to copyright protection:

> '[the following in particular] are considered to be intellectual works: books, brochures and other literary, artistic and scientific writings; conferences, speeches, sermons, pleadings and other works of same nature; dramatic works or dramatico-musical works; choreographies, circus acts and pantomimes whose staging is fixed in writing or differently; musical works with or without words; cinematographic and

other visual works; drawings, pictures, architectural and sculptural works, diagrams and lithography; graphic and typographical works; photographic works and all those realised with similar techniques, fine art, illustrations, maps, frameworks, sketches and software...'

Such a list, not being exhaustive, gives the courts the power to expand the number of items included.

THE ABSENCE OF A REGISTRATION REQUIREMENT

15.5   According to Article L 111-1,[1] protection occurs automatically with the creation of the work. There is no requirement for registration or for any other formality.

1   'L' auteur d' une oeuvre de l'esprit jouit sur cette oeuvre, du seul fait de sa création, d'un droit de propriété incorporelle exclusif et opposable à tous. Ce droit comporte des attributs d'ordre intellectuel et moral, ainsi que des attributs d'ordre patrimonial, qui sont déterminés par les livres I et III du présent code.'

REQUIREMENTS FOR PROTECTION

15.6   The first requirement for protection is originality. A work is original if its author's personality and efforts are apparent. Originality does not mean novelty . The work does not need to be new to be protected:
   (i)   the character of Cinderella was not invented by Walt Disney, and thus was not new, however the way Walt Disney represented her enabled him to claim protection;
   (ii) an anthology of poems is protected even if the poems are not created by the author. The fact that the author chose between several poets and different poems, shows his personality, so the anthology is original and is protected, even if its content (the poems) is not new;
   (iii) a translation is protected as the choice of words to translate a work reveals the personality of the translator. The translated work is not new, but is original and the translator has a copyright in his translation.

So there is 'first hand' and 'second hand' originality: the 'first hand' author (the work is new and original) will be protected, the 'second hand' author (the work is not new but is original) will be also protected, but may have to pay royalties to the 'first hand' author of the work he has used. Such originality is subject to the courts' evaluation which will decide whether a work is original or not, and thus is protected or not. The notion of originality, being subjective (while the notion of novelty is objective: whether there is a preceding work or not), is somewhat vague and protection cannot always be guaranteed.

15.7   The second requirement is that the work must be expressed in a material form. There is no protection for mere ideas. There must be an expression or a realisation of an idea.

15.8   According to Article L 112-1 there is protection no matter the merit, the form of expression, the type or the intended use of the work.[1] Any type of work is protected: literary and musical, as well as graphic works (drawings, sculptures, paintings, etc...).

1   'Les dispositions de la présente loi protègent les droits des auteurs sur toutes les oeuvres de l'esprit, quels qu'en soient le genre, la forme d' expression, le mérite ou la destination.'

15.9   There is no requirement of merit: copyright protects a work irrespective of artistic quality. There is no requirement either as to destination: a work is protected whatever is its intended use – artistic or industrial.

'DROIT MORAL' AND ECONOMIC RIGHTS

15.10   According to Article L 111-1, 'Copyright involves both intellectual and moral rights, as well as economic rights'.

Droit moral

15.11   The 'droit moral' of the author, which is non-assignable and inalienable, covers different categories of rights, which are much wider than the moral rights provided in article 6bis of the Berne Convention:
   (i)   the right to divulge his work, ie to decide whether it shall be made public at his sole discretion (Article L 121-2);
   (ii) the right to be identified as the author of his work (Article L 121-1);
   (iii) the right to the respect of his work (Article L 121-1): the author can object to improper adaptation or treatment of his work by the person to whom he has assigned his rights to reproduce or represent the work (ie a publisher cannot cut out or add paragraphs to the book without the author's authorisation). In a case involving the character 'COLARGOL' (bear stories popular among children), the authors had assigned their rights of adaptation, reproduction and representation for movies, however the assignee had not submitted the new works to the original authors (furthermore there was no reference to the original authors' names) and the Court annulled the contract;[1]
   (iv) the right to repentance and to redemption (withdrawal ?) (Article L 121-4): repentance means that, after he has assigned his rights and before the reproduction or the performance of his work, the author might finally refuse such reproduction or performance, providing that he indemnifies the assignee. Redemption means that, even after the reproduction or the performance of his work, the author might refuse further publication or performance, providing that he indemnifies the assignee.

1   Cour d'Appel de Paris, 26 April 1977, RIDA 131 (1977).

Economic rights

15.12   There are two important kinds of economic rights: the right to reproduce the work and the right to perform it.

15.13 *France*

Reproduction of the work (Article L 122-3)
15.13 Reproduction of the work in order to communicate it to the public is subject to the author's prior authorisation and entitles him to royalties, irrespective of the type (in whole or in part) and the form (Article L 122-3 gives a non-restricted list: printing, drawing, engraving, photography, mechanical, cinematographical and magnetical recordings) of the reproduction:

  (i) the photographing of a sculpture has to be authorised by the sculptor;
  (ii) the transformation of a two-dimensional work such as a drawing into a three-dimensional work is also subject to the authorisation of the artist.[1]

However, reproduction for private use is not subject to the author' s prior authorisation.

1   See A Françon, *La propriété littéraire et artistique*, p 59; also Cour d'Appel de Rennes, 16 October 1984, RTD Com 1985 about an 'ET' puppet.

Performance of the work (Article L 122-2)
15.14 The performance of a work is the direct communication of the work (in whole or in part) to the public, whether by public performance, or by transmission (cinema, television, radio, records) in a public place. Such performance is subject to the author's prior authorisation and entitles him to royalties.

The assignment of economic rights
15.15 The Code protects the author with mandatory rules concerning the assignment of his rights.

15.16 According to Article L 111-3, the sale only of the work does not give any right (reproduction, performance, publication, etc...) to the buyer, who merely owns the material support of the work.

15.17 According to Article L 131-2, a written contract is necessary for the assignment of the rights of performance, publication, audiovisual production, as well as the free authorisation of performance. The contract must specify what rights are assigned, for which territory and for how long.

15.18 Article L 122-7 states that the assignment of the reproduction rights does not involve the assignment of the performance rights, and conversely, the assignment of the performance rights does not involve the assignment of the reproduction rights (eg the assignment of the right to perform a play on the stage, does not involve the right to publish it.[1] Also, the right to adapt a character to cinema does not involve the right to make and sell toys.

1   See C Colombet, *Propriété littéraire et artistique et droits voisins*, p 301.

15.19 Furthermore, under Article L 122-7, when the author assigns totally one of his economic rights, the assignment is limited to the types and forms of exploitation specified in the contract. For example, if an author assigns his performance rights but performance on television is not specified in the contract, the assignee cannot perform the work on television.

DURATION OF PROTECTION

15.20 The author' s economic rights in his work are limited to 50 years[1] from the end of the calendar year of the author's death (Article L 123-1). Thereafter, the work can be freely used. However the duration of the author' s 'droit moral' is not limited.

1   Under the 29 October 1993 Directive, protection is enlarged to 70 years. From 1 July 1995, the Directive is directly applicable in France, so the protection is now 70 years.

INFRINGEMENT OF COPYRIGHT

15.21 According to French Law, 'infringement' of a copyright is a criminal offence.

15.22 Articles L 335-2 and L 335-3 of the Intellectual Property Code deal with these problems. The publication of a written or musical work, drawing, painting or any other printed or engraved work, in whole or in part, is an infringement, as is any reproduction, performance or broadcasting, without the author's prior authorisation. A fine of up to 1,000,000 Francs and imprisonment from three months to two years, or one of these two penalties, can be imposed. These penalties are cumulative with civil remedies, such as damages, if the author suffered a prejudice. It is thus clear that French copyright law provides extensive protection to artistic works. However, to what extent does this protection apply to characters?

Protection of characters by copyright

CHARACTERS ARE PROTECTED APART FROM THE WORKS INCORPORATING THEM

15.23 Characters are generally embodied in written works or artistic works (such as drawings, cartoons, sculptures, etc...). So a character can either be protected as a literary work, or as an artistic work, or as both (cartoons include artistic work as well as literary work). However the problem is that the character is a part of a work. Is it protected apart from the work, is it protected in itself ?

15.24 To be protected in itself, the character must be original and so must have an identity, such identity including name, physical appearance and private life,[1] the originality of such character being subject to the court's evaluation.

1   See Bernard Edelman, *Le personnage et son double*, D 225 (1980).

Name

15.25 Original names are indirectly protected by Article L 112-4. This, article does not refer to names but refers to 'titles'. However, the name of the character can be considered to be his title. Furthermore, the Code protects any original works and a name, provided it is original, will be protected.

15.26 According to the decisions of the courts, the author has a copyright in the name of his character which can be used to annul its registration as a trade mark by third parties.[1] However, when such a name is not original, and thus is not protected by copyright, it may be protected through unfair competition if there is a risk of confusion and if the parties are in a direct competitive relationship.

1   Cour d'Appel de Paris, 26 April 1977, RIDA 131 (1977, COLARGOL).

Physical likeness

15.27 Courts pay a special attention to the physical appearance of the character. The originality of the physical characteristics and clothes entitle, or do not entitle, the character to protection, and the court has to decide whether there is infringement or not.

15.28 In a case involving Donald Duck, the Cour d'Appel de Paris[1] examined precisely the difference between Donald and a real duck, as well as the characteristics of Donald (nose, eyes, arms and hands, etc…), to decide whether such character is original or not.

1   Cour d'Appel de Paris, 15 October 1964, Ann 213 (1965).

15.29 In a case involving Max Headroom,[1] the Tribunal de Grande Instance de Paris, while admitting the originality of Max Headroom, decided that another character having the same characteristics (with differences) was not an infringing copy, as the resemblances between the two characters had their origin in the technical process used in the creation of these characters, such technical process not being protected by the Copyright Act 1957.

1   Tribunal de Grande Instance de Paris, référé, 2 January 1987, unpublished.

15.30 In another case, an advertisement used the photograph of a man dressed only with leopardskin shorts with a scantily dressed woman and a monkey. The Tribunal de Grande Instance de Paris,[1] on the basis of the physical characteristics and clothes, as well as the environment (woman, monkey and the presence of tropical fruits, which are characteristics of the life of Tarzan) decided that such a photograph was a representation of the character Tarzan and his family (Jane and Cheeta) which had to be authorised by the author of Tarzan.

1   Tribunal de Grande Instance de Paris, 21 January 1977, RIDA 179 (January 1978).

15.31 Such protection occurs even when the character is reproduced from a two-dimensional work into a three-dimensional work (such as a puppet).

The 'private life' or nature of the character

15.32 This is the personality of the character, his identity (character for children or for adults, nice or bad, etc).

15.33 In the Donald Duck case (cited above) the court examined the personality and psychology ('sarcastic, coward, boaster, irascible') of Donald and its copy, to decide whether there was infringement or not. In a Tintin case,[1] the court also examined the personality of the character, 'usually imaginative and creative in fighting against adversity', and prohibited its use in a play where he was represented as 'totally impotent to act efficiently'.

1   Cour d'Appel de Paris, 20 December 1990, D 1991 p 532.

15.34 If the character is considered as original, it will be protected against any copying, even when such copy represents the character in an attitude it never had before.[1]

1   Cour d'Appel de Chambery, 10 December 1951, GP 116 (1952).

THE MERCHANDISING OF THE CHARACTER

15.35 Such merchandising is rarely done by the author of the character, and is mainly done by a third person to whom the author partly assigns his rights (right to reproduce or to perform for a specific purpose). Even if he assigned his economic rights, the author retains his moral rights.

15.36 According to Article L 121-1 (author's right to the respect of his work) the author may control the way his character is merchandised: the types of products, distribution, advertising and the way the character is adapted to a commercial exploitation. However, it is preferable to state in the licence agreement the way such control will be exercised.

15.37 The author might also refuse exploitation of his character which could be prejudicial to the reputation of such character.

15.38 However such moral right is restricted by the courts, which keep in mind the necessities of adaptation to the cinema,[1] the necessities of industrial manufacturing and marketing, and the obligation the author assumed in the licence he gave for the merchandising of his character.

1   Tribunal de Grande Instance de Paris, 8 March 1968, D 1968 p. 742: Le Saint.

15.39 In the *COLARGOL* case,[1] the authors had assigned their economic rights and were complaining about the products (yoghurts, mustard pots) reproducing their character (a bear), whose inferiority, they alleged, was prejudicial to their character. The court decided that such products, being appreciated by children, were not prejudicial to the character.

1   Cited above at para 15.11, n 1.

15.40 In the *FANTOMAS* case,[1] the author (Marcel Allain) had assigned the right to adapt the character to the cinema and to create new adventures. It was agreed in the contract that if the author disagreed with the adaptation, the titles of the movie should mention: 'new adventures inspired by the books of Marcel Allain'. Later, the author complained about the denaturating of his character. The court decided that the author always had two targets: the benefits he can get from his work and the respect for the said work, so his moral right was sufficiently protected by the above mentioned, and such moral right could not invalidate the contract signed by the author. The court added: 'to decide differently would make character merchandising impossible'.

1   Cour d'Appel de Paris, 23 November 1970, RIDA 1971 p 74.

15.41   For the Courts, the character's personality is an important factor in deciding whether the way the character is exploited can be prejudicial to its reputation or not.

TRADE MARKS

15.42   The most effective protection, if the character is going to be used in the course of trade, is the registration of the character as a trade mark, if the character is registrable.[1] This is also an important form of protection for personalities, since they cannot usually benefit from copyright protection other than in relation to such things as photographs.

1   According to A Bertrand in *Le droit d'auteur et les droits voisins*, Masson 1991, p 561, in 1988 there were more than 20 registrations of the name 'Mickey' and its graphic representation.

Applicable texts

15.43   Trade marks are, at the present time, governed by the Intellectual Property Code (Articles L 711-1 to L 716-16, Articles R 712-1 to R 718-4).

15.44   France is a party to the Paris Convention, the Agreement of Madrid (international registration of trade marks), the Agreement of Nice (international classification of goods and services in respect of trade marks), the Vienna Agreement (international classification of figurative elements of marks) and the Franco-Italian Trade Marks Agreement.

Legal definition of marks

15.45   Article L 711-1 defines marks as follows:

A trade mark or service mark is a sign capable of graphic representation, used to distinguish the products or services of any person or company.

The following can in particular be considered as such a sign:
(i)   denominations in any form such as: words, combination of words, family names, geographical names, pseudonyms, letters, numbers, acronyms;
(ii)   sound signs such as: sounds, musical phrases;
(iii) figurative signs such as: drawings, stamps, seals, ornamental borders, reliefs, holograms, logotypes, synthetic images; the

characteristic forms of a product or of its getup, or the forms of a service; combinations or dispositions of colours.[1]

This large, non-exhaustive, list gives the opportunity for registration of almost any kind of character, especially names, designs and photographs, as trade marks.

1 'La propriété de la marque s'acquiert par l' enregistrement'.

Necessity of registration

15.46 Registration is necessary in order to become the *proprietor* of the mark and to gain protection for a mark. This is clearly specified by Article L 712-1 which provides 'ownership of a mark occurs by registration...'. Nevertheless, Article L 712-4 provides that the holder of a well-known,[1] but unregistered, mark can contest the registration of a mark which interferes with his well-known mark.

1 Within the meaning of Article 6*bis* of the Paris Convention.

15.47 Articles L 711-4 (a) and L 713-5 also give protection to unregistered but well-known marks . First of all, a sign which interferes with a well-known but unregistered mark cannot be adopted as a mark (Article L 711-4(a). Second, these well-known marks are protected against any prejudicial use of the mark by third parties selling products far removed from their original association (Article L 713-5). So, a right in the trade mark occurs before its registration: unregistered marks are protected, provided that such marks are well-known.

The Registry

15.48 France has adopted a system of ownership based on uncontested registration for a specified period of time: registration gives the right on, and the protection to, the mark (with the exception of well-known marks noted above), provided that such registration has not been contested for a specified period of time.

15.49 Articles L 712-3 and L 712-4 set out the procedure of opposition to registration. During a period of two months following the publication of the application for registration:

(i) Article L 712-3: any person may give his comments to the Director of the INPI (Institut national de la propriété industrielle), such comments have no legal effect but are useful information for the INPI;
(ii) Article L 712-4: the owner of a registered mark, or of a well-known mark, can contest the application for registration. The opposition is made to the Director of INPI. Such opposition is considered as rejected if the Director of the INPI has not settled the dispute within six months. If the opposition is accepted, the application for registration will be rejected.

15.50 According to Articles L 714-3 and L 714-4, if the owner of a registered mark, or the holder of a well-known mark, did not contest the application for registration in time, he can still go to court and apply for annulment and deletion of the registered mark which interferes with his prior mark. Such an action has to be taken within five years of registration of the contested mark by the holder of the well-known mark. The owner of a registered mark cannot claim for annulment if the contested mark was *bona fide* registered and if he has tolerated the usage of such mark for five years.

ASSIGNMENT OF RIGHTS

15.51 According to Article L 714-7, any assignment or modification of rights in registered marks has to be registered in order to be enforceable against third parties.

Specificity of the mark

15.52 The registry is divided into several different classes corresponding to types of goods and services. Such classification is identical with the international classification.

15.53 For a long time, French law protected the mark only in relation to the product within the class for which it is registered. So, there was an infringement only where the infringer used the mark for goods or services within the registration.

15.54 The Intellectual Property Code prohibits (Article L 713-3) the use of the mark by third parties for goods similar to the goods or services within the registration. It also protects (Article L 713-3) famous registered marks, as well as unregistered but well-known marks, against any prejudicial use of the mark by third parties for goods without the registration or removed from the original association (such a use would engage the liability of the user, however, this use is not considered as an infringement).

Duration of protection

15.55 Trade marks and services marks will be protected for ten years after registration, with the privilege of indefinite renewal for ten years.

Lapse of rights

15.56 According to Article L 714-5,[1] the owner of the mark loses his rights if he does not use the mark for a period of five years. Removal will be ordered by the courts at the request of any interested person. However, if the owner of the mark is able to show that he, or a licensee, used the mark, he will not lose his rights.

1   'Encourt la déchéance de ses droits le propriétaire de la marque qui, sans justes motifs, n'en a pas fait un usage sérieux, pour les produits et services visés dans l'enregistrement, pendant une période ininterrompue de cinq ans...'

Infringement of the mark

15.57   According to French law, 'infringement' of a registered trade mark is a *criminal offence.*

15.58   Articles L 716-9 to L 716-14 deal with these problems: reproduction, imitation, use, application, deletion or modification of a trade mark without the authorisation of the owner can be subject to a fine up to 1,000,000 Francs and imprisonment for up to two years. These penalties may be imposed together with civil remedies, such as damages, if the proprietor of the trade mark suffered damage.

15.59   As explained above, the owner of a registered mark can also claim for the annulment of a further registered mark which interferes with and which is capable of causing confusion with his prior mark.

Registration of names and graphic representation

15.60   Trade marks law provides a very efficient protection for characters. According to the Intellectual Property Code, a name alone can be registered.[1] Graphic representation of the character can also be registered.

1   See A Bertrand p 561: 'Astérix', 'Tarzan', 'James Bond 007'.

THE RELATIONSHIP BETWEEN TRADE MARKS AND COPYRIGHT

15.61   According to Article L 711-4 of the Intellectual Property Code and the case law, a mark which infringes prior copyright cannot be validly registered.

15.62   The owner of copyright on a character can apply for annulment and deletion of a trade mark from the register where the mark was registered by the applicant without the prior authorisation of the author. Based on such considerations, the owner of the literary work 'Tarzan' could prohibit the use and the registration of the mark 'Tarzan' which was made without his authorisation.[1]

1   Tribunal de Grande Instance de Paris, 10 July 1973, D Som 32 (1974).

15.63   Special attention has to be paid to the authorisation to be given by the author (Article L 122-7): he must give his authorisation for reproduction as well as performance and adaptation, he must expressly give his consent to the use and the registration of the character as a mark for specified goods and services, and such authorisation must be written.

15.64 Trade marks and copyright not only have a contentious relationship, they may have a harmonious relationship as they are complementary, especially regarding characters[1] and the study of the case law shows that numerous characters were protected by copyright as well as trade mark law.

1   See Marina Ristich de Groote: *Les personnages des oeuvres de l' esprit*, RIDA 19 (October 1986) and *Quelques réflexions sur les personnages de l' esprit et le droit des marques*, RDPI 24 (December 1985).

15.65 First of all, registration of the character as a trade mark gives an indisputable date to the character, while there is no registration system in relation to the Intellectual Property Code and so the date of creation of the character can be hard to prove.

15.66 Second, the duration of protection for the character is not the same: protection by copyright expires 70 years after the death of the author, while protection through trade mark is perpetual (renewal of registration every ten years).[1]

1   André Bertrand in *Le droit d'auteur et les droits voisins*, p 561, points out there is no case law but, in his opinion, trade mark law cannot renew the economic rights of the author's heir when such rights expire.

15.67 Third, copyright does not protect every character: a character whose only feature is its name might not be protected by copyright. The name must be very original. This is a difficult hurdle in practice (the title 'the Godfather' ('Le Parrain'), was not considered to be original and could be registered, without authorisation, as a trade mark for toys[1]). There is also uncertainty arising from the courts having to evaluate the originality of any character. A name or character, on the other hand, is easily protected by trade mark law where there is absolutely no requirement of originality, but special attention has to be given to the rights of third parties.

1   Tribunal de Grande Instance de Paris, 20 March 1975, Ann 55 (1976).

15.68 Finally, trade mark law protects the character only for the goods for which it is registered, so the character and the mark could be used for goods without the registration. But, copyright protects a character against any unauthorised use, so the unauthorised use of the character for goods without the registration will be prohibited.

15.69 Registration of a character as a trade mark should only be effected when the character is going to be used for a commercial purpose, whether by the author or by its licensees. It is possible, however, to register the character and its name as a mark even when there is no immediate possibility of commercial use. Such registration is legal.[1] However, if there is no use of such mark for five years, the owner of the mark might lose his rights (see para 15.56 above). As was pointed out by Mrs Ristich de Groote, in such a case, the trade mark no longer serves the purpose of distinguishing a product or service, but the work itself, since the registration indicates the goods for which the mark is registered, and in relation to which it must be used.

1   Tribunal de Grande Instance de Paris, 3 January 1978, RIDA 119 (April 1978): Tarzan.

THE SEARCH FOR OTHER FORMS OF PROTECTION

15.70   Characters and names (especially the ones created for a commercial purpose) can be protected using the following means.

Trade names

15.71   While trade marks are 'all material signs serving to distinguish products, objects or services of any enterprise', trade names can be considered as signs serving to distinguish the enterprise from any other enterprise.

15.72   There is no specific text regulating trade names, except an Act dated 28 July 1824 which states that the fraudulent application of the trade name to goods which were not made by the enterprise which owns the trade name is a criminal offence. France is also a member of the Union Convention (Article 8: 'trade names will be protected with no obligation of registration').

15.73   Trade names are also protected by Article 1382 of the Civil code. Also, by Article L 711-4 of the Intellectual Property Code, a trade name, known over all the French territory, cannot be adopted as a mark if there is a risk of confusion in the public.

15.74   Trade names can either be an arbitrary, fancy name or a family name. They are protected provided that they are distinctive (they cannot simply be information as to the activities of the enterprise), they cannot be deceptive, generic or descriptive, immoral or misleading.

15.75   Property in trade names occurs with the first public use, a trade name does not need to be registered. The right to a trade name is lost if the name ceases to be used.

15.76   Trade names are protected through the action for unfair competition, but there must be a direct competitive relationship between the parties and thus a risk of confusion: a company making leather clothes chose the trade name 'Creations Bob', later a furs trading company chose the trade name 'Bob-Furs' the courts obliged this second company to change its name.[1]

1   Cour d'Appel de Paris, 14 January 1977.

15.77   For well-known trade names, there is an exception to the requirement of specialty: a pen manufacturer whose trade name 'Waterman' is well-known might suffer a prejudice due to the commercialisation of razor blades by a manufacturer using the same trade name.[1] In other words, there is protection against dilution.

1   Tribunal de Commerce de la Seine, 5 January 1940, Ann 298 (1940-1948).

15.78   Before using a trade name special attention has to be given to the rights of third parties on the same name, whether used as:

    (i) a trade name;

    (ii) a shop sign, if the sign is known on the same territory as the trade name;

    (iii) a trade mark (with the exception of Article L 713-6 of the Intellectual Property Code: *bona fide* use of his own name by a person cannot be enjoined, even if such name is registered as a trade mark by a third person);

    (iv) copyright;

    (v) the name of third parties: a person may authorise the use of his name as a trade name. If the enterprise is later sold, the successors can use the name if it is sold with the enterprise, however they may be obliged to use the name together with their own name and indicate their quality as successors).[1]

1   Cour de cassation, 10 May 1955, Ann 166 (1955).

Shop signs

15.79 A shop sign is the sign which distinguishes a shop from any other shop in the same territory. Rights in the shop sign occur by first usage. But such right is lost if the sign ceases to be used.

15.80 Such a sign can either be an arbitrary, fancy name or a family name (often the name of the trader). It is protected provided that it is distinctive. It must not be deceptive, generic or descriptive, immoral or misleading.

15.81 Protection of shop signs, as for trade names and corporate names, is assured by Article 1382 of the Code Civil (article governing the general principles of liability). It is also protected, like trade names, by Article L 711-4 of the Intellectual Property Code.

15.82 With the exception of well-known shop signs, a shop sign is known in a limited territory, and thus is protected only in such territory. This is the reason why a trader can adopt a sign (whether as a trade mark, a trade name or a corporate name) already used by another trader as a shop sign, provided that the second trader is not located on the same territory as the first one.

15.83 There will be unfair competition only when the two traders who use the same sign have the same activities and are located on the same territory. In such a case, the courts may deny the use of the sign to the second user, and may grant damages to the first user for the prejudice suffered by him.

15.84 There is an exception for well-known shop signs whose protection can cover the whole French territory: the famous Parisian restaurant 'Maxim's' may prevent the use of of its sign by a restaurant in Nice.[1]

1   Cour d'Appel d' Aix en Provence, 12 May 1964, Ann 88 (1965).

15.85 Here again, as in paragraph 15.78 above, before using a shop sign special attention has to be given to the rights of third parties in the same sign.

Corporate names

15.86 A corporate name is the name of an artificial person, such as a company or an association, which gives it individuality.

15.87 The corporate name differs from a trade name, as a trade name serves to distinguish the enterprise, but not the person who carries on such enterprise. The Courts have held that a company has the same rights over its corporate name as a natural person has in his or her name.

15.88 A corporate name can either be an arbitrary, fancy name or the name of a partner (however the corporate name cannot consist only of a partner's name, another word is necessary, such as: Garage..., Etablissement...., Maison......, Groupe....).

15.89 Rights in a corporate name arise by the signature and registration of the articles of the company.

15.90 As with trade marks, corporate names cannot be deceptive, generic or descriptive, immoral or misleading and must be distinctive. Furthermore, the corporate name must take account of the rights of third parties:

    (i) a mark belonging to a third party cannot be chosen as corporate name even when there is no risk of confusion[1] (with the exception of Article L 713-6: *bona fide* use);

    (ii) a prior corporate name is protected by the action for unfair competition under Article 1382 if the second company carries on the same activity in the same territory as the first one, so that there is a risk of confusion;

    (iii) a third party bearing the same name as the corporate name (the corporate name being made with the family name of a partner) can oppose the use of the corporate name when there is a risk of confusion or when there is a fraud (for example, the partner who gave his name to the company is a minor shareholder having no activity in the company).

1   Cour de cassation, 30 October 1973, Bull Cass Civ IV n° 305 p 273 (1973).

Unfair competition and abuse of right

15.91 Characters are also protected by the very general provisions of Article 1382 of the Code civil (the article governing the general principles of liability:

> 'Any act whatsoever of a person which causes damage to anybody else obliges the person by whose fault the damage has been caused to repair it.'[1]

1   'Tout fait quelconque de l'homme qui cause à autrui un dommage, oblige celui par la faute duquel il est arrivé, à le réparer.'

15.92 Article 1382 can be considered as 'the Good Samaritan' for persons unprotected by any other part of the law. Article 1382 was used by the courts, before the Intellectual Property Code came into force, to protect well-known trade marks through the notion of abuse of right even when there is no direct competition between the goods. The use of a well-known mark is wrongful and prejudicial when such use is being made in order to benefit from the mark's reputation, or when such use may dilute the distinctiveness of the well-known mark.

15.93 Unfair competition under Article 1382 is also used to protect characters and personalities, which or who are not otherwise protected, as it does in the case of trade names, corporate names or shop signs. The requirement for protection is that the parties are in a direct competitive relationship (regarding their activities, their goods, their locations, etc...). However, here again, the concept of abuse of right may protect parties which are not in competition. It is thus clear that Article 1382 is an important source of relief where protection is not afforded by trade marks law, or copyright.

15.94 In conclusion, special attention needs to be paid to the rights of third parties, especially personality rights and the rights of the parties bearing the same name as the character, both of which are very well protected in France.

Chapter 16

Germany[1]

Introduction

16.1 The level of protection for characters under German law depends on whether a real person or a fictional character (in whatever form) is the subject of the merchandising operation. The individual enjoys full legal protection against any form of exploitation of his person to which he does not consent and can, with the help of exclusive rights, restrain an unauthorised use. The protection of fictional characters, whether in the form of drawn or sketched figures, cartoons or film and literary characters, is mainly achieved through unfair competition law and is quite extensive, though certainly not total. Protection through industrial property laws is, on the other hand, not very effective because the subject of protection in character merchandising is frequently not the character itself but its advertising value, ie the goodwill that vests in the character.

1   By Bettina Komarnicki of Wessing Berenburg-Gossler Zimmermann Lange, 60323 Frankfurt am Main, Freiherr-vom-Stein-Straße 24-26, Germany.

16.2 The term 'character merchandising' is not yet very widely used in Germany, though cases dealing with the subject of merchandising date back to the 1960s. In a recent decision, however, the Hamburg Court of Appeal used the word 'merchandising' and the courts recognise more and more the necessity to protect the reputation and goodwill in a popular sign, character or name and make sure that no-one gets a free ride on the efforts of the rightful owner of the sign.

PROTECTION OF REAL PERSONS

16.3 A real person is protected against the misuse of his name, picture, image, general get-up, voice and any other feature of his personality through exclusive personality rights, some of which have been given special treatment. The general provision for the protection of an individual's personality is paragraph 823 (1), BGB.

Special personality rights: the right of name and the personal portrait right

16.4 According to paragraph 12, BGB, the lawful bearer of a name can prohibit a misappropriation of his name by an unauthorised user.

16.5. Paragraphs 5 and 15 of the new German Trade Mark Act, MarkenG (in force since 1 January 1995; formerly paragraph 16, UWG) grant more specific relief against misleading use by unauthorised persons in the course of the trade, of business names, symbols and signs which, in the relevant trade circles are taken as a designation of a certain business or enterprise (the classical case of passing-off). Paragraphs 5 and 15, MarkenG are generally superseded by paragraph 12, BGB which does not require a risk of confusion and therefore has become the general means of protection for private as well as commercial names.[1]

1   Baumbach/Hefermehl,16th edn, para 16, UWG, note 1.

16.6 Paragraph 12, BGB originally protected the civil name of natural persons, but has been interpreted by the courts so as to encompass any name used privately or in business. A name is defined as a designation which individualises and identifies a certain person or enterprise. Protection extends to artistic names as well as pseudonyms and any other designation, sign or emblem which is either naturally distinctive as a name, or has acquired distinctiveness through use, ie secondary meaning in the relevant circles where it is used.[1]

1   Palandt-Heinrichs, para 12, BGB, notes 4 et seq; Baumbach/Hefermehl, 16th edn, para 16, UWG, notes 12 and 28.

16.7 The right is violated if the name is used unjustly in order to designate another person, business or goods, provided that the use impairs a legitimate interest of the lawful bearer. The right of a name is not infringed if somebody mentions the name with reference to its lawful bearer, but without the latter's approval. In the context of personality merchandising, for example, an advertisement alleging that celebrity X uses the product Y does not infringe paragraph 12, BGB because the name is not used with reference to the product.[1]

1   BGHZ 30,7 – Caterina Valente; OLG Bremen, GRUR 1986, 838; the use may, however, be a violation of the general personality right, see below.

16.8 The right of name is not transferable as such, but the right to use a name may be licensed. The licence is void if the use of the name by the licensee results in a deception of the public. The licensee may claim prior use as could the bearer of the name.[1]

1   Palandt-Heinrichs, para 12, BGB, note 17.

16.9 Paragraph 22, KUG stipulates that pictures and portraits of a person may only be distributed or publicly exhibited with the consent of that person. Protection lasts until ten years after the death of the person, and the next-of-kin of the deceased are entitled to enjoin the unlawful publication of a portrait. A precondition is, however, that the person can be recognised at least by some people.[1]

1   Von Gamm, Einf, note 99.

16.10 Paragraph 23, KUG allows the publication of pictures and photographs without the consent of the portrayed person if they record contemporary history, ie political, social or cultural events of general interest. This exception covers pictures of contemporary public interest which serve the public's need for information. It does not extend to private, purely commercial purposes nor publication contrary to the legitimate interests of a contemporary personality. The courts have made it clear that the publicising of a celebrity in the context of advertising is not in the public interest and therefore is not covered by paragraph 23, KUG.[1]

1   BGHZ 20, 345 – Paul Dahlke.

16.11   The general personality right has been defined as the exclusive right of the individual to be respected as a human being by the State as well as by the other members of society.[1] The individual is entitled to form and develop freely his personality. That includes the right to be 'left alone', ie to prevent an unwanted interference with one's personality as well as the right to act freely (Handlungsfreiheit). The personality right follows directly from the Basic Law (the German Constitution) which contains an absolute guarantee of the dignity of man in Article 1 (1), GG and grants the Basic Right of personal freedom of action in Article 2 (1), GG.[2] Since the personality right is an absolute individual right, it is protected by the law of torts, paragraph 823 (1), BGB, which stipulates that anyone who negligently violates an exclusive individual right is liable for damages. The courts have determined three different levels of protection of the personality, namely the individual sphere which includes the specific features of the individual in relation to his environment, the private sphere of family life at home and, the most sensitive, intimate sphere of inner feelings and thoughts and confidential matters.

1   BGHZ 13,334.
2   BVerfG, NJW 1973, 1221 – Soraya; Baumbach/Hefermehl, Wettbewerbsrecht, Allg, notes 142 et seq; Palandt/Thomas, para 823 BGB, notes 176 et seq.

16.12   However, not every interference with one of these spheres constitutes a violation of the personality right because, in a society where people live together who each enjoy the protection through Basic Rights, one has to balance the rights of all parties concerned. Therefore, for example, the Basic Right of freedom of speech (Article 5 (1), GG) may justify an infringement of somebody's personality right if the statement serves the legitimate purpose of public information or discussion.[1] The infringement of another's personality rights for commercial purposes can generally not be justified on the ground of overriding interests. With regard to personality merchandising, the courts have frequently stated that it followed from the general personality right that it must be left to the individual to decide whether his name or picture shall be used in advertising and that no-one has to tolerate his name being used in advertising without his consent.[2] The personality right can be invoked, eg against the unauthorised and unwanted mentioning of somebody's name in an advertisement[3] or against the use in an advertisement of the real voice, or the imitation of an actor's characteristic voice.[4] The protection extends to all the personal features and the general get-up of a person and, in the case of an actor, may include his characteristic workstyle.[5] It is not a precondition that the infringement is likely to damage the reputation of the holder of the right.[6]

16.12   *Germany*

1   See Palandt-Thomas, para 823 BGB, notes 185 et seq.
2   BGHZ 20, 345 – Paul Dahlke; BGH, GRUR 1981, 846 – Carrera; OLG Bremen, GRUR 1986, 838.
3   BGHZ 30,7 – Caterina Valente.
4   OLG Hamburg, GRUR 1989, 666 – Heinz Erhardt.
5   OLG Hamburg, as above; OLG Duesseldorf, NJW 1987, 1413 – Heino.
6   BGHZ 81, 75.

16.13   The personality right continues to exist – in an analogy to paragraph 22, KUG – after the death of the person, and his next-of-kin can prevent a distortion of the image of the deceased.[1]

1   BGH, GRUR 1989, 666 – Heinz Erhardt von Gamm, Einf, note 94.

16.14   The remedies against the violation of personality rights are the same in all cases. According to paragraph 1004, BGB, the injured party can move for an injunction to enjoin further infringements and demand *restitutio ad integru* including the retracting of the infringing statements. Even if the infringer did not act negligently, the injured party is entitled to claim a fictional licence fee which he would have earned if the use that was made of his personality had been lawful, ie licensed. The applicable provision is paragraph 812, BGB which gives the injured party the right to demand from the infringer the amount by which the latter is unjustly enriched at the expense of the former. This remedy is particularly useful in the case where an advertising agency publishes a photograph taken by a third party who unjustly represents that the portrayed person has consented to his picture being used in advertising.[1] Even though in that case the advertising agency may not have acted negligently, it will have to pay a reasonable licence fee.

1   BGHZ 20, 345 – Paul Dahlke.

16.15   Damages for negligent violation of the exclusive right are granted via paragraph 823 (1), BGB.[1] It is up to the plaintiff to choose the most suitable of the three possible ways to calculate damages. First, one may claim any real damage, ie the loss of royalties for a licence which, on account of the infringement, could not be granted to a third party (eg a prospective licensee retracts from concluding a contract because the infringer has unlawfully used the name of the licensor in connection with the same kind of goods for which the licensee wanted to use it). This situation is usually difficult to prove in court. The second possibility is to claim as compensation the profits made by the infringer. The infringer is liable to give an account of profits. This method of calculating damages is seldom used however, as infringers tend to be rather inventive in demonstrating that of course they made no profits at all from the infringing act. Therefore, in practice, the third option is the one usually sought by claimants: the injured party may calculate damages amounting to a fictional licence fee which the injured party would have earned if the infringer had acted lawfully, ie had acquired a proper licence. It is not necessary that the injured party would actually have granted a licence for the use made by the infringer, but only that it would, in theory, have been possible to license the actual use of eg the name, picture etc which has actually been made. If such a licence would under no circumstances have been granted, the fictional royalty cannot be claimed. Thus, a famous

284

horse rider whose picture was used to promote a drug said to increase sexual potency was prevented from claiming a fictional licence fee,[2] as he would never have agreed to allow his name being used in this context. In that case, however, it is possible to claim pecuniary compensation for the immaterial damage, in particular the harm to feelings for being made ridiculous, in analogy to paragraph 847, BGB. The wording of this section provides for compensation of immaterial damage when a person suffers bodily harm or unlawful detention. However, the Federal Court of Justice has in the case stated extended by drawing an analogy the scope of this provision to immaterial harm suffered by an individual from an unlawful invasion of privacy which cannot be remedied by other means. The court reasoned that it was necessary to provide a suitable remedy to injured parties in severe cases involving the violation of the right of a person to privacy, as this constitutional right would otherwise be of little value to the individual.[3] A precondition therefore is that the harm to the personality is severe and that there is no other way to compensate the victim. The amount of compensation depends on the nature of the infringement and the gravity of the damage. In the above case, a sum of DM10,000 was deemed to be reasonable (German courts tend to be reluctant to grant awards of high damages).

1   Palandt-Thomas, para 823 BGB, notes 198 et seq.
2   BGHZ 26, 349 – Herrenreiter.
3   BGHZ 30,7 – Caterina Valente; BGH, NJW 1971, 698.

16.16   Further protection exists through various criminal laws, especially paragraph 185 et seq of the Criminal Act (StGB) against libel and slander, and paragraph 824 BGB, paragraphs 14 and 15, UWG against the denigration of commercial reputation. Prosecution depends usually on a request from the injured party.

16.17   German courts and commentators basissally agree that personality rights are bound to the individual and therefore are not transferable.[1] However, it is recognised that the use of a name, portrait or other feature of the personality can be licensed to a third party where the owner of the right waives the assertion of his rights. By a contract of this kind, the holder cannot deprive himself of the personality right, but he can allow eg an agency to exploit and use the right in the way of merchandising.[2] The agreement is legally binding only *inter partes*, since there is no transfer of the exclusive right to the 'licensee'. Therefore, in principle, the agent does not have any means to enjoin the unauthorised use of the name etc by third parties but again, the owner of the personality right can empower the agent to assert his rights. The agent does have a claim of unjust enrichment against an infringer, if it was authorised exclusively to exploit the merchandising possibilities of a person because the latter saved the costs of the royalties at the expense of the agent.[3]

1   Von Gamm, Einf, note 96; for the consequences see Forkel, GRUR 1988, 491; BGH, GRUR 1987, 128 – Nena left the question open.
2   BGH, GRUR 1987, 128 – Nena.
3   BGH, GRUR 1987, 128 – Nena.

16.18   It should be noted that the consent of someone to use his name or photograph for a certain purpose does not cover the use for other purposes.

16.18   *Germany*

The agreement or consent of the rightholder needs to be interpreted and, in case of doubt, does not include the use in an advertisement.[1]

1   BGHZ 20, 345 – Paul Dahlke.

PROTECTION OF FICTIONAL CHARACTERS OF CARTOONS, FILMS AND LITERARY WORKS
Trade mark law

16.19   Trade mark law in Germany is currently undergoing major changes following the implementation of a new Trade Mark Act – MarkenG – on 1 January 1995 in order to comply with the Council Directive of 21 December 1988, 89/104/EEC (OJ 1989 L 40/1), on the harmonisation of trade mark law.

16.20   The former Trade Mark Act of 1968 -WZG – provided for the protection of registered trade marks as well as non-registered but factually distinctive marks, symbols and get-ups used in trade (Ausstattung, paragraph 25, WZG), in their function of distinguishing the goods or services in relation to which they were used as to their commercial origin. Whereas trade mark protection was obtained with the registration of the mark with the German Patent Office (paragraphs 1 and 2, WZG),[1] the protection of get-ups arises merely upon the reputation which the sign has acquired through the use as an indication of origin which related certain goods or services to a particular business (secondary meaning). It was necessary that a significant part of the relevant trade circles recognised the get-up as a distinstive mark of the business which was the source of the goods (a good example of a get-up are the Shell colours, red and yellow).

1   A translation of the provisions of the WZG can be found in volume 6 of the IIC Studies in Industrial Property and Copyright Law, as indicated in the Bibliography.

16.21   Registration could be sought for a sign, symbol, picture or word(s) if they were distinctive.[1] It was thus possible to register as a trade mark, or obtain get-up protection in a drawn figure, cartoon or name of a character as well as the title of a work or film.[2] Protection was acquired by priority of registration or acquisition of the necessary reputation of the get-up. However, paragraph 1, WZG required that in order for a trade mark to be registered, the applicant must have a business concerned with the production or sale of the goods, or offering of the services, for which protection of the mark was sought. Trade marks under the old Trade Mark Act 1968 were thus strictly related to the business of the rightholder.

1   Paragraph 4 (2) WZG; Baumbach /Hefermehl, para 4 WZG, notes 21 et seq.
2   See Walter, pp 97 et seq.

16.22   While the protection of the mark, whether registered or not, extended to the use of similar signs which may cause confusion or deception to the public or the relevant trade circles as to the origin of the goods (paragraph 31, WZG), a prerequisite was that any infringing use must involve the application of the mark to goods identical with or similar to those which were the subject of the lawful trade mark use.

16.23 The above mentioned prerequisites used to make the protection of fictional characters through trade mark law quite ineffective. In order to be unlawful, the infringing use had to be a trade mark use, ie use as an indication of origin of the goods. This requirement is very often not fulfilled in character merchandising cases because the picture or name of a popular character used on the packaging of a product will frequently not be taken as an indication of origin. One would not normally think that a toy or sweet bearing a picture of Mickey Mouse on the label was produced by the Walt Disney Corporation. Besides, for the same reason, there is usually no danger of confusion as to the origin of the goods besause the consumer will in general not expect a trade connection between the goods and the merchandising agency.

16.24 A major problem resulted from the requirement that if the merchandiser wants to acquire trade mark rights, he must deal in the goods for which registration of the mark is sought. Usually, neither a merchandising agency nor the creator of the fictional character will be engaged in the manufacture or marketing of the secondary products, but merely want to exploit the advertising value of the character by way of merchandising. The licensing of the use of the mark was not considered as equivalent to having a business in the goods.[1] Also, if the licensee produces or sells the goods, this will not be taken into account as a business of the licensor.[2] The only way out for the licensor was to become a joint owner of the licensee's business. However, in that case, he was bound to exert constant control over the business which was very inconvenient for an agency with a number of licensees.

1   Pagenberg, p 1081; Walter, pp 87 et seq.
2   BGHZ 18, 175; Baumbach/Hefermehl, para 1 WZG, note 13.

16.25 In addition, trade mark protection extended only to the goods of the class for which the mark is registered and similar goods. That was very unsatisfactory for the merchandiser who wants to license the use of the fictional character for a variety of goods.

16.26 The Federal Supreme Court, in a number of cases, has tried to help the owner of well-known goods or marks – ie of valuable goodwill – against a misappropriation of this goodwill which did not fall within the scope of protection of the old Trade Mark Act by applying paragraph 1 of the Act against Unfair Competition – UWG – prohibiting unfair business conduct (see below). The new German Trade Mark Act 1995 will most probably enhance the protection for creators, owners and merchandisers of fictional characters and thus make at least some of the decisions of the BGH in the field of unfair competition law redundant. This, however, remains to be seen.

16.27 The 1995 Act (English translation available from Martin Aufenanger *Das neue deutsche Markengesetz / The New German Trade Mark Act*, published in October 1994) combines trade mark law and the rules for protection of commercial designations and work titles formerly regulated in paragraph 16 of the Act against Unfair Competition (see below, paragraph 16.36). In relation to trade marks, the Act affords protection in the following way.[1]

1   A detailed outline of the provisions of the new Act is given by Fammler, 1995 1 EIPR 22.

16.28 Paragraph 3 sets out the marks which are eligible for protection. The scope of this provision extends to all marks capable of distinguishing the goods or services of one enterprise from those of another. Marks may consist of any shape or form including three-dimensional marks if the shape of the mark does not consist of features which follow directly from the technical or other nature of the goods to which the mark shall be applied. In other words, the necessary technical design of goods does not qualify for trade mark protection, whereas merely aesthetical features of the goods are protectable.

16.29 Paragraph 4 of the Act sets out the prerequisites for protection: Protection can generally be obtained:

(a) by registering a mark with the German Patent Office;
(b) by using the mark when the same has acquired a secondary meaning; and,
(c) if a mark is well-known (Article 6bis of the Paris Convention).

16.30 Paragraph 9 of the Act provides in accordance with Article 4 of the Directive for relative grounds of refusal of registration, such as identity of the applicant's mark with a prior registration (paragraph 9, sub-section 1, note 1), likelihood of confusion or – and this is a new feature in the Act – likelihood of association of the applicant's mark with a prior mark, following the identity or similarity of both marks and the identity or similarity of the applicant's goods or services with the goods or services of the prior registration (note 2). In cancellation proceedings a third relative ground of refusal may be invoked (paragraph 9, sub-section 1, note 3): if the mark for which registration is sought is identical with or similar to a mark with prior rights which is renowned within the scope of the Act, ie the Federal Republic of Germany, registration of the new mark shall be cancelled even if the goods or services to which the respective marks relate are not similar, if use of the later mark would impair the reputation or distinctiveness of the renowned mark without just cause (ie if the owner of the later mark made unfair use of the mark). It cannot be said so far what constitutes a 'renowned mark'. The Federal Supreme Court will have to establish practical criteria to determine the requirements to be fulfilled in order for a mark to be considered renowned. Paragraph 10 of the Act stipulates the application of the grounds of refusal set out above to well-known marks within the meaning of Article 6bis of the Paris Convention. (It follows from this that the notion 'renowned marks' of paragraph 9 cannot be construed in the same way as 'well-known marks'.)

16.31 Paragraph 6 of the Act provides that priority of either acquisition of the secondary meaning or the application date is decisive. In effect, any conflicting prior intellectual and/or industrial property rights may be invoked against use and registration of a mark.

16.32 The Act confers in paragraphs 14 et seq exclusive rights on the owner of a trade mark. Following Article 5 of the Directive, but in more detail, paragraph 14 defines acts which infringe the said exclusive rights. Namely, third parties are prohibited from using marks identical with or similar to the protected mark in relation to goods or services which are identical with or similar to the goods or services relating to the protected mark, if a likelihood of deception or a likelihood of association of the respective marks arises from the use of the other mark (paragraph 14, sub-section 2, notes 1 and 2). The right of the owner of a renowned mark is also violated if without his consent, an identical or similar mark, no matter whether applied to similar or dissimilar goods or services, is used in a way so as to impair the reputation or distinctiveness of the renowned mark unfairly, ie without just cause.

16.33 According to paragraph 14, sub-sections 5-7, (former paragraph 24, WZG for trade marks and paragraph 25, WZG for trade dress and get-ups), the rightful owner can prohibit the infringing use and obtain an injunction and, in the case of intentional or negligent infringement, may claim damages which are calculated according to the three ways mentioned above,[1] ie the actual loss suffered, a fictional licence fee or the infringer's profits.[2] He can also make a claim of unjust enrichment according to paragraph 812, BGB which does not necessitate negligence on the part of the infringer.[3] In addition, paragraphs 18 and 19 of the new Act confer on the rightholder the right to have unlawfully marked goods destroyed and to demand disclosure of the source and channels of distribution of the unlawfully marked goods.

1   Part A III.
2   Baumbach/Hefermehl, para 24 WZG, notes 30 et seq.
3   BGH, GRUR 1987, 520 – *Chanel No 5.*

16.34 One major limitation on the scope of protection follows from paragraph 25 of the Act which contains the use requirement. If the mark is not used within five years from registration, its owner may not invoke the rights set out above against an infringer. What constitutes use within the meaning of the Act is defined in paragraph 26. The provision has a broader scope than the relevant provisions of the 1968 Act in so far as it allows use of the mark in a form other than the registered form as long as the distinctive character of the registered mark is not affected. Also, paragraph 26 expressly stipulates that the use requirement is met by use of the mark by a third party (licensee) with the consent of the rightholder.

16.35 Paragraphs 146 et seq of the 1995 Act provide for seizure of infringing goods at the frontier.

16.36 In paragraphs 5 and 15, the 1995 Act includes commercial designations and work titles of printed works, film, sound, stage and the like works in its scope of protection. Commercial designations are defined as signs which in the course of commerce are used as the name, company name, special designation of a business or undertaking and any other signs capable of distinguishing a business from other businesses if they have acquired secondary meaning. The subject-matter of the said provisions was formerly granted a similar protection under the Act against Unfair Competition, namely paragraph 16, UWG, but with the reform of trade mark law has been integrated in the Trade Mark Act 1995 which is more appropriate to protect comprehensively marks and designations designed to distinguish their owners in commerce.

16.37 As a precondition of protection, the commercial designation or title must be distinctive as a means of identification of the business or work. The rightful user of the designation or title enjoys exclusive rights paralleling the rights of the owner of a protected mark. In particular, he may enjoin the use of the same or a similar designation or title if that use is deceptive (paragraph 15, sub-section 2 of the 1995 Act), or if the use made, without being deceptive, impairs the reputation or distinctiveness of the protected designation or title in an unfair way (paragraph 15, sub-section 3 of the 1995 Act). The rightholder may also claim damages, destruction of unlawfully marked goods and disclosure of the source and distribution channels.

16.38 In the context of character merchandising, the protection of work titles may in some cases be helpful to protect fictional or real characters, in particular since a likelihood of confusion is not required if the title has a reputation. (Former paragraph 16, UWG was of very little help because the use of a character in relation to the secondary products – eg the name 'Cats' for a perfume – would not be confusing in the sense required by paragraph 16.) The above provisions might for example now be invoked in a case which was formerly decided by the BGH on the basis of unfair competition law where the rightholder to the famous book 'Bambi' sued the producer of 'Bambi' chocolate taking a free ride on the reputation of the book (or rather Walt Disney's animated film) for an injunction.[1] It remains to be seen however, what requirements the Federal Supreme Court will establish in order to afford protection under paragraphs 5 and 15.

1   See BGH, GRUR 1960, 144 – *Bambi.*

16.39 As a part of the general law of tort outside the domain of trade mark law, the courts have developed the doctrine of 'dilution of famous marks' in order to afford protection to marks which have reached a unique distinctiveness and reputation – and therefore advertising force – against the dilution of their commercial magnetism through the use of identical or similar signs or marks on dissimilar goods.[1] The doctrine which covers registered and non-registered marks as well as business designations is founded in paragraphs 823 (1), 1004, BGB which protect the rights of a person in his business, with all its tangible and intangible assets (Recht am Unternehmen) of which the famous mark is a very valuable part, against unlawful interference.

1   BGH, GRUR 1956, 172 – Magirus; BGH, GRUR 1958, 500 – Mecki-Igel I; RGZ 170, 137 – Bayer-Kreuz.

16.40 This doctrine is based on the consideration that the proprietor of a mark who has invested so much effort in acquiring a unique position has an interest worthy of protection in ensuring that the mark keeps its distinctiveness. Since the protection of trade marks beyond the domain of similar goods was considered to be exceptional, the requirements which have to be fulfilled by a mark in order to be eligible for rights under that doctrine are very strict. After the reform of trade mark law, most famous marks will achieve protection under paragraph 14 of the Trade Mark Act 1995 and it is therefore likely that protection under the doctrine will be redundant. It is hard to imagine cases which would not be covered by the 1995 Act, but officially, the 'dilution of famous marks' doctrine has not yet been abolished. The conditions for protection are briefly set out below.

16.41 Firstly, the overwhelming majority of the German population must be aware of the mark (uberragende Verkehrsgeltung). The courts require a level of public awareness – measured in market surveys – of at least 70%-80%.[1] Furthermore, the mark must possess a sole position in the market and a certain amount of originality so as to be distinctive enough to be related in the minds of the public to the specific goods for which it stands. This precondition will usually not be present in character merchandising cases if a licence for the use of the character on certain products is granted to more than one licensee. In addition, the mark must be very highly appreciated by the public and this positive evaluation must have led to an increased demand for the brand, since that is what justifies the extended protection. Finally, the infringing use must actually be capable of endangering the unique advertising force of the famous mark, in the sense that there is a real danger of injury to the competitive position of the brand. On the other hand, a risk of confusion is not required. These preconditions are seldom met. However, a famous figure like 'Mickey Mouse', or other of the Disney characters, may enjoy such protection to the extent that they are also used as trade marks.

1   BGH, GRUR 1966, 623 – Kupferberg; OLG Hamburg, GRUR 1987, 400 – Pirelli.

16.42 As property rights, trade marks protected under the 1995 Act can be assigned (paragraph 27; in contrast, former paragraph 8, WZG permitted the transfer of trade mark rights only together with the transfer of the business itself, or the relevant part thereof to which the mark relates, and provided that any other form of assignment should be invalid) for all or parts of the goods or services to which the mark relates. A trade mark may now be transferred in respect of only a part of the catalogue of goods or services without losing the priority acquired.

16.43 The rights conferred by a trade mark may be pledged as a security and levied in execution (paragraph 29). Paragraph 30 of the 1995 Act contains provisions about the licensing of trade mark rights. The licence may be exclusive or non-exclusive, limited in time, manner of use and territory and shall not be affected by a later transfer or licence of rights in the mark. The licensee may however commence infringement proceedings only with the consent of the owner of the mark. In addition, the owner may invoke under paragraph 30 rights conferred by the Act against a licensee who is in breach of the licence.

16.44 A licence agreement may be invalid if a risk of confusion arises because, in the eyes of the public, the mark stands for a certain standard of quality which is not met by the licensee's products.[1] In that case, a licence would infringe unfair competition law (paragraph 3, UWG which prohibits deceptive advertising and under paragraph 1, UWG the deception of consumers would be considered an improper trading practice) and therefore be invalid for non-compliance with the law, paragraph 134, BGB. In order to avoid such a situation, the licensor would have to provide for and exercise sufficient quality control over the licensee's products.

1   Stumpf, note 468.

16.45   In the case of a get-up licence, the licensee may acquire trade mark rights himself if a secondary meaning in the get-up develops with respect to the licensee's business. That can be avoided if the goods bear an indication that the get-up is used under a licence, and possibly also through a licence limited in time. The BGH has ruled that if the licence expires, the licensee has to stop the use of the mark, even if he has himself acquired a right in the get-up. According to the court, this follows directly from the agreement even if the same does not contain a restriction on use clause.[1]

1   BGH, GRUR 1963, 485 Micky-Maus-Orangen.

16.46   Another problem might be that if many licences are granted, the mark could lose its distinctiveness and, as a result, become generic or fail to meet the requirements for further protection.[1]

1   See Walter, pp 113, 114 Stumpf, notes 473-475.

16.47   There might yet be another drawback to protect fictional characters by trade mark law: at present, registration procedures with the German Patent Office require at least four to six months (if preferred registration is sought for an additional fee). The long registration procedure may outlast the 'life' of the character itself which depends largely on fashion. Film characters like 'ET' or 'Dick Tracy' are usually very popular only for a limited period of time after the marketing of the film, and trade mark protection may come too late to protect the character at the peak of its commercial value.

Copyright

16.48   The Copyright Act of 1965 regulates the protection of intellectual creations in the field of literary, scientific and artistic works (paragraph 2, UrhG) and confers on the creator of the work a number of exclusive rights which are generally divided into two groups: property rights, including comprehensive exploitation rights (in particular paragraphs 15 et seq, UrhG) and the personality rights (droit moral, eg paragraphs 12-14, UrhG). Copyright protection arises upon the creation of the work, ie as soon as the work has found sufficient expression. No formalities need to be complied with. The right is granted within the jurisdiction of the Federal Republic of Germany and expires 70 years after the death of the author (paragraph 64 (1), UrhG).

16.49   Paragraph 2 (1), UrhG contains a catalogue of protected works such as literary works, works of art and applied arts, photographs and the like, films and similar works, technical and scientific illustrations etc which is however not comprehensive. A newly invented fictional character would therefore be eligible for copyright protection, provided the further conditions for protection are met.

16.50 Paragraph 2 (2), UrhG reads:

Works within the meaning of this Act include only personal intellectual creations.[1]

That means that in order to enjoy copyright protection, the work must be an original creation in relation to other already existing works, in the sense that it must be 'distinguishable by its individuality'[2] from other works. There is required a certain 'creative level' which need not be of a very high standard, though it is higher than that required in the UK or France. In order to constitute a work within paragraph 2, UrhG, it is necessary for a literary work to contain an expression of thoughts.[3] For artistic works, the courts require an 'aesthetic content' in order to distinguish copyright protection from the lesser protection under the Design and Utility Model Act.

Only the individual creative features (schoepferische Eigenart) of the work enjoy protection.[4] Both the form or the expression of the content, or the two together, can give the work its individuality.[5] Thus the content of a work – expressed in a particular way – may enjoy copyright protection if it does not consist of general ideas. Invented stories are protected if they are individual creations of the author which were not formerly known.[6] Publicly available ideas, contents, styles or forms are not protected. The work is protected only in its actual concrete form.[7]

1   Translation by Beier et al, IIC-Studies, p 117.
2   Quoted: Schricker, IIC-Studies, p 111.
3   Hubmann, p 87; Fromm/Nordemann, para 2 UrhG, note 10.
4   BGH, GRUR 1958, 500 – Meckilgel I; Hubmann, p 82.
5   See BGH GRUR 1963, 40 – Strassen gestern und morgen; BGH GRUR 1959, 379 – Gasparone; Fromm/Nordemann, para 2, note 25; Schricker, para 2 note 26 et seq.
6   OLG Karlsruhe, GRUR 1957, 395 – Trotzkopf; Schricker, para 2, note 29.
7   Fromm/Nordemann, para 2 UrhG, note 24.

16.51 The above criteria are always to be applied in order to determine whether a work is within paragraph 2, UrhG. On these grounds, parts of works enjoy separate protection if they fulfil these requirements.[1] According to the BGH, there is no requirement that the part of the work be significant or of a certain size as long as it possesses the necessary individuality.[2] Even a title of a work on its own could, in theory, be a protectable intellectual creation, but will usually lack the minimum content of an expressed idea or thought as a title is generally merely descriptive of the content and serves to identify the work. For that reason,the courts are very reluctant to acknowledge copyright protection for a title.[3]

1   Hubmann, p 86, BGHZ 9, 266; Fromm/Nordemann, para 2, note 27.
2   BGHZ 28, 234 – Verkehrskinderlied; Walter, p 119.
3   Fromm/Nordemann, para 2 UrhG, note 41.

16.52 The author of a work in whom copyright vests is the person who created the work (paragraph 7, UrhG). This is true also if the author is an

employee who has created the work in the course of his employment
(paragraph 43, UrhG). If the employer wants to exploit the works created
by his employees, he needs to get a licence from the author. The mere
employment contract cannot generally be construed so as to transfer
exploitation rights to the employer. Collective authorship is possible
(paragraph 8, UrhG), but does not apply if the different contributions to a
work can be exploited on their own, eg the music and the pictures of a film.
A person who does not make an individual creative effort is not regarded
as the author of a work. Accordingly, actors have no copyright in the part
they play because their play is supervised and guided by the artistic
director. Performers do, however, have the right to exploit their efforts
outside cinematographic use.[1] Paragraphs 73 et seq, UrhG contain
neighbouring rights which regulate the performers' rights and allow a
performer to claim royalties for the broadcasting or public distribution of
his performance which is lawful only with the actor's consent. In addition,
the general personality rights of the actor (as mentioned above) will
complement the protection granted by the UrhG.[2]

1   See Hubmann, p 119.
2   von Gamm, paras 73 and 75 UrhG, note 3.

16.53   According to paragraph 11, UrhG, copyright protection extends to
the 'intellectual and personal relations' of the author to his work and also
to the utilisation of the work. Paragraph 15, UrhG grants the author 'the
exclusive right to exploit his work in material form',[1] which are in
particular the rights of reproduction (paragraph 16, UrhG), distribution
(paragraph 17, UrhG) and exhibition (paragraph 18, UrhG). Paragraph
97, UrhG allows the injured copyright owner to bring an action against
the infringer for an injunction and damages. It states that:

> 'In lieu of damages, the injured party may recover the profits derived
> by the infringer from the acts of infringement together with a detailed
> accounting reflecting such profits.'[2]

In the case of negligence, the copyright owner may claim damages for the
violation of an exclusive right in accordance with one of the three methods
explained above.[3] Besides, the UrhG provides for the removal and
destruction of infringing copies. An intentional copyright infringement
constitutes a criminal offence according to paragraph 106 et seq, UrhG.

1   Translation by Beier et al, IIC-Studies, p 119.
2   Translation by Beier et al, IIC-Studies, p 137.
3   Schricker, para 97 note 50 et seq.

16.54   The protection of fictional characters depends on whether they
fulfil the criteria of a work within paragraph 2, UrhG. A cartoon figure
will be protected against unlawful reproduction if the drawing contains a
certain amount of originality and does not simply repeat known forms and
ideas.[1] The figure needs to have some characteristic features which are in
a way exclusive to it and mark it as an individual creation. A certain
amount of imagination is required. It may not be sufficient if the character
displays only the typical features of his genre, eg the horse in an animated
film of 'Black Beauty' would probably not be protected by copyright because
it looks just like any other black horse. Examples of protectable characters

are the drawings of 'Batman', 'Mickey Mouse' or the little fawn 'Bambi' in Walt Disney's animated film.[2] Literary or film characters like 'Sherlock Holmes', 'Kojak' or 'James Bond' will, in general, not be within the scope of copyright. The character's individuality can normally not be separately assessed because it is created all the way through the story or concept of the film or literary work. Therefore the character on its own could only be protected in its actual appearance which is usually not original enough to fall within the definition of a work.[3] Take the example of 'James Bond': his personality may be characteristic, but his external features are just what one commonly expects a successful agent or spy to look like – a cliché which is not protected by copyright.

1   BGH, GRUR 1958, 500 – Mecki-Igel I; Walter, p 122, Fr 2, UrhGH, note 59.
2   See BGH, GRUR 1960, 144 – *Bambi*.
3   See Walter, p 120 et seq.

16.55 Copyright protection is not available for the name of a character, since a name – even an invented one – does not qualify as an intellectual creation. To invent a name is not considered a sufficiently creative effort.[1] The same applies frequently to the title of a work.[2]

1   BGH, GRUR 1958, 402 – *Lili Marleen*; Walter, p 127.
2   BGHZ 26, 52 – *Sherlock Holmes*; von Gamm, Einf, note 42.

16.56 Since the transfer of personality rights is not possible under German law (see above), copyright is not transferable as such (paragraph 29, UrhG). The term 'Sale of Copyright' known from the Anglo-American concept of copyright therefore has no meaning in German copyright law. It is, however, possible to grant exclusive or non-exclusive licences (paragraph 31, UrhG) which may be limited in time or to a certain territory or in respect of the uses that may be made of the copyright work. In order to protect the copyright proprietor, paragraph 31(5), UrhG stipulates the 'purpose of grant' doctrine (Zweckuebertragungstheorie)[1] which helps to limit the scope of the licence. If the permitted manner of exploitation of the work is not fully and 'expressis verbis' stated in the agreement, by applying that doctrine, it is deemed that only those ways of exploitation shall be covered by the licence which are within the purpose of the agreement. For instance, if a licence has been granted by an artist to use his painting to sponsor a charity, the use of the painting in advertisements for goods which are not sold in support of the charity would be outside the licence agreement. It is useful for a licensee to specify in detail any use he wants to make of the licensed work in order to make sure that the licence agreement encompasses all rights necessary. According to the rules of conflict of laws, the availability of copyright protection, the scope of protection and the validity of a transfer of exploitation rights arising from copyright which are considered to be rights *in rem*, are determined in accordance with German law if the territory or nationals of the Federal Republic of Germany are affected (principle of territoriality; ie if German authors or licensees are involved, or if the work is to be exploited in Germany). As German copyright law tends to be rather restrictive as far as the scope of copyright licences is concerned, it is useful for a prospective licensor to include a choice of law clause in the agreement and choose German law as applicable.[2] It follows from the purpose of grant doctrine that the copyright owner is free to grant merchandising licences even if he has previously concluded exploitation licences with other licensees.[3] It is possible for the copyright owner to authorise a third party, preferably an agency, to exploit his personality rights such as the publishing right.[4] An assignment of a licence by the licensee to another party requires the consent of the author (paragraph 34, UrhG).

1 Translation of Schricker, IIC-Studies,p 114.
2 Fromm/Nordemann, para 31 UrhG, note 32.
3 von Gamm, para 31, note 19 et seq ; Schricker, IIC-Studies, p.114.
4 Hubmann p 203 et seq.

Unfair competition

16.57 The protection against unfair competition derives from the Act against Unfair Competition of 1909, designed to prevent unfair business conduct. This has been interpreted very widely by the courts. It can be noted that as a result, competition law serves as the vehicle to protect the goodwill of industrial and commercial enterprise in circumstances where industrial property law typically fails. In cases of the commercial exploitation of another's reputation, paragraph 1, UWG has become the most important means of protection. In view of the new Trade Mark Act which contains express provisions for the protection of the reputation of trade marks, it remains to be seen whether the courts will now award protection against the unfair exploitation of protected trade marks under the more specific 1995 Act rather than under the unfair competition aspect. Unfair competition law will however be the main source of protection if an infringer copies the goods rather than the protected mark.

16.58 Paragraph 1, UWG reads as follows:

'Any person who, in the course of business activity for the purposes of competition, commits acts contrary to honest practices, may be enjoined from these acts and held for damages.'[1]

According to the BGH, paragraph 1, UWG is applicable only in exceptional circumstances because the purpose of the provision is not to confer additional monopoly rights on the owner of industrial or intellectual property such as well-known signs, names, goods etc, but to ensure a proper conduct of the market participants.[2]

1 Translation by Beier et al, IIC-Studies, p 94.
2 BGHZ 26, 52 – *Sherlock Holmes*.

16.59 It is the *unfair* use of another's reputation which, in the view of the BGH, justifies the application of paragraph 1, UWG. The applicability of unfair competition law does not follow from an existing exclusive right of the owner of a well-known name or sign, since there is no general protection of the goodwill of a business.[1] Infringements can usually be dealt with by relevant statutes on copyright and industrial property. Therefore the use or imitation of signs, characters, goods or designations which do not enjoy special legal protection is, as a rule, free and can only be prohibited if the manner in which the use is made is regarded as unfair or dishonest.[2] This has the effect that the owner of the sign, character, goods or name benefits from the application of paragraph 1, UWG as if he had an exclusive right in the goodwill of his sign etc.

1   BGH, GRUR 1963, 485 – *Micky-Maus-Orangen.*
2   Baumbach/Hefermehl, para 1 UWG, notes 439 and 495 et seq.

16.60   The special circumstances which justify the application of paragraph 1, UWG are that the infringer takes a free ride on the success of the owner of the sign etc which the latter has created with great financial investment and advertising efforts. Therefore the owner of the sign etc should be in a position to reap the fruits of what he has sown. The infringer not only saves all these efforts by appropriating another's success for his own purposes, but hinders at the same time the rightful owner in the exploitation of his efforts by licensing the use of his sign, mark etc.[1]

1   BGH, GRUR 1960, 144 – *Bambi*; Baumbach/Hefermehl, para 1 UWG, notes 440, 498 et seq; Pagenberg, p 1100.

16.61   The courts used to rule that an unfair impediment to licensing activities within the scope of paragraph 1, UWG could only occur if the licensor had an exclusive right to license the use of his sign etc.[1] In more recent decisions, however, the BGH extended the application of paragraph 1, UWG to piracy of reputation cases involving marks, goods and designations which did not enjoy special protection by copyright or trade mark law.[2] Thus, in 1985, the court held in the decision 'Ein Champagner unter den Mineralwaessern'[3] that the exporters of French champagne could enjoin the use of advertising slogans by the German importer of 'Perrier' mineral water on the labels declaring 'Perrier from France. As elegant as Champagne' and 'Un Champagne des Eaux Minerales'. The Court found that the defendants had unfairly exploited the reputation of the plaintiffs for the promotion of their own product and recognised that even though the plaintiffs did not have an exclusive property right in the designation 'champagne' which entitled them to license the use of the designation and earn royalties, the mere commercial possibility of granting licences as an actual effect of owning a famous designation deserved to be protected. The court explained that geographical designations could, in practice, be exploited in the same way as a trade mark, although the possibility of granting licences resulted only from a factual monopoly arising out of moral recognition by the market and not from a legal position of the licensor.

1   See eg BGH, GRUR 1960, 144 – *Bambi.*
2   BGHZ 86, 90 – *Rolls Royce*; BGH, GRUR 1985, 550 – *Dimple.*
3   BGHG, NJW 1988, 644; [1988] 8 EIPR D-177; [1988] 19 IIC 192.

16.62   It is probably not now necessary for the infringing use to exploit the quality expectations of the public as former decisions required.[1] There, it was held that a precondition for the application of paragraph 1, UWG was that the infringer exploited the good reputation of the goods of a competitor as an entree for the promotion of his own products, expecting that the popularity of the other brand would reflect positively on his own goods. The reputation, in that case, had to be based on the association by consumers of those products with a high standard of quality. Since the decision of the OLG Hamburg in the 'Cats' case,[2] there is no need to go into the question as to what the popularity and appreciation of the sign, character, goods or name is based on. As far as the unfair exploitation of another's goods is concerned, the BGH requires a certain competitive characteristic feature of the goods which makes them distinguishable from ordinary every day products of the kind, like the famous Rolex 'Oyster' watch.[3] In any case, the protection aims in effect at the image and prestige of the subject-matter of the goodwill as a value of its own, be it the reputation of a name, brand, sign, symbol or of goods or characters.[4]

1   Eg BGHZ 40, 391 – *Stahlexport*; BGHZ 86, 90 – *Rolls Royce*.
2   GRUR 1988, 549 – *Cats*.
3   BGH GRUR 1985 – *Tchibo/Rolex*.
4   Kur, GRUR 1990, 1, 9.

16.63   There is, however, one restriction on the application of paragraph 1, UWG. An unfair exploitation of the popularity of a character etc requires that the character is already well-known and enjoys a good reputation. If, for example, a trade mark consisting of the name of a musical is registered at a time when the musical is not yet very popular, paragraph 1, UWG is not infringed[1] because the use at that time does not exploit the reputation of the musical, nor does it impede an existing possibility for the owner of the name to license its use. The registration A of the mark in those circumstances is lawful and it is not important that the trade mark owner may have registered the mark only with a view to having a popular mark, once the musical has become famous.[2]

1   OLG Hamburg, GRUR 1988, 549 – *Cats*.
2   See BGH, GRUR 1960, 144 – *Bambi*; BGH, GRUR 1981, 277 – *Biene Maja*.

16.64   In order to be applicable, paragraph 1, UWG requires that the infringer and the injured party are involved as competitors in a common field of activity (Wettbewerbsverhaeltnis). In merchandising cases, there is usually no common field of activity in the sense that both the infringer and the proprietor of the character compete in the sale or manufacture of goods. The merchandiser very often does not exploit the character by using it himself in the promotion of secondary products. The BGH recognised very early the need for a common field of activity between the parties.[1] It has only been recently that the BGH has held the economic value which lies in the goodwill achieved through a certain level of creativity and usually high financial investments by a businessman as worthy of protection.[2] In character merchandising the owner of the character tries to exploit the character through licensing its use to third parties and earn royalties. By depriving him of this possibility, the infringer competes with the rightful owner in the field of commercial exploitation of the character.[3] Thus the character itself is seen as a commodity which is the subject of competition. The view of the courts is justified by the fact that the merchandiser will not be able to license the use of this commodity in the field in which the infringer is active. It is recognised now that the possibility of exploiting a character in the way of merchandising creates a competitive relationship between the proprietor of the character and the unauthorised user, not only if the owner intends to merchandise the character himself,[4] but also if the owner does not plan to license the use of the character in the way the infringer used it.[5] A common field of activity exists whenever the commercial exploitation of the reputation of a sign or character under factual market aspects possible.

1   Already in BGH, GRUR 1960, 144 – *Bambi*.
2   See Kur, GRUR 1990, 1, 7.
3   See Walter p 132.
4   OLG Hamburg, GRUR 1988, 549 – *Cats*.
5   See BGH, GRUR 1994, 808 – *Markenverunglimpfung I*.

16.65   Paragraph 1, UWG can also be violated if, as a means of exploiting the reputation of a sign or mark, the infringer uses the mark – or a similar one – in a way which creates an avoidable confusion or deception of the public about the origin of the goods.[1]

1   Baumbach/ Hefermehl, para 1 UWG, notes 450, 486.

16.66   The remedies against infringement of paragraph 1, UWG are the same as in cases of infringement of exclusive rights (see above), ie the injured party can bring an action for an injunction as well as for damages or unjust enrichment.[1] As a result, the injured party stands as if paragraph 1, UWG granted an exclusive right against the unauthorised exploitation of the goodwill that vests in a sign, designation or fictional character.

1   See Baumbach/Hefermehl, Einl UWG, note 225 et seq, 261 et seq.

16.67   A precondition for the protection of fictional characters by paragraph 1, UWG is that the infringer must, through his act, take a free ride on the commercially exploitable reputation or popularity of the fictional character and, secondly, thereby impede the licensing activities of the rightful owner of the character. For example, the use of registered trade mark rights is unfair if registration was sought with the improper aim of depriving the proprietor of the goodwill vesting in the character and exploiting the character at the expense of its rightful owner. In the *Bambi* case,[1] the defendant, a manufacturer of chocolate, had registered the mark 'Bambi' at a time when the 'Bambi' figure was already very popular through Walt Disney's animated film. When later on the plaintiff, Walt Disney Inc, licensed the use of the picture of 'Bambi' to another producer of chocolate, the defendant invoked his trade mark to restrain the use of the picture by his competitor. Walt Disney Inc moved for an injunction, which was granted. The court ruled that the registration of the word 'Bambi' by the defendant was unfair because it not only exploited the popularity of the character which was created by the plaintiff, but also prevented the plaintiff from exploiting his copyright in the figure by way of licensing the picture of 'Bambi' for the use in product promotion, at least for the class for which the defendant's mark was registered. The registration of the mark was said to impede the exploitation of the copyright in the drawn figure, since the use of the figure would have been related by the public to the name – and trade mark – 'Bambi' and would therefore have been deceptive within the provisions of the former Trade Mark Act (paragraphs 31 and 24, WZG).

1   BGH, GRUR 1960, 144 – *Bambi*; see also BGH, GRUR 1985, 550 – *Dimple*.

16.68   The use of a well-known and appreciated character or figure is also anti-competitive if it exploits the creative effort of the author.[1]

1   BGHZ 26, 52 – *Sherlock Holmes*.

16.69   If the use of a character as a product endorsement falsely implies a business connection between the proprietor of the character and the marked goods and on these grounds the public expects the goods to be of a particular standard of quality (qualifizierte betriebliche Herkunftsangabe) which they actually are not, the use of the character may infringe paragraph 3, UWG. The provision prohibits misleading statements in connection with the description of goods. Knowingly making false statements of that kind also constitutes a criminal offence under paragraph 4, UWG.

Bibliography

16.70   The following works provide useful further reading on the areas covered in this chapter.

Baumbach, Adolf / Hefermehl, Wolfgang: Warenzeichenrecht, 12th edn, 1985.
Baumbach, Adolf / Hefermehl, Wolfgang: Wettbewerbsrecht, 16th edn, 1990 and 18th edn, 1995.
Beier, Friedr.-Karl / Schricker, Gerhard / Fikentscher, Wolfgang: IIC-Studies in Industrial Property and Copyright Law, Vol 6, German Industrial Property, Copyright and Antitrust Laws, 1982.
Fammler, Dr Michael: The New German Act on Marks: EC Harmonisation and Comprehensive Reform, in: [1995] 1 EIPR 22 (with further references).
Forkel, Hans: Lizenzen an Persoenlichkeitsrechten durch gebundene Rechtsuebertragung, in: GRUR 1988, pp 491-501.
Fromm Friedkr Karl / Nordemann, Wilhelm: Urheberrecht, 8th edn, 1994.
Hubmann, Heinrich: Urheber-und-Verlagsrecht, 7th edn, 1991.
Kur, Annette: Der wettbewerbliche Leistungsschutz – Gedanken zum wettbewerblichen Schutz von Formgebungen, bekannten Marken und 'Characters', in: GRUR 1990, 1 et seq.
Pagenberg, Jochen: Ausstattung und Character Merchandising, in: Handbuch des Ausstattungsrechts, Festgabe fur Friedrich Karl Beier zum 60, Geburtstag, 1986, pp 1071-1108.
Palandt: Buergerliches Gesetzbuch, 54th edn, 1995.
Schricker, Prof Dr Gerhard: Urheberrecht, Kommentar, Munich 1987.
Stumpf, Herbert: Der Lizenzvertrag, 6th edn, 1993.
von Gamm, Otto-Friedrich: Urheberrechtsgesetz, 1968.
Walter, Wolfgang: Die geschaftliche Verwertung von Werbesymbolen durch Lizenzvergabe, Schriftenreihe zum gewerblichen Rechtsschutz, Band 51, 1979.

Abbreviations

16.71   The following are the meanings of the main abbreviations appearing in this chapter.

BGB   =   German Civil Code, Buergerliches Gesetzbuch.
UWG   =   Act against Unfair Competition, Gesetz gegen den unlauteren Wettbewerb.

StGB	=	Criminal Code, Strafgesetzbuch.
UrhG	=	Copyright Act, Urheberrechtsgesetz of 1965.
WZG	=	Trade Mark Act 1968, Warenzeichengesetz.
MarkenG	=	Trade Mark Act 1995, Markengesetz, in force since 1 January 1995.
KUG	=	Former Copyright Act of 1907 which is not in force any more except for the Personal Rights, Kunsturhebergesetz.
GG	=	Basic Law of the Federal Republic of Germany, Grundgesetz.
BVerfG	=	German Constitutional Court, Bundesverfassungsgericht.
BGH	=	Federal Supreme Court, Bundesgerichtshof.
OLG	=	Court of Appeal, Oberlandesgericht.
GRUR	=	Journal for the Protection of Industrial Property and Copyright, Gewerblicher Rechtsschutz und Urheberrecht.
BGHZ	=	Official Collection of the decisions of the BGH.
NJW	=	Neue Juristische Wochenschrift (Weekly Law Journal).
EIPR	=	European Intellectual Property Review.

Chapter 17

United States[1]

Introduction

17.1 A major source of intellectual property protection in the US is the Constitution, which gives Congress the power to enact laws protecting the writings of authors, and to regulate interstate and foreign commerce (the famous 'commerce clause'). The former provision is the source of copyright law, the latter is the source of the Federal laws on trademarks, designs and unfair competition. In addition to this Federal law, there are state laws both statutory, and non-statutory which are relevant to merchandising.

1   I would like to thank Professor Oliver Goodenough for reading through this section, and for his helpful comments and suggestions. Needless to say, responsibility for errors and omissions is mine.

COPYRIGHT

17.2 Until 1978, copyright law in the US developed along two parallel tracks: federal protection for published works, and state protection for unpublished works. A work written in 1971 enjoyed common law copyright from its creation under state law, and this common law copyright continued until publication.[1] However, since 1978 both unpublished and published works have enjoyed protection under Federal law.[2] The current statute is the Copyright Act 1976,[3] as amended by the Berne Convention Implementation Act 1988 and a number of other Acts. Copyright protection extends generally to 'original works of authorship' that are 'fixed in a tangible medium of expression, now known or later developed, from which they can be perceived, reproduced or otherwise communicated either directly or with the aid of a machine or device'.[4] 'Works of authorship' include the following categories:[5]

    (1) literary works;
    (2) musical works including the accompanying words;
    (3) dramatic works including any accompanying music;
    (4) pantomimes and choreographic works;
    (5) pictorial, graphic and sculptural works;
    (6) motion pictures and other audio-visual works;
    (7) sound recordings.

1   *Nimmer on Copyright* – Overview.
2   S 301(a).
3   17 USC.

4 S 102.
5 S 102(a).

17.3 The requirement that a literary work should consist of words or numbers [emphasis supplied], would appear to exclude single words or numbers as such from copyright protection.[1] Thus the titles of films may not claim federal copyright.[2] It is almost equally clear that, at least since 1978, common law copyright is not available to protect titles,[3] though they may achieve protection under other theories.[4]

1 But see below as to the protection of characters.
2 *Nimmer on Copyright*, para 2.16.
3 Ibid.
4 Ibid.

17.4 Section 101 attempts to draw a distinction between works of the visual arts which are copyrightable, and industrial designs which are not. Copyrightable works include two and three-dimensional works of fine, graphic, and applied art, photographs, prints and art reproductions, maps, globes, charts, diagrams, models and technical drawings including architectural plans. Such works include works of artistic craftsmanship insofar as their form but not their mechanical or utilitarian aspects are concerned. This provision is based on the Supreme Court decision in *Mazer v Stein*.[1] In that case, statuettes representing human figures had been registered for copyright as 'works of art'. The court held that they did not cease to be copyrightable when they were embodied in useful articles, namely, lamp standards. This was the case notwithstanding: (1) their registrability as designs; (2) the intention of the artist that the designs should be mass-produced commercially; (3) their lack of aesthetic value; and (4) their merchandising on a nationwide scale. The result is that virtually all two-dimensional designs are copyrightable. 'A two-dimensional painting, drawing, or graphic work is still capable of being identified as such when it is printed on, or applied to, utilitarian articles such a textile fabrics, wallpaper, containers and the like.'[2] The same is true when a three-dimensional design such as a carving or sculptural work is used to embellish an industrial work or incorporated into a product without losing its ability to exist independently as a work of art.[3] However, where, looking at the article, it is not possible to discern any feature that is capable of independent existence as a purely sculptural or graphic work, then copyright protection is not available.[4] It should also be noted, that since protection is conferred on the expression of an idea, rather than the idea itself, the protection conferred by the copyright in a particular embodiment of an idea may be quite limited.[5]

1 347 US 201 (1954).
2 House Report No 94-1476, September 3, 1976, pp 54-55.
3 Ibid.
4 Eg *Norris Industries Inc v International Telephone and Telegraph Corpn* 696 F 2d 918 (11th Cir) (1983).
5 See para 17.3.

17.5 Photographs are copyrightable as pictorial or graphic works,[1] but a series of slides or film prints constitutes an audio-visual work,[2] and also the sound track.[3] In *Worlds of Wonder Inc v Vector Intercontinental Inc*[4] the plaintiffs manufactured a stuffed toy bear containing motors and a cassette tape with an audio track and a digital command track capable of animating the toy's eyes, nose and mouth. The court held that the defendant had infringed the plaintiff's copyright by marketing rival tapes for insertion in the toy. It is not clear whether the court regarded the 'audio-visual' work as the sights and sounds produced by the tape, or the bear itself.

1 S 102(a)(5).
2 S 102(a)(6).
3 S 101.
4 653 F Supp 135 (ND Ohio 1986); *Worlds of Wonder v Veritel Learning Systems Inc* 658 F Supp 351 (ND Tex 1986).

17.6 Characters are not mentioned as such in the Copyright Act, but there is a considerable body of case law establishing the copyrightability of some characters as independent forms of intellectual property, apart from the copyright works in which they appear.[1] The result is that the licensing of literary and dramatic characters for sequels and 'spin offs' has become an important feature of the motion picture, television and video industries.[2] 'The licensing of pictorial characters from comic strips and periodicals, animated cartoons, motion pictures and television programmes, and even video games, in an inexhaustible variety of copyrightable works and merchandise – toys, games, advertising, live and recorded performances, books, posters, knick-knacks, and so forth – has become a billion dollar business.'[3] In litigation involving characters and their licensing, plaintiffs often rely on both copyright and trademark protection and related doctrines. Cases tend to turn on the similarity between characters, rather than on the copyrightability of the plaintiff's character itself.[4]

1 Ringer and Sandison in 'International Copyright and Neighbouring Rights' ed Stewart, Butterworths (2nd edn, 1989), para 21.12.
2 Eg *Goodis v United Artists Television Inc* 425 F 2d 397 (2d Cir 1970); *Conan Properties Inc v Mattel Inc* 601 F Supp 1179 (SDNY 1984).
3 Ringer and Sandison, loc cit.
4 Ibid.

17.7 Not every character has an independent copyright, however. Where only a character and not other elements of a copyright work is reproduced, protection depends upon a finding that the character is original, creative, and possesses characteristics that are clearly delineated.[1] This is easier to show when the idiosyncratic features of a character are revealed in visual images, rather than in words alone.[2] The copyrightability of pictorial characters as independent works is now established beyond doubt.[3] There is also some authority upholding independent copyright protection for characters originating in purely literary works.[4] However, there is also authority suggesting that literary characters are entitled to autonomous copyright only under sharply limited circumstances.[5] As Nimmer puts it: 'The issue whether a character from a work of fiction is protectable apart from the story in which such character appears, is in a sense more properly framed as relating to the degree of substantial similarity required to constitute infringement rather than in terms of copyrightability *per se*.'[6]

1 Ibid.
2 Ibid. See *Walt Disney Productions v Air Pirates* 581 F 2d 751 (9th Cir 1978) (parodies of Walt Disney characters); *Silverman v CBS Inc* 632 F Supp 1344 (SDNY 1986).
3 *Walt Disney Productions v Air Pirates* above.

4 Eg *Burroughs v Metro-Goldwyn-Mayer Inc* 519 F Supp 60 (SDNY 1981); *Filmvideo Releasing Corpn v Hastings* 509 F Supp 60, affd 668 F 2d 91 (2d Cir 1981).
5 Ringer and Sandison, loc cit. *Warner Bros Inc v Columbia Broadcasting System Inc* 216 F 2d 945 (2d Cir 1970).
6 At para 2.12.

17.8 There is a troublesome question which arises when a character has appeared in a number of works, and some of these have been allowed to fall into the public domain.[1] Proprietors of characters therefore went to extreme lengths to ensure that every manifestation of a character bore a copyright notice, or was registered in the Copyright Office, or both. The implementation of the Berne Convention in the US reduces this problem as it abolishes all formal requirements as a condition of copyright protection, although compliance with the formalities will continue to confer important statutory benefits.[2]

1 The issue was sidestepped in eg *National Comic Publications v Fawcett Publications Inc* 191 F 2d 594 (2d Cir 1951) clarified 198 F 2d 927 (2d Cir 1951); *Silverman v CBS Inc* 632 F Supp 1344 (SDNY 1986) – Ringer and Sandison, loc cit.
2 Ibid.

17.9 Moral rights were not specifically introduced by the 1988 Act, but in 1990 Congress enacted the Visual Artists Rights Act.[1] Analysis of moral rights, so far as works of visual art are concerned, begins with that Act and certain state statutes.[2] For other copyrightable works analysis should proceed through general principles.[3] In relation to the latter, two distinguished commentators have concluded that through some strong and influential decisions the protection of moral rights in the US is now a reality,[4] and that there is a trend towards broader protection.[5] It must be admitted, however, that many practitioners are sceptical of this, and take the view that outside the scope of the Visual Artists Rights Act, moral rights are non-existent. The 1990 Act defines 'works of visual art' to include paintings, drawings and prints.[6] Any such work which exists in a unique original meets the statutory criteria, but works in multiple copies which are signed by the author and consecutively numbered are also included.[7] Photographs qualify only if reproduced for exhibition purposes.[8] The rights conferred by the Act are of paternity ('attribution'),[9] the right to integrity,[10] and the right to object to false attribution of a work.[11] The right of paternity has to be claimed. The implication is that whereas violation of the other two rights will give rise to a claim for damages, violation of the right of paternity will give rise only to injunctive relief.[12] There are several exceptions to these rights.[13] For example, depiction of a protected work on a poster need not bear the artist's name,[14] and if it falsely attributes his name to a depicted work he cannot object under the Act's provisions.[15] Similarly in the case of a work reproduced on packaging material. Newspapers, books and magazines are not liable for the manner in which they display, portray or reproduce a work.[16] A museum can sell postcards of an artists work attributed to him, but cropped in a way he finds offensive, and he cannot invoke the Act.[17] There are also other exceptions.[18] The effect of these exceptions is effectively to confine the utility of the Act to such situations as where an original painting is displayed in an art gallery without attribution. In such a case the artist can assert the right of paternity. The exceptions severely limit the relevance of the Act to the merchandising context.

1   Effective 1 June 1991.
2   *Nimmer on Copyright*, para 8.21.
3   Ibid.
4   Ibid.
5   Ibid.
6   17 USC, para 101.
7   Ibid.
8   Ibid.
9   17 USC, para 106A(a)(1)(A).
10 17 USC, para 106A(a)(2).
11 17 USC, para 106A(a)(1)(B). Similarly an author can prevent the use of his name in relation to a distorted or mutilated work.
12 *Nimmer on Copyright*, para 8.21[B].
13 Nimmer, loc cit.
14 Ibid.
15 Ibid – he might of course have other remedies.
16 Ibid.
17 Ibid.
18 Ibid.

17.10   Copyright vests in the author of a work.[1] But in the case of works made 'for hire' the employer or other person for whom the work is prepared is considered the author.[2] A work 'made for hire' is either a work prepared by an employee in the course of his employment, or certain commissioned works.[3] Commissioned works enjoying 'for hire' status include contributions to collective works, and parts of motion pictures or other audio-visual works.[4] Works outside the specified categories do not enjoy 'for hire' status,[5] and proper assignments must be taken.[6] For a work within the specified categories to be considered a 'for hire' work, it must be expressly agreed in writing that it is to be so considered.

1   1976 Act, s 201(a).
2   S 102(b).
3   S 101.
4   S 101.
5   *Mister B Textiles Inc v Woodcrest Fabrics Inc* 523 F Supp 21 (SDNY 1981).
6   Complying with s 204(a) requiring a conveyance or memorandum in writing signed by the copyright owner. Assignments can be subject to the complex reversionary provisions which are a feature of US copyright law, but it is beyond the scope of an outline of this sort to discuss these.

17.11   The term of protection (subject to the transitional provisions) is now the life of the author plus 50 years.[1] Registration of copyrights is still possible but it 'is not a condition of copyright protection',[2] although certain practical benefits can accrue from registration, and it is believed that most practitioners are advising their clients to register.

1   The transitional provisions are complicated – see Copyright Code, ss 302-305.
2   Copyright Code, s 408(a).

DESIGNS

17.12   The present statute covering design patents is the Patents Act of 1952.[1] There is no definition of a design for the purposes of this Act, but the Patent and Trademark Office currently considers that a design of an object 'consists of the visual characteristics or aspects displayed by the object'.[2] There is however a conflict between the practice of the Office, and the courts' definition. In *Re Zahn*[3] it was held that an article may well have portions which are immaterial to the design claimed. The Office must look at the article that is being claimed, rather than the article itself.[4]

1   35 USC, paras 171-173.
2   Manual of Patent Examining Procedure, para 502 (5th edn, 1983).
3   617 F 2d 261, 204 (CCPA 1980).
4   *Walker on Patents*, ed Lipscomb, para 16:4.

17.13   A design patent cannot be granted merely for the purpose of identifying an article of manufacture which would function in effect as a trademark.[1]

1   *Re Koehring* 37 F 2d 421 (1930); *North British Rubber Co v Racine Rubber Tire Co* 271 F 936 (CA2NY 1921).

17.14   The design must be new in the US.[1] The applicant must in general be the inventor of the design, and the design must involve a degree of inventiveness. It is not sufficient that it is new.[2] These requirements are more rigorous than those in operation in the equivalent laws of Australia, Canada and the UK. This obviously limits its utility somewhat in the context of merchandising. Nevertheless, it has some utility. In *Louis De Jonge & Co v Breuker & Kessler Co*[3] a design from a water colour painting which was adapted for fancy paper for covering boxes for the holiday season was patentable. The court also held that the painting for use as a design could at the owner's election be protected by copyright or by patent.

1   Para 171.
2   *Berlinger v Busch Jewelry Co* 48 F 2d 812, 813 (CA2NY 1931).
3   182 F 150 (CCPa 1910).

17.15   Given the fairly extensive protection afforded to characters by copyright law, the need to register designs is presumably not much felt. This, together with the rather rigorous requirements for securing a design patent may explain why it seems to be comparatively little used in this context.

17.16   It should be noted that under the Copyright Office Regulations copyright registration may not be obtained subsequent to a design patent for the same design, whereas copyright registration does not preclude subsequent issuance of a design patent.[1]

1   See *Yardley's Application* 219 F 2d 1389 (CCPA 1977).

PASSING OFF AND UNFAIR COMPETITION

17.17   In *Boston Professional Hockey Association Inc v Dallas Cap & Emblem Manufacturing Inc*[1] the defendants had sold embroidered patches bearing the plaintiff's emblem. These patches could be attached to clothing etc. The plaintiffs had licensed the National Hockey League Services Inc as their exclusive licensing agent. The defendant tried to obtain a licence to manufacture embroidered emblems from NHLS, but they were refused.

Nevertheless, they went ahead and manufactured and sold them. The plaintiffs sued inter alia for infringement of their registered trade mark and unfair competition. It was held that the plaintiffs were entitled to relief on both grounds. As to the latter the District Court had held that the defendant's use of the plaintiffs' marks 'had ... the prospect of trading on the competitive advantage the mark originator has to the public which desires the "official product"'. This decision was affirmed. The species of unfair competition involved in this case is, of course, passing off. In order to succeed in this species of unfair competition, it is necessary not merely to show confusion amongst the public as to the source of a product, as where eg two virtually identical articles are marketed which do not infringe other intellectual property rights of the plaintiff, there must also be evidence that the public associate the goods with the plaintiff.[2] Merely to copy an industrial design is not enough. Nor would this appear to amount to unfair competition in the sense discussed below.[3] Of course, if the design has acquired a trade mark function the position is different.[4]

1   510 F 2d 1004 (USCA 5th Cir 1975).
2   *Sears Roebuck & Co v Stiffel Co* 376 US 225 (SC 1964).
3   *Cheney Bros v Doris Silk Corpn* 35 P 2d 279 (2d Cir 1929).
4   See *Compco Corpn v Day-Brite Lighting Inc* 376 US 234 (USSC 1964).

TRADE MARKS

17.18   The present law is contained in the Lanham Act 1946, as amended. A US registration covers the 50 states of the Union, American Samoa, Guam, Panama Canal Zone, the Virgin Islands, Puerto Rico, and the Northern Mariana Islands.

17.19   Some individual states have registration systems. Many of these state laws provide criminal sanctions, whereas Federal law provides only for civil remedies.

17.20   'Trademark' means any word, name, symbol, or device or any combination thereof used by a person, or which a person has a bona fide intention to use in commerce and for which he applies for registration on the principal register, to identify and distinguish his goods, including a unique product, from those of others and to indicate the source of the goods, even if that source is unknown. Service marks may also be registered.

17.21   A *bona fide* intention to use the mark is required, and evidence of use must be submitted within six months of the Notice of Allowance (ie grant). This period can be extended for a further six months on written request. Upon cause being shown, this period can be extended for further six monthly periods up to 24 months. Thus the total period within which a mark must be used is 36 months. It would appear that efforts to find licensees would suffice for the purpose of getting an extension.

17.22   Licences can be registered, but as in the UK such registration is permissive, not obligatory.

17.23 As noted above, the use of trade marks in merchandising is well established, and trade mark infringement actions are commonly joined with copyright infringement actions in proceedings against pirates. However, the licensor must exercise quality control. It has been stated that naked licensing without quality control is a fraud on the public and unlawful.[1] Subject to this, it would not appear that a merchandiser who exercises quality control would in any way endanger his application,[2] or registered marks.

1   *Société Comptoir v Alexander's Dept Store* 299 F 2d 299 (CA2 1962).
2   Compare *Re American Greetings Corpn* [1984] RPC 329.

17.24 Confusion of source or sponsorship is the primary concern of conventional trade mark law. But there is also a persistent view that regards the identification function of trade marks as secondary, emphasising instead the undoubted advertising and commercial values that inhere to successful symbols.[1] More than 20 states accordingly have passed statutes aimed at preventing dilution of marks. The Model State Trademark Bill, paragraph 12 provides:

'Likelihood of injury to business reputation or of dilution of the distinctive quality of a mark registered under this Act, or a mark valid at common law or a trade name valid at common law, shall be a ground for injunctive relief notwithstanding the absence of competition between the parties or the absence of confusion as to the source of goods or services.'

These statutes can be used to prevent the defendant from using their mark to threaten the distinctiveness of the plaintiff's mark in relation to the products they licensed (as in the *Boston Hockey* case). Such use hardly goes beyond the traditional bounds of trade mark law. But the Acts can also be used to stop people using a mark generically, or tarnishing a mark's reputation by using it on products which are inferior, or which are incompatible with the products of the trade mark owner.

1   *Schechter* 40 Harvard LR 813 (1927); Martino 'Trade Mark Dilution' OUP 1996.

DEFAMATION

17.25 The law of defamation in the US is based on English common law. However, decisions of the Supreme Court have changed and restricted the tort. According to the Restatement on Torts[1] a public figure can maintain an action for defamation only if the defendant (a) knows that the statement is false and that it defames the other person, or (b) acts in reckless disregard of these matters.[2] So far as defamation of private individuals is concerned, there is a division in state laws as to whether an action for defamation can be sustained only upon clear and convincing proof that the defamatory falsehood was published with knowledge that it was false or with reckless disregard of whether it was false or not,[3] and on the other hand a negligence standard.[4] In *Gertz v Robert Welch Inc*[5] it was held that the First and Fourteenth Amendments to the Constitution prohibit the imposition of liability without fault on a publisher or broadcaster of a defamatory falsehood injurious to a private individual. In addition, the scope of conditional and absolute privileges have been increased, and proof of special damage has come to be required.

1   Para 580A.
2   See *Times v Sullivan* 376 US 254 (1963) on which the principle stated in the Restatement is largely based.
3   *Rosenbloom v Metromedia Inc* 403 US 29 (USSC 1971).
4   See eg *Thomas H Maloney & Sons v EW Scripps* 334 NE 2d 494 (Ohio 1974).
5   418 US 323 (USSC 1974).

INVASION OF PRIVACY

17.26   In some states the tort of invasion of privacy prevents the appropriation of the plaintiff's name or likeness for the defendant's benefit.[1] Indeed, such appropriation was the first form of the tort.[2] The tort was introduced by statute in New York,[3] and other jurisdictions followed either through case law or statutes.

1   The key modern American article is by Prosser 48 Cal LR 383 (1960). For English literature on the subject see P Russell (1979) 129 NLJ 791; *Privacy* ed JB Young (1979) Wiley & Sons, Essay 5 by G Dworkin; Wacks *The Protection of Privacy* (1980) Sweet & Maxwell; J Thomas McCarthy 'Protection of Names and Likenesses' (1986) Trade Mark World (December) p 14.
2   See *Prosser on Torts* (5th edn, 1984) West Publishing Co, p 849.
3   NY Sess Laws 1903 Ch 132 ss 1-2 – following its rejection by the New York Court of Appeals in *Robertson v Rochester Folding Box Co* 64 NE 442 (1890). Two earlier decisions had recognised the right – *Manola v Stevens & Myers* New York Times 14, 18, 21 June 1890; *Mackenzie v Soden Springs Co* 18 NYS 240 (1891).

17.27   A celebrated article by Warren and Brandeis was influential in this development.[1] After examining a number of cases on defamation, invasion of a property right and breach of confidence,[2] Warren and Brandeis concluded that these cases were really based on a broad principle of 'a right to privacy'. This view does have some attraction on the basis of the English cases examined by the authors. If you employed a photographer to take your picture, the use of the negative to make further unauthorised prints could be restrained. In *Pollard v Photographic Co*[3] North J based his decision, in part, on breach of faith.[4] In *Wyatt v Wilson*[5] Lord Eldon is supposed to have said 'If one of the late King's physicians had kept a diary of what he heard and saw, this Court would not, in the King's lifetime, have permitted him to print and publish it'. Brandeis and Warren concluded from these cases and other authorities that:

> 'The protection afforded to thoughts, sentiments , emotions, expressed through the medium of writing or of the arts, so far as it consists in preventing publication, is merely the instance of the enforcement of the more general right of the individual to be left alone.'[6]

1   'The Right of Privacy' 4 HLR 193 (1890).
2   Including *Prince Albert v Strange* (1849) 1 Mac & G 25; *Abernethy v Hutchinson* (1825) 3 LJOS Ch 209.
3   (1888) 40 Ch D 345.
4   The unauthorised use of photographs in the UK is now controlled by the Copyright, Designs and Patents Act 1988, s 85, which confers a right to privacy of certain photographs and films.
5   Unreported, cited by Cottenham LC in *Prince Albert v Strange* above.

6   4 HLR 193, at 205 (1990).

17.28   Important limitations on this tort arise from the freedom of speech provision of the First Amendment to the Constitution, and from the fact that newspapers, periodicals and other media repeatedly use the names of celebrities in items of news and other features. Although this helps to sell the newspapers etc, it also keeps the celebrities in the public view, and makes their names marketable commodities. Clearly, they cannot be allowed to charge for the very publicity which helps to make them celebrities. Attempts to charge the newspapers etc for using celebrity names in this way were met with very early in the history of this tort, and it was held that the celebrities were not entitled to payment in such cases.[1]

1   *Colyer v Richard Fox Publishing Co* 146 NYS 999 (1914).

EXPROPRIATION OF PERSONALITY AND VIOLATION OF A RIGHT TO PUBLICITY

17.29   At the outset it must be said that there is some need to establish the jurisprudential categorisation of these rights. If they are property rights they are assignable or transferable;[1] if they are rights arising by virtue of tort law they are merely releasable. The right to publicity appears to be a property right, the other rights to be based on tort, but the division of labour between these principles in relation to any given fact situation may be difficult to establish.

1   *Haelan Laboratories v Topps Chewing Gum Inc* 202 F 2d 866 (1953).

17.30   The problem with a tort based on a 'right to be left alone' or a 'right to privacy', is that it is difficult to see how publishing or using a celebrity's name, likeness or other indicia of identity, involves its commission. The unauthorised use of a celebrity's name would not appear to involve an invasion of privacy, in that it involves neither intrusion, public disclosure of anything confidential, nor the misuse of confidential information.[1] Strictly speaking, therefore, it ought logically to be of limited value in personality merchandising where the complaint is really the unpaid for exploitation of a celebrity's name.[2] Indeed, far from wanting to be 'left alone' celebrities thrive on publicity.[3] In consequence, some jurisdictions have recognised a property right in a name. This is based on the view that unauthorised use violates the celebrity's right to the commercial exploitation of their name or likeness.[4] The right thereby created is often referred to as the 'right to publicity'.

1   See Wacks, op cit, p 10; Murumba, op cit, p 91 – citing inter alia the Ghanaian case of *University of Cape Coast v Anthony* [1971] 2 Ghana L Rep 21.
2   Gordon 55 NWULR 553 (1961).
3   Pannam (1966) 40 ALJ 4.
4   See Nimmer 19 Law and Cont Prob 203 (1954). *Munden v Harris* 134 SW 1076 (1911); *Uhlaender v Henricksen* 316 F Supp 1277 (1970); *Haelan Laboratories v Topps Chewing Gum Inc* 202 F 2d 866 (1953); *Cary Grant v Esquire Ltd* 367 F Supp 876 (1973); *Bela Lugosi v Universal Pictures* Cal 603 P 2d 425 (1979), 172 USPQ 541; *Price v Hal Roach Studios* 400 F Supp 836 (1975); *Ali v Playgirl Inc* 447 F Supp 723 (1978); *Presley's Estate v Russen* 513 F Supp 1339 (1981); *Martin Luther King Jr Centre for Social Change v American Heritage Products* 694 F 2d 674 (1983).

17.31 The basis of this tort, whatever it is called, seems to be the advantage gained by the defendant from the unauthorised use of the plaintiff's name.[1] As it was put in an old case, if the defendant sees value in the plaintiff's likeness to exploit it for profit it is 'the property of him who gives it value from whom the value springs'.[2] On this basis the action is, in principle, available to private individuals as well as to celebrities.[3]

1 Prosser, op cit, p 851 et seq.
2 *Munden v Harris* 134 SW 1076 (1911).
3 *Erick v Perk Dog Foods Co* 106 NE 2d 742 (1952); *McAndrews v Roy* 131 So 2d 256 (1961).

17.32 Having regard to the First Amendment, this tort is subject to the same limitations as invasion of privacy in respect of the unauthorised use of celebrities' names in news items etc.

CONCLUSION

17.33 Even allowing for the fact that they are federal jurisdictions, there are quite close similarities between the laws of Australia, Canada and the UK both as regards character merchandising and as regards personality merchandising. The development in Canada of a tort of appropriation of personality, is perhaps on close examination less significant than it appears at first sight, because it is by no means clear that at present it goes beyond the extended tort of passing off as it has developed in Australia and in England. The most significant difference between Canadian law on the one hand, and Australian and UK law on the other, is in the prohibition on the licensing of unregistered marks, and on the licensing of registered marks outside the statutory scheme.

17.34 US law is perhaps the most developed of these common law jurisdictions. Its copyright law has developed in a way which not only facilitates character merchandising, but which to some extent covers image merchandising. These advantages outweigh the more limited scope for protecting designs through the law of design patents, than exists in the design registration systems of the other jurisdictions. US trade marks law is also more generous in allowing merchandisers a period of up to 36 months to find licensees. It does not treat the mere fact that a licensor is seeking to register the name of a character as evidence in itself of a lack of *bona fide* intention to use.[1] Through the development of the torts of invasion of privacy and of expropriation of personality, it also offers the most favourable situation for personality merchandising of any of the jurisdictions studies. The development of these torts outweighs the reduced scope of the tort of defamation in the US.

1 See *Pussy Galore* [1967] RPC 265 – a case decided under the Trade Marks Act 1938. The requirement under the 1994 Act is that registration should be sought in good faith, and it is unclear whether or not this requirement will be interpreted any differently – see para 3.43.

Section III
Precedents

Precedent 1

Licence agreements[1]

THIS AGREEMENT is made the   day of   19

BETWEEN:

(1)

('the Licensor')

(2)

('the Licensee')

RECITALS

(A) The Licensor is the sole owner of the Intellectual Property.

(B) The Licensor has the right to grant licences of the Intellectual Property in the Territory.

(C) The Licensee has requested a Licence to use the Intellectual Property in order to manufacture and distribute the Products.

(D) The Licensor has agreed to grant such a licence to the Licensee upon the terms set out in this Agreement.

1. Definitions and Interpretation

1.1 In this Agreement the following expressions shall have the following meanings:

1.1.1	'Intellectual Property'	:	the copyrights trade marks and other rights listed in Schedule [1]
1.1.2	'Notice'	:	Notice in writing served in accordance with the provisions of sub-clause [21.8]
1.1.3	'Products'	:	the goods listed in Schedule [2]
1.1.4	'Royalties'	:	the payments to be made to the Licensor by the Licensee under clause 5.
1.1.5	'Specifications'	:	the specifications set out in Schedule [3].
1.1.6	'Term'	:	the period or periods set out in

---

1   No stamp duty – see para 9.156 et seq above.

			clause 4.
1.1:7	'Territory'	:	the area designated in Schedule [4]

1.2 Unless the context requires otherwise:

    1.2.1   words importing the singular number shall include the plural and vice versa;

    1.2.2   words importing any particular gender shall include all other genders;

    1.2.3   references to persons shall include bodies of persons, whether corporate or incorporate;

    1.2.4   references to clauses and the Schedules shall be to clauses of and the Schedules to this Agreement;

    1.2.5   any reference in this Agreement to any statute or statutory provision shall be construed as referring to that statute or statutory provision as it may from time to time be amended, modified, extended, re-enacted or replaced (whether before or after the date of this Agreement) and including all subordinate legislation from time to time made under it;

    1.2.6   The expression 'copyright' shall mean the entire copyright subsisting under the laws of the United Kingdom and all analogous rights subsisting under the laws of each and every jurisdiction throughout the Territory.

2. Grant

In consideration of the obligations undertaken by the Licensee under this Agreement and SUBJECT TO the CONDITIONS set out in clauses 7 to 21 inclusive the Licensor grants to the Licensee a[n] [sole and] [non-]exclusive licence to use the Intellectual Property to manufacture distribute and sell the Products in accordance with the specifications and instructions given or approved by the Licensor under the terms of this Agreement throughout the Territory during the Term.

3. Non-exclusive/exclusive licence

[The Licensor reserves the right to grant licences of the Intellectual Property within the Territory to other licensees] *or* [This licence is sole and exclusive and the Licensor shall not grant other licences of the Intellectual Property for the Products in the Territory [nor itself sell the Products in the Territory] but nothing in this clause shall be construed as preventing the parallel importation of the Products into the Territory from another member state of the European Free Trade Area].[2]

4. Term

4.1 This Agreement shall extend for an initial period of [   ] from [   ] until [   ].

---

2   See para 8.23 et seq. Where exclusive rights are granted, the provisions of the Restrictive Trade Practices Act 1976 need to be considered – see para 8.19.

4.2   If the aggregate Royalties paid by the Licensee to the Licensor during such initial period shall exceed £[   ] then this Agreement shall continue for one further period of [   ] unless either of the Parties shall have given to the other Notice of determination not less than three months before the expiry of such initial period.

5.   Royalties

5.1   In consideration of the rights granted by the Licensor to the Licensee the Licensee shall pay to the Licensor the following sums.

    5.1.1   Upon the signing of this Agreement an advance royalty of £ [   ] which shall not in any circumstances be repayable either wholly or partly by the Licensor but which may be set off against the royalty payments due under the following sub-clause.

    5.1.2   In addition a royalty of [ ]% ([ ] per cent) on the net selling price of each unit of the Products sold by the Licensee calculated by deducting from the price at which each unit was sold by the Licensee Value Added Tax or other governmental taxes and levies [and trade and cash discounts].

    5.1.3   If royalties (exclusive of Value Added Tax or other governmental taxes and levies) payable under sub-clause 5.1.2 shall in any year of the Term be less than £ [   ] then the shortfall shall be due and payable on the date for delivery of the final statement of account under clause 5.5 in respect of that year.

5.2   The provisions of sub-clauses [5.1.1, 5.1.2 and 5.1.3] shall apply to any further period granted in accordance with the provisions of clause 4.2 save that in sub-clause 5.1.1 for the words 'signing of this Agreement' there shall be substituted the words 'commencement of the further period'.

5.3   The Licensee shall within 30 days of the expiration of each calendar quarter during the subsistence of this Agreement commencing three months after the signing of this Agreement deliver to the Licensor a statement giving particulars of all sales of the Products effected by the Licensee during the quarter and showing the total royalty payable to the Licensor and at the same time deliver to the Licensor a remittance for the full amount of that royalty.

5.4   The Licensee shall allow the Licensor or a firm of [chartered] accountants on the Licensor's behalf to examine the books and records of the Licensee in so far as they relate to sale of the Products and to take copies and extracts of such books and records. Any such inspection shall be during normal office hours and not carried out more than twice in any calendar year and shall be at the Licensor's expense unless such inspection shall reveal an underpayment to the Licensor of more than £ [   ] in which event the Licensee shall bear the costs of such inspection.

5.5   In the event of late payment of any money due to the Licensor under the terms of this Agreement (including without limitation any moneys found on an inspection carried out under clause 5.4 to have been underpaid) the Licensee shall pay to the Licensor interest accruing from day to day calculated at the annual rate of [   ]% above the base rate from time to time of [   ] Bank plc on all such money overdue from the due date for payment until the actual date of payment.

6.   Signature[3]

Signed

The Licensor (1)

Signed

The Licensee (2)

CONDITIONS
7.   Licensee's Obligations as to Conformity to Specification and Quality

7.1   The Licensee shall manufacture the Products according to the Specifications or such other specifications as the Licensor may from time to time substitute and at all times ensure that the Products are of the highest quality attainable within such specifications.

7.2   The Licensee shall deliver to the Licensor free of charge samples of each unit of the Products including their wrappings and packaging and shall not commence distribution of any unit of the Products until it has received written approval from the Licensor of its design standard of workmanship quality of presentation and intrinsic merit.

7.3   The Licensee shall ensure that all other units of the Products including their wrappings and packaging of the same description as the samples correspond to the samples approved by the Licensor in accordance with the previous sub-clause.

7.4   The Licensee shall supply to the Licensor free of charge such further samples of the Products as the Licensor may reasonably require from time to time.

8.   Requirements Contract[4]

The Licensee shall supply to the Licensor or to such other persons as the Licensor shall require any of the Products that the Licensor may require up to the quantities and at the prices specified in Schedule [5].

---

3   If the signature block is placed in this position, a clause must be added to incorporate Conditions – see clause 2 above.
4   See para 6.10.

9. Use and Protection of Intellectual Property

9.1 COPYRIGHT MATERIAL

9.1.1   Every unit of the Products copied from any copyright material comprised in the Intellectual Property and all packaging advertising and point of sale materials used in connection with the Products shall bear the following copyright identifications ['© (year of first publication)[name of Licensor]'] or with the prior written consent of the Licensor an abbreviated version, the terms of which must first be approved in writing by the Licensor, may be used on such Products but not on the packaging or other material.

9.1.2   The date to be placed in brackets after '©' shall be the year specified for that purpose for the particular copyright material by the Licensor or in the case of combination design the year of first marketing by the Licensee in which case the Licensor shall be notified in writing of such year by the Licensee.

9.1.3   No copyright material comprised in the Intellectual Property may be altered or amended by the Licensee without the prior written consent of the Licensor but the Licensee may use a combination of such materials even where such a combination has not previously been used.

9.1.4   No artwork other than that comprised in the Intellectual Property shall be used in relation to any of the Products without the prior written consent of the Licensor.

9.1.5   No copyright material comprised in the Intellectual Property may be used in connection with the manufacture distribution or marketing of any goods other than the Products for which the use of such material is specified.

9.2 TRADE MARKS

9.2.1   Each unit of the Products for which a trade mark comprised in the Intellectual Property is specified shall display that mark in a manner first approved by the Licensor.

9.2.2   No other trade mark shall be affixed by the Licensee to the Products or to any associated packaging advertising and point of sale materials without the prior written consent of the Licensor.

9.2.3   The Licensee shall not use in relation to or affix to any goods other than the Products for which such marks are specified any of the trademarks comprised in the Intellectual Property.

9.3   The Licensee shall not use any of the Intellectual Property as part of the Licensee's name or the name of any entity associated with it without the prior written consent of the Licensor.

9.4   The Licensee shall not during the subsistence of this Agreement or at any time subsequently register or use any of the Intellectual Property in its own name as proprietor.

319

Precedent 1   Licence agreements

9.5   The Licensee recognises the Licensor's title to the Intellectual Property and shall not claim any right title or interest in the Intellectual Property or any part of it.

9.6   The Licensee shall promptly call to the attention of the Licensor the use of any part of the Intellectual Property by any third party or any activity of any third party which might in the opinion of the Licensee amount to infringement or passing off.

9.7   The Licensee shall not assign, mortgage, charge or otherwise deal with (whether wholly or in part) the benefit of this Agreement or grant any sub-licence[5] without the prior written consent of the Licensor.

9.8   The Licensee shall hold all goodwill generated by its operations under this Agreement as bare trustee for the exclusive benefit of the Licensor.

9.9   Any designs or other works derived by the Licensee from the Intellectual Property or any part of it shall be held by it as bare trustee for the Licensor and at the Licensor's request shall be assigned to it without compensation.[6]

9.10   Every unit of the Products shall bear the statement 'manufactured by [*the Licensee*] under licence from [*the Licensor*]'.[7]

10. Registration of licence[8]

When required by the Licensor the Licensee shall join with the Licensor at the [Licensee's] [Licensor's] expense to register this licence of the Intellectual Property or any part of it in any part of the Territory and on termination of this Agreement the Licensee shall co-operate with the Licensor in securing the cancellation of any such registration.

11. Licensee Not to Use the Licensor's Name

The Licensee shall not except with the prior written consent of the Licensor make use of the name of the Licensor in any connection otherwise than is expressly permitted by this Agreement nor under any circumstances apply to register it as a company name.

12. Licensee's Obligations as to Marketing

12.1   The Licensee shall ensure that a full range of the Products shall be on sale to the public within [six] months of the date of this Agreement.

5   As to the problems to which sub-licences can give rise, see para 6.26.
6   This provision could constitute a breach of Art 85 of the Treaty of Rome, and should be avoided if the licensing programme is likely to exceed the guidelines set out in the Notice on Agreements of Minor Importance – see para 8.25.
7   See para 7.16 – an alternative form of words is suggested there.
8   See para 6.3.

12.2 The Licensee undertakes that the Products will be sold only to recognised wholesale firms for resale to retail firms or to retail firms for resale to the public or direct to the public.

12.3 The Licensee shall ensure so far as it is reasonably practicable that the Products are not supplied for re-sale as an integral part of another product and shall not be supplied either directly or indirectly to other manufacturers or to hawkers pedlars street vendors and the like or to any person intending to distribute the Products gratuitously for publicity.

12.4 The Licensee shall at all times during the Term use its best endeavours to promote and sell the Products throughout the Territory.

13.   No Premiums

13.1 The Licensee shall not sell or otherwise dispose of any of the Products as premiums to any person or persons whatsoever.

13.2 The right of sale as premiums is expressly reserved by the Licensor and if the Licensee shall receive any approach for the purpose of the use or sale of the Products as premiums it shall as soon as possible notify the Licensor and furnish it with the names and full particulars of the person or persons making the approach.

13.3 For the purposes of this clause 'premium' means a product or products combined with a service which is sold or supplied in association with the promotion of another product or service offered in association with the sales promotional activities of retailers wholesalers or manufacturers' associations with incentive programmes of all kinds.

14.   Action Against Third Parties

14.1 The Licensor shall have the sole right to take action against third parties in respect of any infringement of its rights in the Intellectual Property[9] and if required to do so by the Licensor the Licensee shall co-operate fully with the Licensor in any such action and the Licensee's expenses incurred in doing so shall be borne by the Licensor.

14.2 If the Licensor fails to take any such action against third parties or to require the Licensee to do so the Licensee may serve Notice on the Licensor and on the expiry of 30 days after the service of such Notice the Licensee shall be entitled to prosecute such action itself and at its own expense provided that the Licensor has not served Notice within the 30 day period of its own intention to take action.

---

9   But note that an exclusive licensee of copyright has the same rights and remedies as if the licence had been an assignment – Copyright, Designs and Patents Act 1988, s 101 (see para 10.11 et seq). The effect of a contractual provision of this sort would appear to be that an exclusive licensee exercising its rights under s 101 would be in breach of contract.

14.3   The Licensee shall in no circumstances settle any claim or action against third parties without the prior written consent of the Licensor.

14.4   All damages recovered from third parties shall be the exclusive property of the Licensor provided that the Licensee shall be entitled to set off any expenses which it is able to claim from the Licensor under this Clause against damages recovered by itself.

15.   Termination

This Agreement shall terminate:

15.1   TIME

On the expiry of the Term

15.2   FUNDAMENTAL BREACH

On the occurrence of any of the following events which are fundamental breaches of this Agreement:

15.2.1   failure on the part of the Licensee to comply with the terms of any Default Notice (as defined by clause [16]) within the time stipulated

15.2.2   failure on the part of the Licensee to make any payment due to the Licensor under this Agreement for [21 days] after such payment shall have become due

15.2.3   any breach by the Licensee of clause [9] of this Agreement

15.2.4   any challenge by the Licensee to the validity of any part of the Intellectual Property[10]

15.2.5   (*specify other events*)

provided that the Licensor may waive any breach of this Agreement by the Licensee

15.3   INSOLVENCY

If the Licensee goes into liquidation either compulsorily or voluntarily (save for the purposes of reconstruction or amalgamation) or if a receiver is appointed in respect of the whole or any part of its assets or if the Licensee makes an assignment for the benefit of or composition with its creditors generally or threatens to do any of these things

15.4   CHANGE OF MANAGEMENT OR CONTROL

If any change occurs in the management or control of the Licensee and in particular any change of directors [or shareholders] without the prior approval of the Licensor

---

10   Although 'no challenge' clauses are generally contrary to Art 85 of the Treaty of Rome, it is permissible to make an agreement terminate on challenge – see para 8.24.

322

15.5 TERMINATION ON CESSER OF RIGHTS

15.5.1   If at any time the Licensor shall cease to have the right to grant licences of the Intellectual Property the Licensor may forthwith terminate this Agreement by giving Notice to the Licensee.

15.5.2   The Licensee shall have no claim against the Licensor in respect of such termination and the rights of the Licensee set out in clause 16 shall only have effect if the Notice provides that they are to apply.

16.   Default Notice

In the event of a breach by the Licensee of any of the provisions of this Agreement other than a fundamental breach specified in clause [15.2] the Licensor may serve notice (a Default Notice) requiring the breach to be remedied within the time stipulated in that notice at the discretion of the Licensor (but nothing in this clause shall require the Licensor to serve notice of any breach before taking action in respect of it)

17.   Termination Consequences

17.1   The Licensee shall forthwith pay to the Licensor the balance of any Royalties accrued up to the date of termination, together will any other sum due under clause 5

17.2   Subject to the following sub-clauses upon termination of this Agreement whether by expiry of the Term or otherwise the Licensee shall discontinue all use of the Intellectual Property.

17.3   If the Licensee shall have any remaining stocks of the Products at the time of termination [and if this Agreement shall have terminated by expiry of the Term and shall not have been terminated by reason of the Licensee's breach of any of its obligations under this Agreement] they may be disposed of by the Licensee in compliance with the terms of this Agreement but not otherwise on a non-exclusive basis for a period of [4] months from the date of termination ('the sell-off period').

PROVIDED THAT:

17.3.1   the price charged by the Licensee for each Product during the sell-off period is not less than the price charged by the Licensee during the six months prior to the termination of this Agreement; and

17.3.2   all other provisions of this Agreement (including those relating to payment of royalties) are observed by the Licensee in respect of items sold during the sell-off period.

17.4   Any Products in the course of manufacture at the time of termination may be completed within [30] days and disposed of during the sell-off period in compliance with the terms of clause 16.2 of this Agreement but not otherwise.

18.   Indemnity

18.1   LICENSOR'S RIGHT TO INDEMNITY

The Licensee shall indemnify the Licensor against all actions claims costs damages and expenses which it may suffer or sustain as a result of the actions of the Licensee.

18.2   LICENSEE'S RIGHT TO BE INDEMNIFIED

The Licensor shall indemnify the Licensee against all actions claims costs damages and expenses arising out of the Licensee's use of the Intellectual Property in accordance with the terms of this Agreement.

19.   Inspection

The Licensee shall permit the Licensor [and its servants or agents] at all reasonable times to inspect the Licensee's premises in order to satisfy itself that the Licensee is complying with its obligations under this Agreement.

20.   Product Liability Insurance

The Licensee shall at its own expense obtain and maintain product liability insurance in an amount of not less than £[ ], with both the Licensor and Licensee as beneficiaries under the policy, and providing cover for claims, demands and causes of action arising out of Products sold during the Term, whether such claims, demands or causes of action arise or are notified during or after the Term.

21.   Miscellaneous

21.1   RECEIPT

The receipt of any money by the Licensor shall not prevent the Licensor from questioning the correctness of any statement in respect of any money

21.2   FORCE MAJEURE

    21.2.1   If either party is prevented from fulfilling its obligations under this Agreement by reason of any supervening event beyond its control (including, but not by way of limitation, war, national emergency, flood, earthquake, strike or lockout (other than a strike or lockout induced by the party so incapacitated)) the party unable to fulfil its obligations shall immediately give notice of this to the other party and shall do everything in its power to resume full performance

    21.2.2   Subject to the previous sub-clause, neither party shall be deemed to be in breach of its obligations under this Agreement

21.2.3   If the period of incapacity exceeds [six] months then this Agreement shall automatically terminate (unless the parties first agree otherwise in writing) in which case the provisions of clause [17] shall apply

21.3 WHOLE AGREEMENT

This Agreement contains the whole agreement between the parties and supersedes any prior written or oral agreement between them in relation to its subject matter and the parties confirm that they have not entered into this Agreement upon the basis of any representations that are not expressly incorporated into this Agreement

21.4 RESERVATION OF RIGHTS

All rights not specifically and expressly granted to the Licensee by this Agreement are reserved to the Licensor

21.5 HEADINGS

Headings contained in this Agreement are for reference purposes only and shall not be incorporated into this Agreement and shall not be deemed to be any indication of the meaning of the clauses and sub-clauses to which they relate

21.6 PROPER LAW AND JURISDICTION

This Agreement shall be governed by English law in every particular including formation and interpretation and shall be deemed to have been made in England and the parties agree to submit to the [non-]exclusive jurisdiction of the English courts

21.7 ARBITRATION

Any difference between the parties concerning the interpretation or validity of this Agreement or the rights and liabilities of either of the parties shall in the first instance be referred to the arbitration of two persons (one to be nominated by each party) or their mutually agreed umpire in accordance with the provisions of the Arbitration Acts 1950-1979.[1]

1   Note that the Arbitration Act 1996 is due to come into force before the end of 1996.

21.8 NOTICES

21.8.1   Any notice, consent or the like (in this clause referred to generally as 'notice') required or permitted to be given under this Agreement shall not be binding unless in writing and may

be given personally or sent to the party to be notified by pre-
paid first class post (if posted from an address within the UK
to an address also within the UK) or by air mail (if posted
from an address within the UK to an address within the USA
or vice versa) or by telex electronic mail or facsimile
transmission with confirmation copy by pre-paid first class
post or air mail as appropriate at its address as set out in
this Agreement or as otherwise notified in accordance with
this clause

21.8.2   Notice given personally shall be deemed given at the time of
delivery

21.8.3   Notice sent by first class post in accordance with this sub-
clause shall be deemed given at the commencement of business
of the recipient on the second business day next following its
posting

21.8.4   Notice sent by air mail in accordance with this sub-clause shall
be deemed given at the commencement of business of the
recipient on the seventh business day next following its posting

21.8.5   Notice sent by telex, electronic mail or facsimile transmission
in accordance with this sub-clause shall be deemed given at
the time of its actual transmission

21.9   No modification

This Agreement may not be modified except by an instrument in
writing signed by both of the parties or their duly authorised representatives

21.10   Waiver

The failure by either party to enforce at any time or for any period any
one or more of the terms or conditions of this Agreement shall not be a
waiver of them or of the right at any time subsequently to enforce all terms
and conditions of this Agreement

21.11   Severance

In the event that any provision of this Agreement is declared by any judicial
or other competent authority to be void, voidable, illegal or otherwise
unenforceable or indications of this are received by either of the parties
from any relevant competent authority the remaining provisions of this
Agreement shall remain in full force and effect

21.12   Survival of terms

The warranties and indemnities contained in this Agreement and the
provisions for payment of and accounting in respect of Royalties and other
moneys due to the Licensor under the terms of this Agreement shall
survive the termination of this Agreement.

21.13   VAT

All sums payable to the Licensor under this Agreement are exclusive of Value Added Tax which shall where applicable be paid in addition at the rate in force at the due time for payment, subject to the Licensor supplying VAT invoices to the Licensee when necessary

21.14   RIGHTS AND REMEDIES CUMULATIVE

All rights and remedies available to either of the parties under the terms of this Agreement or under the general law shall be cumulative and no exercise by either of the parties of any such right or remedy shall restrict or prejudice the exercise of any other right or remedy granted by this Agreement or otherwise available to it

21.15   BINDING EFFECT

This Agreement shall bind and enure to the benefit of the Licensor and its assigns and successors in title

21.16   NO AGENCY OR PARTNERSHIP

The parties are not partners or joint venturers nor is the Licensee entitled to act as the Licensor's agent nor shall the Licensor be liable in respect of any representation act or omission of the Licensee of whatever nature.

SCHEDULES

1.   Intellectual Property [list]
2.   Products [list]
3.   Specifications [list]
4.   Territory [specify]
5.   Prices of Products to be supplied to Licensor [specify]

Precedent 2

Representation agreement[1]

THIS REPRESENTATION AGREEMENT is made the   day of   19
BETWEEN:

(1)
whose [registered office or principal place of business is at] *or* [whose address for service within the jurisdiction of the courts of [England] is] (address)

('the Owner')

and

(2)
[whose [registered office or principal place of business is at] *or* [whose address for service within the jurisdiction of the courts of [England] is] (address)

('The Agent')

RECITALS

(A)   The Owner owns the Property set out in Schedule 1
(B)   The Owner has the exclusive right to grant licences for the production, marketing, advertising and distribution of goods [and provision of services] based upon, or related to, or connected with, or incorporating all or any part of the Property and for the use of them for promotional purposes.
(C)   The Owner wishes to appoint the Agent as its agent to negotiate the grant of such licences to manufacturers or any other interested persons and the Agent wishes to accept such appointment on the terms of this Agreement.

1.   Definitions and Interpretation

1.1   The following terms shall have the following meanings for the purposes of this Agreement:

1   So long as the agent is not negotiating the sale and purchase of goods on behalf of the principal, the agreement will not be subject to the Commercial Agents Regulations 1993, SI 1993/3053 – see para 6.8.

328

1.1.1	'Accounting Day	:	(date) in each year of the Term.
1.1.2	'Business'	:	the negotiation of Licences of the Merchandising Rights by the Agent as agent for the Owner and all matters relating thereto.
1.1.3	'Commencement Date'	:	[(date) or the date of this Agreement].
1.1.4	'Commission'	:	in relation to any one licence, [ ]%of the gross royalties (excluding any Value Added Tax or any sales tax or other similar tax on royalties) received by the Owner pursuant to any such licence during the Term [after deduction from such royalties of any amounts paid to the Agent by the Owner pursuant to clause [3.3.1]].
1.1.5	'Conditions'	:	the provisions [set out overleaf] *or* [contained in Clauses 3 to 7]].
1.1.6	['Excluded Products'	:	the products listed in Schedule [3]].
1.1.7	'Expiry Date'	:	(date) or such later date as shall result from any extension of the Term pursuant to Clause[3.8].
1.1.8	'Licence'	:	a licence upon the Owner's Standard Form of licence agreement to use or exploit the Merchandising Rights granted by the Owner to a licensee procured or introduced by the Agent within the Territory during the Term.
1.1.9	'Merchandising Rights':		the rights commercially to exploit the Property by way of the production, distribution and sale of Products [or the provision of Services].
1.1.10	'Payment Dates'	:	[eg the last business day (being a day on which banks are open for business in England) of each calendar month].
1.1.11	'Products'	:	the products specified in Schedule 2 which are based upon, related to or connected with or incorporating all or any part of the Property.
1.1.12	'Property'	:	the property set out in Schedule 1.
1.1.13	'Services'	:	the services specified in Schedule 4 which are based upon, related to or connected with or incorporating all or any part of the Property.
1.1.14	'Standard Form'	:	the form of Licence set out in Schedule 5.

1.1.15	'Term'	:	the period starting on (and including) the Commencement Date and ending on (and including) the Expiry Date unless extended or earlier terminated as provided in the Conditions.
1.1.16	'Territory'	:	the territory defined in Schedule [6].

1.2   Unless the context requires otherwise:

1.2.1   words importing the singular number shall include the plural and vice versa;

1.2.2   words importing any particular gender shall include all other genders;

1.2.3   references to persons shall include bodies of persons, whether corporate or incorporate

1.2.4   references to clauses and the Schedules shall be to clauses of and the Schedules to this Agreement

1.2.5   any reference in this Agreement to any statute or statutory provision shall be construed as referring to that statute or statutory provision as it may from time to time be amended, modified, extended, re-enacted or replaced (whether before or after the date of this Agreement) and including all subordinate legislation from time to time made under it

[1.2.6   the expression 'copyright' shall mean the entire copyright subsisting under the laws of the United Kingdom and all analogous rights subsisting under the laws of each and every jurisdiction throughout the Territory]

2.   Grant and reservations

2.1   The Owner grants to the Agent for the Term the [exclusive *or* sole *or* non-exclusive] right to negotiate with manufacturers [or specify in case of services] and other interested parties Licences in relation to the manufacture of the Products (other than the Excluded Products) [provision of the Services] pursuant to the terms of this Agreement including the Conditions.

2.2   Without prejudice to the remaining provisions of this Agreement the Owner reserves the right:

2.2.1   to vary its Standard Form in respect of any one or more prospective licensees;

2.2.2   at its sole discretion to decline [without giving reason] to enter into any one or more Licences negotiated by the Agent on its behalf][2]

2.2.3   at its sole discretion to vary the list of Excluded Products set out in Schedule [3] by written notice to the Agent provided that

---

2   Some agreements provide that the Owner's approval shall not be unreasonably withheld in respect of proposed licence agreements submitted to the Owner in conformity with the terms of the Representation Agreement.

no addition shall be made to that Schedule in respect of a product forming the subject matter of a Licence granted pursuant to this Agreement prior to the date of such notice [or in respect of a product forming the subject of negotiations between the Agent and a prospective licensee at that date].

[Signature block if Conditions are to be printed overleaf][3]

3. Owner's obligations

The Owner agrees with the Agent throughout the Term:

3.1   [SOLE OR EXCLUSIVE AGENT[4]

[Provided that none of the events referred to in Clause 5 has occurred] not to appoint any third party as agent for the negotiation of Licences in the Territory [nor itself to negotiate any such Licence whether directly or indirectly]].

3.2   SUPPORT AND INFORMATION

To support the Agent in its efforts to promote the Business and in particular [at its own expense or at the expense of the Agent]
[3.2.1   to supply transparencies...]
[3.2.2   ... other].

3.3   ADVERTISING AND PROMOTION

3.3.1   To reimburse the Agent for expenditure incurred by the Agent in advertising and promoting the Merchandising Rights in the Territory provided that the aggregate of such expenditure shall not have exceeded the budget limit agreed between the parties;

3.3.2   To refer to the Agent any enquiries from prospective licensees or other leads in the Territory;

3.3.3   To supply to the Agent information which may come into its possession which may assist the Agent in carrying on the Business.

3.4   INDEMNITY

To indemnify and keep the Agent indemnified from and against any and all loss, damage or liability suffered [and reasonable legal fees and costs

3   If the signature block is placed in this position, a clause must be added to incorporate the Conditions attached - see clause 2.1.
4   The terms 'sole' and 'exclusive' are not terms of art. If it is intended that the Owner should be able to operate in the Territory (a 'sole' agency) the Agreement should reserve this right expressly. Similarly if it is intended that the agent alone should have the selling right (an 'exclusive' agency) this should be spelled out. Refer also to discussion of competition law in Chapter 8.

incurred] by the Agent in the course of conducting the Business and resulting from:

    3.4.1   any act neglect or default of the Owner or its agents employees licensees [or customers];

    3.4.2   the proven infringement of the intellectual property rights of any third party;

    3.4.3   any successful claim by any third party alleging libel or slander in respect of any matter arising from the conduct of the Business in the Territory

PROVIDED that such liability shall not have been incurred through any default by the Agent in relation to its obligations (express and implied) under this Agreement.

3.5   ENTRY INTO LICENCES

Subject to Clause 2.2.2, forthwith to execute Licences negotiated by the Agent in conformity with the terms of this Agreement.

[3.6   PAYMENTS

To pay promptly without demand deduction or set-off:

    3.6.1   the Commission on the Payment Dates[5]

    3.6.2   any other sum payable by the Owner to the Agent under this Agreement].

3.7   MAINTENANCE OF RIGHTS

[Subject to Clause 4.6 of this Agreement] [to maintain the Owner's Merchandising Rights during the Term and not to cause or permit anything which might damage or endanger them or the Owner's title to them or assist or suffer others to do so] *or* [to consult with the Agent if the Owner's Merchandising Rights are or appear likely to be damaged or endangered].

[3.8   EXTENSION OF TERM

To extend the Term for [one] further period[s] of ... [years] without any break in continuity provided that:

    3.8.1   none of the events described in clauses 5.2 to 5.6 has occurred and is continuing; and

---

5   Consider whether or not to insert a clause along the following lines:
The Owner may request the Agent to collect the royalties due from any licensee appointed under the terms of this Agreement and for this purpose only the Agent shall have the same rights to collect payments due under the Licence as if the Licence had been entered into between the Agent and the licensee;
The Agent shall hold the sums collected pursuant to the previous sub-clause on trust to pay the same to the Owner;
Commission on such sums shall be payable as if the Owner had collected the sums directly from the licensee and payment of Commission shall be in accordance with the terms of this Agreement.

[3.8.2   The Agent pays to the Owner a renewal fee of £ (amount)]; and

3.8.3   The Agent serves written notice on the Owner requiring such extension not later than [ ] months before the Expiry Date; and

3.8.4   The Agent [acknowledges that the terms of this Agreement (other than this clause 3.8) shall apply to any extension of the Term] *or* [executes a new agreement on the Owner's standard terms current at the Expiry Date].]

4.   Agent's obligations

The Agent agrees with the Owner throughout the Term at its own expense:

4.1   DILIGENCE

At all times to work diligently to protect and promote the interests of the Owner.

4.2   SCOPE OF ACTIVITY AND AUTHORITY

4.2.1   Not without the previous consent in writing of the Owner to be concerned or interested either directly or indirectly in the conduct of any business which is similar to or competitive with the Business;

4.2.2   Not to deal directly or indirectly with any prospective licensee located outside the Territory or with any person located in the Territory knowing or having reason to believe that goods produced under a Licence granted to such person would be resold outside the territory;[6]

4.2.3   Not to describe itself as agent or representative of the Owner except as expressly authorised by this Agreement;

4.2.4   Not to pledge the credit of the Owner in any way;

4.2.5   Not to make any profit from the conduct of the Business other than by means of the Commission;

4.2.6   Not to make any representations or give any warranties to prospective licensees other than those contained in the terms of the Licence.

4.3   PROMOTION

To use its best endeavours to induce manufacturers to make use of the Property in relation to the manufacture, promotion or sale of goods [provision of services] and in all such cases to take Licences from the Owner for that purpose by:

4.3.1   personal visits to and correspondence with potential licensees;

4.3.2   advertising and distribution of publicity matter subject however to the specific prior approval in writing in all cases

---

6   See discussion of competition law in Chapter 8.

by the Owner of the form of and extent of such advertising and publicity matter (without recourse to the Owner pursuant to Clause [3.3.1] for any expense incurred unless such expense is specifically authorised by the Owner in writing);

4.3.3   attendance at trade shows and other sales outlets.

PROVIDED that in considering prospective licensees the Agent shall investigate, take into account [and report to the Owner as to] the credit-worthiness and status of all such prospective licensees including without limitation the amount of product liability insurance already held and additional cover that would be required by such prospective licensees in the event that a Licence were to be granted to any of them.

4.4   NEGOTIATIONS

To negotiate the terms of Licences with manufacturers and other interested persons and in that connection:

4.4.1   to make clear to prospective licensees that the Owner reserves the absolute right in its discretion to refuse to grant a Licence without the need to give any reason for such refusal;

4.4.2   to submit to the Owner at the earliest practicable opportunity [the names and addresses of the prospective licensees concerned and any terms proposed during such negotiations together with particulars of the Products[Services] in respect of which a Licence is sought] [details of the proposed agreement on the form set out in Schedule [7]]; and

4.4.3   to ensure that the terms negotiated with each prospective licensee conform as closely as is practicable to those set out in the Standard Form.

4.5   PASS ON INFORMATION

To refer to the Owner any inquiries which may come into its possession which may assist the Owner to grant Licences for the use of the Property outside the Territory.

4.6   PROTECTION OF PROPERTY

4.6.1   Not to do, cause or permit anything which may damage or endanger the Property, the Merchandising Rights or the Owner's title to them or assist or allow others to do so;

4.6.2   To notify the Owner of any suspected infringement of the Merchandising Rights or any of them;

4.6.3   To take such reasonable action as the Owner may direct at the expense of the Owner in relation to any such infringement;

4.6:4   To compensate the Owner for any use by the Agent of the Merchandising Rights otherwise than in accordance with this Agreement;

4.6.5   To indemnify the Owner for any liability incurred to third parties for any use of the Property otherwise than in accordance with this Agreement;

4.6.6   On the expiry or termination of this Agreement forthwith to cease to use the Property save as expressly authorised by the Owner in writing;

4.6.7   Not to apply for registration of any part of the Property as a trade mark but to give the Owner at the Owner's expense any assistance it may require in connection with the registration of any part of the Property as a trade mark in any part of the world and not to interfere with in any manner nor attempt to prohibit the use or registration of any part of the Property or any name device or design resembling it by any other licensee of the Owner;

4.6.8   Not to use the Property otherwise than as permitted by this Agreement;

4.6.9   Not to use any name or mark similar to or capable of being confused with any part of the Property;

4.6.10 Not to use the Property except directly in the Business;

4.6.11 Not to use any part of the Property or any derivation of it in its [trading or] corporate name;

4.6.12 To hold any additional goodwill generated by the Agent for the Property or the Business as bare trustee for the Owner.

4.7   GOOD FAITH

In all matters to act loyally and faithfully towards the Owner.

4.8   COMPLIANCE

4.8.1   To obey the Owner's reasonable orders and instructions in relation to the conduct of the Business;

4.8.2   To conduct the Business in an orderly and businesslike manner maintaining at its own expense an office and organisation suitable and sufficient for the proper timely and efficient conduct of its obligations under this Agreement and to comply in the conduct of the Business with all applicable laws (including, without limitation, EC competition law) bye-laws and requirements of any governmental or regulatory authority applicable to the Business.

4.9   DISCLOSURE

Before entering into this or any other agreement or transaction with the Owner during the Term or any extension of it to make full disclosure of all material circumstances and of everything known to it respecting the subject matter of the relevant agreement or transaction which would be likely to influence the conduct of the Owner including in particular the disclosure of other agencies in which the Agent is interested directly or indirectly AND THE AGENT WARRANTS TO THE OWNER that the Agent has made full disclosure of all such information before entering into this Agreement.

4.10 SECRECY

4.10.1 Not at any time during or after the Term to divulge or allow to be divulged to any person any confidential information relating to the business or affairs of the Owner other than to persons who have signed a secrecy undertaking in a form approved by the Owner;

4.10.2 Not to permit any person to act or assist in the Business until such person has signed such undertaking.

4.11 ACCOUNTS

To keep full, accurate and separate records and accounts in respect of the conduct of the Business in accordance with good business and accountancy practice [in England] and:

4.11.1 have them audited by qualified auditors once a year during the Term;

4.11.2 submit copies certified by such auditors to the Owner within [ ] days of each Accounting Day during the Term;

4.11.3 keep them for not less than [   ] years; and

4.11.4 within 14 days of submission or receipt to supply to the Owner a copy of each VAT return or assessment in respect of the Business.

4.12 CUSTOMER LIST

To keep and regularly update a list of actual and potential licensees (including name, address, telephone and fax numbers and main contact personnel) and to supply a copy of it to the Owner from time to time upon request.

4.13 INSPECTION OF BOOKS AND PREMISES

To permit the Owner or its representatives at all reasonable times to inspect all things material to the Business [and to take copies of any relevant documentation] and for this purpose to enter any premises used in connection with the Business.

4.14 SUB-AGENTS

Not to employ sub-agents without the prior written consent of the Owner and to be responsible and indemnify the Owner for any loss or claims resulting from the activities of any properly appointed sub-agents.

4.15 ASSIGNMENT

4.15.1 Not to assign charge or otherwise deal (whether wholly or in part) with this Agreement in any way without the prior written consent of the Owner;

4.15.2　In the case of an intended assignment by the Agent such consent shall not be unreasonably withheld in cases where the proposed assignee shall covenant directly with the Owner in writing to be bound by the terms of this Agreement and where the proposed assignee can show to the Owner's satisfaction that it is credit-worthy and reputable.

4.16 DELEGATION

Not to delegate any duties or obligations arising under this Agreement otherwise than may be expressly permitted under its terms.

4.17 PAY EXPENSES

To pay all expenses of and incidental to the carrying on of the Business.

5. Termination

[*see Precedent 1 clause 15*]

6.　　Termination consequences

6.1　LICENCES SUBMITTED PRIOR TO TERMINATION

[Termination of this Agreement shall not apply to any proposal for a Licence submitted in accordance with the terms of this Agreement prior to such termination] [but the entitlement of the Agent to Commission on Licences granted after the date of such termination shall depend upon Clause[6.3]].

6.2　PROCEDURE

On the termination of this Agreement the Agent undertakes:

6.2.1　to return to the Owner all samples, drawings, publicity, promotional and advertising material used in the Business;

6.2.2　not to make any further use of nor reproduce nor exploit in any way the Property, the Merchandising Rights or the Owner's name or any mark or representation confusingly similar to the Property or any part of it.

6.3　COMMISSION ON TERMINATION

Provided that termination is not due to a breach of this Agreement by the Agent the Agent shall be entitled to Commission in respect of Licences granted by the Owner before the date of termination [but not in respect of Licences granted by the Owner after that date notwithstanding that the

Agent may have been responsible in whole or in part for the, negotiation of the terms of any such Licence] [or as the case may be].

6.4   COMPENSATION FOR TERMINATION

If this Agreement is terminated by the Owner pursuant to Clauses [5.[ ]] the Owner shall pay to the Agent compensation as follows:
6.4.1   nothing if less than l year of the Term has been completed since the Commencement Date;
6.4.2   otherwise an amount equal to [one-half of] the average annual Commission earned by the Agent up to [   ] years from the Commencement Date;
6.4.3   if more than [   ] years of the Term have been completed since the Commencement Date the amount of the compensation shall be increased by [   ]% in respect of each completed year of the Term in excess of [   ];
6.4.4   the compensation shall be paid by the Owner to the agent not later than [   ] days after the date of termination.

6.5   NO COMPETITION[7]

For a period of [   ] years after expiry or termination of this Agreement the Agent undertakes:
6.5.1   not to engage directly or indirectly in any capacity in any business venture competitive with the Business in the Territory;
6.5.2   not to solicit actual or potential licensees with the intent of taking their custom as licensees of properties for products which may compete with the Products;
6.5.3   not to employ any employees or former employees who were employed in the Business by the Owner or any other representative of the Owner and to procure that all directors and shareholders of the Agent enter into direct covenants of a similar nature with the Owner.[8]

6.6   EXISTING RIGHTS

The expiry or termination of this Agreement shall be without prejudice to any rights which have already accrued to either of the parties under this Agreement.

7. Miscellaneous

[*insert as required from Clause 21 of Precedent 1 making appropriate changes*]

---

7   Refer to discussion of restraint of trade.
8   Refer to discussion of Restrictive Trade Practices Act, para 8.42 et seq.

SCHEDULES

1.   The Property [list]
2.   Products
3.   Excluded Products [list]
4.   [Services [list]]
5.   Licence Agreement [annex Standard Form]
6.   Territory [specify - a map may be helpful]
7.   Form of particulars of proposed Licence (see clause 4.4.1)
[*Signature block if not placed before Conditions*]

LICENSING CHECKLIST[9]

1.   Licensee – if company, where incorporated? – address of registered office – if partnership, names of partners or other information sufficient to identify partnership

Business address:

[including telex, telephone, facsimile, electronic mail etc]

Licensor's representative for dealing with licensing enquiries, and other matters arising out of licensing

Licensee's or agent's representative for dealing with queries arising in connection with licence

2.   Territory – specify by reference to legally designated area if possible eg United Kingdom (but remember choice of law where jurisdictions other than England & Wales included for example)

Is Agreement of exclusive territory? Is it exclusive both as regards manufacture and distribution?

3.   Language of Territory – what languages is Licensee permitted to apply to packaging or to the associated materials?

4.   Goods or services to which Licence applies

5.   Sub-contracting – is Licensee going to sub-contract, if so, to whom?

6.   Supply to Licensor – is Licensee going to supply goods to the Licensor or persons designated by Licensor? – if so insert requirements term and remember to cover potential liability under Sale of Goods Act etc – see chapter 7

---

9   This list does not purport to be comprehensive - it is merely intended to focus attention on the matters which commonly need to be thought about.

Precedent 2   Representation agreement

7. Distribution – is Licensee going to distribute to retail outlets directly or through further distributors? Agreements with distributors should safeguard the Licensor's Merchandising Rights

8. What Intellectual Property is included in the Merchandising Rights? Specify

9. What materials is the Licensor providing? – eg transparencies, photographs, promotional material. How are such things to be paid for by the Licensee?

10. Royalties – what is a reasonable commercial rate?

11. Currency of payment

12. Starting dates
    1)   production
    2)   sales
    3)   promotion
When does liability commence?

13. When is initial fee payable?

14. Quality control – samples to be provided by Licensee (including packaging etc). Quantities of samples, and when to be provided?

15. Term – automatic renewal for one further term, or renewal only on notice by Licensee?

16. Trade marks – is Licensee to be registered user? Who is to pay costs of this?

17. Other Licensees – is this Agreement in conformity with other existing Agreements especially with regard to Territory?

Precedent 3

Commissioning agreement for the preparation of artwork[1]

THIS AGREEMENT is made the   day of   19
BETWEEN:
(1)
        of

('the Illustrator')
(2)
[whose registered office/principal place of business] is at/whose address
for service within the jurisdiction of the courts of England is]

('the Purchaser')

IT IS AGREED as follows:

1. Definitions and Interpretation

1.1 In this Agreement the following terms shall have the following
meanings:

1.1.1	'Artwork'	:	The illustrative material which the Illustrator shall prepare and deliver/has delivered to the Purchaser which is described in the Schedule
1.1.2	'Completion Date':		[*specify date*]
1.1.3	'Price'	:	£[*amount*]
1.1.4	'Rights'	:	all vested contingent and future rights of copyright and all rights in the nature of copyright and all accrued rights of action and all other rights of whatever nature in and to the Artwork whether now known or in the future created to which the Illustrator is now or may at any time after the date of this Agreement be entitled by virtue of or pursuant to any of the laws in force in each and every part of the Territory

---

1   As to the importance of having an agreement of this kind when commissioning artwork,
     see para 1.82 above. As to stamp duty see para 9.156 et seq.

| 1.1.5 | 'Term' | : | the full period of copyright in the Artwork[2] [and all renewals reversions extensions and revivals of such period subsisting or arising under the laws in each and every part of the Territory and afterwards so far as permissible in perpetuity]. |
| 1.1.6 | 'Territory' | : | [the world] |

1.2   Unless the context requires otherwise:
  1.2.1   Words and expressions that are defined in the Copyright Designs and Patents Act 1988 shall bear the same meanings in this Agreement;
  1.2.2   Words importing the singular number shall include the plural and *vice versa*;
  1.2.3   Words importing any particular gender shall include all other genders;
  1.2.4   References to persons shall include bodies of persons, whether corporate or incorporate
  1.2.5   References to clauses and the Schedules shall be to clauses of and the Schedules to this Agreement
  1.2.6   Any reference in this Agreement to any statute or statutory provision shall be construed as referring to that statute or statutory provision as it may from time to time be amended, modified, extended, re-enacted or replaced (whether before or after the date of this Agreement) and including all subordinate legislation from time to time made under it
  1.2.7   The expression 'copyright' shall mean the entire copyright subsisting under the laws of the United Kingdom and all analogous rights subsisting under the laws of each and every jurisdicition throughout the Territory

2.   The Illustrator's Obligations

The Illustrator agrees with the Purchaser:

2.1   Preparation and delivery of Artwork
To prepare and deliver to the Purchaser the Artwork in a form suitable for reproduction and subject to the Purchaser's approval (which approval shall not be unreasonably withheld or delayed) as detailed in the Schedule.

2.2   To deliver to the Purchaser roughs of the Artwork not later than [date] and the finished Artwork by the Completion Date, time being of the essence.

2.3   If the Illustrator shall otherwise than by reason of circumstances beyond his control fail to complete and deliver the Artwork to the Purchaser by the Completion Date or by any subsequent date to which the Purchaser may consent in writing, then the Purchaser may by summary notice to the Illustrator terminate this Agreement, and any

2   As to the term of copyright see para 1.48 et seq above.

342

moneys previously paid by the Purchaser to the Illustrator shall then immediately be repayable to the Purchaser.

3.   Assignment of copyright

3.1   In consideration of the Price the Illustrator with full title guarantee[3] ASSIGNS the Rights to the Purchaser, its successors and assigns absolutely throughout the Territory[4] for the Term [by way of present assignment of [existing or] future copyright].

3.2   The Illustrator acknowledges the Purchaser's right throughout the Territory during the Term to license the exploitation of all or any part of the Rights to third parties.

3.3   The Parties agree to do all such things and to sign and execute all such documents and deeds as may reasonably be required in order to perfect, protect or enforce any of the rights assigned and granted to the Purchaser pursuant to this Assignment in any part of the Territory.

4.   Payment of the Price

The Purchaser shall pay to the Illustrator the Price by the following instalments:

4.1   [£   ] (   ] pounds) on the date of this Agreement (receipt of which the Illustrator acknowledges);

4.2   [£   ] (   ] pounds) on delivery and approval of the roughs; and

4.3   [£   ] (   ] pounds) on delivery and approval of the finished Artwork.

5.   Warranties and Indemnity

The Illustrator warrants to the Purchaser that:

5.1   The Illustrator is the sole owner of the Rights and has full power to enter into this Agreement and to give the warranties and indemnities contained in this Agreement;

---

3   These words replace the former formula 'as beneficial owner' – Law of Property (Miscellaneous Provisions) Act 1994 which is dealt with at para 6.3 above.

4   In certain jurisdictions, such a provision may be ineffective to assign copyright – see eg Chapter 16 (Germany). This does not prevent a contractual obligation subject to the law of England and Wales from arising between the parties. The main disadvantage of copyright remaining in the Illustrator in a particular territory is in relation to potential infringement proceedings against a third party. The Illustrator would have to be persuaded to take action in his or her own name. When therefore target territories have been established for the merchandising programme, it is advisable to check with local lawyers what needs to be done to perfect the Purchaser's title (if anything can be done, that is). The Illustrator is under an obligation by virtue of clause 3.3 to sign any necessary documentation for this purpose.

5.2   The Illustrator will at all times during the creation of the Artwork be a 'qualifying person' within the meaning of section 154 of the Copyright, Designs and Patents Act 1988 and the sole author of the Artwork which will be original in him and has not previously been published in any form anywhere in the Territory;

5.3   The Artwork contains nothing obscene, blasphemous, libellous or otherwise unlawful and the exploitation of the Rights by the Purchaser will not infringe the copyright or any other rights of any third party; and

5.4   The Illustrator will keep the Purchaser fully indemnified against all actions claims proceedings costs and damages (including any damages or compensation paid by the Purchaser on the advice of its legal advisers [and after consultation with the Illustrator] [and after approval by the Illustrator] to compromise or settle any claim) and all legal costs or other expenses arising out of any breach of any of the above warranties [or out of any claim by a third party based on any facts which if substantiated would constitute such a breach].

6.   Reservation of Rights

The Purchaser reserves the following rights:

6.1   LIKENESSES OF LIVING PERSONS

If the Artwork contains a recognisable likeness of any living person, to require the Illustrator to explain to such person the use to which the Artwork will be put and to obtain and deliver to the Purchaser a written form of release from each such person in a form satisfactory to the Purchaser.

6.2   ALTERATIONS AND DELETIONS

6.2.1   To require the Illustrator to alter or delete from the Artwork any part of it which the Purchaser or its legal advisers considers to be objectionable or likely to be actionable at law, and if the Illustrator fails promptly to do so or refuses or is for any reason unable to do so, the Purchaser may [make such alteration to the Artwork as it thinks fit, notwithstanding the moral rights of the Illustrator pursuant to section 80 of the Copyright, Designs and Patents Act 1988][5] [by summary written notice to the Illustrator terminate this Agreement, in which case the Illustrator shall without delay return to the Purchaser any moneys already paid by the Purchaser under clause 4];

6.2.2   Any such deletion or alteration shall, if made by the Illustrator, be without prejudice to and shall not in any way affect the

---

5   As to which see para 1.90 above. See also clause 8 below.

Illustrator's liability under the warranties and indemnities given to the Purchaser by the Illustrator in Clause 5 of this Agreement

6.3   RIGHT NOT TO USE THE ARTWORK

In its absolute discretion to use or not use the Artwork

6.4   RIGHT TO SELL THE ARTWORK

To sell the original Artwork (as distinct from any rights in the Artwork)

7.   Cancellation

7.1   The Purchaser may terminate this Agreement and cancel the commission in respect of the Artwork by giving written notice to the Illustrator PROVIDED THAT the Purchaser shall pay to the Illustrator a cancellation fee proportional to the degree of completion, in accordance with clause 7.2.

7.2   The cancellation fee shall be calculated as the following percentage of the Price:

    7.2.1   [   ] per cent of the Price if cancellation takes place between signature of this Agreement and approval of roughs; or

    7.2.2   [   ] per cent of the Price if cancellation takes place between approval of roughs and approval of finished Artwork.

7.3   Any sums paid by the Purchaser under Clause 4 shall be set off against any cancellation fee arising under this Clause and a repayment by the Illustrator to the Purchaser shall be made if the cancellation fee is less than the sums paid under Clause 4.

7.4   The Purchaser shall have no rights in the Artwork so cancelled.

8.   Waiver of Moral Right of Integrity

8.1   The Illustrator hereby irrevocably and unconditionally waives all moral rights in respect of the Artwork to which he may now or at any time in the future be entitled under sections 77, 80, 84 and 85 of the Copyright, Designs and Patents Act 1988[6] and under any similar laws in force from time to time during the Term in any part of the Territory[7] and the Illustrator declares that this waiver shall operate in favour of the Purchaser, its licensees, assignees and successors in title.

---

6   As to which see para 1.90 above.
7   Waiver of the moral right of integrity is not possible in some jurisdictions, but this does not prevent this provision operating contractually in England and Wales. Thus, if the Illustrator were to insist on enforcing his or her moral rights, for example in France, it would be a breach of this agreement – see Chapter 15.

8.2   Where in any part of the Territory waiver in accordance with the previous sub-clause is not possible, the Illustrator agrees not to enforce such moral rights and that any attempt to enforce them shall constitute a breach of this Agreement.[8]

9.   Miscellaneous

[*See Precedent 1 clause 20*]

10.   Certificate of value[9]

It is hereby certified that this transaction does not form part of a larger transaction or series of transactions in respect of which the amount or value or the aggregate amount or value of the consideration involved exceeds £60,000 (sixty thousand pounds)

11.   AS WITNESS the hands of the Assignor and the Assignee or their duly authorised representatives on the date first mentioned above.[10]

Signed by
[for and on behalf of]

....

In the presence of:

....
WITNESS SIGNATURE

.............................Name
.............................Address
....
.............................Occupation

Signed by
[for and on behalf of]
....

In the presence of:

....
WITNESS SIGNATURE

.............................Name

---

8   See previous note.
9   See para 9.165.
10   The formalities for a written contract to be effective as a deed are set out in s 1 of the Law of Property (Miscellaneous Provisions) Act 1989: a seal is no longer required.

.............................Address
....
.............................Occupation

THE SCHEDULE
The Artwork (clause 1.1)

The Artwork shall consist of:
     [   ] Illustrations in black and white.
     [   ] Illustrations in [   ]colours.
     [   ] Black and White photographs.
     [   ] Colour transparencies.
Medium:
Method of Reproduction:
Size/proportion:
Description of nature of illustrations:

Precedent 4

Assignment of copyright, design right and/or a right in a registered design

THIS ASSIGNMENT is made the   day of   19

BETWEEN:

(1)   (   ) [whose [registered office or principal place of business] is at (*address*) or whose address for service within the jurisdiction of the courts of England and Wales is (*address*)] ('the Assignor') and

(2)   (*name of assignee*) [whose [registered office or principal place of business] is at (address) or whose address for service within the jurisdiction of the courts of England and Wales is (*address*)] ('the Assignee')

RECITALS

The Assignor is the owner of the Rights and has agreed to assign them to the Assignee on the following terms and conditions

IT IS AGREED as follows:

1.   Definitions

The following terms shall have the following meanings:

'Design[s]'   the design[s] of which [an example is or examples are] set out or particulars are set out in the Schedule

'Rights'   [the full rights in the registered Design[s]]

the full design rights in the Design[s]]

[and full copyright in the design documents of the Design[s]] together with all the Assignor's rights and interests in respect of such rights

348

2.   Assignment

In consideration of the sum of £(amount) paid by the Assignee to the Assignor (the receipt of which the Assignor acknowledges) the Assignor with full title guarantee ASSIGNS to the Assignee the Rights

3.   Assignor's Obligations

The Assignor agrees with the Assignee at the direction and expense of the Assignee to sign all documents and do all such acts to vest in the Assignee the Rights and any form of industrial property protection (other than a patent for an invention) relating to them in any country in which such protection exists

4.   Assignor's warranties and Indemnity

The Assignor warrants that:

4.1   The Assignor is the sole owner of the Rights and has full power to enter into this Assignment

4.2   The Assignor has not granted any licences in respect of any of the Rights in any part of the world nor suffered any of the Rights to be the subject of any charge mortgage or other incumbrance [except (specify incumbrances and licences)]

4.3   The Assignor will keep the Assignee fully indemnified against all actions claims proceedings costs and damages (including any damages or compensation paid by the Assignee on the advice of its legal advisers to compromise or settle any claim) and all legal costs or other expenses arising out of any breach of the above warranties or out of any claim by a third party based on any facts which if substantiated would constitute such a breach

5.   Miscellaneous

[*See Precedent 1 clause 20. Choose from: Whole Agreement; Headings; Joint and Several; Proper Law and Jurisdiction; Interpretation; Arbitration; VAT*]

6.   Certificate of Value[1]

[*See Precedent 3 clause 10*]
[*Conclude as in Precedent 3 clause 11*]

---

1   As to stamp duty see para 9.156 et seq above.

SCHEDULE

The Design[s]

[set out example(s) of unregistered design[s] in which copyright or design right subsists and / or particulars of registered design(s)]

Full assignment of copyright in existing artistic work for lump sum

THIS ASSIGNMENT is made the   day of   19

BETWEEN:

(1) (   ) [of [*address etc*]

('the Assignor')

(2) (   ) [whose [registered office/principal place of business] is at][whose address for service within the jurisdiction of the courts of England is] (*address*)

('the Assignee')

RECITALS

The Assignor owns the Rights and has agreed to assign them to the Assignee on the terms and conditions set out in this Assignment

1.   IT IS AGREED as follows:

The following terms shall have the following meanings:

1.1	'Price'	:	[£]
1.2	'Rights'	:	all vested contingent and future rights of copyright and all rights in the nature of copyright and all accrued rights of action and all other rights of whatever nature in and to the Work whether now known or in the future created to which the Assignor is now or may at any time after the date of this Assignment be entitled by virtue of or pursuant to any of the laws in force in each and every part of the Territory
1.3	'Term'	:	the full period of copyright in the Work and all renewals reversions extensions and revivals of such period subsisting or

			arising under the laws in each and every part of the Territory and afterwards so far as permissible in perpetuity
1.4	'Territory'	:	[the world]
1.5	'Work'	:	the artistic work created by the Assignor [entitled '[ ]'] a photograph of which is attached as the Schedule to this Assignment

2   Assignment

2.1   In consideration of the Price now paid by the Assignee to the Assignor (the receipt of which the Assignor acknowledges) the Assignor with full title guarantee[1] ASSIGNS to the Assignee the Rights TO HOLD the same unto the Assignee, its successors and assigns absolutely throughout the Territory[2] for the Term

2.2   The Assignor acknowledges the Assignee's right throughout the Territory during the Term to license the exploitation of all or any part of the Rights to third parties

2.3   The parties agree to do all such things and to sign and execute all such documents and deeds as may reasonably be required in order to perfect, protect or enforce any of the rights assigned and granted to the Assignee pursuant to this Assignment in any part of the Territory

3.   Warranties and Indemnity

The Assignor warrants to the Assignee that:

3.1   The Assignor is the sole owner of the Rights and has full power to enter into this Assignment and to give the warranties and indemnities contained in this Assignment

3.2   The Assignor was at all material times during the creation of the Work a 'qualifying person' within the meaning of section 154 of the Copyright, Designs and Patents Act 1988 and is the sole author of the Work which is original in him and has not previously been published anywhere in the Territory

3.3   The Work contains nothing which is obscene blasphemous libellous or otherwise unlawful and the exploitation of the Rights by the Assignee will not infringe the copyright or any other rights of any third party

3.4   The Assignor will keep the Assignee fully indemnified against all actions claims proceedings costs and damages (including any damages or

---

1   These words replace the former formula 'as beneficial owner' – Law of Property (Miscellaneous Provisions) Act 1994 which is dealt with at para 6.3 above.
2   See Precedent 3, note 4 above.

compensation paid by the Assignee on the advice of its legal advisers [and after consultation with the Assignor] [and after approval by the Assignor] to compromise or settle any claim) and all legal costs or other expenses arising out of any breach of any of the above warranties [or out of any claim by a third party based on any facts which if substantiated would constitute such a breach]

4.   Waiver of Moral Rights

[*See Precedent 3 clause 8 above*]

5.   General

[*See Precedent 1 clause 20 above. Choose from: Whole Agreement; Headings; Joint and Several; Proper Law and Jurisdiction; Interpretation; Arbitration; VAT as required*]

6.   Certificate of Value[3]

[*See Precedent 3 clause 10 above*]

7.   [*Conclude as in Precedent 3 clause 11*]

SCHEDULE
The Work

[*attach photograph of the Work*]

---

3   As to stamp duty see para 9.156 et seq above.

Precedent 6

Short form of assignment of registered trade marks without the goodwill of the business in which they are used[1]

THIS ASSIGNMENT is made the   day of   19

BETWEEN:
1.   'The Assignor':

2.   'The Assignee':

RECITALS

The Assignor is the proprietor and beneficial owner of the UK registered trade marks set out in the Schedule ('the Trade Marks')

IT IS AGREED as follows:

In consideration of the sum of £[   ] now paid by the Assignee to the Assignor (receipt of which the Assignor acknowledges) the Assignor with full title guarantee[2] ASSIGNS and transfers to the Assignee all right title and interest in the Trade Marks with the goodwill attaching to the Trade Marks but without the goodwill of the business in the goods in respect of which the Trade Marks are registered and have been used by the Assignor.
[*Certificate of value: see Precedent 3 clause 10*][3]
[*Conclude as in Precedent 3 clause 11*]

---

1   As to assignments of trade marks see para 3.70 above.
2   These words replace the former formula 'as beneficial owner' – Law of Property (Miscellaneous Provisions) Act 1994 which is dealt with at para 6.3 above.
3   As to stamp duty see para 9.156 et seq above.

Precedent 6   Short form of assignment of trade marks without goodwill

THE SCHEDULE
Registered Trade Marks

Mark	No	Class	Goods/Services

Precedent 7

Cross-border licences: exchange control and withholding of tax[1]

WITHHOLDING OF TAX

1.   The Licensee shall be entitled to deduct from any payment(s) due to the Licensor any sum(s) that are required to be withheld by reason of any law or statute or any decree in any part of the Territory.

2.   In the event of any such deduction the Licensee shall notify the Licensor and shall give the Licensor all assistance necessary to recover the same [the costs of such assistance being borne by the Licensor].

3.   If the Licensee obtains a tax credit for taxes so withheld in respect of any sums due to the Licensor the proportion of such credit attributable to such sums shall promptly be paid or credited to the Licensor.

EXCHANGE CONTROL

In the event that because exchange control are in force or for other reasons the Licensee is unable to procure the payment of any moneys due to the Licensor the Licensee shall at the written request of the Licensor discharge its obligation to the Licensor to make payment of such moneys by producing evidence of their payment [at the Licensee's expense] into such bank account in the Territory as the Licensor may direct in writing subject to any applicable exchange control or other regulatory or official restriction consents and provision.

1   See para 9.61 et seq.

Index

References are to paragraph numbers. References in *italic* type refer to page numbers in the Precedents.

Index

Corporation tax *see* INCOME AND
    CORPORATION TAX
Corporations
    cinematographic films, and 2.18
        unpublished pre-1957 2.26, 2.27
    copyright, and 2.15-2.18
    photographs, and 2.17
    sound recordings, and 2.18
    subsistence of copyright, and 2.15-2.18,
        2.26-2.27
Court of Chivalry
    coats of arms, use of, and 5.16
Criminal and regulatory protection
    conspiracy 12.21
    Copyright, Designs and Patents Act
        1988 12.20
    customs law 12.19
    deception 12.17-12.18
    misleading advertising 12.8-12.16
    trade descriptions *see* TRADE
        DESCRIPTIONS
Cross-border licences
    exchange control *356*
    tax, withholding of *356*
Crown copyright
    generally 1.85

Damages
    see also CIVIL REMEDIES
    account of profits, and, election
        between 11.17
    adequacy of, on application for
        injunction 11.5
    compensatory only 11.10
    computation of 11.11
    copyright infringement, for 11.10
        innocent infringement 11.17
        primary infringement 11.15
        secondary infringement 11.16
    exemplary 11.14
    forestalling exploitation of markets,
        compensation for 11.12
    generally 11.10-11.16
    Germany 16.15, 16.66
    importing of pirated goods 11.16
    intellectual property rights,
        infringement of 11.10
    interest on 11.13
    jury assessment of 11.11
    passing of, for 11.11, 11.14
        Australia 13.20
    patent, infringement of 11.11, 11.14
    trade marks, infringement of 11.11, 11.14
    value added tax, and 9.146-9.149
Deception
    generally 12.17-12.18
Defamation
    Australia 13.23
    Canada 14.24
    generally 5.8-5.9
    United States 17.25
Defective products
    liability for *see* PRODUCT LIABILITY

Delivery up
    see also CIVIL REMEDIES
    affidavit supporting 11.6
    destruction, for 11.7
    generally 11.6-11.9
    infringing parts, severance of 11.9
    interlocutory stage, ordered at 11.3,
        11.6
    moulds, of 11.8
    whole, of 11.9
Derivative works
    see also FILMS; SOUND
        RECORDINGS
    ownership of 1.6
    term of copyright 1.67-1.75
    United States, protection of UK works
        in 2.70
Design documents
    copyright in 1.16
Design right
    assignment of *348-350*
        assignor's obligations *349*
        assignor's warranties and
            indemnity *349*
        certificate of value *349*
    owner of 1.82
Designs
    articles made to 1.16
    commissioner of 1.82
    industrial *see* INDUSTRIAL DESIGNS
    international protection of 2.72
    Paris Convention, and 2.72
    registered *see* REGISTERED
        DESIGNS
    title to 1.89
    United States 17.12-17.16
Destruction
    order for 11.6, 11.7
Dolls
    see also PUPPETS; THREE-
        DIMENSIONAL OBJECTS; TOYS
    Australia 13.3, 13.7
    cartoon characters, reproduction of 1.18
        Australia 13.3
Dramatic works
    characters in
        see also FICTIONAL
            CHARACTERS; LITERARY
            CHARACTERS
        no copyright in 1.40
        United States 17.6
    copyright, and 1.40
    quality of 1.40
    subsistence of copyright 2.19
        Australia 13.5
    Taiwan, first published in 2.49
    term of copyright
        anonymous or pseudonymous works
            1.64-1.65
        known author 1.49-1.54
        original 1.49-1.54
        'Peter Pan' 1.53
        unpublished at death 1.51-1.53